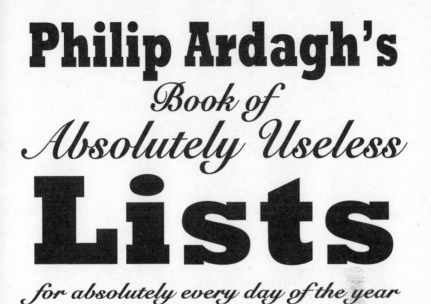

Philip Ardagh's
Book of
Absolutely Useless
Lists
for absolutely every day of the year

'Not worth the paper it's printed on'
THOMAS CAXTON

'[T]he most beautiful things in the world are the most useless'
THOMAS RUSKIN

'This book is rubbish!'
THE NATIONAL COUNCIL FOR RECYCLING

'A waste of time'
THE ROYAL HOROLOGICAL SOCIETY

'I'd rather eat it than read it'
A BOOKWORM

'[U]seless and need not be preserved'
CALIPH OMAR

'There's only one thing more useless than these lists,
and that's my good-for-nothing layabout son'
MRS ARDAGH (author's mother)

'More, please!'
ALFRED THE GEEK

*Also by Philip Ardagh
from Macmillan*

WOW: inventions that changed the world
WOW: discoveries that changed the world
WOW: events that changed the world
WOW: ideas that changed the world

The Truth About Christmas
The Truth About Love
The Truth About Fairies
The Truth About Cats

Philip Ardagh's

Book of *Absolutely Useless*

Lists

for absolutely every day of the year

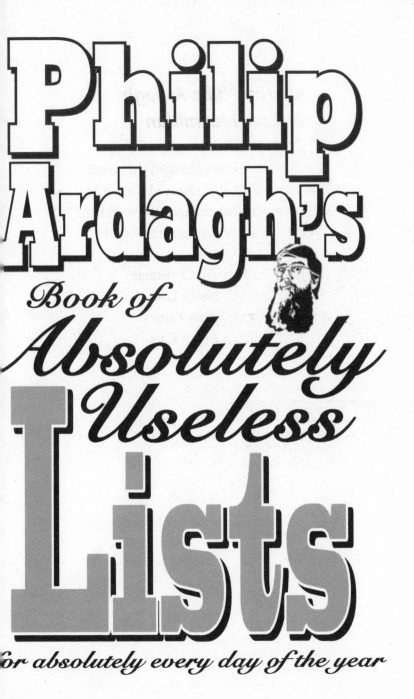

MACMILLAN

First published 2007 by Macmillan Children's Books
a division of Macmillan Publishers Limited
20 New Wharf Road, London N1 9RR
Basingstoke and Oxford
www.panmacmillan.com

Associated companies throughout the world

ISBN: 978-0-230-70050-5

1 3 5 7 9 8 6 4 2

A CIP catalogue record for this book is available from
the British Library.

Typeset by Perfect Bound Ltd and Tony Fleetwood
Printed and bound in Great Britain by Mackays of Chatham plc, Kent

How it all began

One day I was having lunch with my Macmillan editor, Gaby, when she said, 'How about writing us a book of lists?' 'What kind of lists?' I asked. 'Whatever kind you like,' she replied. 'Facts, instructions, rankings, ideas . . . Lists about anything and everything.' I stabbed a potato with a fork and pushed it around my plate. 'Well . . .' I said, doubtfully. 'You're a font of useless information,' she said, 'and here's your chance to get a lot of it down on paper.' 'Well . . .' I said. 'And that's not all,' said Gaby, wiping her mouth with an impressively large napkin. 'We want you to write a list for every day of the year!' 'Wow!' I said. 'Three-hundred-and-sixty-six lists, allowing for leap years?' 'Exactly.' 'This could be great,' I said. 'I could link each list to an event that occurred on a particular day.' 'For instance?' asked Gaby. 'For instance – er – the World Health Organization came into existence on 7 April 1948, so under 7 April we could list all the actors who have played the character of Doctor Who.' Gaby gave me a funny look over the pepper grinder. 'I'm not entirely sure I follow.' 'World Health Organization,' I said. 'W.H.O.' She smiled. 'I like it!' she said. 'For 16 March, I could list sad and nasty nursery rhymes where terrible things happen, because that was the date in 1973 that the new London Bridge was officially opened!' 'As in "London Bridge Is Falling Down"?' Gaby laughed. 'Spot on!' I said. 'I *really* like it!' she said. 'Then let's get started!' I said. So we did. We didn't even stay for pudding.

A message from the author

There will be mistakes. There will be differences of opinion. It's a fact of life that facts are open to interpretation. Any errors are, of course, mine. Please forgive me. I have used an enormous number of sources to sniff out information and/or try to check and verify various useless gobbets and/or nuggets wherever possible, but *Book of Days* (Chambers, 2004) has been particularly invaluable for the on-this-day aspect. My thanks to Gaby Morgan and 'accessories after the fact' Emma Young, Fliss Stevens, Talya Baker, Louisa Sladen, Debbie Gill, Pippa Durn, Dan Newman, Tony Fleetwood and everyone else in the 'absolutely useless' team at Macmillan who was involved in bringing this big fat man's big fat book to fruition. It's been fun.

Philip Ardagh
Tunbridge Wells

An important note from our lawyers

Neither the author nor Macmillan Publishers Limited accepts any responsibility or liability for any content or material published on or accessible from any of the websites for which addresses are given in this book. It is for readers to make their own judgement about these websites, and readers visit them at their own risk. If you purchase or acquire goods, services or advice from any of these websites then that is a matter between you and them. We have no liability for and make no recommendation as to the quality or type of goods, services or advice provided by any of these websites or by anyone to whom they may be linked. Neither can we accept any responsibility for any loss or damage caused by any viruses or other technologically harmful material that may infect your computer equipment or programs because of your use of such websites. It is for you to make your own judgement about them.

A note to readers who couldn't be bothered to read 'How it all began', and who could blame you?*

This book contains 366 lists: one for every day of the year, and not just this year: any year, from 1 January to 31 December. If it's a leap year, there are just enough to go around. If it isn't, then you have a bonus list to do with as you will.

Beneath each date is an event that occurred on that day in history, or is associated with that date. Beneath that is a list, somehow connected to the event. Sometimes the connection is obvious – I mean really, *really* obvious – and sometimes less so. But there is a connection, I promise you. Not that it really matters. They're absolutely useless.

* That was a rhetorical question.**
** In other words, it doesn't require an answer.

1 January

Ten things that get some people hot under the collar (if they're wearing one)

1. The state of schools/roads/antelope/hospitals/prisons/ swimming pools/dungeons/parks/haircuts/whatever today.*
2. The 'misspelling' and lack of punctuation in text messages.
3. Unjust wars.
4. Anyone wearing a hood unless they are:
   (i)   Taking a basket of food to their grandmother in the forest, whilst trying to dodge wolves
   (ii) Living in a monastery
   (iii) Stealing from the rich to give to the poor, whilst hanging with Little John.
5. Adding apostrophes to words for no apparent reason, and particularly being unaware that *it's* is short for 'it is'.
6. People who say that they don't want their own chips, then end up eating far too many of yours.**
7. People who 'borrow' your clothes without remembering to ask, then return them without remembering to tell you about the nail-varnish/hot-chilli-sauce stain they got on them.
8. People who abuse animals.
9. People who let their animals abuse you – biting/drooling/ snarling/far worse – and choose not to notice.
10. Whether 'scone' should be pronounced *skon* (to rhyme with Don) or *skown* (to rhyme with phone).

* Take your pick.
** This also applies to kebabs and just about everything else, come to think of it.

2 January

1959: USSR launches Luna 1, the first human-made object to escape the Earth's gravity

Nine things you might not have known about Sir Isaac Newton*

1. He was born on Christmas Day 1642.
2. His father was also called Isaac Newton, dying before he was born.
3. He was a failed farmer/estate manager.
4. His university education was interrupted by the plague.
5. He once made a list of his sins, which included squirting water and making pies on a Sunday, punching his sister and, more seriously, wishing to burn his mother and stepfather 'and the house over them'.**
6. He had a terrible temper and bore grudges. (You might just have guessed that from No. 5.)
7. He once suffered from a nervous breakdown.
8. The story about him developing his theory about gravity when watching an apple fall was probably – 'shh!' – made up or, at the very least, a bending of the truth.
9. He refused the last rites on his deathbed.

* It might be more usual to list ten things, but I thought nine would make a nice change.
** Which, fortunately, he never did.

3 January

1888: the first paper drinking straw is patented, in the USA, by Marvin C. Stone of Washington, DC

Some facts about burping

- On average we – and, yes, that includes you – are thought to burp about fifteen times a day.

- Some are big burps that everyone notices. Some are small ones that we hardly know we're doing. A burp can contain up to 80 ml of gas.

- This gas is air. As well as swallowing food and drink, we swallow air (which contains nitrogen and oxygen).

- The air goes down into the stomach. What goes in must come out. Some of this unwanted gas is forced out of the stomach through the tube which connects the back of the throat to the tummy – the oesophagus – and out of the mouth. This can happen very quickly, almost without warning, and a burp is born.

- Drinking fizzy drinks can greatly increase the likelihood of burping . . . because they contain carbon dioxide: yet more gas.

- The remaining unwanted gas escapes through the bottom. But that's a different story.

- Animals burp too. Cows produce about 50 million tonnes of methane gas every year, accounting for 22% of global emissions.

- It's possible to deliberately burp by swallowing air and forcing it out again.

- Girls' burps are not naturally quieter than boys' burps. It's just that girls may do more to try to stifle the sound and, anyway, boys are more likely to practise making their burps as loud as possible.*

* Oh, what a surprise!

4 January

1809: Louis Braille, inventor of the
alphabet for the blind, is born
1813: Isaac Pitman, inventor of Pitman
Shorthand English, is born

An A to Z listing
of the phonetic alphabet

The phonetic alphabet is used by, among others,
the emergency services to spell out names,
locations, numberplates, etc. over the radio or
phone, to avoid mishearing.* It is comprised of:

Alpha	November
Bravo	Oscar
Charlie	Papa
Delta	Quebec
Echo	Romeo
Foxtrot	Sierra
Golf	Tango
Hotel	Uniform
India	Victor
Juliet	Whisky
Kilo	X-ray
Lima	Yankee
Mike	Zulu

* Saying 'B' might be mistaken for saying 'D', for example,
but no one's going to mistake 'Bravo' for 'Delta'.

5 January

*1941: pioneer airwoman Amy Johnson disappears
after crashing in the Thames estuary*

Three famous disappearances

1. Roanoke

In 1586 Sir Walter Raleigh founded the first English colony
in North America on the island of Roanoke (in what was then
Virginia but is now North Carolina). Virginia was named after
Queen Elizabeth I of England, the Virgin Queen. The colony's
leader was Sir Richard Grenville, who returned to England
for supplies. While he was gone, the colonists suffered the
consequences of a terrible drought, and worsening relations
with the local Native Americans. When Sir Francis Drake
turned up at the island after a raid in the Caribbean, he agreed
to take them all home to England . . . which is why Sir Richard
found the place deserted on his return!*

Grenville left fifteen crew members on Roanoke to maintain
an English presence there, then he too headed back home. On
22 July 1587, a second group of 115 colonists arrived under
the leadership of John White. Their plan was to join up with
the fifteen people already there. Of fourteen there was no sign.**
They found the fifteenth, but only his bones.

Soon two babies were born in the colony. The first of these
was White's granddaughter, Virginia Dare, on 18 August
1587, making her the very first European to be born in North
America. Once again, relations with the local Native Americans
were far from good, and one of the colonists was killed. White
decided to return to England for help.

He didn't get back to Roanoke until 1588, to find the place
deserted. There wasn't a single member of the colony to be
found. The only clue was the word 'Croatoan' (*sic*) carved into
a tree. The Croatan were a local Native American tribe. Had
the colonists joined them on a nearby island? Perhaps they had
been massacred by them? Or by the English settlers' deadly

---

* But this isn't the disappearance Roanoke is famous for.
** But this isn't the disappearance Roanoke is famous for either.

rivals, the Spanish? Perhaps the colonists had given up, tried to sail home and drowned? Nobody knows to this day. Roanoke is remembered as the Lost Colony. And that's the disappearance it's famous for.

2. The *Mary Celeste*

Originally named the *Amazon* and registered in Nova Scotia, Canada, in 1860, this 280-ton half-rig ship became American-registered and renamed the *Mary Celeste* some ten years later.

On 7 November 1872, the ship set sail from New York under the command of Captain Benjamin Briggs. Also aboard were his wife Sarah and their daughter Sophia, and a crew of seven. (Their son Arthur stayed behind to go to school.) The cargo was around 1,700 barrels of raw, undiluted alcohol to fortify wine. They were bound for the port of Genoa in Italy.

On 5 December the *Mary Celeste* was spotted drifting between the Portuguese coast and the Azores by the *Dei Gratia*. Her captain ordered the *Mary Celeste* to be boarded. The men found her deserted. The legend was born.

Many people today are under the false impression that the ship was called the *Marie* (rather than *Mary*) *Celeste*. They also believe stories about the boarding party finding the table laid for a meal, with cups of tea still steaming. This is down to Arthur Conan Doyle – later Sir Arthur and creator of Sherlock Holmes – and his wonderfully convincing fictional version of events in the short story 'F. Habakuk Jephson's Statement', which reads like a piece of journalism.

The truth is rather more straightforward, but still intriguing. In December 1872, the Vice Admiralty Court in Gibraltar heard a very different story. Much of the ship's interior was soaking wet, kitchen utensils thrown about, and there was not a single lifeboat on board. Neither the ship's chronometer nor sextant were found – both instruments a captain is likely to have taken with him when leaving his ship. It looked like everyone had left in a hurry.

The most likely explanation is that the Briggs family and crew climbed aboard a boat, possibly attached to the ship by the main halyard (a very thick rope) which was found broken hanging over the side. But why? Raw alcohol is a highly flammable and explosive cargo. Perhaps there had been a small explosion or fire in the hold (later extinguished by the sea), or something which the captain mistook for an explosion, so he ordered everyone into the 'safety' of a boat, which then broke free in a storm. The disappearance remains a mystery, and young Arthur Briggs became an orphan.

3. Amelia Earhart

US aviator Amelia Earhart's dream was to be the first woman to fly around the world. In 1928 she had been the first woman to fly across the Atlantic. In 1932 she had been only the second person to fly the Atlantic solo. On 1 June 1937 she and her navigator, Fred Noonan, set off from Miami to begin her attempt at circling the globe. By 29 June they had only 7,000 of the 29,000 miles to go. They landed in Lae, New Guinea, and then prepared for the 2,500-mile flight to Howland Island in the mid-Pacific.

Everyone knew the dangers of this leg of the journey. Earhart herself described Howland Island as 'such a small spot in the Pacific'. She not only had her twin-engine Lockheed Electra stripped to its bare essentials so that she could carry extra fuel, she also arranged for a US Coastguard vessel and three other US ships to be positioned along the way as 'route markers'.

On 2 July Earhart and Noonan took off from Lae at 12.30 a.m. The weather forecast was good, but the skies soon became overcast and it started to rain. Radio contact between the Coastguard ship *Itasca* became patchy. At 7.25 p.m. Earhart reported, 'We must be on you, but cannot see you . . . gas is running low . . .' At 8.45, she reported, 'We are running north and south.' This was her final message. Amelia Earhart and Fred Noonan were never seen again.

The US government spent a massive $4 million and searched over 250,000 square miles of the Pacific before finally calling off the rescue operation on 19 July.

There are many theories about what happened to Earhart and Noonan. The two main conspiracy theories are that they were actually on a spying mission for the US government, trying to find out what the Japanese were up to in the Pacific. According to this theory, the so-called 'search and rescue mission' resulting from their disappearance was really the cover for a huge, hi-tech surveillance operation. The other theory is that they were taken prisoner by the Japanese.

What's most likely, though, is that Earhart and Noonan ran out of fuel and their plane ditched into the ocean, where they drowned.

1841: the Penny Red replaces the Penny Black stamp

A dozen philatelic fundamentals

1. The average lick of glue off the back of a postage stamp contains 0.1 of a calorie.

2. The first non-royal person to appear on a British postage stamp was Britannia (though she did, of course rule the waves) in 1913. The first animal was a dragon, along with his sidekick St George, in 1929.

3. The first person to appear on a British postage stamp who was neither royalty, mythical nor scaly was William Shakespeare, but not until 1964.

4. Self-adhesive stamps are nothing new: they were introduced in Sierra Leone, also in 1964.

5. In 1973, the Himalayan kingdom of Bhutan issued a series of stamp that not only looked like tiny records but could be played like records. Tunes included folk songs and Bhutan's national anthem.

6. At the time of writing, the world's largest stamps measure 21cm by 6.5cm and were issued in China in the 1900s.

7. The world's smallest stamps to date measure just 9.5 mm by 8 mm, and were issued in Bolivia back in 1863.

8. There used to be an underwater post office off the Bahamas, established in 1939. The postmark read 'SEA FLOOR BAHAMAS'.

9. Strangely, in 1879 in Belgium over thirty cats were employed to carry bundles of letters to villages. The practice was soon dropped because they were so bad at it!

10. Britain is the only country which issues stamps without its name on them. The Universal Postal Union requires all other countries to do so. Britain is exempt because it was the first country to issue stamps so it didn't need to name them, because stamps didn't exist anywhere else in the world!

11. For sixty years, the only image allowed on British postage stamps was that of Queen Victoria.

12. One of the world's most valuable stamps was a 3-skilling Banco Yellow issued in Sweden in 1857 which sold for $2.26 million in 1996.

7 January

1536: Catherine of Aragon (first ex-wife of Henry VIII) dies*

Hat Facts**

CROWN***
The part of the hat which covers the top of the head

BRIM
A stiff horizontal projection around the circumference of the hat

SWEATBAND
The part of the hat which touches the head

HATBAND
A strip where the crown joins the brim

PEAK (aka VISOR)
A projection at the front of a hat (to shade the eyes)

* She became his 'ex' by divorce. Anne Boleyn and Catherine Howard were less fortunate. They were beheaded!

** Well, they do say, 'If you want to get ahead, get a hat'.

*** Not to be confused with a crown of the type worn by a king or queen around the house.

8 January

1935: Elvis Presley* is born in Tupelo, Mississippi, USA

People whose names make them sound ennobled or like royalty (though they're neither), who can be counted on the fingers of one hand**

1. Nat KING Cole

Probably most famous for singing 'When I Fall In Love', 'Mona Lisa' and 'Unforgettable', Nat King Cole was a remarkable singer and pianist, and was the first black person to have his own TV show in the US. He was born Nathaniel Adams Coles in 1919, and gained his 'new' name in 1937. He died in 1965.

2. DUKE Ellington

Born Edward Kennedy Ellington in 1899 in Washington DC, he became one of the world's most famous jazz musicians and composers. By the time he died in 1974, he'd played over 20,000 performances around the world.

3. Screaming LORD Sutch

Founder of Britain's Monster Raving Loony Party, David Edward Sutch was born in 1940 in Kilburn, London. He changed his name in the 1960s when he recorded a number of very strange comedy records. He stood for parliament 39 times but was never elected. A number of the Monster Raving Loony Party's proposals did, however, later become law.**** He died in 1999.

* aka 'The King'.
** OK, OK, so I could only think of five offhand.***
*** The hand pun was not intended.
**** Including reducing the age of voting to 18, passports for pets and all-day pub openings. These were deemed very loony ideas at the time!

4. LORD Haw-Haw

William Joyce was born in New York in 1906 to an Irish father and English mother. A Fascist, he went to Nazi Germany in 1939. During the Second World War he broadcast anti-British propaganda, always beginning with the words 'Germany calling,' and earned the nickname Lord Haw-Haw because of his accent. After the war, he was found guilty of treason and executed in January 1946.

5. COUNT Basie

Born in 1904 in New Jersey, USA, the jazz musician's real name was William Basie. He started out as a drummer before becoming a pianist. He had his own jazz orchestra and recorded with many jazz greats, including Ella Fitzgerald, before dying aged 79 in 1984.

9 January

1894: a film showing Thomas Edison's assistant, Fred Ott, sneezing, becomes the world's first copyrighted 'motion picture'

Some facts about sn-sn-sn-sneeeeeeezing

- A sneeze is a great way of spreading germs. The material – yerch! – fired out of your nose and mouth can travel a distance of 2 to 3 metres, at explosive speeds.

- A big sneeze can expel air from your lungs at an impressive 100 mph.

- It can also throw your head back with the same G-force experienced when riding a rollercoaster.

- A sneeze is a reflex action (intended to stop us inhaling things that could damage our lungs). We have no control over it, though we can deliberately cause sneezing by, for example, sniffing pepper.

- Scientists have recently discovered a 'sneeze centre' in the brain stem, in a part called the medulla.* This controls our sneezing reflex.

- It is thought to be near impossible – if not impossible – to sneeze with your eyes open.**

- Around one in four people sneeze when they go out in the sun. This condition is called photic sneezing and is often inherited.

- The longest recorded attack of the sneezes started on 13 January 1981 and ended on 16 September 1983. This extraordinary world record for sneezing – which lasted over TWO-AND-HALF YEARS – is held by Donna Griffiths from Worcestershire.

* It's amazing what scientists spend their time doing nowadays, isn't it?
** WARNING: There's an old wives' tale saying that if you did your eyes would pop out!

10 January

1863: the first stretch of London Underground opens to the public

A feast of fossorial beasts*

Aardvarks
Ants
Armadillos
Badgers
Bilbies (aka rabbit-eared bandicoots)
Bunnies (aka rabbits)
Chipmunks
Cicadas (a type of flying insect)
Clams (yup: clams)
Conies (aka pikas)
Coypus
Desert Tortoises
Earthworms
Ferrets
Foxes
Gerbils (if you let them)
Groundhogs (aka woodchucks**)
Hamsters
Jerboas
Kangaroos
Meerkats
MOLES (of course!)
Mongooses (not mon*geese*)
Nutrias (aka coypus)
Pikas (aka conies)
Prairie Dogs (not really a dog at all)
Pupfish
Rabbit-Eared Bandicoots (aka bilbies)
Rabbits (aka bunnies)
River Otters
Sand Dollars
Sea Cucumbers
Shrews
Slow-Worms
Tarantulas
Woodchucks** (aka groundhogs)

* Animals that burrow underground.

** As in: 'How much wood could a woodchuck chuck, if a woodchuck could chuck wood?'***

*** The answer to which is: 'As much wood as a woodchuck would chuck if a woodchuck could chuck wood.'

11 January

1974: the first surviving sextuplets are born in Cape Town, South Africa

Ten pairs of well-known and not-so-well-known twins

1. Mary-Kate and Ashley Olsen (US actresses famous for being famous).
2. Kara and Shelby Hoffman (shared the role of Sunny Baudelaire in the film of Lemony Snicket's *A Series of Unfortunate Events*).
3. Gabriella and Monica Irimia (The Cheeky Girls).
4. Alanis Morissette (Canadian singer) and her lesser-known brother Wade.
5. Maurice and Robin Gibb (The Bee Gees).
6. Nicholas Brendon (Xander in *Buffy the Vampire Slayer*) and his brother Kelly.*
7. Matt and Luke Goss (Bros).
8. Craig and Charlie Reid (The Proclaimers).
9. Elvis Presley and Jesse (who died at birth).
10. James and Oliver Phelps (Fred and George Weasley in the *Harry Potter* films).

* Both Nicholas and Kelly use their middle names as their stage names: Nicholas Brendon and Kelly Donovan. Their surname is Schultz.

12 January

Twenty films and TV shows in which Oscar-winning Sir Michael Caine played bit parts before 1964*

1956
Yield to Night
The Caine** Mutiny Court Martial
The Lark
Taffy

1957
Bayonet
Requiem for a Heavyweight
Mister Charlesworth
Joyous Errand
Dixon of Dock Green

1958
Ice Cold in Alex
Women of Mystery
The Two-Headed Spy
Carve Her Name with Pride
The Key
Blind Spot
The General's Daughter
The Prisoner
Dixon of Dock Green II

1959
Dixon of Dock Green III

1961
Somewhere in the Night
The Ship That Couldn't Stop

* When he played Lt Gonville Bromhead in Zulu.
** No relation.

13 January

A handful of Hardys

Thomas Hardy (novelist and poet)

Oliver Hardy (film partner of Stan Laurel of 'Laurel and Hardy' fame)

Keir Hardy (politician)

Vice Admiral Sir Thomas Masterman Hardy* (as in Nelson's 'Kiss me, Hardy'**)

Bert Hardy (*Picture Post*'s chief photographer)

Godfrey Harold Hardy (mathematician)

Hardy Ha-Ha*** (cartoon colleague of fellow cartoon Lippy the Lion)

* Many people assume that the Hardy Monument in Dorset, England, was erected in memory of Thomas Hardy, the county's most famous resident. It was, in truth, erected to this particular Hardy.

** Over the years there's been much debate about whether Nelson actually said 'Kismet, Hardy', as in 'This is fate, Hardy'. The general consensus nowadays is that he did, in fact, ask for a kiss (and probably got one).

*** Who, despite the name, wasn't himself very funny. Being a hyena, he laughed, but he didn't particularly make the viewers laugh along with him.

1939: The Grapes of Wrath *by John Steinbeck*
is first published

Seven titles Steinbeck might possibly have considered* before settling on *The Grapes of Wrath***

1. *The Wrath of Khan*

2. *The Really Angry Grapes*

3. *The Really Angry Caterpillar*

4. *The Little Grapes on the Prairie*

5. *What's Eating the Grapes of Wrath?*

6. *The Raisins of Wrath*

7. *Depression****

* Though it's highly unlikely.
** The title is a quote from 'The Battle Hymn of the Republic' by Julia Ward Howe:

'Mine eyes have seen the glory of the coming of the Lord:
He is trampling out the vintage where the grapes of wrath are stored.'

(Wrath means extreme anger.)
*** If you read it, you'll know why.

15 January

1559: Queen Elizabeth I is crowned in Westminster Abbey

A variety of interesting facts about Britain's most famous abbey (which, incidentally, isn't really an abbey)

- Westminster Abbey hasn't been an abbey – a place for monks – since the 16th century.

- The Abbey's correct title is the Collegiate Church of St Peter, Westminster.

- For a normal service, the Abbey seats some 2,000 people. For a coronation, they can squeeze in about 8,200 seats.

- During the Second World War over 60,000 sandbags were used to protect the royal tombs, the Coronation Chair was sent to Gloucester Cathedral, and the Stone of Scone was secretly buried somewhere in the Abbey.

- The Stone of Scone was stolen in 1950 and reinstated a year later. In 1996, it was returned to Scotland, where it originally came from. Scottish Kings were traditionally crowned on it.

- Around 3,300 people are buried in the Abbey and cloisters (excluding monks buried in the cemetery behind the Chapter House).

- Thomas Parr, buried in the Abbey in 1635, was said to have been 152 years, 9 months old.

- Elizabethan poet Ben Jonson is thought to have been buried standing up.

- Oliver Cromwell was originally buried in the Abbey. After the restoration of the monarchy he was dug up. His body was hanged at Tyburn, decapitated and reburied somewhere else.

- Thomas Hardy's body is buried in the Abbey but his heart is buried in Dorset or may have been eaten by a cat.

- Since 1906 only a person's *ashes* can be buried in the Abbey.

16 January

*1957: the Cavern Club, later made famous by
the Beatles, opens its doors in Liverpool*

UK number one Christmas singles with body parts and/or colours in the song title

1952 Al Martino, 'Here in My **Heart**'

1959 Emile Ford and the Checkmates, 'What Do You Want to Make Those **Eyes** at Me For?'

1963 The Beatles, 'I Want to Hold Your **Hand**'

1966 Tom Jones, 'The **Green** Green Grass of Home'

1968 The Scaffold, 'Lily the **Pink**'

1970 Dave Edmunds, 'I H**ear** You Knockin''

1972 Jimmy Osmond, 'Long-**Hair**ed Lover from **Liver**pool'

1987 The Pet Shop Boys, 'Always on My **Mind**'*

* Hang on! Hang on! This last one would only count if it was called 'Always on My Brain'!

17 January

1929: Popeye first appears in a comic strip

Some not-so-eye-popping facts about Popeye

- Popeye started with a 'walk-on' part in a long-running comic strip called *Thimble Theatre* by Elzie Segar.
- In the beginning, Olive Oyl and her family were the main characters.
- Olive soon became Popeye's 'goil' and he adopted an 'infink' called Swee'Pea.
- Other characters included tough-gut Bluto and J. Wellington Wimpy, who would 'gladly pay you Tuesday for a hamburger today'.
- Popeye first appeared in a film in *Popeye the Sailor*, a Betty Boop* cartoon.
- His first live-action outing was in the 1980 film, with Robin Williams in the title role and Shelley Duvall as Olive.**
- Popeye's amazing strength comes from spinach. In 1937, 'America's spinach capital' Crystal City, Texas, erected a statue to his honour!
- Spinach sales were said to have increased by a third when Popeye was at the height of his popularity.

* Betty Boop's catchphrase was 'Boo-boop-ee-doo'. At least, that's what it sounded like. Whether it's actually spelled that way is another matter.

** This film was, somewhat surprisingly, directed by Robert Altman, better known for such films as *Gosford Park* and *M*A*S*H*.

18 January

*1912: Captain Robert Falcon Scott reaches the South Pole
(Roald Amundsen having already beaten him to it)*

The many different South Poles (and there you were thinking that there was only one)

1. **The Geographic South Pole:** one of two points where the Earth's axis of rotation intersects the surface, the other being the Geographic North Pole.* It is marked by a small sign and a stake. Because the ice cap moves up to ten metres a year, it's moved back to its correct position each New Year's Day. This was the South Pole first reached by Amundsen on 14 December 1911.

2. **The Ceremonial South Pole:** an area marked by a sphere on a stripy plinth, surrounded by the flags of the countries signed up to the Antarctic** Treaty. It's here that official 'South Pole' photos are taken. It's only a few metres from the Geographic South Pole.

3. **The South Geomagnetic Pole:** determined by the Earth's magnetic field, the location of this pole is constantly moving as the Earth's magnetic field is constantly changing.

4. **The South Magnetic Pole:** the point on the Earth's surface where the geometric field lines are directed upward vertically.

---

* On a globe, the two Poles are the points at which the bar running through the globy part stick out at either end, to attach to the stand.

** The South Pole is in the Antarctic, where the penguins are. The North Pole is in the Arctic, where the polar bears are. Neither has both. (**S**outh Pole = **S**ome Penguins/ **N**orth Pole = **N**o Penguins)

19 January

A palette-ful of artistic styles and movements to bandy about when talking about Western art, to make it sound like you know what you're talking about*

Abstract art
Art in which shapes, lines and colour are non-representational. In other words, they don't represent anything. They're not trying to be realistic.

Arts and Crafts
A 19th-century movement dedicated to recapturing and recreating the skill and quality of medieval craftsmanship. Created everything from architecture and furniture to wallpaper and books.

Art deco
A highly decorative and angular style made popular during the 1920s and 1930s.

Art nouveau
Late 19th-/early 20th-century ornamental style which incorporated vegetable forms into architecture and furniture.

Baroque
See Rococo.

Britart
A modern art movement created by a group of young British artists, starting in 1988.

* Oh dear! This list is supposed to be absolutely useless but it might come in handy, which means that this book isn't necessarily what it claims to be. How absolutely useless!**

** Oh, phew! That's all right then.

Cubism
The first big step away from painting figuratively – how people looked – in Western art. Started by Picasso and Braque in 1907.

Dada
Art designed to outrage the viewer or, at the very least, make them feel uncomfortable. Started in the First World War, it is sometimes described as 'an anarchic form of Expressionism'.

Environmental art
Art in which the landscape itself is somehow altered or decorated, often using natural objects such as wood or stone.

Expressionism
Early 20th-century movement in which the artist expresses his/her emotion through, among other things, distortion and exaggeration.

Impressionism
Art aimed at conveying an impression of what your eyes actually see rather than what your brain is telling you is in front of you. Developed in France and given a name in 1874, it has gained popularity over time.

Modern art
A general term for the development of art from the birth of Impressionism to today.

Neoclassicism
A late 18th-century reaction against the over-the-top Rococo style, going for 'noble simplicity'.

Performance art
An art form combining visual art with a dramatic performance.

Pointillism
The employment of small dots to create blocks of colour, form and subject from a distance.

Post-Impressionism
Born of Impressionism, this is an umbrella term for artistic movements which rejected naturalism, including the likes of Pointillism.

Pre-Raphaelite
The intention of this short-lived movement, started in 1848, was to return to the simplicity of painting before Raphael (1483–1520). Its inspiration was medieval myth and legend.

Realism
A 19th-century style depicting real life – including poverty and hardship – realistically (in other words, without idealizing light, colour or even circumstances).

Rococo
An extremely decorative, ornate style of 18th-century France.

Surrealism
Founded in 1924, surrealism explores dream, fantasy, and objects out of context.

20 January

1961: J. F. Kennedy is sworn in as
President of the United States

US presidents who have died in office (so far)

1841   William Henry Harrison, pneumonia

1850   Zachary Taylor, indigestion (not arsenic
poisoning, as suspected)

1865   Abraham Lincoln, assassinated by John
Wilkes Booth

1881   James A. Garfield, assassinated by Charles
J. Guiteau*

1901   William McKinley, assassinated by Leon
Czolgosz

1923   Warren G. Harding, heart attack

1945   Franklin D. Roosevelt, cerebral haemorrhage

1963   John F. Kennedy, assassinated by Lee
Harvey Oswald (according to the Warren
Commission)

* Or as a result of the inadequate medical care
following the shooting.

21 January

*1793: King Louis XVI is guillotined,
ending the monarchy in France*

Some upbeat last words*

'I want nobody distressed on my account.'
Ulysses S. Grant, US soldier and president

'I hope to see you on Tuesday at 10.30 a.m.'
Earl Douglas Haig, British general in the First World War

'Cheer up, children, I'm all right.'
Franz Joseph Haydn, composer

'Am I dying or is this my birthday?'
Lady Nancy Astor, British politician

'That was the best ice-cream soda I ever tasted.'
Lou Costello (of Abbot and Costello)

'Get my swan costume ready.'
Anna Pavlova, Russian ballerina

'God bless you all, I feel myself again.'
Sir Walter Scott, British novelist

* For obvious reasons, my favourite final utterance didn't qualify:
'Dying is a very dull, dreary affair. My advice to you is to have nothing to do with it.'
W. Somerset Maugham, author

22 January

1901: Queen Victoria dies

A shower of monarchs
(well, they did reign)

- William the Conqueror used to be known as William the Bastard. He later, of course, became William I of England.

- William I's wife Matilda was only 1.27 metres (4 feet 2 inches) tall, making her Britain's smallest monarch (so far).

- Edward II was the first British king to abdicate (give up his throne). He was forced to by his French wife Isabella in 1327. (Later, she and her mother probably had him murdered.)

- Henry VI was less than a year old when he became King of England and just over a year old when he became King of France.

- During the reign of Henry VII (aka Henry Tudor), two 'pretenders' claimed to be the rightful king. The first, Lambert Simnel (a baker's son), ended up a kitchen hand. The second, Perkin Warbeck, was less lucky. He was hanged for treason.

- Henry VIII's wife Anne Boleyn had six fingers on one hand, giving her a grand total of eleven. Well, nine fingers and two thumbs to be more accurate!

- Lady Jane Grey was the great-granddaughter of Henry VII. (Her mother was one of Henry VIII's sisters.) She ruled England as queen for just nine days.

- Elizabeth I was way ahead of her time. She had a bath four times a year – whether she needed one or not – instead of the more usual once-a-year or never approach.

- Mary Queen of Scots was bald when she died. (This was discovered after her execution.)

- Though George III is famous for his madness – hence the film *The Madness of King George* – he wasn't the only one: Henry VI also had serious bouts of insanity.

- William IV (who was the monarch just before Queen Victoria) lived with an actress and they had ten children together!
- Queen Victoria was the first monarch to make Buckingham Palace (formerly Buckingham House) her official London residence.*
- When Edward VIII abdicated to marry a divorcee, his brother became King George VI. George's first name was actually Albert.

* George IV died before he could move in and William IV hated the place.

23 January

1931: Russian ballerina Anna Pavlova dies

Famous food named after famous folk

Peach Melba and Melba toast: Dame Nellie
Melba

Garibaldi biscuits: Giuseppe Garibaldi,
Italian nationalist leader

Beef Wellington: the Duke of Wellington,
hero of the Battle of Waterloo

Banoffi pie: Count Ricardo Banoffi,*
Italian statesman

Pavlova: Anna Pavlova, ballerina

Victoria sponge cake: Queen Victoria,
queen (believe it or not)

Earl Grey tea: Earl Grey, aristocrat

Apple Charlotte: Queen Charlotte (wife of
George III)

* IMPORTANT NOTE: I'm lying. The name Banoffi is
a corruption of banana and toffee, the pie's two
key ingredients.

24 January

AD 41: Roman Emperor Caligula assassinated*

What those descriptions of the colours of horses actually mean (in alphabetical order)

Bay: brown with a black mane and legs

Chestnut: reddish-brown all over

Dun: sandy with a black mane

Palomino: golden with a pale mane

Piebald: black and white

Skewbald: brown and white

Strawberry roan: chestnut and white

* He's the one who made a horse a senator.

25 January

1533: Henry VIII secretly marries Anne Boleyn

Memorable marriages

- Film-stars Richard Burton and Elizabeth Taylor married each other twice, as did Don Johnson and Melanie Griffith, and Robert Wagner and Natalie Wood.

- Sir Termulji Bhiacaji Nariman and Lady Nariman of (what was then) Bombay, India, were married in 1853. They were cousins and both just five years old. Sir Temulji died in 1940. They had been married for 86 years.

- Lazarus Rowe and Molly Webber were also, apparently, married for 86 years. It's claimed that they married in Greenland, New Hampshire, USA in 1743. Rowe died in 1829.

- King Mongkut of Siam* (1804–68), had 39 wives (and 82 children).

- Glynn 'Scotty' de Moss Wolfe (1908–97) holds the US record for the most marriages: 29. His last wife, Linda Essex, holds the US record for the most-married woman: 23 weddings.

- According to the Bible, King Solomon had 700 wives and 300 concubines (partners he wasn't married to). This is a hard number to beat.

* Played by Yul Brynner in the film *The King and I.*

32

26 January

1915: Rocky Mountain National Park is established in the US

A pile of well-known rocks that aren't really rocks of the stony variety at all

Peter the Rock: In the Bible, Christ changes Simon's name to Peter and says 'and upon this rock I will build my church' (Matthew 17:18.) This is a pun which only works if you know that the Latin for rock is *petra*, from which the name Peter comes.

The Rock of Ages: This refers to Jesus Christ himself, as the unshakeable and eternal foundation. Augustus Montague Toplady later wrote the well-known hymn 'Rock of Ages', first published in 1775. One version of its origins has him writing it in Burrington Combe, Somerset, with the mighty rocks in the Cheddar Gorge on one side and the Mendip Heights on the other. Another has him jotting down the lyrics for the first verse on a ten of diamonds* in a break between two rubbers of whist.

Rock English: The mixture of English and Spanish spoken by people living on the Rock of Gibraltar.

Seaside Rock: Hard cylindrical peppermint-flavoured sticks, sold at the seaside, often with the name of the resort running all the way through it. George Formby Jr sang about 'My Little Stick of Blackpool Rock'.

Brighton Rock: Not a rock, not seaside rock. Not even a collective term for music to come out of Brighton, but the name of a book by Graham Greene which later became a British film starring Richard Attenborough.

Rock and Roll: A type of popular music originating in the 1950s.

Rocky: A boxing character played by Sylvester Stallone in the films of the same name.

* Well, diamonds are highly polished rocks, of course.

27 January

1995: Footballer Eric Cantona is fined
for aiming a kick at a fan

What those cool martial arts names actually mean

kung fu: hobby or leisure time*

tae kwon do: way of the foot and fist

judo: gentle way**

kyudo: way of the bow***

karate: way of the empty hand****

* No, honestly it does!
** Though not that gentle, mat or no mat.
*** I think we've worked out that the 'do' part means
'way of' by now.
**** Hang on, where's the 'do' in that?

28 January

*1980: the original Ants (of Adam and the Ants) split
up with Adam (of Adam and the Ants)*

Thirteen well-known sporting activities not included in the official Olympics

1. Egg and spoon racing
2. Sack racing
3. Three-legged racing
4. The cruel and disgusting outlawed art of trying to burn ants with the aid of the sun's rays and a magnifying glass
5. Synchronized belly-flopping and dive-bombing
6. Conkers
7. Hopscotch
8. Marbles
9. Mud-wrestling
10. Pillow fighting (feather stuffing)
11. Pillow fighting (synthetic filler stuffing)
12. Wellington-boot throwing (distance)*
13. Wellington-boot throwing (freestyle)

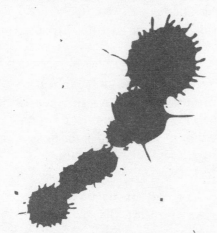

* The editor's husband once hit a spectator when taking part in such an event.

29 January

1929: first US guide-dog (Seeing Eye) school opens

Famous fictional dogs of all shapes and sizes

Timmy: one of Enid Blyton's *Famous Five*, along with humans Julian, Ann, George and Dick.

Snowy: Tintin's snow-white sidekick in Hergé's books.

Dougal: close friend of Florence, Zebedee, Brian the snail and Dylan the rabbit in TV's *The Magic Roundabout*.

Snoopy: Charlie Brown's beagle in the PEANUTS© cartoons, who slept ON rather than in his kennel.

Spike: Snoopy's brother, who looks suspiciously like Snoopy but with a droopy moustache and a hangdog look.

Goofy: a Disney cartoon dog.

Pluto: Mickey Mouse's pet dog. (For some reason, Mickey – a mouse – is larger than him!)

Rebel: the dog in TV's *Champion the Wonder Horse* who seems more wonderful than Champion.

Belle: a St Bernard from *Belle and Sebastian*,* a book by Cecile Aubrey who both wrote the original story and the TV series,** and now the name of a pop group.

Beethoven: another St Bernard, this time in the title role of at least two films (starring Charles Grodin).

Sandy: Ahhhh! The little dog belonging to Little Orphan Annie in *Annie*.

Lassie: who came home.

Rin Tin Tin: whom I've never seen, but was a big movie star.

Spottie Dog: of TV's *The Woodentops* fame. A string puppet, he waves goodbye with his ear rather than a hand (or paw).

The Hound of the Baskervilles: in *The Hound of the Baskervilles* plus, of course, the dog who impersonates him.

K9: the robot dog*** in *Doctor Who*.

Toto: Dorothy's dog in *The Wizard of Oz*.

* Originally spelled Sebastien.
** Cecile Aubrey's son played Sebastien in the series.
*** So technically not a real fictional dog . . . if you see what I mean.

30 January

1790: first lifeboat is launched in England

An 'A to Z' of different types of vessel*

A is for AIRCRAFT CARRIER
A large warship on which aircraft – helicopters and planes – can take off and land.

B is for:
BARGE
A confusing term this, because a barge can be a *canal boat*, a sailing cargo ship or even an ornately decorated rowing boat used by royalty (as in a royal barge).

BATTLESHIP
A large, heavily armed warship.

C is for:
CANAL BOAT
A long flat-bottomed boat used for pleasure or cargo (such as a coal barge) on human-made waterways, called canals.

CAR FERRY
A *ferry* which also carries cars.

CATAMARAN
A boat with two separate hulls, side by side.

CONTAINER SHIP
A cargo ship especially designed to carry standard-sized cargo containers. These containers can easily be loaded and unloaded, and even attached to cabs to form container lorries.

CRUISER
A fast, medium-sized warship. Larger than a *destroyer*, less heavily armed than a *battleship*.

CRUISE SHIP
But there are far too many Cs here already, so see *L is for LINER*.

* Well, an A to Y with plenty of gaps.

D is for DESTROYER

A small, fast warship, primarily with a defensive role against submarines and aircraft.

F is for:
FERRY

A ship taking passengers from one port to another.

FRIGATE

A small warship specifically designed to protect convoys of cargo (supply) ships from attack by submarines.

G is for:
GALLEON

A large sailing ship, typically square-rigged with three or more masts and decks, used from the 15th to 18th centuries.

GALLEY

Not only an ancient warship propelled by oars (the oarsmen often being slaves), but also a large open rowing boat kept on board a naval vessel, used by the captain. To add further confusion 'the galley' is a name given to a ship's kitchen.

H is for:
HOVERCRAFT

A boat crossing water on a cushion of air created by a downward blast, surrounded by a skirt.

HYDROFOIL

A boat with vanes (foils) which lift the hull clear of the water when it reaches speed, reducing surface tension, thus making it travel *faaaaaaaaster*! (The vanes themselves are also referred to as hydrofoils.)

J is for JUNK

No, not some rusty old hulk, ready for the scrap heap but a Chinese or Japanese flat-bottomed sailing ship with a high stern (back end) and two or three masts.

L is for:
LAUNCH

Both a large motorboat and, in the past, the largest rowing boat carried on a *man-of-war*.

LINER
Now also known as cruise ships, liners were once ocean-going ships designed to take passengers on long journeys (such as England to America). Later, these became more luxury vessels designed to take people on holiday cruises (stopping off to visit the sights).

M is for:
MAN-OF-WAR*
A historical nickname for a warship.

MINESWEEPER
A naval vessel designed to sweep for (search for) mines (floating bombs) and to destroy them.

P is for PADDLE STEAMER
A boat powered by steam and propelled by a paddle which turns through the water.

S is for SUBMARINE
A vessel designed to operate underwater for long periods of time. Military submarines are used to avoid detection and to fire torpedoes at ships on the surface and to fire missiles into targets in the air or on land. Civilian submarines are employed for underwater exploration and the study of wrecks and marine life.

T is for TANKER
A ship designed to carry liquids in huge quantities, such as an oil tanker carrying oil from an oil field to a refinery.

Y is for YACHT
A sailing or engine-powered vessel used for both pleasure cruising or racing.

* Not to be confused with a Portuguese man-of-war, which is a stinging jellyfish-type thingy.

31 January

1953: storms and flooding across the east coast of the UK leave thousands homeless

How windy is that wind?
(the Beaufort Scale, devised
by Francis Beaufort in 1805)

0	Calm
1	Light air
2	Light breeze
3	Gentle breeze
4	Moderate breeze
5	Fresh breeze
6	Strong breeze
7	Moderate gale
8	Fresh gale
9	Strong gale
10	Whole gale
11	Storm
12	Hurricane

1 February

1979: Trevor Francis becomes the first £1-million footballer when he signs for Nottingham Forest*

Some footballing facts

- In a Sheffield v. Glasgow match in 1930, the referee's uniform matched the Sheffield players' kit and they kept passing the ball to him! Eventually, he went off to change into something less confusing.

- Another problem with strips arose when both Coventry City and Southend United played in blue and white in 1962. The game was stopped after three minutes, and Coventry changed into red shirts before play was resumed.

- In 1958, Spurs captain, Danny Blanchflower, became the first person to refuse to appear on the UK version of the TV show *This Is Your Life*.

- George Best was the first player to receive a red card and be sent off in a football league game, in 1976.

- Millwall's fanzine is called *No One Likes Us*.

- Derby County and Charlton Athletic had a football burst on them twice in the same year, 1946. Firstly during the FA Cup final, and then in a league match less than a week later.

* Though someone told me that his actual transfer fee was £999,999. Cheapskates!

2 February

1996: dancer, movie star, choreographer,
director Gene Kelly dies

Movie actors and actresses with the top five most Oscar nominations (so far)

1. Meryl Streep (13 nominations, 2 Oscars)
2. Katharine Hepburn (12 nominations, 4 Oscars)
3. Jack Nicholson (12 nominations, 2 Oscars)
4. Bette Davis (10 nominations, 2 Oscars)
5. Jack Lemmon (8 nominations, 2 Oscars)
   Marlon Brando (8 nominations, 2 Oscars)

NOTE: Ingrid Bergman had only 7 nominations, but did win 3 Oscars.

3 February

1966: Russia makes first controlled landing of (unmanned) spacecraft on the Moon

Some of the items an alien might be intrigued by on the gold-plated records to be found on *Voyagers* 1 and 2 in outer space

- Animal sounds
- Human-made sounds
- Sounds from nature (wind, rain, crashing waves, etc.)
- Greetings in 55 different languages
- Messages from (then) US President Jimmy Carter and (then) UN Secretary General Kurt Waldheim
- The first movement of Bach's *Brandenburg Concerto* No. 2 in F
- Chuck Berry's 'Johnny B. Goode'
- Bagpipe music from Azerbaijan
- Over 100 images of 'scenes from everyday life' from playing sport to watching television

NB The discs predate DVD and CD-ROM technology and can be played by using a cartridge and needle provided. Each disc is in an aluminium sleeve cover, on which appear the image of a naked male and female, and a map to help find our solar system. (Let's hope those aliens are friendly.)

4 February

People who are so famous that they're known by one name

Beyoncé: US singer Beyoncé Knowles

Björk: Icelandic singer and actress Björk Gudmundsdottir

Bono: Irish front man of rock group U2, Paul Hewson

Canaletto: 18th-century Italian painter Giovanni Antonio Canale

Cher: US singer Cherilyn Sarkisian

Dido: English singer Dido Armstrong

Eminem: US rap singer Marshall Mathers

Enya: Irish singer Eithne ní Bhraonáin

Evita: 20th-century Argentinian politician Eva Perón

Houdini: US escapologist and magician Ehrich Weiss

Liberace: pianist Wladziu Valentino Liberace

Lulu: Scottish singer Marie McDonald McLaughlin Lawrie

Madonna: US singer Madonna Louise Ciccone

Meatloaf: US singer Marvin Lee Aday

Michelangelo: Italian painter Michelangelo Buonarroti

Pelé: Brazilian footballer Edson Arantes do Nascimento

Pink: US singer Alecia Moore

Ronaldo: Brazilian footballer Ronaldo Luiz Nazário de Lima

Sting: English singer Gordon Matthew Sumner

5 February

1953: Disney's film version of Peter Pan *is released*

Peter Pan, Barrie and the Llewelyn Davieses

- The original story of *Peter Pan* was written by Scottish author and playwright J. M. Barrie. *Peter Pan* existed as a play (1904) long before Barrie rewrote it as a book (1911).

- 37-year-old actress Nina Boucicault was the first person to play the character of Peter Pan on stage.

- The character of Peter Pan first appeared in Barrie's novel *The Little White Bird* (1902), though he had told stories about him to the Llewelyn Davies brothers: George, Jack, Michael, Peter, and, later, Nicholas* (Nico).

- The actor Gerald du Maurier, the boys' uncle (their mother Sylvia** was his sister) played Captain Hook in the original play.

- Tragedy seemed to strike those closely associated with the early life of *Peter Pan*:

  ◆ The Llewelyn Davies boys' father, Arthur, died of cancer in 1907.

  ◆ Their mother, Sylvia, died of cancer in 1910.

  ◆ George died in Flanders in 1915 in the First World War.

  ◆ Michael, Barrie's favourite – and on whom the Peter Pan statue*** in London's Kensington Gardens is modelled – drowned while at university in 1921.

  ◆ Peter committed suicide in 1960, aged 63. He had described *Peter Pan* as 'that terrible masterpiece'.

* Nicholas's daughter had a bit part in the 2004 film *Finding Neverland*.

** Sylvia Llewelyn Davies was born Sylvia du Maurier and was the aunt of Daphne du Maurier, author of, among others, *Rebecca* and *My Cousin Rachel*.

*** Though Barrie didn't think that the features captured any of Michael's impishness.

- Charles Frohman, the theatre impresario behind the staging of *Peter Pan*, was aboard the *Lusitania* when it was torpedoed and sunk by a German U-boat* in 1915. Mirroring Peter Pan's words 'To die would be an awfully big adventure,' he was reported to have said, 'Why fear death? It is the most beautiful adventure in life.'
- J. M. Barrie died at the age of 77 in 1937. He bequeathed the royalties of *Peter Pan* to the Great Ormond Street Children's Hospital.**

* A submarine.

** These, like all royalties, expired 70 years after his death (in 2007). Royalties from the official sequel, *Peter Pan in Scarlet* (2006), are shared between its author, Geraldine McCaughrean, and the hospital.

46

6 February

A list showing the categories of the UFO 'Close Encounter' ('CE') scale, as devised by J. Allen Hynek in 1972 (and later expanded)

The higher the 'CE' number, the closer the contact:

CE1: The witness sees objects or very bright lights from less than 457 metres away.

CE2: The UFO physically affects the environment, leaving traces of its presence (such as marks from its landing gear or even a 'sunburnt' witness).

CE3: Witness actually sees – or even meets! – the alien occupants of the spaceship.

CE4: Witness actually enters the alien craft (more often than not against his or her will).

CE5: The witness encounters paranormal activity such as telepathy with the aliens.

CE6: The witness takes part in a show-stopping song and dance number with the aliens, climaxing with a beautifully choreographed high-kicking chorus line.*

* IMPORTANT NOTE: I made up CE6.

7 February

1649: the office of king officially ceases
to exist in Britain (as far as Cromwell and
the Parliamentarians are concerned)

A Scotch mist of
non-existent items

Left-handed screwdrivers*
Elbow grease*
Pigeon milk*
Rick moulds*A
Cats' footfalls**
Women's beards**
Birds' spittle**
Fishes' voices**
Mountains' roots**

* Items that workmates traditionally sent a greenhorn/
novice/apprentice to find, as a practical joke.

A During harvesting, back in the days when the hay was
gathered into neatly shaped thatched stacks called ricks,
there was a tradition of sending a youth to 'fetch the
rick mould' (as though, like a jelly, these haystacks were
somehow moulded into their distinctive shape). When the
unsuspecting victim returned lugging a very heavy sack
under a hot summer's sky, it would be opened to reveal
that it had been filled with nothing but the nearest heavy
objects. There's no such thing as a rick mould.

** According to Norse mythology, these existed in the world
until they were used as the magical ingredients to create
the rope Gleipnir, which bound the mighty wolf Fenris.

8 February

A nosebag of well-known horses (some real, some imaginary)

Aldaniti: a horse who recovered from a serious leg injury and went on to win the 1981 Grand National at Aintree, ridden by Bob Champion (recently recovered from cancer)

Black Beauty: star of Anna Sewell's book, and of film and TV fame

Boxer: the hardworking carthorse in George Orwell's *Animal Farm*

Champion, the Wonder Horse: star of a US TV series of the same name

Pegasus: the winged horse

Red Rum: champion racehorse, whose name is 'murder' backwards

Seabiscuit: a very famous American horse indeed (and subject of a film of the same name)

Silver:* the Lone Ranger's horse. (Tonto, the Lone Ranger's sidekick, had a horse called Scout)

Trigger: horse of film-star Roy Rogers (now stuffed)**

* Also referred to as 'White Fella' in an early episode.

** The horse, not Mr Rogers.

49

9 February

A series of unfortunate deaths

- Francis Bacon, the Elizabethan philosopher – and the man some claimed actually wrote Shakespeare's plays – died in 1626 as a result of having stuffed a plucked chicken with snow. He wanted to see if freezing the meat would preserve it as well as packing it in salt did. Sadly, he caught a fatal chill.

- Isadora Duncan was famous for her dancing and for her fashion style, which included wearing very long scarves. Unfortunately, in 1927, one such scarf became entangled in the rear wheel of a sports car in which she was a passenger.

- Sir Thomas Urquhart, a Scottish author, is said to have died laughing when he heard the news that King Charles II had been restored to the throne of England.

- In 1920 King Alexander of Greece died of an infection as a result of being bitten by his pet monkey.

- Harry Houdini, the great escapologist, died in 1926 of a ruptured appendix. Many believe that this was as a result of a punch in the stomach from a university student. He had told (or permitted) the student to punch him, but hadn't been quite ready for him.

- Aeschylus, the Greek dramatist, was said to have died in 456 BC when a passing vulture dropped a tortoise on his head, hoping to crack the animal's shell. The bird is thought to have mistaken the bald man's shiny, smooth head for a nice hard rock.

- Jack Daniel (of *Jack Daniel's* sipping whiskey fame) kicked his safe when he couldn't remember the combination to open it, in 1911. He hurt his toe, ended up with blood poisoning and died.

- Jerome Cardan (aka Gerolama Cardano) was an astrologer who foresaw his own death. In 1576 he killed himself to make sure that his prediction was correct!

- Pope Clement VII died in 1534 as a result, it is claimed, of having eaten death cap mushrooms. A matter of days before his death, he had commissioned Michelangelo to paint *The Last Supper* in the Sistine Chapel.

- Henry Purcell, the composer, died in 1695 after returning home from the theatre late one cold evening to find that his wife had locked him out. It's believed that the chill he caught eventually killed him. (Others claim he died from too much chocolate or from tuberculosis. Or, perhaps, all three.)

- David Douglas, a Scottish botanist, was killed in 1834 when he fell in a pit, dug as a trap. It wasn't the fall that killed him but the bull that fell on top of him.

- Allan Pinkerton, founder of the Pinkerton Detective Agency, stumbled on a pavement, bit his tongue and died of the resulting gangrene in 1884.

10 February

1997: world chess champion Garry Kasparov is beaten in a match by IBM computer Deep Blue (though Kasparov will go on to win the tournament)

French and German names for chess pieces, according to my mate Dave

English	French	German
Pawn	Pion (*pawn*)	Bauer (*peasant*)
Rook/Castle	Tour (*tower*)	Turm (*tower*)
Knight	Cavalier (*horseman*)	Springer (*jumper*)
Bishop	Fou (*fool*)	Laufer (*runner*)
King	Roi (*king*)	König (*king*)
Queen	Reine, Dame (*queen, lady*)	Königin (*queen*)

11 February

1858: Bernadette Soubirous (later St Bernadette) has her first vision of the Virgin Mary at Lourdes, France

Twenty patron saints and what they're patrons of

St Adjutor: Swimmers

St Agatha: Volcanoes and Nurses

St Andrew: Scotland

St Anthony: Gravediggers and Pig-herders

St Apollonia: Dentists and Toothache

St Bartholomew: Plasterers

St Catherine (and **St Gregory**): Teachers

St David: Wales

St Fiacre: Haemorrhoids (piles) and Cab Drivers

St Francis of Sales: Writers

St George: Scouts and England

St Hippolytus: Prison Officers

St John of God: Booksellers

St Joseph of Cupertino: Astronauts

St Jude: Lost Causes

St Martin of Porres: Hairdressers

St Michael: Policemen

St Nicholas: Children

St Vitus: Comedians and Dancers

12 February

1831: in Boston, rubber galoshes go on sale for the first time

Some lesser-known firsts

- The first dinner jacket to be worn in the US was at the Tuxedo Park Country Club in New York in 1886 (which is why Americans refer to them as a tuxedo or tux).

- The first officially named zebra crossing was introduced on Halloween 1949 in Slough.

- The very first woman prime minister in the world was Mrs Sirimavo Bandaranaike of Ceylon (now Sri Lanka) in 1960.

- The very first duke in the UK was Edward, Duke of Cornwall, in 1337.

- The world's first credit card was the Diners Club card in New York in 1950.

- The first sex-change operation took place in 1952 when George Jorgensen became Christine Jorgensen.

- The first MOT test on cars in the UK was in 1960.

- The first UK television licence was introduced in 1946.

13 February

*1692: members of the MacDonald clan are
killed at the Massacre of Glencoe*

A few famous 'Scottish' items borrowed from elsewhere*

Kilts: It's now generally accepted that kilts were invented by the Irish, though the word itself comes from *kilte op*, the Danish for 'tuck up'.

Bagpipes: These are a very old musical instrument indeed. They turn up in the Old Testament in the Bible and in ancient Greek poetry. They're thought to have originated in Central Asia.

Porridge: This basic oaty meal has been discovered in the stomach of bodies of Neolithic people (preserved) in the peat bogs of Europe for over 5,000 years.

Haggis: Similar such 'sausages' were certainly around in ancient Greece.

Whisky: Neither a Scottish nor Irish invention – though only Scottish whisky is Scotch – it was first made by the Chinese, and was made in Ireland (whiskey with an 'e') before reaching Scotland.

* Even the name Scotland isn't strictly from Scotland. The country is named after the Scoti, who were an Irish tribe (which is why Scots Gaelic is a dialect of Irish).

14 February

St Valentine's Day

The universal language of love

Afrikaans Ek is lief vir jou!
Albanian Te dua!
Amharic Afekrishalehou!
Arabic Ohiboke (*to female*), Nohiboka (*to male*)
Armenian Yes kez si'rumem!
Basque Maite zaitut!
Bengali Ami tomake bahlobashi!
Bosnian Volim te!
Bulgarian Obicham te!
Catalan T'estimo!
Creole Mi aime jou!
Croatian Volim te!
Czech Miluji te!
Danish Jeg elsker dig!
Dutch Ik hou van je!
English I love you!
Esperanto Mi amas vin!
Estonian Mina armastan sind!
Farsi Tora dost daram!
Filipino Iniibig kita!
Finnish (Mä) rakastan sua!
French Je t'aime!
Frisian Ik hald fan dei!
Galician Querote!
German Ich liebe dich!
Greek S'ayapo!
Gujarati Hoon tane pyar karoochhoon!
Hawaiian Aloha wau ia 'oe!

Hebrew Anee ohev otakh (*male to female*),
  Anee ohevet otkha (*f to m*), Anee ohev otkha (*m to m*),
  Anee ohevet otakh (*f to f*)
Hindi Mai tumase pyar karata hun (*male to female*),
  Mai tumase pyar karati hun (*female to male*)
Hungarian Szeretlek!

Icelandic Eg elska thig!
Indonesian Saya cinta padamu!
Irish-Gaelic T'a gr'a agam dhuit!
Italian Ti amo!
Japanese Kimi o ai shiteru!
Korean Dangsinul saranghee yo!
Latin Te amo!
Latvian Es teవi mílu!
Lithuanian As tave myliu!
Malaysian Saya cintamu!
Mandarin Wo ai ni!
Marshallese Yokwe Yuk!
Norwegian Jeg elsker deg!
Polish Kocham ciebie!
Portuguese Eu te amo!
Romanian Te iubesc!
Russian Ya tyebya lyublyu!
Sanskrit Twayi snihyaami
Serbian Volim te!
Sesotho Kiyahurata!
Slovak Lubim ta!
Slovenian Ljubim te!
Spanish Te amo!
Swahili Nakupenda!
Swedish Jag älskar dig!
Tagalog Mahal kita!
Thai Khao raak thoe
Turkish Seni seviyorum!
Ukrainian Ya tebe kokhayu!
Urdu Main tumse muhabbat karta hoon!
Vietnamese Anh yeu em (*male to female*)
      Em yeu an (*female to male*)
Welsh Rwy'n dy garu di!
Yiddish Kh'hob dikh lib!
Zulu Ngiyakuthanda!

15 February

1965: Canada celebrates its new national flag: a red maple leaf on white, between two red stripes

A case of champagne bottles in order of size*

Magnum: equivalent to 2 bottles
Jeroboam: equivalent to 4 bottles
Rehoboam: equivalent to 6 bottles
Methuselah: equivalent to 8 bottles
Salmanazar: equivalent to 12 bottles
Balthazar: equivalent to 16 bottles
Nebuchadnezzar: equivalent to 20 bottles

* Cause enough for celebration.

16 February

1906: J. H. and W. K. Kellogg found the Battle Creek Toasted Corn Flake Company

Twenty common (and not-so-common) reasons for missing breakfast

1. **Oversleeping.** (*'Zzzzzzzzzzzzzz.'*)
2. **Undersleeping.** (*'I'm toooooo tired!'*)
3. **Alien abduction.** (*'Aaargh!'*)
4. **Loss of memory.** (*'What?'*)
5. **Loss of dignity.** (*'Who glued my pants to my head?'*)
6. **Loss of sanity.** (*'I don't eat cornflakes since I became one.'*)
7. **Poor planning.** (*'This is my wallpapering-the-hallway time of day.'*)
8. **Too full from last night.** (*'I shouldn't have eaten that pizza and the box that it came in.'*)
9. **Too empty.** (*'I don't have the strength to get to the breakfast table.'*)
10. **Too lazy.** (*'Could someone please carry me to my chair?'*)
11. **Just Plain Weird.** (*'I'm a cocker spaniel . . .'*)
12. **In too much of a hurry.** (*'Wheeeeeeeeeeeeeeeeeeeeeeeeeeeee!'*)
13. **Still shut in the loo.** (*'Weeeeeeeeeeeeeeeeeeeeeeeeeeee!'*)
14. **Helping others.** (*'I'll climb through that open window and open the front door for you.'*)
15. **Helping the police with their enquiries.** (*'I thought they'd locked themselves out, Officer. How was I to know that it wasn't their house?'*)
16. **Texting.** (*'Will I C U 4 lunch?'*)
17. **Waking up in a parallel universe where breakfast is thought   to be the least important meal of the day.** (*'Television, however, is full of goodness . . .'*)
18. **Having something better to do.** (*'I have until sundown to achieve world peace.'*)
19. **Being dead to the world.** (*'Huh?'*)
20. **Being dead.** (*'–'*)

17 February

1924: BBC uses the chimes of Big Ben as a radio time signal

Ten common fallacies exposed

The following are facts, whatever you might think:

1. The clock tower at the Houses of Parliament is not called Big Ben. (The big bell inside it is.)

2. The Bayeux Tapestry is not a tapestry. (It's an embroidery.)

3. Mustard gas is not a gas and doesn't contain mustard. (It's a liquid that gives off a terrible vapour.)

4. Catgut isn't made from cats' guts. (It's sheep gut.)

5. Spaghetti is not an Italian invention. (It's probably Etruscan.)*

6. Rice paper isn't made of rice. (It's made from the pith of a shrub.)

7. Richard III was not a hunchback. (This was enemy propaganda.)

8. The idea of moonshine is technically moonshine. (Moonlight is actually sunlight reflected off the Moon.)

9. Glass is a solid – though clever people, and some dictionaries – will tell you that, in its normal state, it's a liquid. (It's an amorphous solid.)

10. A centipede has nowhere near 100 legs. (Count them yourself.)

* Though some people are convinced that it's Chinese – a variation on noodles.

18 February

1930: the planet Pluto is discovered by Clyde Tombaugh, an American astronomer

Six things you may not have known about Area 51 (if you've even heard of it)

1. Area 51 is US government land located in Nevada, north of Las Vegas.
2. It contains Groom Lake Base, a secret air force testing facility.*
3. The U2 spy plane and F-117A Stealth bomber were developed and test-flown there under tight security.
4. It borders military facilities such as the site of the US's original atom-bomb tests.
5. Civil aviation is banned from the airspace around Area 51. This no-go area is nicknamed 'Dreamland'.
6. There are claims that Area 51 is also where the US government takes crashed UFOs to be studied for their advanced alien technology (which might then be applied to US hardware), in a process known as reverse engineering.
7. The US government deny No. 6 above, which is hardly surprising because, understandably, they deny the existence of alien spacecraft.

---

* If I know about it, the base itself can't be that secret, but what they actually test there is secret, at the time of testing, anyway.

19 February

1910: Manchester United play their first game on their new ground at Old Trafford

A few sporting firsts which don't involve people coming first in a sport

How some of the most famous games in sport came about are lost in the mists of time, but a few can be traced back to one specific person. These include:

- **Basketball:** invented by Dr James Naismith in Springfield, Massachusetts, USA, in 1891.
- **Bowls:** the rules of the modern game were drawn up in 1848 by William Mitchell of Glasgow.
- **Softball:** this indoor version of baseball was invented by George Hancock in Chicago, USA, in 1887.
- **Volleyball:** invented in 1895 by William Morgan, also of Massachusetts, and originally known as 'mintonette'.

Two bonus sporty facts:
1. US Civil War general Abner Doubleday is credited as having invented baseball in New York State in 1839. This is strange when you consider that the game is described in an English book published in 1744 called *A Little Pretty Pocket Book*, which came out in America 18 years later. Modern baseball was developed by Manhattan bookseller (and volunteer fireman) Alexander Cartwright in the 1840s.
2. Jockeys are not allowed beards (at least, not on their faces). There's probably nothing to stop them from keeping one in a jar on a shelf at home.

20 February

1947: Earl Mountbatten of Burma is appointed India's last Viceroy (in advance of India's independence from Britain in August)

The order of British nobility (with the poshest one first)

1st. Duke
2nd. Marquess
3rd. Earl
4th. Viscount
5th. Baron
6th. Baronet

Popular mnemonic for remembering it: Did Mary Ever Visit Brighton Beach?*

* Good, huh? The best I could come up with was 'Dame Melba Eats Very Big Buns' and 'Don't Mind Everyone Vilifying Big Brother'.

21 February

Eight humungously huge statues

Christ the Redeemer, Rio de Janeiro, Brazil
Vital statistics: 38 metres tall, 1,163 tonnes
Unveiled: 1931
Point of interest: Officially unveiled by Guglielmo Marconi

The Statue of Liberty, New York, USA
Vital statistics: 46 metres tall (including pedestal: 93 metres),
229 tonnes
Unveiled: 1886
Point of interest: Made in France, it was originally called Liberty
Enlightening the World

The Sphinx, Giza, Egypt
Vital statistics: 20 metres tall, 73 metres long
Built: probably about 2,500 BC
Point of interest: Famous for its missing nose

The Angel of the North, Gateshead, England
Vital statistics: 19.8 metres tall, wingspan 53.3 metres, 200
tonnes.
Built: 1998
Point of interest: Designed by Antony Gormley

Leshan Giant Buddha, China
Vital statistics: 71 metres high
Built: between AD 713 and 803
Point of interest: Its ears are 7 metres long

Mount Rushmore, South Dakota, USA
Vital statistics: four massive heads, each around 18.3 metres
high
Carved: Between 1927 and 1939
Point of interest: representing the heads of US presidents
Washington, Jefferson, Lincoln and Roosevelt, it's still one of
America's most popular tourist attractions

Abu Simbel, Egypt

Vital statistics: four seated statues, each 20 metres high
Carved: 13th century BC
Point of interest: All four statues were dismantled and relocated
 when the Aswan High Dam was built (and their original site
 was flooded)

Crazy Horse Memorial, South Dakota, USA

Vital statistics: 172 metres high, 195 metres long
Carved: Begun 1948 and still going
Point of interest: THE BIGGEST MONUMENT ON EARTH

22 February

*1879: in Utica, New York, Frank Woolworth
opens his first 'five-cent' store**

Twenty things which our American cousins say kinda different to us

UK	US
aubergine	eggplant
macaroni cheese	macaroni *and* cheese
bowler hat	derby
bum-bag	fanny pack
caravan site	trailer park
chemist's shop	drug store
chips	French fries
crisps	potato chips
courgette	zucchini
curtains	drapes
estate agent	realtor
foyer	lobby
funny bone	crazy bone
garden	yard
ice lolly	Popsicle
jam	jelly
jelly	jello
ladybird	ladybug
merry-go-round	carousel
nappy	diaper
tadpole	pollywog (sometimes)
tap	faucet
telephone box	phone booth
trousers	pants
waistcoat	vest
wallet	billfold
windscreen	windshield

* When Woolworth's stores first opened in the UK, nothing cost more than 6d. (six old pennies), so they were 'sixpenny' stores.

23 February

1792: English painter Joshua Reynolds dies
1817: English painter Sir George Watts is born
1987: US pop artist Andy Warhol dies

A splatter of painters and paintings

- The painter Caravaggio had to flee Rome in 1606 having killed a man in an argument.
- The painter Richard Dadd murdered his own dad in 1843.
- *Red Vineyard* was the only painting by Van Gogh sold in his lifetime.
- Munch's *The Scream* was stolen from the National Gallery, Oslo, in February 1994 and recovered in May 1994. It was also stolen from the Munch Museum in Norway in August 2004, and recovered in August 2006.*
- Renoir suffered from rheumatism so badly in later life that he had to tie the paintbrush to his fingers.
- Velázquez's *Rokeby Venus* was slashed by a suffragette in the National Gallery, London, in 1914, to draw attention to the cause of votes for women.
- Graham Sutherland's portrait of Sir Winston Churchill was destroyed by Churchill's widow, she hated it so much.
- James Whistler sued John Ruskin for his comments on Whistler's painting *Falling Rocket*. Whistler won the case but was awarded only a farthing (a quarter of an old penny).

* There is more than one version of the painting.

24 February

Nine Bibles containing misprints of varying degrees of seriousness

The Ears to Ear Bible so called because this 1810 edition contains the misprint 'Who hath ears to *ear*, let him hear' (instead of 'Who hath ears to *hear* . . .') in Matthew 13:43.

The Forgotten Sins Bible (of 1638) in which Luke 7:47, 'Her sins which are many, are forgiven', reads: 'Her sins which are many, are *forgotten*'.

The Judas Bible (of 1611) in which Judas Iscariot's name appears in Matthew 26:36, instead of Jesus's!!!

The Lions Bible (of 1804) which contained an enormous number of printers' errors, including, most famously, 'but thy son that shall come forth out of thy *lions*' instead of 'out of thy loins', hence its name.

The Printers' Bible (of c.1702) in which Psalms 119:161, 'princes have persecuted me without cause', appears as '*printers* have persecuted me without cause' . . . due to a printer's error!

The Sin On Bible (of 1716) is probably the most famous of the misprinted Bibles. John 5:14, should read 'sin no more', but appears as 'sin on more', meaning quite the opposite!

The To-Remain Bible (of 1805) is particularly interesting because an editor's comment written in the margin of the proof pages – pages which are corrected before the final printing – ended up in the final bound Bible. Galatians 4:29, should read: 'persecuted him that was born after the spirit, even so it is now'. It appeared as: 'persecuted him that was born after the spirit *to remain*, even so it is now'. The words 'to remain' were a note from an editor that the comma after the word spirit was to remain. The printer thought it meant that he should add the words to the text!

The Unrighteous Bible (of 1653) also contains a serious altering of meaning. Instead of I Corinthians 6:9 stating 'the unrighteous shall not inherit the Kingdom of God', it claims: 'the unrighteous shall inherit the Kingdom of God'!

The Wicked Bible (of 1631) contains the unfortunate commandment: 'Though shalt commit adultery.' The printers were fined the then HUGE sum of £300 and went out of business.

25 February

1899: F. R. Sewell becomes the first driver of a car ever to be killed in a car crash, while test-driving a Daimler in Harrow

People better known by their initials, and what these initials stand for

J. S. Bach Johann Sebastian (composer)

J. M. Barrie James Matthew (most famous for *Peter Pan*)

W. C. Fields William Claude (comedy actor)

K. C. Gillette King Camp (most famous for his safety razor)

W. G. Grace William Gilbert (the big-bearded cricketer)

P. D. James Phyllis Dorothy (crime writer)

J. B. Priestley John Boynton (novelist)

J. K. Rowling Joanne Kathleen (author of Harry Potter books)

E. H. Shepard Ernest Howard (illustrated *Winnie-the-Pooh*)

J. R. R. Tolkien John Ronald Reuel (author)

P. G. Wodehouse Pelham Grenville (comic novelist)

26 February

Four things to do with one million one-pound coins (now that there are no longer one-pound notes)

1. Line them up in a neat row, edge to edge, to make a 13.98-mile (22.5-km) line of them.
2. Melt them down – which is illegal, because you mustn't deface legal tender – and make a 9.5-tonne statue of your favourite children's author, beard and all.*
3. Take them to your local bank or building society and have them changed for exactly 356 tonnes of one-penny pieces.
4. SPEND THEM!!!

PS
- The average adult in the UK has four credit and/or debit cards.
- Holograms first appeared on credit cards on Visa cards in the US. This was a security measure – making cards that much harder to forge – introduced in 1984.
- The first cards to have built-in microchips were introduced as long ago as 1975. This was in France.
- The world's very first credit card was the Diners Club card, invented by Frank McNamara and introduced in 1950.

* Neither author nor publisher recommend such action, of course.

27 February

1933: the German parliament building, the Reichstag, is burnt down. Hitler's government blames the Communist Party

Fourteen folk better known by other names (plus three others)

Archie Leach = Cary Grant (suave movie star)
Taidje Khan Jr = Yul Brynner (bald movie star)
Damon Gough = Badly Drawn Boy (singer/songwriter)
Christopher Wallace = Notorious B.I.G. (singer)
Derek Van Den Bogaerde = Dirk Bogarde (actor/writer)
David Jones = David Bowie (cool rock legend)
Charles Dodgson = Lewis Carroll (*Alice in Wonderland* author)
Vincent Furnier = Alice Cooper (worrying rock star)
Denis Pratt = Quentin Crisp (writer/style guru)
Caryn Johnson = Whoopi Goldberg (actress)
Adolf Schicklgruber = Adolf Hitler (evil dictator)
Julius Marx = Groucho Marx (very funny man)
Demi Guynes = Demi Moore (actress)
Theodre Seuss Geisel = Dr Seuss (author/illustrator)
Chris Collins = Frank Skinner (comedian/TV host)
Robert van Winkle = Vanilla Ice (rapper/actor)
Steveland Judkins = Stevie Wonder (singer/songwriter/ musician)

*1784: the rules of the Methodist Church are issued
by John Wesley in the Deed of Declaration*

Just what those different types of religious building really are

Church: a building used by Christians for public worship

Chapel: a place of worship inside a larger building (sometimes a private house); or the name of a nonconformist Christian building

Basilica: a kind of early Christian church

Cathedral: the seat of a Christian bishop – all towns with cathedrals are actually cities – and the main church in the area

Meeting House: a meeting place for certain religious groups, most notably the Quakers

Abbey: a building full of Christian monks or nuns (but not both at the same time), under the care/control of an abbot or abbess

Friary: the home of Friars (a Christian brotherhood)

Priory: a religious house overseen by a prior, sometimes under the overall control of an abbey

Monastery: a building housing a religious community of monks

Nunnery: a building housing a religious community of nuns (as is a **convent**)

Shrine: a place of worship, often containing sacred relics, associated with a particular saint or holy person

Dagoba: a Buddhist shrine

Mosque: a building used by Muslims for public worship

Synagogue: a building used by Jews for public worship

Tabernacle: a Jewish house or tent used as a place of worship. Its name comes from the tent covering the Ark of the Covenant

Temple: sometimes used by Jews in place of a synagogue; also, a place of worship dedicated to a particular deity. The majority of Hindu temples are dedicated to a presiding deity – the primary deity – and subordinate deities (though others are dedicated to several)

29 February

An odd list for an odd day of the year

Five words beginning with the letter 'b' that don't actually mean what they look as though they might mean

burpee: *not* someone who's burped at, rather than one who burps, *but* a squat thrust used in an agility test created by psychologist Royal H. Burpee in the 1930s.

burro: *not* a burrow which has collapsed at the far end, *but*, in the US, a small donkey used as a pack animal.

baldachin: *not* a clean-shaven person who is, in other words, 'bald on the chin', *but* a ceremonial canopy over a throne, doorway or even an altar.

blanquette: *not* a posh French blanket used instead of a duvet, *but* a dish of white meat in a white sauce.

bruit: *not* a violent fruit, *but* to spread a rumour widely.

boatel: *not* a hotel reached by boat . . . Oh, hang on: it IS!

1 March

International emergency 'help me!' messages for use at sea*

1. An article of clothing – ideally a coat – tied to a mast or upright oar. (Make sure the coat isn't better served keeping you warm.)
2. An ensign – flag on a ship – flown upside down. (But, be warned, some people might not *notice* it's the wrong way up.)
3. Flying a square ensign with a ball either above or below it. (Hmm. It rather depends what you have with you.)
4. Flames on a vessel. (If the ship's already on fire – hence the emergency – you don't have to do much to create this one. If you do set fire to an oil-soaked rag, though, be sure not to make matters worse by burning yourself or the vessel. Or both.)
5. Firing a red flare. (Don't leave home without one!)
6. Firing a rocket that gives off red stars at intervals. (So long as it's not mistaken for a firework display.)
7. Creating orange smoke signals. (First, take one smoking orange . . .)
8. Flying the international code signal NC (November Charlie). (Using your handy pack of international flags – from A to Z – for just such a purpose.)
9. Blowing a continuous whistle (though you are allowed to pause for breath) or sounding a siren.
10. Radio signalling the Morse code message: SOS (. . . ___ . . .). (But only if the situation is REALLY life-threatening.)
11. Broadcasting the word MAYDAY. (Again, only if it's a matter of life or death.)
12. Slowly raising and lowering your arms again and again and again. (Though you do run the risk of being mistaken for someone doing arm exercises up on deck.)

* And the problems accompanying them.

2 March

Those silly-sounding names for numbers so large you'll never get around to counting up to them from zero anyway

Trillion: 1,000,000,000,000 (12 zeros)

Quadrillion: 1,000,000,000,000,000 (15 zeros)

Quintillion: 1,000,000,000,000,000,000 (18 zeros)

Sextillion: 1,000,000,000,000,000,000,000 (21 zeros)

Septillion: 1,000,000,000,000,000,000,000,000 (24 zeros)

Octillion: 1,000,000,000,000,000,000,000,000,000 (27 zeros)

Nonillion: 1,000,000,000,000,000,000,000,000,000,000 (30 zeros)

Decillion: 33 zeros

Undecillion: 36 zeros

Duodecillion: 39 zeros

Tredecillion: 42 zeros

Quattuordecillion: 45 zeros

Quindecillion: 48 zeros

Sexdecillion: 51 zeros

Septendecillion: 54 zeros

Octodecillion: 57 zeros

Novemdecillion: 60 zeros

Googol: 100 zeros

3 March

1802: Beethoven's Moonlight Sonata *(Piano Sonata No. 14 in C-sharp minor) is published*

Giant leaps in Moon history

- Only 12 human beings have (so far as we're aware) set foot on the Moon.

- The most popular first names for Moonwalkers are Charles (2) and Alan (2).

- The longest time any astronaut has spent outside the lunar module (landing craft) on the Moon is 22 hours and 4 minutes in total (not all in one go). This time was achieved by the astronauts of *Apollo 17*.

- All Moonwalks took place between July 1969 and December 1972. No one has been back since.

- The Moonwalkers were, in order of steps:
  1. Neil Armstrong,* *Apollo 11*, July 1969
  2. Edwin 'Buzz' Aldrin, *Apollo 11*, July 1969
  3. Charles Conrad Jr, *Apollo 12*, November 1969
  4. Alan Bean, *Apollo 12*, November 1969
  5. Alan Shepard, *Apollo 14*, Jan/Feb 1971
  6. Edgar Mitchell, *Apollo 14*, Jan/Feb 1971
  7. David Scott, *Apollo 15*, July/August 1971
  8. James Irwin, *Apollo 15*, July/August 1971
  9. John Young, *Apollo 16*, April 1972
  10. Charles Duke Jr, *Apollo 16*, April 1972
  11. Eugene Cernan, *Apollo 17*, December 1972
  12. Harrison Schmitt, *Apollo 17*, December 1972

- *Apollo 13* never made it to the Moon as planned after an oxygen tank exploded, but all three astronauts returned safely to Earth.

---

* Many history books report that Neil Armstrong's first words when setting foot on the Moon were: 'This is one small step for a man, one giant leap for mankind.' Others claim that he actually fluffed the line, saying: 'This is one small step for man, one giant leap for mankind.' Because 'man' and 'mankind' mean the same thing, this would have made the statement somewhat meaningless. In 2006, tests on the recording suggested that Armstrong may well have said 'a man', but that static covered the word 'a'.

1890: the Forth rail bridge, spanning
the Firth of Forth in Scotland, is
opened by Edward, Prince of Wales

Ten of the many different names by which the current Prince of Wales (at the time of compiling this list) is known:

1. Charles (by his parents HM Queen Elizabeth II and Prince Philip, the Duke of Edinburgh)

2. Charles Philip Arthur George (by marriage celebrants)

3. His Royal Highness (HRH)

4. Duke of Cornwall

5. Earl of Carrick and Baron Renfrew

6. Lord of the Isles

7. Duke of Rothsay

8. Prince and Great Steward of Scotland

9. Heir apparent/Heir to the throne

10. Prince of Wales*

* This title was bestowed in 1958, but he wasn't inaugurated until
his investiture at Caernarfon Castle in Wales in 1969.**
** I was given a nice, bright yellow, commemorative mug to mark
the occasion.

5 March

1998: water, in the form of ice, is discovered by NASA on the Moon

A dip of the toe into the world of lakes

- Morar in Scotland is the deepest lake in Great Britain: 1,017 ft (310 m).

- The deepest lake in England is Wastwater in Cumbria, at only 260 ft (79 m) deep.

- The deepest lake in Wales is Baba (Llyn Tegid) at a meagre 125 ft (38 m).

- The deepest lake in the whole world is Lake Baikal in Russia, with a depth of 5,314 ft (1,620 m).

- The Dead Sea, in Israel and Jordan, is the world's lowest body of water. A salt lake, it's actually 1,312 ft (400 m) below sea level.

- Lake Titicaca, in Peru and Bolivia, is around 12,500 ft (3,810 m) above sea level.

- Lake Winnipeg in Manitoba, Canada, actually means 'muddy water' in Cree Indian.

- Lake Mweru in Zambia and the Democratic Republic of Congo is simply the Bantu word for 'lake'!

- Neah is the largest lake in the British Isles (England, Scotland, Wales and the whole of Ireland). It borders five of the six counties which make up Northern Ireland. (The only county to miss out is County Fermanagh.)

- Lake Kariba in Zambia and Zimbabwe covers 2,000 square miles (5,180 sq km) and was created when the Zambesi river was dammed.

6 March

1863: the Siege of the Alamo ends with the
deaths of Davie Crockett (of hat fame) and
Jim Bowie (of Bowie knife fame)

Three familiar things around the house named after Americans

HOOVER: actually the brand name of a vacuum
cleaner, named after the American engineer
William H. Hoover, though people often talk about
'hoovering' even though they're vacuuming with
other branded vacuum cleaners, such as Dyson
(named after its British inventor).

POINSETTIA: a red-leaved flower people have
around at Christmas, named after the American
diplomat Joel R. Poinsett. (He was a botanist too.)

PHILLIPS SCREWS: screws with a cross-shaped
notch rather than the usual single line notch,
giving a better grip and requiring, of course, a
Phillips screwdriver. Named after the American
inventor Henry F. Phillips.*

* Today, they're also referred to as 'cross-head screws'.
Shame.

7 March

1876: Alexander Graham Bell is issued with a US patent for the first telephone

Some phone-related facts or telephonic truths

1. It was US inventor and entrepreneur Thomas Edison who invented the word 'hello' with an 'e' as a greeting, primarily for answering the telephone. (The word 'hullo' with a 'u', which already existed, was more an exclamation of the 'what-have-we-here?' variety.)

2. Alexander Graham Bell preferred to answer his early phone calls with 'Ahoy, hoy!'

3. The first telephone call – on Bell's equipment, at least – was 'Mr Watson! Come here. I want you!' This wasn't planned. Bell had spilled battery acid on his trousers and called out to his assistant for help. He hadn't realized the message would be heard on Watson's telephone receiver.

4. Antonio Meucci demonstrated a prototype of his own *teletrofono* as early as 1860. He filed a caveat – the first stage of the patenting process – in the US in 1871, which he needed to renew in 1874 to protect his invention. Sadly, he was injured in an accident, and so too poor and too poorly to do this.

5. Meucci sued Bell once Bell's patent had been registered. He died in 1889 before the case was settled.

6. For those who think Nos. 4 to 5 are an unlikely tale, you might be interested to learn that, as recently as 2004, the US House of Representatives passed an official resolution that the 'achievements of Antonio Meucci should be recognized, and his work in the invention of the telephone should be acknowledged'.

8 March

1859: Kenneth Grahame, author of
The Wind in the Willows, *is born*

Twenty-four rivers, and the cities that they run through

Arno: Florence, Italy
Avon: Bristol, England and Christchurch, New Zealand*
Chao Phrya: Bangkok, Thailand
Clyde: Glasgow, Scotland
Danube: Vienna, Austria, and Budapest, Hungary
Dnieper: Kiev, Ukraine
Hudson: New York, USA
Liffey: Dublin, Eire
Main: Frankfurt, Germany
Mississippi: Memphis, USA
Moskva: Moscow, Russia
Nile: Cairo, Egypt**
Ohio: Cincinnatti, USA
Po: Turin, Italy
Potomac: Washington, DC, USA
Rhine: Bonn, Germany
St Lawrence: Quebec, Canada
Shannon: Limerick, Eire
Seine: Paris, France
Tagus: Lisbon, Portugal
Thames: London, England
Tiber: Rome, Italy
Tigris: Baghdad, Iraq
Tyne: Newcastle, England

* Though not the same one.
** The Nile, measuring 4,160 miles (6,695 km) is the world's longest river, 111 miles (179 km) longer than its nearest rival, the Amazon, which measures 4,050 miles (6,516 km).

9 March

*1796: Napoleon Bonaparte marries Josephine
(of 'Not tonight, Josephine')*

The enigma of the Great Sphinx at Giza

- The Sphinx is a mythical beast with the head of a human, the body of a lion and the wings of a bird.

- Carvings of the Sphinx were very common in ancient Egypt. Probably the most famous surviving 'avenue of Sphinxes' can be seen at the entrance to the temple of Luxor.

- The most famous carving of the Sphinx is the Great Sphinx at Giza in Egypt, apparently carved from an outcrop of rock. Even its age is disputed, though most Egyptologists settle on it being between 4,500 and 6,500 years old.

- Some New Age believers claim that the Sphinx is, in fact, hollow and contains some of the most important secrets of the universe. (I don't.)

- The Sphinx is missing its nose. Many people – including me in other books – have claimed that it was blown off by Napoleon's army. It has been pointed out, however, that there were sketches made in 1737 showing the Sphinx without its nose . . . Napoleon wasn't born until 1769!

10 March

Stars who appear in cameo roles in *The Great Muppet Caper**

- Jack Warden, as Mike Tarkanian, the editor-in-chief boss of 'identical twin' reporters Fozzie Bear and Kermit the Frog at *The Daily Chronicle*, who (reluctantly) sends them – along with press photographer Gonzo – to England to interview top fashion designer Lady Holiday.

- Robert Morley, as an unnamed gentleman on a park bench who suggests free places in London for Kermit, Fozzy and Gonzo to stay: '. . . riverbank . . . bus terminal . . . Happiness Hotel.' They choose the hotel.

- John Cleese, as Neville, an English gent living at 17 Highbrow Street, London SW7 (which Miss Piggy tricks Kermit into believing is her own home, when masquerading as Lady Holiday following a misunderstanding).

- Peter Ustinov, as the unnamed driver of a truck hijacked by Miss Piggy on her way to try to prevent the theft (by Nicky Holiday) of Lady Holiday's fabulous Baseball Diamond at the Mallory Gallery, following her escape from prison on the back of a 'Big House Laundry' laundry van.**

- Oscar the Grouch (from *Sesame Street*), as a – er – creature whose dustbin home Peter Ustinov comes crashing into when ejected from his truck.

- Peter Falk,*** as an unnamed down-at-heel man in a Columbo-type**** raincoat (who tries to sell Kermit a watch) in a London park.

* Well, it is a film about theft and it *does* have an Oscar in it. It stars all the main members of the late great Jim Henson's Muppets, along with Diana Rigg and Charles Grodin as sister and brother Lady and Nicky Holiday . . . and I did see it four times in the same seat in the same cinema (in St Martin's Lane, London) in the same (first) week when it was first released in the UK.

** Exciting, or what!?!

*** His role is uncredited. (In other words, the name Peter Falk doesn't appear anywhere in the credits and/or titles.) He doesn't even appear in the Book of the Film.

**** Of course, he IS Columbo!

11 March

*1819: Sir Henry Tate, art patron and philanthropist, is born
(He is also the Tate of Tate & Lyle, the sugar company)*

An A–Z* of well-known people and their lesser-known jobs

Aesop of fable-writing fame: a slave

Robbie Burns the poet: an excise officer

Lewis Carroll, author of *Alice in Wonderland*: a maths lecturer

Christopher Dean of 'Torvill and Dean': a policeman

T. S. Eliot the poet: a bank clerk

Sam Goldwyn of 'Metro Goldwyn Meyer': a glove salesman

Harry Hill the comedian: a doctor

Henrik Ibsen the playwright: a pharmacist

Andrew Johnson, 17th President of the United States: a tailor

Wassily Kandinsky the artist: a lawyer

Burt Lancaster the actor: an acrobat

St Matthew the apostle: a tax collector

Thomas Newcomen, the inventor of the atmospheric steam engine: a blacksmith

George Orwell the novelist (born Eric Blair): a policeman in Burma

Peter the Great, the Russian tsar: a shipbuilder

Peter Roget of *Roget's Thesaurus* fame: a doctor

Delia Smith the cookery writer: a hairdresser

Pyotr Tchaikovsky the composer: a civil servant

Liv Ullmann the film star: UNICEF ambassador

Vincent Van Gogh the painter: a trainee priest

George Washington, 1st President of the United States: colonel in the British Army

Brigham Young the Mormon leader: a carpenter

Count von Zeppelin of airship fame: a soldier in the US Civil War

* Without an F, Q or X.

12 March

1930: in British-ruled India, Mahatma Gandhi begins his campaign of passive resistance and civil disobedience by leading a march to collect salt from the sea, against government regulations

Some salty ponderings

- Salt is sodium chloride. For every gramme of salt, almost 40 per cent is sodium and just over 60 per cent is chlorine.
- Although salt is soluble (it 'dissolves') in water, it isn't soluble in sulphuric acid.
- Humans need salt to survive, not just to flavour our food.
- If not the very first, salt must have been *one* of the world's first traded commodities. If not available locally it would have been brought great distances by anything from packhorse or boat to camels.
- The 4,700ish-year-old Chinese writings the Png-tzao-kan-mu records more than 40 different types of salt, and describes two methods of extracting and processing it, similar to those still used today.
- The word 'salary' comes from the Latin *sal* meaning salt. This is because Roman soldiers used to be paid in salt, or given an allowance to buy it.
- Until the 19th century, one of the main uses of salt was to preserve food for the winter months. (The rich had ice houses, but there were no fridges or freezers, remember.)
- In 1807, Sir Humphry Davy managed to separate salt into its constituent parts of sodium and chlorine, the only problem being that nobody knew what to do with them. Today they're used in everything from baking soda to PVC.
- Too much salt can be bad for people, especially young children.
- 'Sitting below the salt' means being of a lower social standing. This dates back to the time when salt was a very valuable commodity and placed in ornate salt cellars (often shaped like ships) in the centre of the table, with the host and posh folk up one end, and the less important people at the other end, 'below' it.

13 March

1759: Halley's Comet passes its closest point to the Sun

1066 and all that

- The man who was to become William the Conqueror was born the son of a tanner's daughter. A tanner rubs leather with animal dung to make it brown . . . So it wasn't the classiest of jobs.

- William's father, Robert, was – most historians agree – a little barmy. He had a reputation of coming up with very inventive ways of being horrible and cruel to his enemies. He had the nickname of 'Robert the Devil'.

- William married a woman called Matilda. She was to become Britain's smallest monarch, being only 4ft 2in (1.25 metres) tall. They had four sons and five or six daughters. (Today, no one seems quite sure!)

- On the death of King Edward the Confessor, Harold took the English throne. William claimed that Edward had promised *him* the crown, while standing on saints' bones, no less, which made the promise binding and official.

- According to the scenes on the Bayeux Tapestry, created by William's half-brother, Bishop Odo (after William's victory at the Battle of Hastings), a shooting star had appeared as a bad omen at the time of Harold's coronation.

- Halley's Comet did, indeed, appear in the sky in 1066, but not until much later – 24 April – but, perhaps more puzzling, shooting stars were traditionally seen as good luck.

- The Battle of Hastings didn't actually take place in Hastings but at a place called Battle . . . Though, of course, it wasn't called Battle at the time. And it was near-ish to Hastings. The battlefield survives today within the walls of Battle Abbey, where the 1,040th anniversary of William the Conqueror's victory was marked in 2006.

14 March

Public Enemies

The then Director of the Federal Bureau of Investigation, J. Edgar Hoover, started the 'Top Ten Fugitive Program' with its TEN MOST WANTED lists, intended to be a cooperative measure between US law enforcement and the media to catch the country's 'most violent and elusive fugitives'.

The three main criteria for a fugitive to be placed on the list were:

1. They must have a violent criminal history.
2. There must be a federal (rather than state) warrant issued for their arrest.*
3. The nature of the case must be such that additional publicity will significantly increase the chances of their being caught.

The methods by which a fugitive could be removed from the list included:

1. Apprehension (being caught).
2. Death (self-explanatory).
3. Dismissal of the federal warrant.
4. Or if they no longer met the 'Top Ten' criteria listed above.

Similar criteria exist for the lists today.

NB The FBI has never issued a list ranking fugitives in order of their danger to the public. In other words, there's never been an official list of Public Enemy No. 1, No. 2 and so on.

* A federal warrant can be enforced right across the US; a state warrant only in a particular state.

15 March

A queue of car stuff

- Car theft is one of the world's biggest crimes.

- The Morris Minor became Britain's first million-selling car in December 1960.

- Britain's first parking meters were installed in the London borough of Westminster in July 1958. The world's first were put up in Oklahoma City, USA, in 1935.

- The first motorway was constructed in Italy in 1925. It was called an *autostrada*. Britain's first motorway was the M1. The first stretch was opened near Preston in Lancashire in 1958.

- There were no official speed limits on British roads between 1932 and 1934.

- Car number plates were introduced in Paris in 1893. They appeared in Britain in 1903, the very first one being 'A1'.

- The self-starter for cars was invented in 1911. Before that, cars were started with a crank handle. Many cars still had to be started with the crank on wet or cold days.

- Officially, there are no roads in the City of London (as opposed to London in general). When a road runs into the City area, it becomes a street!

16 March

1973: the new London Bridge is officially opened, the old bridge having been sold and relocated to Arizona, USA

Sad and nasty nursery rhymes

Three Blind Mice
They have their tails cut off with a carving knife

Ding Dong Bell
Pussy is drowned in a well

Who Killed Cock Robin?
Cock Robin is killed by a sparrow with a bow and arrow

Tom, Tom the Piper's Son
A pig gets eaten and a boy gets beaten

There Was An Old Woman (Who Lived In A Shoe)
The living conditions are overcrowded, the children are undernourished and abused

There Was An Old Woman (Who Swallowed A Fly)
A whole variety of creatures get eaten and the old woman in question dies

London Bridge Is Falling Down
A collapsing bridge is never a laughing matter

Humpty-Dumpty*
After a fall from a wall, he's so badly damaged that even all the king's horses and all the king's men are unable to reassemble him

Old Mother Hubbard
She's undoubtedly poor, and her dog goes hungry

Jack and Jill
A boy sustains a serious head injury and receives primitive, if not inadequate, medical treatment

Rock-a-bye Baby
A very young child is, rather foolishly, left up a tree, with the inevitable consequences

---

* The rhyme never says that he was an enormous egg. It's more likely that he was a cannon.

17 March

1845: the rubber band is patented as an invention by Stephen Perry of London

Dumbo, the flying elephant

- Dumbo was due to appear on the cover of *Time* magazine in December 1941 when the film was released. Unfortunately, the bombing of Pearl Harbour* by Japan meant the Japanese general Yamamoto took that spot instead.

- The film took only 18 months to produce (despite a strike at the Disney studios).

- Some claim that, in the film, some of the not-so-nice clowns who are asking their boss 'for a raise' were caricatures of the studio strikers.

- Bill Tytla was the key animator for *Dumbo*. He said that he based Dumbo the elephant's expressions and behaviour on those of his own two-year-old son.

- The film premiere was on 23 October 1941, at the world-famous Broadway Theater, and it was an instant hit with the critics.

- Walt Disney had made numerous short films, but *Dumbo* was only his fourth full-length animated feature. The first three were *Snow White and the Seven Dwarfs* (1937), *Pinocchio* (1940) and *Fantasia* (1940). The fifth was to be *Bambi* (1942).

- In a song sung by some crows, there's plenty of wonderful word play, including:

  *'I seen a peanut stand / And heard a rubber band / I seen a needle that winked its eye / But I've been, done, seen about everything / When I see a elephant fly.'***

* Spelled Pearl Harbor (without the 'u') in the US, so this is an English translation.

** Though the obvious racial stereotyping/caricaturing of black people may be uncomfortable to a 21st-century audience.

18 March

1967: oil tanker Torrey Canyon *runs aground off Land's End, Cornwall*

The best places to spot mermaids in the British Isles

- Mermaids live in salt water, not fresh water, so forget streams and rivers. Concentrate your searches on the sea and beaches. (Though, it must be said, that they have been known to swim short distances upstream.)

- 'Eyewitnesses' have often reported mermaids sitting on rocks, so areas of sea with rocky outcrops and rocks at the water's edge are a better bet than clear expanses of water.

- Mermaids are said to regularly tend to their hair with 'a comb and a glass in [their] hand', a glass being a looking glass or (in this instance) hand-held mirror – though this makes little sense, seeing as how they'll mess their hair up again as soon as they go back underwater – so they'll need places with enough light to work by.

- Unlike their relatives the sirens, who lure sailors to their deaths with their hypnotic voices and wily women's ways, mermaids are thought to be shy of human contact and are likely to stick to more deserted coves and hard-to-reach beaches. (Binoculars could be a useful asset to the mermaid hunter.)

- There are differing views about what it is exactly that mermaids eat, so looking for regions with particular types of seaweed, for example, is not necessarily very helpful. There are reported incidents of mermaids being lured inland by the sound of humans singing (particularly males), so a CD could come in handy.

- The West Country – particularly Cornwall – has more than its fair share of mermaid legends and folklore. One of the most famous stories is of the mermaid at Zennor, who lured away local villager Matthew Trewhella. There's even a carving of her in the local church. This would be as good a county to start as any.

- Reports of people finding mermaids' purses on the beach are of little use in your search. They are, in reality, just the egg cases of rays, skates or sharks.
- Irish folklore has many a tale about the merrow, another name for a mermaid, so you could try your luck there.
- There are, of course, those who argue that you'll be equally successful (or unsuccessful) wherever you look for a mermaid, for the simple fact that they don't exist.*

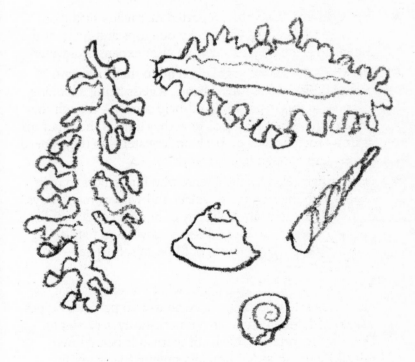

* Spoilsports.

19 March

What destroyed six of the Seven Wonders of the Ancient World*

1. The Hanging Gardens of Babylon
Created in around 600 BC by Nebuchadnezzar II. They are thought to have been a series of terraced gardens on the banks of the river Euphrates, near present-day Baghdad, Iraq.
Destroyed by: Erosion, time and lack of interest.

2. The Temple of Artemis, Ephesus, Asia Minor (Turkey)
Originally built in the 6th century BC in honour of Artemis, goddess of hunting (and the Moon), and rebuilt in the 4th century BC.
Destroyed by: The Goths in the 3rd century BC.

3. The Statue of Zeus at Olympia, Greece
A statue 13 metres high, it had a wooden frame covered in gold and ivory.
Destroyed by: Fire in AD 462.

4. The Mausoleum at Halicarnassus, Asia Minor
A 4th-century-BC tomb built for Mausollos – from whom the term mausoleum comes – by his widow.
Destroyed by: Earthquake damage, probably some time in the 14th century, which led to it being demolished in 1522.

5. The Colossus of Rhodes, eastern Mediterranean
Built between 294 BC and 282 BC, this colossal 33-metre-high bronze statue of Helios the sun god stood for less than a century.
Destroyed by: Yup, another earthquake, this time in 226 BC.

6. Pharos of Alexandria, eastern Mediterranean
The world's first lighthouse – or certainly the first one we *know* about – was built at the entrance to Alexandria harbour, in Egypt, in 280 BC.
Destroyed by: Earthquake damage (yet *again*). Severely weakened, it toppled over (and into the sea) in 1357.

---

* And what destroyed the seventh wonder? Nothing. The oldest of all the ancient wonders, the Great Pyramid at Giza, Egypt, still stands.

20 March

1852: Uncle Tom's Cabin *by Harriet Beecher Stowe is published. Later 'Uncle Tom' becomes derogatory slang in the US*

23 Cockney Rhyming Slang* phrases that appear to be food-related but actually refer to something else

biscuits and cheese = knees
mince pies = eyes
butcher's hook = look
field of wheat = street
apples and pears = stairs
loaf of bread = head
apple fritter = bitter (as in beer)
bacon and eggs = legs
jam jar = car
plates of meat = feet
chopsticks = six
Bath bun = son
rabbit and pork = talk
sausage and mash = cash/crash
macaroni = pony
bees and honey = money
currant bun = son/sun
bread and butter = gutter
Brussels sprouts = scouts
carving knife = wife
china plate = mate
cocoa = say so
tea leaf = thief

---

* Cockney Rhyming Slang was developed as a code so those eavesdroppers not in the know would have no idea what was being talked about. When talking in rhyming slang, only the first word of the phrase is used, so '*Hello, my old mate. Got any money? My son tripped over his feet, fell down the stairs with a mighty crash, and hurt his head. I want a doctor to take a look*' might be: '*Hello, me old china. Got any bees? My currant tripped over his plates and fell down the apples with a mighty sausage, and hurt his loaf. I want a doctor to take a butcher's*' – which is, I'm sure you agree, suitably confusing for the uninitiated.

21 March

1829: a duel occurs between the Duke of Wellington and the Earl of Winchilsea in Battersea Park, which becomes famous for the fact that each deliberately misses

A few bite-sized chunks about Battersea Dogs Home

- In 1860, a Mrs Mary Tealby opened the Temporary Home for Lost and Starving Dogs in a stable yard. She had decided to do this after seeing the large number of strays roaming the streets of London.

- Rather than praise her for her charitable efforts, Mrs Tealby and the dogs' home received plenty of bad press when it first opened. Victorians thought she should be helping fellow human beings living in dreadful conditions – and there were numerous such people in London at the time – rather than channelling her efforts into helping 'dumb animals'.

- In 1862, author and campaigner Charles Dickens published an article throwing a positive light on the home. Called 'Two Dog Shows', the article contrasted the difference between an exclusive dog show (for pure breeds and wealthy owners) with one held at the Temporary Home for Lost and Starving Dogs. Slowly but surely, the public was won over.

- Mary Tealby died in 1865.

- In 1871 the home moved to its present site and became the Dogs' Home Battersea.

- In 1883 it started taking in cats too.

- In 1885 Queen Victoria became its royal patron.

- Although officially the Battersea Dogs and Cats Home, it's still referred to by most as 'Battersea Dogs Home'. Its current patron is Queen Elizabeth II.

- In addition to the Battersea HQ, the home now has two satellite centres: Battersea Dogs & Cats Home, Old

Windsor, Berkshire, and Battersea Dogs & Cats Home, Brands Hatch, in Kent.

- Since the home first opened, they've taken in over three million animals.
- It takes around £10 million a year to run the home.
- In 2004 alone, they found homes for 5,814 animals, as well as reuniting owners with their lost pets.
- They use over 1,000 blankets a day.
- Their official website is: www.dogshome.org

22 March

Terrible accents in film and television

- Keanu Reeves's English accent in *Bram Stoker's Dracula*
- Dick Van Dyke's 'cockney' accent in *Mary Poppins*
- Peter Sellers's French accent as Inspector Clouseau in the *Pink Panther* films*
- Don Cheadle's 'cockney' accent in *Ocean's 11* (the remake)
- Humphrey Bogart's 'Irish' accent as a stablehand in *Dark Victory*
- Renée Zellweger's English accent in the *Bridget Jones* films**
- Sean Connery's 'Irish' accent in *The Untouchables****
- Julia Roberts's 'Irish' accent in *Mary Reilly*
- Peter Postlethwaite's 'American' accent in *The Usual Suspects*
- Meryl Streep's Danish (apparently?!?!?!) accent in *Out of Africa*
- Brad Pitt's accent in *Seven Years in Tibet*****
- Tom Cruise and Nicole Kidman's 'unusual' Irish accents in *Far and Away*

---

* But it's supposed to be terrible . . . even though he's supposed to be French!

** Though only pretty terrible rather than terribly terrible.

*** Connery came top of a bad-accents poll conducted by *Empire* magazine in 2003.

**** In fact most English actors trying to sound American, and American actors trying to sound English.

23 March

1839: the first appearance of the slang word 'OK' in print (in the Boston Morning Post)

15 Cockney Rhyming Slang phrases that appear to be nothing to do with food but which are really*

stand at ease = cheese
Sexton Blake = cake/fake
tiddly wink = drink
stammer and stutter = butter
army and navy = gravy
Conan Doyle = boil
kidney punch = lunch
Doctor Crippen = drippin'
fine and dandy = brandy
you and me = tea
Uncle Fred = bread
Harvey Nichols = pickles
Jack the Ripper = kipper
Kate and Sydney = kidney
Lilley and Skinner = dinner

* So 'Let's have cheese and pickles for lunch with brandy to drink' would be: 'Let's have stand and Harvey for kidney with fine to tiddly'.

24 March

Some great escapes

- On this very day – 24 March – in 1944, 76 prisoners of war escaped from the Stalag Luft III prison camp. This daring escape was later turned into the 1963 film *The Great Escape* which, among others, starred Steve McQueen . . . who was *also* born on 24 March.

- In 1998 a pet called Fido went upstairs and scratched on the bedroom door of its owner to warn her that the house in Devon was on fire. The owner, her two daughters and Fido all escaped unharmed. What makes this all the more amazing was that Fido wasn't a dog. He was a pet rat.

- One of the greatest escapes of all time was of around 338,000 Allied soldiers and civilians from Dunkirk on the north coast of France. Between 27 May and 4 June 1940, a fleet of naval vessels and small boats of every conceivable shape and size, that could make it across the English Channel, came to their rescue.

- *The Scarlet Pimpernel* by Baroness Orczy was based on the exploits of a real man: Barton de Bats, who escaped the guillotine himself not once but twice. The first occasion was in 1793, after trying to rescue the King of France. He then tried to rescue the Queen. The second escape came in 1795 after he had finally been arrested. This time he decided to keep a low profile, re-emerging when the monarchy was reinstated in 1814.

- During the Second World War, the artworks at the National Gallery escaped to the safety of some mines in Wales, to avoid the German bombs.

- In May 2003, pinned down by a boulder in a remote canyon in Utah, US mechanic Aron Ralston decided to break the bones in his trapped arm before amputating it. After being trapped for five days, he managed to cut off his arm and escape with his life.

25 March

A web of information

- Spiders are arachnids. All arachnids have eight legs, including scorpions. (All insects have six legs. Centipedes, for example, aren't insects but molluscs.)

- There are over 35,000 different species of spider. Most of these are harmless. But not all.

- The banana spider from Central and South America produces enough venom to kill six adults. They have been known to turn up in bananas exported to other countries.

- The black widow and the tarantula are probably the most famous of the deadly spiders.

- The Australian funnel-web spider is particularly dangerous. They often turn up in the dunny (an outside toilet). They get their name from their tightly-woven funnel-shaped webs (where they lurk in the hole at the bottom).

- The world's biggest spider is the South American Goliath bird-eating spider. Goliath was, of course, the name of the giant in the Bible. This spider is well named. Its legs can grow up to 25 cm long!

- In England, it was believed that a common cure for jaundice was to swallow a large, live household spider rolled up in butter. Although this probably did the patient no real harm – though it certainly didn't help matters – it was very bad news for the poor spider.

- A spider is said to have helped to save Mohammed from the Koreishites when he fled from Mecca. Hiding in a cave, a tree sprang up in the opening, in full leaf and with a pigeon nesting in its branches. A spider then span its web between tree and the cave, making the opening seem undisturbed. The Koreishite saw this and, believing that no one had entered the cave lately, didn't bother searching it and moved on.

26 March

1874: Robert Frost, the US poet, is born
1923: the BBC begins its daily weather forecasts

Cold weather

- Fabulous old names for a snap of cold weather include 'blackthorn winter' and 'peewit's pinch'. These refer to the cold spell in March when blossoming blackthorn and ground-nesting peewits feel the pinch of the cold.

- 'Ice Saints' or 'Frost Saints' are the saints whose saints' days fall during this period in March. Like most things, the actual days are disputed, and therefore which saints can be included. One of them is St Boniface.

- According to German legend, St Boniface 'invented' the idea of one of winter's most enduring symbols: the Christmas tree. On discovering a group of pagans about to sacrifice a baby to the spirit of an oak tree, he chopped down the tree. There, among its roots, was a tiny young fir tree. Boniface thought that the new tree rising from the remains of the now-dead one symbolized life after death, and Jesus's resurrection . . . and the conifer became the Christmas tree.

- The coldest place on Earth is the Russian research base at Polus Nedostupnosti (better known as the Pole of Cold) in Antarctica, with temperatures of −57.8°C.

- Unlike the Cold Pole, where – for obvious reasons! – no one lives, the coldest place on the planet with a regular population is Norilsk in Russia. Here the average temperature is a mind-numbingly low −10.9°C.

- The greatest depth of snow ever recorded, however, was in, of all places, California. At 11.46 metres deep, it was measured in Tarmarac in March 1911.

- The South Pole has six fewer days of (possible) sunshine than the North Pole does every year.

27 March

*1914: the first successful blood transfusion using
stored blood treated with an anticoagulant**

Vlad Dracula

- Vlad Dracula was a real person. He lived in Romania from 1431 to 1476.
- 'Dracula' means 'son of a dragon'.
- It also means 'son of the devil'.
- Vlad became ruler of the Wallachia region of Romania when he was about 25.
- His nobles hated him and his family. They buried his family alive. This was a foolish thing to do. In revenge, he had their wives and children stuck on to spiked stakes.
- Vlad Dracula soon earned the nickname Vlad the Impaler.
- Once, some foreign ambassadors failed to remove their skull caps, explaining that it was their custom to keep them on at all times. Vlad thought this was disrespectful. On his orders, Vlad's men then nailed the caps into their skulls.
- Vlad liked to tour his country under the cover of darkness, wearing a flowing cape. People lived in fear of his turning up.
- Up to 100,000 people died on his orders or at his own hand.
- Vlad himself was eventually impaled. Killed by the Turks, his head was chopped off and sent to Turkey, where it was displayed on a spike.
- In 1897, Bram Stoker borrowed the name Dracula for his fictional blood-sucking vampire. And what was the only way to kill him? With a pointed stake through the heart.

* An anticoagulant stops the blood from congealing, in other words, from thickening.

28 March

1881: Rivals P. T. Barnum and James A. Bailey join forces to create the Barnum and Bailey Circus, 'The Greatest Show on Earth'*

Types of boxers

1. Rebelling Chinamen

Members of a secret society of nationalistic Chinese determined to oust Westerners (and their influence) from China in the 19th century, resulting in the Boxer Rebellion of 1900.[1]

2. Pugilists

People who put on big gloves and punch each other in a boxing ring, following a strict set of rules.[2] The most famous of which must be Mohammed Ali,[3] officially one of the most recognized faces on the planet.

3. Underwear

Pants[4] resembling shorts rather than briefs.

4. Flat-faced pooches

Smooth-coated dogs with pug-like faces.

* As well as circus acts, Barnum and Bailey also presented 'Grand Boxing and Wrestling Tournaments'.

[1] So-called because the secret society was referred to in Chinese as *yi he quan* or *yi ho tan* – 'righteous harmony fists'.

[2] The most famous of which are the Marquess of Queensberry rules.

[3] Born Cassius Clay.

[4] In the US trousers are called 'pants', so the pants they wear under their pants are called 'underpants' . . . but, because we call trousers 'trousers', we should be calling pants 'pants' not '*under*pants', whatever the dictionary might say . . . though, of course, we could try calling them 'undertrousers'.

29 March

A matter of marathons

- A Snickers bar used to be called a Marathon in the UK.

- Marathon races are called marathon races in recognition of a non-stop run made by an ancient Greek runner – sometimes referred to as Pheidippides, and sometimes Eucles – from the Plain of Marathon to the city of Athens in 490 BC. The reason for the run was to deliver the message that the Athenians had defeated the Persians in battle. The runner promptly dropped down dead.

- The distance from the Plain of Marathon to the city of Athens is over 23 miles (37 km).

- The modern marathon race, however, is now set at exactly 26 miles and 385 yards (around 42 km).

- This modern length was determined at the 1908 Olympic Games in London. The start of the race was outside a window at Windsor Castle (from which some of the royal family could watch) and the finishing line was in front of the royal box in the White City stadium (where other royals were waiting).

- The first London Marathon in 1981 had 6,255 runners crossing the finishing line. Today, on average 30,000 people take part. So far, 2002 saw the most people cross the finishing line: an impressive 32,899.

- Far more people apply to run in the London Marathon than can be accepted. In 2004, 98,500 people applied for 46,500 places.

- Many charities are allocated places in advance, to be sure of having people running for them on the day. People can then apply directly to the charities to run for them.

- It's estimated that over £200 million has been raised for charities to date since the London Marathon began. Over three-quarters of those running are sponsored for some charity or other.

- The fastest runners have completed the London Marathon in well under 2 hours 10 minutes.

- The world's other major city marathons are in Berlin, Boston, Chicago and New York.

- The official London Marathon website can be found at: www.london-marathon.co.uk

30 March

A series of jokes supposedly told (if not created) by comedian Tommy Cooper*

- Apparently, one in five people in the world is Chinese. And there are five people in my family, so there must be one of them. It's either my mum or my dad. Or my older brother Colin. Or my younger brother Ho-Cha-Chu. But I think it's Colin.

- I went to the doctors the other day and I said, 'Have you got anything for wind?' So he gave me a kite.

- I went to the doctor and I said, 'It hurts when I do that.' He said, 'Well, don't do it.'

- Man goes to the doctor, with a strawberry growing out of his head. The doctor says, 'I'll give you some cream to put on it.'

- Two aerials meet on a roof – fall in love – get married. The ceremony was rubbish but the reception was brilliant.

- A man goes to a doctor and says, 'I can't pronounce my "f"s, "t"s and "h"s,' and the doctor says, 'Well, you can't say fairer than that, then.'

- What do you call a fish with no eyes? A fsh.

- The phone was ringing. I picked it up, and asked, 'Who's speaking, please?' And a voice said, 'You are.'

- So I rang up my local swimming baths. I said, 'Is that the local swimming baths?' He said, 'It depends where you're calling from.'

- So I rang up a local building firm. I said, 'I wanna skip outside my house.' He said, 'I'm not stopping you.'

☞

* Britain's most famous fez-wearer.

- So I was getting into my car, and this bloke says to me, 'Can you give me a lift?' I said, 'Sure, you look great. The world's your oyster. Go for it.'

- Police arrested two kids yesterday. One was drinking battery acid. The other was eating fireworks. They charged one and let the other one off.

- My dog was barking at everyone the other day. Still, what can you expect from a cross-breed?

- I went to the butcher's and I bet him fifty quid that he couldn't reach the meat off the top shelf. And he said, 'No, the steaks are too high.'

- It's strange, isn't it? You stand in the middle of a library and go 'Aaaaaaagghhhh!' and everyone just stares at you. But you do the same thing on an aeroplane, and everyone joins in.

- I saw this man and the back of his anorak was leaping up and down, and people were chucking money to him. I said, 'Do you earn a living doing that?' He said, 'Yes, this is my livelihood.'

- I went down my local ice-cream shop, and said, 'I want to buy an ice cream.' He said, 'Hundreds and thousands?' I said, 'We'll start with one.'

- You know, somebody actually complimented me on my driving today. They left a little note on the windscreen. It said 'Parking Fine'. So that was nice.

31 March

1836: the first monthly instalment of Charles Dickens's Pickwick Papers *is published*

The ten silliest names in Charles Dickens's novels, as chosen by me (unless I come up with some even sillier ones)

10th M'Choakumchild (Hard Times)

9th Mrs Colonel Wugsby (Pickwick Papers)

8th Tom Tootle (Our Mutual Friend)

7th Peg Sliderskew (Nicholas Nickleby)

6th Peepy Jellyby (Bleak House)

5th Chevy Slyme (Martin Chuzzlewit)

4th Major Hannibal Chollop (Martin Chuzzlewit)

2nd Kit Nubbles (The Old Curiosity Shop)

2nd Snittle Timberry (Nicholas Nickleby)

1st Conkey Chickweed (Oliver Twist)

1 April

April Fool's Day

Some foolish thoughts for All Fools' Day

- April Fool's Day originally had nothing to do with the month of April. It was named after April Tregoose, the 18th-century Cornish prankster who famously tricked George I, 'the pudding king', into eating his own suet-coated wig. (Apparently, he was under the impression that it was the very latest delicacy from the Continent.)*

- Back in the real world, experts seem unable to agree on the origins of All Fools' Day and how it came to fall on 1 April. Some believe that its roots lie in the Roman festival of Cerealia, honouring Ceres (aka Mother Earth). Others claim it harks back to the switch in continental Europe to the Gregorian calendar in 1582, when many were convinced that the new dates were a joke! It's also been linked to the Holi festival, with its playful pranks, celebrated in India in late February or early March.

- In Mexico, I'm fairly reliably informed, All Fools' Day falls on 28 December, and centres on an even more specific kind of trickery. This is the day to ask to borrow your neighbour's car, in the hope that he's forgotten the date and agrees to let you have it: for an item borrowed on All Fools' Day down Mexico way doesn't have to be returned.

- One of the most fondly remembered British April fools is undoubtedly Richard Dimbleby's 1957 *Panorama* television report on the spaghetti growers of Switzerland. This was back in the days of black and white TV, when such broadcasters were deeply respected. If Dimbleby was narrating a piece about picking strands of limp spaghetti from bushes, then that was where it jolly well came from. The genius was in the detail: the fear of the frost affecting flavour, drying the strands in the sun and the equal length of said strands being down to the skill of generations of growers. Spaghetti Bolognese was still a strange and exotic dish back in the 1950s!

* And if you believe any of that, you'll believe anything!

- In 1977, the *Guardian* started a spate of national newspaper April Fool's Day hoaxes when it created a whole supplement about the republic of San Seriffe – actually named after 'sans serif', a printing term – in the Indian Ocean, its two main islands being Upper Caisse and Lower Caisse. (Upper case being capital letters and lower case ordinary letters in printing, and a 'serif' being the horizontal stroke at the top and bottom, for example, of the capital letter I.) Even the advertisers got in on the act. The brewers Guinness ran an advertisement saying that on San Seriffe, the islanders preferred their pint to have its distinctive white head at the bottom of the glass.

- Two other wildly contrasting April Fool's pranks, one Australian, one American, show how such different approaches can have equally satisfying results. The former relied on the building of an enormous prop, while the latter relied on the power of the written word alone.

    ◆ On 1 April 1978, what appeared to be a huge iceberg was towed into Sydney Harbour. This was no surprise to locals who'd known for some time that food mogul Dick Smith had been planning to tow one all the way from Antarctica, to be diced up and sold as ice-cubes . . . and here it was! Local radio stations were whipped into a frenzy of excitement, until the so-called iceberg got close enough to reveal its secret. It was nothing more than a mixture of firefighters' foam and shaving cream sprayed over plastic sheeting on a frame.

    ◆ The American prank of 1998 required nothing more than an advertisement in *USA Today* proclaiming the advent of a new left-handed Whopper at Burger King. It contained the same ingredients as the usual burger, they revealed, but they were rotated 180 degrees to cater for America's 32 million left-handers. And, yup, you guessed it, plenty of people went and asked for one over the counter – many of them right-handed, simply wanting to see if they could taste the difference.

- People tricked on All Fools' Day get called different things in different countries. In France, the victim who doesn't spot anything fishy and is successfully tricked is called a *poisson d'avril*, or 'April fish'. In Scotland, so a Glaswegian friend tells me, they're called a *gowk*, which apparently means 'cuckoo', but I'd look it up for yourself to be on the safe side.

- According to myth, Ceres (later of April festival fame) thought she heard the screams of her daughter Proserpina as she was being dragged to the underworld by Pluto – not the cute Disney dog, but the ruler of the dead – and went in search of her. What she didn't realize was that it was only the echoes of the screams she was hearing, so there was no way that she could have reached her daughter in time to save her. Ceres had been on a fool's errand . . . or, as the Scots say, 'hunting a gowk'. Perhaps that should be hunting a cuckoo's *nest*, which really would be a fool's errand, wouldn't it? Hence the link between the festival and pranks.

- Today, the April Fool's Day tradition of the fool's errand is alive and well in Britain. (Think of the poor people sent out in droves to ask for left-handed screwdrivers – if not burgers – and the like, but save your real pity for the victims of the crueller practical jokes: the clingfilm over the loo bowl, the inky soaps . . . This is a tradition which caters for all tastes and ages, and leaves me feeling a little uneasy. I don't 'do' April Fool's pranks, for fear of having them done to me.*

* There, now I've put it down in black and white, you can believe every word I say on 1 April.**

** Would I lie to you?

2 April

Some juicy facts and pithy thoughts concerning oranges

1. Hollywood (originally known as Hollywoodland)* was built on what were predominantly orange groves.

2. The only word in the English language to rhyme with 'orange' (other than various proper nouns) is borrange, which means 'a word created for the sole purpose of rhyming with orange; having no other function or meaning'.**

3. Either oranges are called oranges because they're orange in colour, or the colour orange is called orange because it's the colour of oranges.***

4. According to the title of Jeanette Winterson's rites-of-passage novel – and to common sense and observation – oranges are not the only fruit.

5. An orange a day is about as likely to keep the doctor away as an apple, should apples become unavailable.

6. The word 'orange' comes from the Sanskrit *narang*, and – according to one of my old English teachers – was referred to in English as 'a norange' before, eventually, becoming 'an orange'.

7. The biggest grower of oranges is Brazil, producing over twice as many tonnes of fruit as the US, which comes second. Mexico is third. Not surprisingly, Brazil also produces the most orange juice in the world.

---

* Even the famous sign used to read HOLLYWOODLAND until the letters L, A, N and D were removed.

** The first recorded use of the word 'borrange' was in *Philip Ardagh's Book of Absolutely Useless Lists for absolutely every day of the year* (2007, Macmillan).

*** It would seem that the fruit name came first, and the colour orange wasn't called orange until the mid-16th century. (So what colour did they call carrots before then?)

8. The orange blossom is the state flower of Florida.*

9. A typical raw Florida orange contains 50 kcal/190 kg per 100 g (3.5 oz).

10. Marmalade is usually made from Seville oranges.**

* My favourite US state flowers include:
    Maine: the white pine cone and tassel
    Oregon: the Oregon grape
    New Mexico: the Yucca plant
** Contain your excitement! I always save the best till last.

3 April

A postbag of legal letters

A letter of safe conduct: allowing the bearer of the letter safe passage through enemy territory.

A letter of Marque: a commission authorizing a privately owned ship to retaliate against a hostile/enemy nation until satisfaction – or restitution – has been made for financial loss or injury.

A letter of Slains: a petition made to the Crown by a murder victim's family, in old Scottish Law, asking for a pardon for the murderer because they've 'received satisfaction'.

A letter of Uriah: a letter which, on the face of it, seems helpful and friendly but which is really a death warrant.

Letters of Credence: documents, signed by a sovereign or head of state, officially appointing the bearer to a position – such as ambassador – to a foreign government. The bearer isn't officially 'recognized' – doesn't officially take up the role – until these letters have been presented.

Lettre de Cachet: warrants issued under the French King's name. In the 18th century, these got a bad reputation when they were often left blank so that the authorities and (rich) parties could fill them in as they wished! Such letters were often used by families against their own relatives with whom they didn't see eye to eye. They were finally abolished in 1790, as a result of the French Revolution.

Letters of Administration: a letter of authority, granting a person the right to administer the estate of a person who has died without leaving a will.

Letters of Bellerophon: any letters which are a danger or will cause prejudice to those who hold them. (Named after the Greek myth of Bellerophon, who carried letters urging King Iobates of Lycia to put him to death. Instead, Iobates set him numerous death-defying tasks which he succeeded in completing.)

4 April

Animal males, females and babies

ANIMAL	MALE	FEMALE	BABY
Alligator	bull	cow	hatchling
Antelope	buck	doe	calf
Ape	*male*	*female*	baby
Armadillo	*male*	*female*	pup
Badger	boar	sow	kit, cub
Bat	*male*	*female*	pup
Bear	boar	sow, she bear	cub
Bee	drone	queen, worker	larva
Bird (general)	cock	hen	hatchling, chick
Bison	bull	cow	calf
Camel	bull	cow	calf
Cat	tomcat	queen	kitten
Chicken	cock, rooster	hen	chick, pullet (*female*), cockrell (*male*)
Deer	buck, stag	doe	fawn
Dog	dog	bitch	pup
Dolphin	bull	cow	pup, calf
Donkey	jack, jackass	jennet, jenny	colt, foal
Dove	cock	hen	chick, squab
Duck	drake	duck	duckling
Eagle	*male*	*female*	eaglet, fledgling
Elephant	bull	cow	calf
Falcon	tercel	falcon	chick
Ferret	hob	jill	kit
Fox	reynard, tod dog fox	vixen	kit, cup, pup
Frog	*male*	*female*	tadpole, polliwog, froglet
Gerbil	buck	doe	pup
Giraffe	bull	doe	calf
Goat	buck, billy	doe, nanny	kid, billy*
Goose	gander	goose	gosling
Guinea pig	boar	sow	pup

* Not to be confused with Billy the Kid.

Hare	buck	doe	leveret
Hawk	tiercel	hen	eyas
Horse	stallion, stud	mare, dam	foal, filly (*female*), colt (*male*)
Jellyfish	*male*	*female*	ephyna
Kangaroo	buck, jack, boomer, roo	doe, jill	joey
Leopard	leopard	leopardess	cub
Lion	lion	lioness	cub
Llama	*male*	*female*	cria
Moose	bull	cow	calf
Mouse	buck	doe	pup, pinkie, kitten
Mule	jack	hinney	foal
Opossum	jack	jill	joey
Otter	*male*	*female*	whelp, pup
Platypus	*male*	*female*	puggle
Porpoise	bull	cow	calf
Quail	cock	hen	chick
Rabbit	buck	doe	bunny, kitten, kit
Rat	buck	doe	pup, pinkie, kitten
Seal	bull	cow	pup
Sheep	buck, ram	ewe, dam	lamb, lambkin, cosset
Snake	*male*	*female*	snakelet, neonate (*newly born*); hatchling (*newly hatched*)*
Squirrel	buck	doe	pup, kit, kitten
Swan	cob	pen	cygnet, flapper
Turkey	tom	hen	poult
Wasp	drone	queen (*fertile*), worker (*infertile*)	larva
Whale	bull	cow	calf
Wolf	dog	bitch	pup, whelp
Wren	cock	jenny	chick
Zebra	stallion	mare	colt, foal

* Some snakes are born live, others hatch from eggs.

5 April

1916: US actor and film star Gregory Peck is born

A mouthful of tongue twisters

1. Three grey geese in a green field grazing
   Grey were the geese and green was the grazing.

2. Robert Rowley rolled a round roll round.
   A round roll Robert Rowley rolled round.
   Where rolled the round roll
   Robert Rowley rolled round?

3. Swan swam over the sea.
   Swim, swan, swim!
   Swan swam back again.
   Well swum, Swan!

4. Peter Piper picked a peck of pickled pepper.
   A peck of pickled pepper Peter Piper picked.
   If Peter Piper picked a peck of pickled pepper,
   Where's the peck of pickled pepper Peter Piper picked?

5. Betty Botter bought some butter.
   'But,' she said, 'the butter's bitter;
   If I put it in my batter,
   It will make my batter bitter.
   But a bit of better butter,
   That would make my batter better.'
   So she bought a bit of butter,
   And she put it in her batter,
   And the batter was not bitter.
   So 'twas better Betty Botter
   Bought a bit of better butter.

6. Moses supposes his toeses are roses,
   But Moses supposes erroneously;
   For nobody's toeses are posies of roses
   As Moses supposes his toeses to be.

6 April

1938: Teflon is invented

A few fascinating facts about Teflon which will never stick

1. Teflon – the non-stick coating on saucepans and frying pans – is the trade name of polytetrafluroethylene (aka fluoropolymer resin).

2. Polytetrafluroethylene is also known as PTFE, and PTFE tape is often used by plumbers to give an extra-tight-fitting seal to pipe joints.

3. The story that Teflon was a by-product of the NASA space programme is untrue. It's a falsehood. It's a lie. It's an urban myth. But that won't stop people from continuing to perpetrate* it.

4. Roy Plunkett, an employee of the company DuPont, was experimenting with chlorofluorocarbons (aka CFCs of old fridges fame). He accidentally produced a waxy, white(-ish) solid which was very slippery indeed. This was what DuPont was to market as Teflon in 1946.

5. Some bullets are coated in Teflon, not for the bullet's own sake, but to reduce the friction and wear and tear on the barrel of the weapon firing it.

6. One of the problems of a non-stick material such as Teflon is getting it to stick to the cookware in the first place! The only way is to create a very rough, scratched surface on to which a thin layer of liquid Teflon is sprayed. Once caught in the scratches, it is baked and hardened and coated with a sealant (which still retains its slippery properties).

7. Teflon was used on components in the Manhattan Project (the secret development of nuclear weapons by the US from 1941 to 1946), and for wire insulation on the US's *Apollo* space missions. It is extremely heat-resistant.

* Which is what people who spread myths do.

7 April

All the actors who have played the character of Doctor Who on television (so far), excluding Richard Hurndall who played the first doctor in 'The Five Doctors' in 1983; that lot in the Red Nose Day and/or Children in Need spoof episodes; and any stuntmen or stand-ins.

1st. William Hartnell (1963-6)

2nd. Patrick Troughton (1966-9)

3rd. Jon Pertwee (1970-74)

4th. Tom Baker (1974-81)

5th. Peter Davidson (1981-4)

6th. Colin Baker (1984-6)

7th. Sylvester McCoy (1987-9, 1996 in TV movie starring Paul McGann)

8th. Paul McGann (1996, in one-off made-for-TV movie)

9th. Christopher Eccleston (2005)

10th. David Tennant (2005-)

8 April

*1904: Britain and France sign the Entente Cordiale,
settling differences in foreign policy*

Thirteen or more historical facts about thirteen places that the UK leg of the Tour de France bicycle race passed through on 8 July 2007

Westminster: Westminster Abbey, the Houses of Parliament and Westminster School were built on what was once Thorney Island, an island in the middle of the Thames. Over time, land and water levels have changed and the river island and its buildings have become part of the mainland.

Greenwich: Greenwich has a longitude of 0° 0' 0", 'the Prime Meridian' (agreed by many countries – excluding France! – as an international standard in 1884). It passes directly through Greenwich's Royal Observatory, where they came up with Greenwich Mean Time.

Woolwich: The Royal Arsenal in Woolwich was set up in the 17th century and became England's biggest supplier of fuses, explosives, shot, and ammunition in general. (The football club is named after it.)

Erith: The name is Saxon and means either 'muddy harbour' or 'gravelly landing place', neither of which is terribly exciting. The (few remaining) ruins of Lesnes Abbey* are nearby.

Dartford: The birthplace of Mick Jagger (26 July 1943), lead singer of the Rolling Stones.

Gravesend: The Native American princess Pocahontas – later of Walt Disney fame – died on a ship anchored off Gravesend in 1617.

Medway: The Medway towns are Rochester, Strood, Chatham, Gillingham and Rainham. The Royal Victoria and Bull Hotel in Rochester was actually stayed in by the queen whose name it bears (when it was still the plain old Bull

---

* Which my parents dragged me around one New Year's Day when I was a child, and which I was greatly disappointed by (though I may be thrilled beyond belief by if I ever decide to revisit them as an adult).

Hotel and she was still a princess). It was an unscheduled stop in 1836, when the princess and her party couldn't cross a bridge damaged by a storm.

Maidstone: Much of Maidstone – the capital of the county of Kent – used to have a distinctive smell coming from its toffee factory (variously known as the Trebor* and Sharp's factory). It closed in 1998. The appealing smell went with it.

Tonbridge: The town's name probably comes from the Old English tun meaning 'enclosure, farmstead, village, manor, estate' and brycg, meaning 'bridge', combining to mean 'bridge belonging to the estate', which would have been the best place to cross the river.

Tunbridge Wells:** The water in the wells after which the town is named, supplied by the Chalybeate Spring, tastes pretty dreadful. Trust me, I've tried it in both the Pantiles*** and Dunorlan Park, but it's free! (You only pay if you have it served to you.)

Tenterden: Although Tenet-ware-den means 'pig-pasture of the men of Thanet', Tenterden's later prosperity came from the dyeing and weaving of sheep's wool in the 14th century. Today, it's probably better known for its steam railway.

Ashford: The town gets a mention in the Domesday Book, but as Essetesford. In 1911, it became the site of one of the UK's earliest purpose-built cinemas (rather than being a converted theatre or other building).

Canterbury: The city suffered much bomb damage during the Second World War and, among the genuinely old and fascinating buildings are many heavily restored or completely rebuilt fascinating buildings . . . or so they whisper. Though the 'seat' of the Archbishop of Canterbury, his main residence is at Lambeth Palace in London.****

---

* The Trebor brand – probably most famous as Trebor Mints (as in 'are a minty bit stronger') and Soft Mints were part of Robertson & Woodcock Ltd, founded in 1907. Although Trebor is the name Robert spelled backwards, the sweets apparently got their name from the building in which they were first (hand)made. They're now a part of Cadbury.

** The race went right past the bottom of my road.

*** The Pantiles is a 17th-century colonnade of shops, updated in the 18th and 19th centuries.

**** The Archbishop of Canterbury is not, as is so often incorrectly stated, the head of the Church of England. That role goes to the reigning monarch.

9 April

Ten fascinating facts about (plastic) flying saucers

1. The most common ways of playing Frisbee are Freestyle, Ultimate, Guts and Double Disc Courts.
2. The official and original Frisbee was the Wham-O Frisbee. (It's a registered trademark.) Other Frisbees should really be called flying discs or flying saucers.
3. There are now even 'Disc dog' competitions where dogs catch Frisbees and/or flying discs in their mouths!
4. Flying Saucers were originally invented by Fred Morrison and financed and developed by Warren Franscioni in 1948.
5. In 1955 Morrison brought out an improved version.
6. In 1957 Wham-O bought the rights, selling them as Pluto Platters.
7. In 1958, Wham-O changed the name to Frisbee. Some suggest that this was as a tribute to the Frisbie (with an 'i') Pie Company of Connecticut whose empty pie tins were often thrown by Yale University students.
8. Fred Morrison earned over a million dollars in royalties.
9. Nowadays, the Frisbee trademark is owned by toy-makers Mattel.
10. Wham-O sold over ONE HUNDRED MILLION Frisbees before selling Mattel the rights.

* Without seeing a single alien spacecraft.

10 April

1710: the Copyright Act comes into effect, protecting authors' rights to their works, even for a period after their death

An A to Z of noisy book titles (with footnotes for the first ten, then a further smattering as the mood takes me)

Airport by Arthur Hailey[1]
Birdsong by Sebastian Faulks[2]
The Bottle Factory Outing by Beryl Bainbridge[3]
The Call of the Wild by Jack London[4]
Captain Corelli's Mandolin by Louis de Bernières[5]
Chitty Chitty Bang Bang by Ian Fleming[6]
The Devil Rides Out by Dennis Wheatley[7]
The Executioner's Song by Norman Mailer[8]
The Fall of the House of Usher by Edgar Allan Poe[9]
Gone With the Wind by Margaret Mitchell[10]
Heavy Weather by P. G. Wodehouse
The Hornet's Nest by Patricia Cornwell
The Hound of the Baskervilles by Arthur Conan Doyle
I Hear Voices by Paul Ableman

[1] Well, have you ever been to a quiet airport?
[2] The dawn chorus can be very noisy indeed.
[3] Imagine all that chinking of glass.
[4] Howling and braying and the like, I suppose.
[5] He may play softly, of course, but I doubt it.
[6] A veritable cacophony!
[7] The clattering of hoofs, perchance?
[8] A wailing lament?
[9] CRASH!
[10] No obvious rude jokes about this one, please. Who made that noise? Was it you at the back?

Jonathan Livingston Seagull by Richard Bach[1]
The Kraken Wakes by John Wyndham[2]
The Little Drummer Girl by John le Carré
The Man Who Watched Trains Go By by Georges Simenon
Night Train by Martin Amis
Only When I Larf by Len Deighton
Paddy Clarke Ha Ha Ha by Roddy Doyle
The Postman Always Rings Twice by James M. Cain
Rosemary's Baby by Ira Levin[3]
Shout at the Devil by Wilbur Smith
To Kill a Mockingbird by Harper Lee[4]
Under the Volcano by Malcolm Lowry
The Van by Roddy Doyle
The War of the Worlds by H. G. Wells
When Eight Bells Toll by Alistair MacLean
Wild Swans by Jung Chang
Year of the Tiger by Jack Higgins
Zen and the Art of Motorcycle Maintenance by Robert Pirsig

[1] SQUAWK!
[2] Yawn . . .
[3] Waaaaaah! Waaaaaah!
[4] SQUAWK! Bang! Thud!

11 April

A plethora* of palindromes (in this case, sentences that read the same backwards as forwards)

Madam I'm Adam

Never odd or even

Do geese see God?

Was it Eliot's toilet I saw?

Able was I ere I saw Elba

Murder for a jar of red rum

Some men interpret nine memos

Go hang a salami – I'm a lasagna** hog!

A man, a plan, a canal – Panama!

Was it a car or a cat I saw?

Tuna roll or a nut?

* Lots.
** You can't spell it lasagne (with an 'e') for this one to work!

126

12 April

1961: Soviet cosmonaut Yuri Gagarin becomes the first human being in space as he orbits the Earth for 108 minutes

A short list of facts about taking the long – as in slow – way around the world

1. The first officially recognized circumnavigation of the world *on foot* was by American David Kunst.
2. He started on 20 June 1970.
3. He finished on 5 October 1974.
4. That's a long time.
5. The walk was actually 14,450 miles (23,250 km) long.
6. Mr Kunst took around 20 million steps.
7. He wore out 21 pairs of shoes.
8. No. 7 is not surprising!

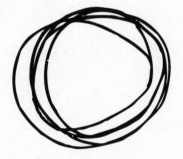

13 April

1598: Henry IV of France signs the Edict of Nantes, granting rights to Protestants

Feathers used as quill pens*

- The most common quill pen was made from a goose's feather.

- A swan's-feather quill pen was more rare, more expensive and wrote that little bit better.

- Crows' feathers made the quills which produced the finest line. They're the classiest quill pens of all.

- Other quills were made from:
  - eagle
  - owl
  - hawk
  - turkey

* Quill pens were invented in about AD 700. The most suitable feathers were the five outer wing feathers, plucked from a live bird in the spring. (The left wing was best because the feathers curved away from the writer if s/he was right-handed, as most people are, rather than tickling the nose.)

14 April

Languages more widely spoken than English* (and I'll bet you thought it was just Chinese)

1st: Mandarin Chinese
Spoken by approximately 874 million people

There are many Chinese dialects, but Mandarin is the most widely spoken. Next comes Wu, spoken by around 77 million people. Very few non-Chinese speak Mandarin.

2nd: Hindustani
Spoken by approximately 426 million people

Hindustani incorporates the two very similar languages of Hindi and Urdu. Hindustani is the official language of both India and Pakistan. In India, its written form is Devanagari and it's called Hindi. In Pakistan, its written form is Urdu.

3rd: Spanish
Spoken by approximately 358 million people

What makes the use of Spanish so different from Mandarin and Hindustani is that it's so widely spoken *outside* its country of origin. In addition to Spain, it's also widely spoken in the USA, South America and the west coast of Africa.

* English comes fourth with around 341 million. Having said that, around one billion people – 1,000,000,000 – are thought to be learning English worldwide.

15 April

1452: Leonardo da Vinci is born

A bunch of famous Browns, excluding Gordon

Paddington Brown, aka Paddington Bear, adopted by the Brown family (having arrived in England from darkest Peru) in the books written and created by Michael Bond. His aunt lives in a home for retired bears in Lima.

Mr Brown (who went off to town on the 8.21), a member of the Home Guard referred to in 'Who do you think you are kidding, Mr Hitler?' sung by Bud Flanagan as the theme tune to long-running BBC TV comedy *Dad's Army*, written by Jimmy Perry and David Croft.*

Mr Brown (played by Richard Wattis), the round-glasses-wearing neighbour of Eric and Hattie in the incredibly long-running TV comedy series *Sykes*, written by and starring Eric Sykes.

Mr Brown from *Mr Brown Can Moo! Can You?*, a 'book of wonderful noises' by Dr Seuss. This Mr Brown is a man and not a bull.

John Brown, one of Queen Victoria's ghillies,** who became an extremely close friend of the monarch. (In the film *Mrs Brown*, staring Judi Dench as Queen Victoria and Billy Connolly as Brown, the title refers to the queen herself and was an unflattering nickname at the time.)

John Brown, a larger-than-life abolitionist during the American Civil War. (Abolitionists wanted to abolish slavery.) According to a popular song at the time, his body 'lies a-mouldering in his grave' but 'His soul goes marching on'.***

Dan Brown, author of the HUMUNGOUS bestseller *The Da Vinci Code*.

James Brown, the late 'Godfather of Soul'. Need I say more?****

* The TV series, not the theme tune. That was written by Jimmy Perry alone.
** Male Scottish servants.
*** Though the song, sung to the tune of 'The Battle Hymn of the Republic', might also have been referring to a lesser known (unpopular) John Brown for comic effect, as a morale-booster.
**** Probably.

16 April

A list of flightless birds, many of which are extinct, probably because they couldn't run away fast enough

Adzebill (extinct)
Auckland Island Teal
Bar-winged Rail (extinct)*
Calayan Rail
Cassowary
Chatham Rail (extinct)
Dieffenbach's Rail (extinct)
Dodo (extinct)
Elephant bird (extinct)
Emu
Falkland Flightless Steamer Duck**
Flightless Cormorant**
Gough Island Moorhen
Great Auk (extinct)
Guam Rail
Gulls and relatives
Hawaiian Rail (extinct)
Henderson Island Crake
Inaccessible Island Rail
Invisible Rail
Junin Flightless Grebe**
Kagu
Kakapo
Kangaroo Island Emu (extinct)
King Island Emu (extinct)
Kiwi
Kosrae Island Crake (extinct)
Laysan Rail (extinct)
Lord Howe Swamphen (extinct)*

Lord Howe Woodhen
Magellanic Flightless Steamer Duck**
Makira Wood Rail
Moa-nalo (extinct)
Moa (extinct)
New Britain Rail
New Caledonian Rail
New Guinea Flightless Rail**
North Island Takahe (extinct)
Ostrich
Penguin
Petrel-like birds
Red Rail (extinct)
Rheas
Rodrigues Rail (extinct)
Rodrigues Solitaire (extinct)
Roviana Rail ***
Samoan Wood Rail
Snoring Rail
Spectacled Cormorant (extinct)
Stephens Island Wren (extinct)
Tahiti Rail (extinct)
Takahe
Titicaca Flightless Grebe**
Tristan Moorhen (extinct)
Wake Island Rail (extinct)
Weka
White-headed Flightless Steamer Duck**
Woodford's Rail (extinct)*

* Probably flightless.
** The clue is in the name.
*** Probably as near to flightless as made no difference.

17 April

A few common-sense tips on avoiding being struck by lightning

1. Stay inside during thunderstorms.

2. If you do go out, don't wear a metal suit of armour, or a lightning conductor strapped to your head.

3. Avoid high places. Lightning is more likely to strike a tall building, hill or tree than someone hiding in a ditch. If it's raining hard, however, the ditch may fill with water and drown you.

4. Avoid metal. That includes wire fences, corrugated-iron sheds, golf clubs, fishing rods, cars, bicycles and even that suit of armour I already mentioned.

5. If possible, avoid using a land-line telephone during a thunderstorm if the phone wires are above ground (on telegraph poles). If lightning hits one of these wires, it can conduct electricity down it, right into the hand of anyone holding their phone. OUCH!

6. During a thunderstorm, don't fly a kite with a metal key tied to the wet string.*

7. Throw yourself to the ground if your hair stands on end. Hair standing on end and/or a tingling sensation are possible warnings that lightning is about to strike. The throwing-yourself-to-the-ground part is official advice, and not an old wives' tale.

---

* Benjamin Franklin did. Some of the others who were foolish enough to repeat his experiment – to prove that storm clouds were charged with static electricity – were killed. DON'T TRY THIS. IT IS EXTREMELY DANGEROUS.

18 April

1949: the Republic of Ireland is born

Popular souvenirs for sale in an Irish airport

- Giant green foam hats.
- Giant foam hats shaped like pints of Guinness.
- Cuddly leprechauns (in a variety of sizes).
- Leprechaun keyrings.
- Leprechaun bookmarks.
- More leprechaun stuff.
- Small pieces of reconstituted stone with the message, 'I kissed the Blarney Stone'.
- Shamrock keyrings.
- Shamrock paperweights.
- Shamrock lucky trinkets.
- Yet more leprechaun stuff.
- Gaelic jewellery.
- More shamrock stuff.
- T-shirts (including ones of shamrock, Guinness - er - leprechauns, and Gaelic designs).
- Fudge.

19 April

St Paul's Cathedral

- The first St Paul's was built in 604 during the reign of England's first Christian king, St Ethelbert of Kent. It burned down.

- It was rebuilt twice. This third building was also burned down, this time in the Great Fire of London in 1666.

- The only monument to survive this fire was to the metaphysical poet John Donne (who had been the Dean of St Paul's).

- The fourth building on this site – the present one – was built between 1675 and 1708, with the first service taking place in it in 1697.

- It was built by court architect Sir Christopher Wren, who had to submit a number of plans before being given the go-ahead. (He then changed the designs further during the building process.)

- St Paul's was the first British cathedral to be designed by one person and completed in his lifetime. (The final stone was laid on Wren's 76th birthday, which was nice.)

- Wren originally designed a stone canopy to go above the main altar but this was not built. After a bomb destroyed this area of the cathedral during the Blitz in the Second World War, the altar was later rebuilt with the canopy in place.

- Much of the interior of the cathedral is covered in brightly coloured mosaics which many find – OK: which *I* find – garish and out of keeping. These were added in the Victorian era when Her Majesty complained that the interior was 'most dreary, dingy and unemotional'.

- The dome of St Paul's is 111.3 metres high and weighs around 65,000 tons. The dome you see outside isn't the one you see inside. It has an inner shell.

- Many of the outer walls of the cathedral are simply there to hide the flying buttresses Wren required to support the inner walls. These buttresses would have looked very out of keeping with his classical design.

- The body of Admiral Nelson lies in the middle of the crypt (directly beneath the centre of the dome). He was buried in the coffin that he actually had with him at the Battle of Trafalgar* (just in case).

- The Duke of Wellington and Wren himself are also buried in the cathedral.

- The Prince of Wales and Lady Diana Spencer married in St Paul's Cathedral in 1981.

- Author Philip Ardagh – oh, that's me – was baptized in the cathedral on 10 February 1962.**

* Also fought off Cadiz.
** There was no national holiday.

20 April

Films centred on apes and/or monkeys in a big way

King Kong (1933)
starring Fay Wray, Robert Armstrong and Bruce Cabot
directed by Merian C. Cooper and Ernest B. Schoedsack
featuring giant gorilla

Monkey Business (1952)
starring Cary Grant, Marilyn Monroe and Charles Coburn
directed by Howard Hawks
featuring chimpanzees

Planet of the Apes (1968)
starring Kim Hunter, Charlton Heston and Roddy McDowall
directed by Franklin Schaffner
featuring (talking) gorillas and chimpanzees

King Kong (1976)
starring Jessica Lange, Jeff Bridges and Charles Grodin
directed by John Guillermin
featuring giant gorilla

Every Which Way But Loose (1978)
starring Clint Eastwood, Ruth Gordon and Sondra Locke
directed by James Fargo
featuring orang-utan

Any Which Way You Can (1980)
starring Clint Eastwood, Ruth Gordon and Sondra Locke
directed by Buddy Van Horn
featuring orang-utan

Project X (1987)
starring Helen Hunt and Matthew Broderick
directed by Jonathan Kaplan
featuring chimpanzees

Planet of the Apes (2001)
starring Mark Wahlberg and Tim Roth
directed by Tim Burton
featuring (talking) gorillas and chimpanzees

King Kong (2005)
starring Naomi Watts, Jack Black and Adrien Brody
directed by Peter Jackson
featuring giant gorilla

21 April

753 BC: the traditional date for the founding of Rome by Romulus (having killed Remus)

Four simple mnemonics* for trying to remember the Seven Hills of Rome**

1. Canny Queen Victoria Eats Carrots And Peas
2. Certain Questions Vile Edward Cannot Answer Properly
3. Court Quashes Viscount Edmund's Challenge Against People
4. Count's Quirky Vampire Experiences Change Attitudes Permanently

The Hills are: Capitoline, Quirinal, Viminal, Esquiline, Caelian, Aventine and Palatine.

* All my own work!
** I find it hard enough trying to remember the mnemonics.

1860: John McDouall Stuart becomes the first
European to reach the middle of Australia

Twenty things I learned about Australia and Australians from watching *Neighbours* and *Home & Away*

1. Very few Australian children actually live with their parents.

2. An Australian twin will instinctively know where to locate the other twin after an accident, even if (years later) it turns out that there was a mix-up at birth and they're not twins at all.

3. Most Australian light aircraft and helicopter trips end in crashes.

4. It's not worth the professional rescuers looking for survivors after such crashes, as nine times out of ten, friends or relatives 'acting on a hunch' will be the ones who find them.

5. There is only one bed in an Australian hospital (except on very special occasions). The door to the hospital room nearly always looks out on to the nurses' station.

6. An Australian part-time teacher can very quickly end up a headteacher and an Australian GP can be performing operations in a local hospital before you can say, 'But are you qualified to do this?'

7. Cults are a regular nuisance in Australia, with their leaders usually trying to lure someone called Tasha or Angel to join them (so long as they're blonde and a girl).

8. In Australia, serious injuries don't seem to remain serious for long.

9. Australians regularly arrange their clandestine meetings and lovers' trysts by the same stretch of water, be it pond or sea.

10. Most young Australian males are forever coming up with hare-brained money-making schemes which backfire on them, and which are more annoying than amusing.

11. People who run pubs/coffee shops/general stores often have bets with other people who run pubs/coffee shops/general stores about which of them can run faster or make the better barbecue sauce.

12. Sometimes, an Australian comes home looking completely and utterly altered – from height, hair and eye colour to completely different features – and no one (from their family to the local policeman) seems to notice.

13. All fridges in Australia have some surf-related item (postcard, bumper-sticker, magnet) stuck to the front of them.

14. Everyone in Australia gets married before they've left school.

15. At some time or other, an Australian child will write and perform his – but usually *her* – own song.

16. Australian nightclubs contain very few people, most of whom look very embarrassed when trying to dance.

17. Australians regularly discover that the person they thought of as being their father *isn't* their father.

18. With a few notable exceptions, in Australia, people who've been away for a while rarely come back to attend funerals or weddings of loved ones. It's as if they've somehow been 'written out' of life.

19. The most secret conversations are always overheard (and often misunderstood).

20. A surprising number of Australians have brothers or sisters who are never mentioned until a couple of weeks before they turn up unexpectedly.

23 April

St George's Day

A dozen different uses for a pet dragon

1. For company.
2. To impress your friends.
3. One-upmanship (if the Joneses next door don't have one).
4. To raise/lower local house prices (depending on locals' reaction).
5. As a cheap source of heating and lighting.
6. As a fire-breathing, giant flying lizard substitute for a guard dog.
7. As a mobile barbecue/for roasting marshmallows.
8. As living proof that some mythological beasts are actually real.
9. To attract knights on quests (and get their autographs).
10. To attract media attention.
11. For cheap flights abroad (simply climb on its back).
12. To wipe that smug smile off your vet's face.

24 April

1990: the Hubble Space Telescope is launched

A cluster of famous alleged UFO* sightings

June 1947: the Kenneth Arnold Sighting, Washington State, USA

Pilot Kenneth Arnold reported having seen 'a chain of nine peculiar-looking aircraft' moving like 'saucers skipping over water' and flying 'at tremendous speed'. A newspaper printed the claim using the phrase 'FLYING SAUCERS' for the first time. For weeks afterwards, thousands of claims of similar sightings came from across the globe.

July 1947: Roswell, New Mexico

One of the most famous UFO incidents of all time. The US military themselves issued a press release claiming that a flying saucer had crashed. They later changed their story, saying that it was, in fact, a weather balloon. Soon rumour spread that it *had* been an alien spaceship which was taken back to the Roswell airforce base (where autopsies were carried out on its dead alien occupants).

September 1961: the Interrupted Journey, New Hampshire, USA

Barney and Betty Hill reported having seen a flying saucer. Under hypnosis, they claimed to have been abducted by the alien occupants and probed. This was the first 'alien abduction' story to receive such widespread publicity.

---

* A UFO is simply an unidentified flying object. If you catch sight of a dustbin lid (thrown from a multi-storey car park) hurtling through the sky, and don't know that it's a dustbin lid (thrown from a multi-storey car park), then – to you – it's a flying object which is unidentified so is, quite legitimately, a UFO. In that sense, they can't fail to exist. Whether any UFOs have anything to do with aliens from other planets is quite a different matter. Reports of UFO sightings fall into a variety of categories from 'made-up' and hallucinations to 'very-difficult-to-explain'. None has, so far, been spotted through the Hubble telescope.

October 1978: the Valentich Incident, Tasmania/Australia

While flying over the Bass Strait between Tasmania and Australia, Australian pilot Frederick Valentich radioed in that he'd spotted an enormous UFO. Neither he nor his aircraft were ever seen again.

December 1980: the Rendlesham Forest Incident, Suffolk, England

Soon labelled 'the British Roswell', members of the local USAF base reported a number of UFO sightings (from the ground) on consecutive nights. What is significant about this case is the sheer number of apparently highly credible witnesses to the events, and official supporting evidence. The *News of the World* ran the headline:

UFO LANDS IN SUFFOLK – AND THAT'S OFFICIAL

25 April

1599: Oliver Cromwell is born

First names* with fruit and veg in them

Melony with a melon
Oliver with an olive
Apple** with an apple
Peaches*** with peaches

THIS SPACE HAS KINDLY BEEN PROVIDED BY THE
AUTHOR FOR YOU TO ADD TO THE LIST YOURSELF****

* Thus excluding the likes of Halle Berry, Gilbert Grape and
William Shakespeare (who has a pear in there somewhere).
** The name of film star Gwyneth Paltrow's and musician Chris
Martin's firstborn.
*** As in Peaches Geldof, one of Bob Geldof's daughters.
**** OK! I confess. The list seemed like a good idea at the time, and
is a lot harder than I imagined!

26 April

Some strange-but-true facts about hair

- Except at the root, hair is dead. It is non-living material made from the protein keratin.
- Because of this, British advertisers are not allowed to talk about their products 'putting life' into your hair.
- Autumn is the time of greatest natural hair loss and growth.
- Hair actually grows faster in warm weather.
- More dandruff is created in the colder months.
- Hair doesn't continue growing after death (it's just that the body tissue around the hair roots shrinks, thus making the hair look longer).
- Egg shampoos can turn bleached hair green. (So can chlorine and fluoride in water.)
- Cutting hair doesn't make it grow thicker or quicker.
- Eyebrow hairs and eyelashes grow in ten-week spurts, then stop for months.
- Fingernails are also made from keratin, and also grow faster in the heat.
- Tsar Peter the Great banned beards, ordering that anyone who dared enter St Petersburg wearing one would have it cut off by his guards immediately.

* He of, among other things, the impressive beard.

27 April

1759: writer and feminist Mary Wollstonecraft* is born

Some famous monsters, excluding those from classical mythology***

1. Those involved in the wild rumpus with Max in *Where the Wild Things Are.*

2. The Gruffalo in *The Gruffalo* and *The Gruffalo's Child.*

3. The majority (by headcount) of the characters in *The Lord of the Rings* trilogy.

4. The Great Big Red Rock Eater (the answer to the question: 'What's big, red and eats rocks?').

5. The one under your bed.[1]

6. Many of the life forms Doctor Who encounters.

7. The cast of *Monsters, Inc.*

9. An enormous number of nasties in *Buffy the Vampire Slayer.*

10. Hang on just one big-clawed, sharp-toothed minute! There are no such things as monsters . . . I'm going to make a cup of tea.[2]

---

* Mother of Mary Wollstonecraft Shelley,** who wrote *Frankenstein.*

** Born Mary Wollstonecraft Godwin, she married poet Percy Bysshe Shelley.

*** I'm not counting huge things such as giants, ogres or King Kong because they're just larger than usual, and so am I. And I'm not a monster . . .

[1] If it's not there, check the bedroom wardrobe.

[2] WOW! This really could turn out to be one of the most absolutely useless lists in the book!

28 April

The more famous Monroe

- Elton John's 'Candle in the Wind' (first line: 'Goodbye, Norma Jean') is about film-star Marilyn Monroe, her having been born Norma Jeane Mortenson.

- Marilyn married three times:
  1. James Dougherty (aircraft factory worker)
  2. Joe DiMaggio (baseball player)**
  3. Arthur Miller (playwright)

- Monroe's father was Norwegian. There is a statue of her in Haugesund, Norway, where he came from.

- She didn't legally change her name to Marilyn Monroe until 1956, though she started using it back in 1946.

- Her marriage to Joe DiMaggio officially lasted a year but they split after just eight months.

- In a career of 15 years, she appeared in 29 films including *Some Like It Hot*, *Gentlemen Prefer Blondes* and *The Misfits*.***

- Her 30th film would have been *Something's Got to Give* but she died before they were even halfway through shooting it.

- She died aged 36 in 1962.

- Marilyn Monroe's image has appeared on a 32-cent stamp in the US.

* On her mother's side, Marilyn Monroe was a direct descendant of US President James Monroe.

** Joe DiMaggio is mentioned in Simon and Garfunkel's 'Mrs Robinson'.

*** Written by third husband, Arthur Miller.

29 April

Five number-crunching facts

1. If you multiply 111,111,111 by 111,111,111 you get 12,345,678,987,654,321.

2. If you take any three-digit number in which the difference between the first and last digit is greater than 1 (for example, 422 or 934 would do) . . .

   . . . then reverse the number (so 422 becomes 224 and 934 becomes 439) . . .

   . . . then subtract the smaller from the larger number: (422 – 224 = 198, 934 – 439 = 495) . . .

   . . . and finally take this total and add it to the same number (the total) reversed, you'll find the answer is *always* 1,089. If it isn't, you've done something wrong! (Let's double-check that with my two examples: 198 + 891 = 1,089; and 495 + 594 = 1,089. Yup, it works!)

3. To convert a temperature in degrees Fahrenheit to degrees Celsius, subtract 32, multiply by 5 and then divide by 9. Try that with –40°F, and you'll find you end up with –40°C: –40 –32 = –72; –72 x 5 = –360; –360 ÷9 = –40. (So –40°F and –40° C must both be the same extremely c-c-cold temperature!)

4. If you multiply 142,857 by any number between 1 and 6, you'll find the answer contains the same digits (142,857) but in a different order:

   1 x 142,857 = 142,857

   2 x 142,857 = 285,714

   3 x 142,857 = 428,571

   4 x 142,857 = 571,428

   5 x 142,857 = 714,285

   6 x 142,857 = 857,142

If you multiply that original number (142,857) by 7, however, you get the very satisfying figure of 999,999!

5. Without changing the order, it's possible to make the digits 123456789 equal 100 in an extraordinary number of ways, simply by putting plus and minus signs between them:*

$1 + 2 + 34 - 5 + 67 - 8 + 9 = 100$

$12 + 3 - 4 + 5 + 67 + 8 + 9 = 100$

$123 - 4 - 5 - 6 - 7 + 8 - 9 = 100$

$123 + 4 - 5 + 67 - 89 = 100$

$123 + 45 - 67 + 8 - 9 = 100$

$123 - 45 - 67 + 89 = 100$

$12 - 3 - 4 + 5 - 6 + 7 + 89 = 100$

$12 + 3 + 4 + 5 - 6 - 7 + 89 = 100$

$1 + 23 - 4 + 5 + 6 + 78 - 9 = 100$

$1 + 23 - 4 + 56 + 7 + 8 + 9 = 100$

$1 + 2 + 3 - 4 + 5 + 6 + 78 + 9 = 100$

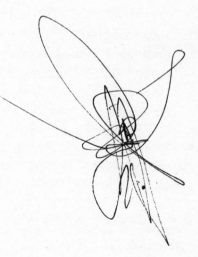

* If minus numbers can be included, then there's also:

$-1 + 2 - 3 + 4 + 5 + 6 + 78 + 9 = 100$

30 April

Injuries to people and property following the crash of 'Train No. 1' driven by Casey Jones,* according to A. S. Sullivan, General Superintendent of the Illinois Central Railroad Company**

People:
1. Simon Webb, Fireman Train No. 1, body bruises [arising from] jumping off Engine 382.
2. Mrs W. E. Breaux, passenger, 1472 Rocheblabe Street, New Orleans, slight bruises.
3. Mrs Wm. Deto, passenger, No. 25 East 33rd Street, Chicago, slight bruises [to] left knee and left hand.
4. Wm. Miller, Express Messenger, injuries to back and left side, apparently slight.
5. W. L. Whiteside, Postal Clerk, jarred.
6. R. A. Ford, Postal Clerk, jarred.

Property (and cost of repair):
7. Engine No. 382 ($1,396.25).
8. Caboose No. 98119 ($430.00).***
9. Two freight cars ($455.00).
10. I.C. baggage car 217 ($105.00).
11. I.C. mail car 51 ($610.00).
12. Railroad track ($102.50).
13. Freight ($100.00).

* The railway company's formal report concluded that Casey Jones 'was solely responsible for the accident as a consequence of not having properly responded to flag signals'.****

** The reason why Casey Jones had songs written about him, along with a TV series, films and giving his name to a chain of burger outlets in UK stations, was because he remained on the footplate – probably trying to stop the engine – rather than jumping clear and saving himself.

*** A caboose is the carriage at the very rear of the train.

****Jones had been suspended for a total of 145 days as a result of nine previous incidents of breaking company protocol.

1 May

A cluster of icy discoveries

1. In 2004 amateur historian and member of the local mountain-rescue team Maurizio Vincenzi found three bodies preserved in ice on San Matteo mountain in Italy. They were three Austrian soldiers from the First World War, still wearing their uniforms. It seems likely they were killed by a grenade in 1918.

2. In 2005 Clarence Stowers bought a pint tub of chocolate ice cream from a drive-through store in Wilmington, North Carolina, USA. Once home, he discovered a severed human finger in it. The finger turned out to belong to store employee Brandon Fizer. Mr Fizer had accidentally put his finger into the ice-cream mixing machine. While some of his workmates were rushing to his aid, another, an attendant at the drive-through window, unknowingly served Mr Stowers a measure of ice cream containing the finger. In the previous year, an employee at the same store had lost a finger in the same machine!

3. In 1991 two hikers discovered a frozen body high up near the Austrian/Italian border. Later found to be 5,300 – yes, 5,300 – years old, he was named Ötzi the Iceman. He was found with a number of beautifully preserved items including a copper axe. In June 2001 Italian scientists discovered a stone arrowhead embedded in his shoulder (something missed in all earlier scientific investigations). They concluded that, having been attacked or frightened, Ötzi fled, was shot from behind as he ran, but made it up into the mountain, where he died.

4. On 19 May 1845 129 men and officers aboard the HMS *Terror* and the HMS *Erebus* set sail to explore the North-west Passage, under the command of Sir John Franklin. After 18 months, they disappeared. In 1981 their bodies were discovered in their permafrost graves by a team led

by the forensic anthropologist Owen Beattie. Their bodies were so well preserved in the ice that it was possible to carry out tests on them to try to determine the cause of death. They contained larger than usual amounts of lead. (One body was found to contain over 100 times the acceptable amount!) It seemed that they died of lead poisoning. Where from? The cans of food which had contained their meagre supplies. In those days, they were made from a combination of lead and tin.

2 May

1882: Baron Manfred von Richthofen, the First World War German flying ace, better known as the Red Baron, is born

Some important firsts in the life of the PEANUTS cartoon, according to its official website: www.snoopy.com

16 November 1952: Lucy first holds an American football for Charlie Brown, which she then pulls away when he tries to kick it.

1 June 1954: Linus's security blanket first appears.

5 January 1956: Snoopy first gets off all fours and walks on two legs.

11 March 1960: Charlie Brown's father is revealed to be a barber by profession.

19 November 1961: Charlie Brown first pines for the little red-haired girl at school.

4 April 1967: a bird strongly resembling Woodstock, though not actually referred to as 'Woodstock', puts in its first appearance.

20 July 1971: Marcie first calls Peppermint Patty 'Sir'.

28 June 1979: The First World War Flying Ace (Snoopy) first visits the 'cute little French girl' (Marcie).

7 January 1980: Peppermint Patty gives a correct answer in her class!

30 March 1993: Charlie Brown hits his first-ever home run in baseball.

6 August 1993: Sally discovers that her family is 'famous' . . . because their name is in the telephone directory!

3 May

1493: Pope Alexander VI issues the first of a number of papal bulls this year, dividing up ownership of the 'New World'

A dozen famous splits

1. Banana (as in the food).
2. *The Banana* (as in Fleegle,[1] Bingo,[2] Drooper[3] and Snorky[4] from the 1968–70 US TV series).
3. As in doing the (which can be painful).
4. Ireland (the Irish Free State – later the Republic of Ireland – and Northern Ireland in 1922).
5. As in getting out of here.
6. The Beatles (in 1970).
7. The Prince and Princess of Wales (divorced 1996).
8. The infinitive (as in 'To boldly go . . .').
9. Jennifer Aniston and Brad Pitt.
10. One's sides (as in laughing).
11. Hairs (as in arguing over petty details).
12. The Grand Canyon.

[1] A kind of dog.
[2] A kind of gorilla.
[3] A kind of lion.
[4] A kind of elephant.[5]
[5] Though they all could have been people dressed up.

4 May

International Star Wars Day and, if it isn't, it should be. Why? 'May the Fourth be with you' of course!*

My favourite lines attributed to movie mogul Sam Goldwyn

'A verbal contract isn't worth the paper it's printed on.'

'Tell me, how did you love the picture?'**

'Anyone who goes to a psychiatrist should have his head examined.'

'I had a monumental idea this morning, but I didn't like it.'

'In two words: im-possible.'

'Let's bring it up to date with some snappy 19th-century dialogue.'

'Gentlemen, include me out.'

'Directors are always biting the hand that lays the golden egg.'

* If you'd like a genuine on-this-day event for 4 May, how about the UK's first-ever general strike in 1926?

** Though film guru Leslie Halliwell questions whether Goldwyn really said this one.

5 May

Some ropy old traditions and sayings

- There was the commonly held belief that carrying a piece of rope from a hangman's noose in your pocket would make you lucky at cards. But only if the noose had actually been used to hang someone.

- Marines were nicknamed 'Mistress Roper' by British sailors, for they way in which they (allegedly) handled the ropes so badly, 'like a girl'! (Yup, an insult to the marines *and* to women.) 'Marrying Mistress Roper' meant enlisting in the Royal Marines.

- The phrase 'a taste of the rope's end' has nothing to do with sucking a piece of rope (in much the same way one might a flannel in the bath) but being whipped with one: once a common punishment for sailors.

- The Rope-walk used to be the nickname barristers had for having a practice at London's Old Bailey law courts. It got its nickname from those found guilty of serious crimes being hanged. (People were *hanged*, by the way. It's pictures that are hung.)

- A person really down on their luck/on the verge of collapse is said to be 'on the ropes' because that's what an exhausted boxer/prize-fighter clings on to to stay upright at the edge of the ring.

- 'Learning the ropes' when you start a new job, and 'knowing the ropes' once you've been there a while, come from sailors having to learn all that rigging.

- To get roped into something – involved in some activity against your will – comes from roping an animal with a lasso.

- In Australia, the word 'ropeable' means *really* angry, suggesting that the person needs to be restrained . . . with ropes!

6 May

1954: Roger Bannister becomes the first human to run a mile in under four minutes

The six elements combining to make a standard staircase

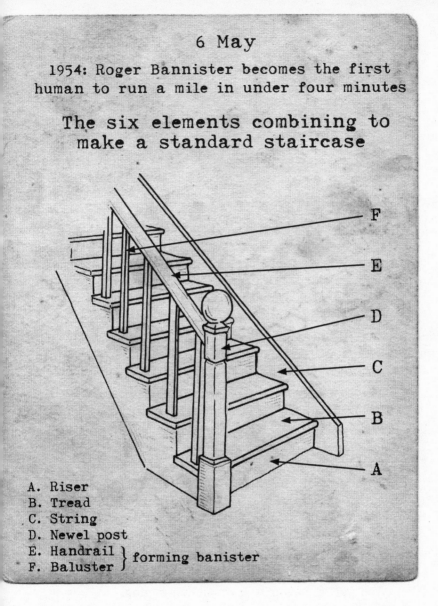

F

E

D

C

B

A

A. Riser
B. Tread
C. String
D. Newel post
E. Handrail ⎫ forming banister
F. Baluster ⎭

7 May

A few facts about *Batrachomyomachia*, which you've probably never heard of anyway

1. It's pronounced *ba-trak-o-mi-o-ma-kya*.
2. It's the name of a mock Greek epic, once attributed to Homer (author of the *Iliad* and the *Odyssey*).
3. It means *The Battle of the Frogs and Mice*.
4. It was later thought to have actually been written by a chap called Pigres of Caria or Pigres of Halicarnassus . . . who was either the brother or son – big difference – of Queen Artemisia of Caria.
5. More recently, some scholars believe it to have been written by some unknown/unnamed author in the time of Alexander the Great.
6. The plot is great! The King of the Frogs is giving the King of the Mice a lift across a lake on his back, when along comes a water snake. Forgetting his passenger, the frog dives underwater to protect himself, and the mouse drowns. Mice, witnessing the accident from the bank, believe it was a deliberate act: murder. War breaks out. The King of the gods, Zeus, wants the gods to take sides but they refuse. The mice are winning the battle and are clearly going to decimate the frogs, so Zeus intervenes: he sends in the crabs to fight alongside the amphibians. The mice can't defeat these armoured mercenaries, so peace breaks out.
7. *Batrachomyomachia* has come to signify a storm in a teacup: a great fuss about nothing . . . which it is unless, of course, you're a frog or a mouse.

158

8 May

Some stuff about volcanoes

- There are more than 1,500 potentially active volcanoes in the world today.
- Over 380 have erupted since the year 2000.
- Every day there's at least one volcano erupting somewhere in the world. (Look out!)
- The world's largest volcano is Mauna Loa in Hawaii.
- One of the world's most famous volcanic eruptions was from Vesuvius, which covered the towns of Pompeii and Herculaneum in molten lava and ash in AD 79.
- Pliny the Younger witnessed the eruption from afar. He wrote that the air was not black like a moonless night 'but the darkness of a sealed room'.
- Mount Etna has been erupting on and off for somewhere between 2,500 and 5,000 years.
- Two of the biggest eruptions were at Tambora in 1815 and Krakatoa in 1883 (both of which are in Indonesia).
- The Krakatoa eruption caused a tsunami which killed over 36,000 people. At Tambora, the initial blast killed around 10,000 people but a resulting famine killed a further 80,000.
- Volcanic eruptions can be measured using the Volcanic Explosivity Index (also known as the VEI), 8 being the highest measure. The explosion of Tambora had an incredible VEI of 7.
- Based on geological evidence, scientists believe that the world's biggest volcanic eruption probably occurred in Yellowstone, Wyoming, USA, around 2.2 million years ago, ejecting a staggering 2,500 km^3 of ash into the Earth's atmosphere.
- The study of volcanoes is called vulcanology. This has little to do with pointy-eared Mr Spock of *Star Trek*.

9 May

1785: Englishman Joseph Bramah
patents the beer pump for pubs

Three theories about how the pub name the 'Goat and Compasses' came into being

1. It was based on the coat of arms of the Wine Coopers Company of Cologne.*

2. The pub was originally called the Goat and somebody added the Masonic emblem of the Freemasons: a pair of compasses.**

3. It is a corruption of the phrase 'God encompasseth us'.***

* Boring!

** But why?

*** I like it! Even if this isn't the real reason, it's the most satisfying one!

10 May

1798: English explorer George Vancouver (of Canada fame) dies

Seven things beginning with the letters 'ca' that aren't necessarily what you'd expect them to be

1. A dog that isn't a dog
cant dog: a hinged hook at the end of a long pole, used by lumberjacks for gripping and rolling logs.

2. An uncle that isn't an uncle
caruncle: a fleshy outgrowth, such as a bird's wattle.*

3. A cat that isn't a cat
cat-o'-nine-tails: a rope whip with nine knotted cords, used for flogging (on board ship).

4. A mate that isn't a mate
casemate: a small room in the thickness of a fortress's walls from which guns or missiles can be fired.

5. A doctor that isn't a doctor
Cape doctor: the strong prevailing south-east wind in South Africa's Western Cape Province.

6. A trip that isn't a trip
cantrip: a (Scottish) playful act or trick.

7. A noodle that isn't a noodle
canoodle: to kiss and cuddle.

* Not to be confused with a carbuncle.

11 May

Bands formed in Britain whose names have a previous existence*

- **Jethro Tull** was the inventor of the seed drill, a piece of equipment used for planting crops. It is also the name of a pop group founded in the 1960s.

- Today, **Iron Maiden** is best known as the name of a heavy metal band. In the past, an iron maiden referred to an instrument of torture: a coffin-shaped box lined with iron spikes.

- A Zeppelin was a type of airship named after its inventor, Count von Zeppelin. Choosing the name **Led Zeppelin** suggests that the super-group thought their music might go down like a lead balloon.

- **The Police** were a well-known band in the 1970s and 1980s, but there were actual police forces thousands of years ago. The Romans even had police dogs.

- The Latin phrase *status quo* simply means 'the existing state of affairs'. To their fans, however, **Status Quo** is a four-piece pop group.

- 'A rolling stone gathers no moss.' In the case of the **Rolling Stones**, however, they just seem to keep (rocking and) rolling along.

* I'd love to include the Beatles and insects, but the six-legged variety are spelled 'beetles' with two 'e's.

12 May

*1907: author and creator of 'The Saint',
Leslie Charteris, is born*

Damsels in distress (who do get rescued)

Andromeda: in classical mythology, she was rescued from a sea monster by that general-all-round-hero Perseus.

Rapunzel: according to the Grimms' fairy tale she was rescued from a tower by a passing prince who had to climb her long tress of hair to reach her!

Sleeping Beauty (aka **Princess Aurora**): had to be woken from her enchanted sleep by a kiss from a prince.

Snow White: was awoken from her deathlike sleep when the piece of apple which had 'poisoned' her was dislodged from her mouth as a prince carried off her glass coffin.

The dragon's captive: probably the most famous damsel in distress of all, this was the princess rescued from a dragon by Saint George himself.

13 May

1857: Sir Ronald Ross, discoverer of the cause of malaria, is born

A few sickening thoughts

- A single can of corned beef from South America led to the death of three people and the infection of 512 others in Aberdeen, Scotland, in 1964. The corned beef was cut on a supermarket slicer which had been used for meat infected with typhoid.

- Powdered unicorn horn was believed to be a guaranteed cure for the plague in the 14th century.*

- Malaria comes from the Italian *mala aria*, meaning 'bad air'.**

- Some people believe that Richard II died of anorexia.

- Before Hungarian doctor Ignaz Semmelweis came up with the idea, people didn't wash their hands before or after delivering a baby!

- The world's most common disease is tooth decay.

- The plague could possibly have been prevented with penicillin.

- Up until the 1850s no one knew germs existed. Hospitals didn't use to change sheets between patients, and surgeons would wear blood-stained aprons with pride, to show how many operations they'd performed.

* Hmm. Difficult to prove this one, methinks.
** Malaria is actually transmitted by the bite from the female mosquito.

14 May

1796: Edward Jenner innoculates a boy against smallpox with a cowpox vaccine

Things I realize I know about cows without particularly knowing how

- With their big goo-goo eyes, cows look gentle but have been known to trample unsuspecting hikers to death.
- Occasionally, cows get so full of gas that they need to be punctured (by a professional) to relieve the trapped wind.
- Milking a cow isn't as easy as it looks. Some people practise on a surgical glove filled with water.
- Well-known cow jokes include those with the punchlines: 'Because their horns don't work' and 'Pull the udder one'.
- Once cows start producing milk, they need to be milked every day.
- Cows mainly eat grass and lick big blocks of salt called 'salt lick'. They do a great deal of burping and farting.
- Scientists reckon a diet of fish would cut down on cows' flatulence.
- Cows' soft-looking pink tongues are actually quite rough.
- You're supposed to be able to tell whether it's going to rain or not by whether the cows in a field are lying down or standing up. The suggestion is that, if they're lying down, they're trying to keep a patch of ground dry from up-coming rain. I think. Perhaps it's the other way round.

15 May

1957: Britain's first hydrogen bomb is tested over Christmas Island in the Pacific Ocean

A town called Santa Claus

- The town of Santa Claus can be found in southern Indiana, USA.

- It has a 7-metre-high statue of Santa Claus (in all his colourful glory) surrounded by fields of maize.

- The idea for the name for the town was put forward in the mid-19th century when, according to most versions of events, someone appeared dressed as Santa at the council's Christmas party. Someone suggested that they name the town after him. It was put to the vote and passed unanimously.

- In 1856 the US Postal Service officially recognized the town being called Santa Claus.

- In 1946 Indiana industrialist Louis J. Koch opened a theme park in Santa Claus. (He might have opened one earlier, but the Second World War got in the way.) Walt Disney didn't open Disneyland until 1955.*

- Koch had nine children of his own and thought it only right that Santa Claus be celebrated in a town that bore his name.

- The theme park was originally called Santa Claus Land. In 1984, this changed to Holiday World.

- Today, all letters posted in the US that are addressed to Santa Claus or Father Christmas – over three million – are sent to the town of Santa Claus, where, one assumes, they make sure that they're then passed to the real Santa Claus.

---

* Apparently, Disneyland's grand opening wasn't a great success. There was a heatwave with temperatures of up to 43°C (110°F) and, because of a plumbers' strike, most of the cooling water fountains weren't actually working. The asphalt, which had been laid on the ground the night before, was still soft and steaming – trapping people's shoes!

16 May

A few fictitious people inspired by real ones (and who those real ones might have been)

BIGGLES: Captain W. E. Johns's ace pilot Biggles (aka James Bigglesworth) seems to have been inspired by a certain Air Commodore Cecil Wigglesworth. According to literary detective William Amos, in 1949 Captain Johns gave a radio interview in which he said that his Biggles/ Bigglesworth was based on a pilot with a similar name . . . and Amos found Wigglesworth to be the only one to fit the bill. They are, indeed, very similar sounding . . . though Biggles sounds a far more manly nickname than Wiggles ever would!

JAMES BOND: The name for Ian Fleming's master spy came from the author of *Birds of the West Indies*, but whom he based much of the character on is still disputed. Possible candidates include: Commander Wilfred Dunderdale, Lt-Commander Michael Mason and Yugoslav double agent Dusko Popov. Reilly 'Ace of Spies' has also been suggested, though Fleming himself pooh-poohed this one.

ROBINSON CRUSOE: The castaway hero of Daniel Defoe's novel of the same name seems to have been based on Alexander Selkirk. In 1704, Selkirk had such a bad argument with his ship's captain, William Dampier, he asked to be put ashore on Juan Fernández, an uninhabited island! He ended up living there for four years before being picked up by another ship.

SHERLOCK HOLMES: One of the most famous people who never existed, Sherlock Holmes was the creation of Sir Arthur Conan Doyle. He was based on Dr Joseph Bell, a professor at Edinburgh University when Conan Doyle was there as a medical student. (*An aside*: The most famous illustrations of Sherlock Holmes were drawn by Sidney

Paget. Paget was given the job by mistake: it was supposed to have been given to his brother Walter. But Walter Paget plays his own part in the Sherlock Holmes legend. Sidney based Holmes's appearance in his illustrations on Walter.)*

THE ANCIENT MARINER in Samuel Taylor Coleridge's poem may well have been based on Fletcher Christian, the man who led the mutiny against Captain Bligh in the mutiny on the *Bounty*!

* Walter Paget actually got to illustrate one Sherlock Holmes story after brother Sidney died in 1908. It was 'The Adventure of the Dying Detective' in 1913.

17 May

National Independence Day in Norway

Norwegian heads of government between 1971 and 2001 with surnames beginning with the letter B*

1. Trygve Bratteli (1971-2, 1973-6)
2. Gro Harlem Brundtlan d (1981, 1986-9, 1990-96)
3. Kjell Magne Bondevik (1997-2000, 2001-5)

NOTE: During this time, there have been two monarchs (heads of state): Olav V (1957-91) and Harald V (1991-present)

* Contain your excitement!**
** We did say that these lists were useless, remember?

18 May

A slick of 1970s major maritime disasters and their environmental impact*

1. **1970** The tanker *Othello* collided in Tralhavet Bay, Sweden, spilling somewhere between 17.6 million and 29.4 million gallons of oil.

2. **1972** The collision of the tanker *Sea Star* in the Gulf of Oman led to 33.81 million gallons of oil being spilt.

3. **1976** The grounding of the supertanker *Urquiola* off La Coruña, Spain, resulted in a spillage of 29.4 million gallons of oil.

4. **1977** A fire aboard the *Hawaiian Patriot* in the north Pacific caused a 29.1-million-gallon spill of oil.

5. **1978** The tanker *Amoco Cadiz* was grounded at Porstall, France, spilling 65.56 million gallons of oil.

19 May

A short selection of assassinations, (some unsuccessful)

- The only British prime minister to be assassinated in office, so far, was Spencer Perceval on 11 May 1812. He was killed with a single shot from a pistol in the lobby of the House of Commons. The assassin was a businessman whose French business interests were ruined by war with France.

- On 28 February 1986, Olof Palme, the prime minister of Sweden, was assassinated in a street in the capital, Stockholm.

- On 13 May 1981, Pope John Paul II survived an assassination attempt in St Peter's Square, Rome. Some claim that his predecessor, Pope John Paul I (who was pontiff for only 33 days), was actually murdered.

- So far, around 26 popes are believed to have been assassinated. These include:
  - John VIII (872–82), who was poisoned, then clubbed to death.
  - St Adrian III (884–5), who was also poisoned. (No mention of clubbing.)
  - Stephen VI (896–7), who was strangled.
  - John X (914–28), who was suffocated with a pillow.
  - Stephen VIII (or IX) (939–42), who was so badly mutilated that he died from his injuries.
  - John XII (955–64), who was said to have been murdered by 'an outraged husband'.
  - Benedict VI (973–4), who was strangled.*
  - John XIV (983–4), who either starved to death or was poisoned.**
  - Gregory V (996–9), who was rumoured to have been poisoned, though it might actually have been malaria.
  - Boniface VIII (1294–1303), who died while a captive of the French.

* By a – er – priest, I'm afraid to say.
** Neither of which is pleasant.

20 May

1685: Titus Oates, concocter of the fictitious 'Popish Plot', is flogged from Aldgate to Newgate Prisons

A nosebag of Oates

Captain Lawrence Oates: nicknamed Titus Oates, a member of Captain Scott's ill-fated expedition to the South Pole in 1912, and a 'very gallant gentleman'. In temperatures of −40°* he crawled from the tent on to the ice, announcing, 'I am just going outside and may be some time.' He died. It was 17 March 1912, his 32nd birthday. The remaining three men, Scott, Wilson and Bowers, died only a matter of days later.

John Oates: (born in 1949 in New York City) along with Daryl Hall, formed Hall and Oates, the R&B band which, between 1972 and 1990, produced numerous records.

Joyce Carol Oates: (born 1938) US academic and novelist with a prolific output, but modest approach. Having written almost forty novels, a wealth of short stories and poems, plus a number of academic papers, she's been quoted as saying that it seemed like a small thing 'in the great scale of being'.

Titus Oates: once an Anglican minister (dismissed for 'drunken blasphemy'), then a ship's chaplain (from which he was also dismissed). In 1678, he declared that he'd uncovered a Roman Catholic plot to kill King Charles II. Oates claimed that Catholics intended to replace Charles with his Roman Catholic brother, James. Oates argued that this could lead to Protestants being killed in their thousands. As a result, many Catholics were arrested and a number, including the Archbishop of Armagh in Ireland, were executed . . . only for the plot to be uncovered as a pack of lies. In 1683 Titus Oates received a massive fine and was imprisoned 'for life' . . . only to be released in 1688. He lived until 1705.

---

* Celsius or Fahrenheit, take your pick. They're both the same at −40°.

21 May

Quotes attributed to Bogart in life, and spoken by him on film*

'I made more lousy pictures than any actor in history.'

'A hot dog at the ball park is better than steak at the Ritz.'

'All you owe the public is a good performance.'

'The only point in making money is, you can tell some big shot where to go.'

'I was born when you kissed me. I died when you left me. I lived a few weeks while you loved me.'

'It doesn't take much to see that the problems of three little people doesn't add up to a hill of beans in this crazy world.'

'The problem with the world is that everyone is a few drinks behind.'

'You're not a star until they can spell your name in Karachi.'

'I don't approve of the John Waynes and the Gary Coopers saying "Shucks, I ain't no actor, I'm just a bridge-builder or a gas station attendant." If they aren't actors, what are they getting paid for? I have respect for my profession. I worked hard at it.'

'I came out here with one suit and everybody said I looked like a bum. Twenty years later Marlon Brando came out with only a sweatshirt and the town drooled over him. That shows how much Hollywood has progressed.'

'Things are never so bad they can't be made worse.'

* But I'm not telling you which are which.**
** So there!

22 May

AD 337: Constantine I, Roman emperor, dies

Twelve things you may not have known about Roman fashion

1. Some upper-class Roman women wore wigs made from their slaves' hair.

2. Men shaved without soap or oil.

3. Women often coloured their lips with red plant dye or even wine.

4. To make their skin seem fashionably pale, women often covered their face, necks and arms with chalk powder. Ash was used for eyelids.

5. Both men and women wore rings but, starting at the top and working down, women also wore:
   ◆ hairpins
   ◆ earrings
   ◆ necklaces
   ◆ brooches
   ◆ bracelets
   ◆ anklets

6. The average Roman's clothes were made from linen or wool. Only rich Romans could afford cotton or silk.

7. It was fashionable for men to oil and curl their hair.

8. Men and women just *loved* wearing perfume.

9. Most Roman men and women wore tunics. Some women wore a *stola*, a simple dress, instead of a tunic. Over this, they wore a colourful robe called a *palla*.

10. For that hoody look, sometimes the *palla* could be worn over the head.

11. Togas were reserved for Roman citizens, all of whom were men. Senators wore togas with purple edging.

12. To wear a sheet as a proper toga, you'd have to cut it into a semi-circle first (which probably wouldn't make you very popular).

23 May

1931: Whipsnade Park Zoo opens to the public

Ten types of tiger which aren't (tigers, that is)

Tiger moth: a type of moth which is extremely brightly coloured and, I am reliably informed, has extremely unpleasant-tasting body fluids.

Tiger Moth: a biplane used during the Second World War for the majority of the elementary training of RAF pilots.

Paper tiger: someone who seems brave and powerful but is actually weak and ineffectual.

Paper Tiger: a 1975 film starring David Niven, about a chap who isn't all he's cracked up to be, but finally makes good. (What ho!)

Tiger lily: a type of lily.

Tiger Lily: a 'Red Indian' (Native American) girl rescued by Peter Pan in J. M. Barrie's play.

Tamil Tigers: a Sri Lankan rebel group.

Flying Tigers: the nickname of a volunteer group of US airmen, formed in August 1941 under General C. L. Chennault, who supported China against the Japanese, before the USA's entry into the Second World War.

Tiger shark: once one of the most common and most dangerous – as far as people are concerned – of the bigger sharks, now endangered.

Tiger prawns: yup, big prawns. There are huge tiger-prawn farms in Vietnam.

24 May

Some of the Eurovision Song Contest winning entries with the most annoying names

'La La La' sung by Massiel from Spain in 1968.

'Boom Bang-A-Bang' sung by Lulu from the UK in 1969 (joint winner).

'Ding A Dong' sung by Teach In from Holland in 1975.

'A-ba-ni-bi' sung by Izhar Cohen and the Alpha-Beta from Israel in 1978.

'Diggi Loo-Diggi Ley' sung by Herreys from Sweden in 1984.

25 May

1850: the first live hippopotamus in Europe since Roman times arrives at London Zoo

Four types of gladiator you might encounter if you ever go back in time and find yourself in an arena in ancient Rome*

1. **A Murmillo:** armed only with a short sword, he has to fight close up, hence his wearing a helmet, shield, and some arm and leg armour for protection.
2. **A Samnite:** with similar weapon and armour to a *murmillo*, they're most easily told apart by their different-shaped helmets. (The two types of gladiator were very similar.)
3. **A Retarius:** with next to no armour but a three-pronged spear (called a trident) and a net with weights around the edges. He can throw the net and spear you from afar, so tries to keep his enemy at a distance.
4. **A Thracian:** with very little metal armour and just a small wooden shield and short-sword, he might seem the least threatening . . . but many *Thracians* were good fighters by all accounts.

* Good luck. I don't rate your chances.

26 May

1966: English actress Helena Bonham Carter is born*

A greengrocer's dozen** of films with fruit in the title (not the word 'fruit', but a named fruit, and not that fruit alone, OK?)

1. *Attack of the Killer Tomatoes*[3]
2. *Fried Green Tomatoes*[3]
3. *What's Eating Gilbert Grape?*
4. *The Lemon Drop Kid*
5. *The Grapes of Wrath*
6. *Journey to Banana Land*[4]
7. *A Clockwork Orange*
8. *The Apple Dumpling Gang Rides Again*
9. *Top Banana*[5]
10. *The Quince Tree Sun (aka El Sol del membrillo)*
11. *Herbie Goes Bananas*
12. *The Lemon Sisters*
13. *James and the Giant Peach*

* Helena Bonham Carter is married to film director Tim Burton.[1]

** Plus one dropped on the floor and rolled under a display of cabbages.

[1] Tim Burton has directed a number of films starring Johnny Depp.[2]

[2] Johnny Depp starred in the film *What's Eating Gilbert Grape?* (Hence the choice of list.)

[3] Often mistaken for vegetables, tomatoes – killer or otherwise – are fruit.

[4] A corporate film made in 1959 by United Fruit.

[5] This film was originally shot in 3-D, but was released as an ordinary (flat!) film.

27 May

1930: Adhesive tape made from cellophane
is patented

Ten things I wouldn't try to fix with my trusty roll of Sellotape (which, by the way, is a registered trademark)

1. A broken heart
2. A broken arm
3. The wing of a Boeing 747
4. A leak in a swimming pool
5. A loose tooth in a crocodile's jaw
6. A stress fracture in a glass tank at the London Aquarium*
7. The Grand Canyon
8. A four-foot tear in the envelope of a hot-air balloon
9. A hole in the road
10. A broken promise

* Not that I'm suggesting that they have had, or will ever have, a stress fracture in a glass tank at the London Aquarium . . .**

** The publishers' lawyers made me add this.

28 May

Seventeen things* you may not have known about James Bond – the character, the books and the films – based on information supplied by super-fan** Grant Weston

1. Ian Fleming didn't write his first James Bond book, *Casino Royale* (which was also his first novel), until he was 43.

2. He based it on his experiences in the Second World War, notably the time he lost a large sum of money when gambling in Lisbon.

3. His publisher, Jonathan Cape, didn't like the novel, but published it anyway . . . as a favour to Fleming's older brother, Peter, who was already published by them!

4. Fleming named his secret agent 'James Bond' after an ornithologist who'd written a book entitled *Birds of the West Indies*.

5. A copy of *Birds of the West Indies* can be seen – very briefly – in the film *Die Another Day*.

6. Although Fleming originally gave James Bond an English background, after he became friends with Sean Connery (the first film Bond), Fleming decided to give 007 a Scottish heritage as a tribute to the Scottish actor.

7. As readers of Charlie Higson's *Young Bond* series will probably be well aware, James Bond was educated at Eton (as was his creator, Fleming). What they may not know is that Master James wasn't there that long, though, and continued his education at Fettes College in Edinburgh, Scotland, his father's old school.***

8. The first Bond movie was *Dr No* (named after the villain).

* There were 20 things, but three have been classified as . . . TOP SECRET.
** Of James Bond, not of me (though I am rather lovely).
*** Where Tony Blair was educated.

Ian Fleming offered the role of Dr No to his friend Noel Coward. Coward responded: 'Dear Ian, No! No! No!' (Coward did, however, play the chief villain in the original *Italian Job* movie.)

9. When Ian Fleming created James Bond's arch-enemy Ernst Stavro Blofeld, he gave the villain the same birthday as his own, right down to the year.

10. Fleming bought a gold-plated typewriter after the success of the first Bond novel. It was later owned by Bond actor Pierce Brosnan.

11. Bond's favourite food is scrambled eggs.

12. The oft-repeated line 'Bond. James Bond' is just outside the Top 20 of the most famous movie quotes of all time, as compiled by the American Film Institute. It comes in at No. 22.

13. A scene in the 2006 *Casino Royale* shows an Aston Martin DBS rolling an amazing 7.75 times after Bond swerves to avoid Vesper Lynd lying, tied up, in the road. This is a world record.

14. The first 21 Bond films have been watched by more than 1.6 BILLION people in the cinemas alone. Add those who've seen them on TV, video and DVD, and the total must be even more mind-boggling.

15. The title of the film *The World Is Not Enough* comes from the English translation of the Bond family's Latin motto, *Orbis non suffict*, which was established and adopted by James Bond in the novel (and later the film) *On Her Majesty's Secret Service*.

16. Bond lives in an apartment just off the King's Road in London.

17. Bond married once. That was in the film *On Her Majesty's Secret Service* (when Bond was played – for that one film only – by George Lazenby). The marriage lasted barely two minutes on screen, until Tracy di Vicenzo (Mrs Bond) – played by Diana Rigg, best known as Mrs Peel in *The Avengers* – was killed by Irma Bunt, accomplice to arch-villain Ernst Stavro Blofeld.

29 May

Singles which have topped the charts for eight weeks or more since I was born

(The month denotes when each song first reached No. 1.)

Mar 1962: 'Wonderful Land', the Shadows, 8 weeks.

Oct 1969: 'Sugar Sugar', the Archies, 8 weeks.[1]

Nov 1975: 'Bohemian Rhapsody', Queen, 9 weeks.[2]

Dec 1977: 'Mull of Kintyre', Wings, 9 weeks.[3]

Jun 1979: 'You're the One That I Want', John Travolta & Olivia Newton-John, 9 weeks.[4]

Jun 1984: 'Two Tribes', Frankie Goes To Hollywood, 9 weeks.

Jul 1991: '(Everything I Do) I Do It for You', Bryan Adams, 16 weeks.[5]

Feb 1992: 'Stay', Shakespears Sister, 8 weeks.

Dec 1992: 'I Will Always Love You', Whitney Houston, 10 weeks.[6]

Jun 1994: 'Love Is All Around', Wet Wet Wet, 15 weeks.[7]

Apr 2006: 'Crazy', Gnarls Barkley, 9 weeks.[8]

May 2007: 'Umbrella', Rihanna (featuring Jay-Z), 10 weeks.[8]

PS Bing Crosby's 'White Christmas' may not have been No. 1 in the UK charts for eight weeks or more, but it is one of the bestselling non-charity singles of all time. And it's lovely.

---

[1] The Archies were an animated cartoon pop group. We never actually saw the performers.

[2] Reissued in 1991, it was No. 1 for a further five weeks.

[3] Wings frontman was former Beatle Paul McCartney. The Beatles were the first recording artists to have 17 UK No. 1 singles. (Equalled by Elvis Presley in 1977, he then went on to beat their record.)

[4] From that lovely film *Grease*.

[5] The theme tune to *Robin Hood: Prince of Thieves*, starring Kevin Costner, this song has the record for the longest number of consecutive weeks at No. 1.

[6] The theme tune to *The Bodyguard*, starring – er – Kevin Costner (and Miss Houston herself, of course).

[7] The theme tune to a film, but NOT one starring Kevin Costner.

[8] I know nothing about these, I'm afraid, because I'm far too old and crusty to listen the charts any more. Instead, I sit in my saggy old armchair muttering about 'the youth of today'.

30 May

1966: US unmanned spacecraft Surveyor 1 *makes a soft landing – rather than crashing – on the Moon*

Ten things I think I know about the Moon, without looking them up or up at it

1. It is not made of cheese.

2. No mice have ever really built their own rocket and landed there.

3. No Moon monster has ever really popped its head about the rim of a crater then ducked down again (just before an astronaut turned around and looked in that direction).

4. It does not really house the moonbase for SHADO (Supreme Headquarter Alien Defence Organization). That was just in a TV series.

5. It doesn't really shine like the Sun, just reflects the Sun's light off it.

6. It somehow affects the tides here on Earth.

7. A lot of space junk has been left on the Moon's surface by visiting humans.

8. You CAN'T see the Great Wall of China from the Moon, whatever anyone says.*

9. The Moon's weaker gravity (relative to Earth) means you can leap around in semi-slow motion, which is cool.

10. According to a joke book I read as a kid, you'd only need one ball of string to reach the Moon from here. But it would have to be a big one.

* Though you can see it when orbiting Earth in space, which is a big difference.

31 May

Ten things you may not know about the Houses of Parliament buildings in London (unless you've read my book *Terrible Times*)*

1. Where Guy Fawkes failed, a ridiculous accident succeeded. On 16 October 1834, the furnaces were over-fed and the parliament buildings caught alight.

2. The furnaces had been stoked with 'tally sticks': wooden sticks used to work out taxes right up until the 1820s. Now redundant, they decided to use them as fuel . . . but got carried away!

3. The famous artist Turner painted images of the fire from across the Thames. They're mainly smoke, flame and reflections in the water.

4. A few important buildings were saved: Westminster Hall, the crypt of St Stephen's Chapel, the adjacent cloisters and the Jewel Tower.

5. The fire was (mainly) put out by the London Fire Engine Establishment, London's first single fire service – rather than lots of little private ones – which had, fortunately, been formed in the previous year.

6. Leading operations was Lord Melbourne, the prime minister at the time! He knew where things were and what needed saving.

7. There was a competition to design and build the new Houses of Parliament. For political reasons, Roman Catholics were not allowed to enter!

8. The winning design was by Charles Barry (1795–1860) and his assistant Augustus Welby Pugin (1812–52), though Pugin's contribution was enormous.**

* Available from all good bookshops. Hurry while stocks last!

** Shhh! Don't tell anyone, but Pugin had become a Roman Catholic in 1834!

9. The surviving buildings were incorporated into the current – at time of writing – buildings.

10. It took 30 years to complete.

11. The House of Commons chamber was destroyed in a German air raid in 1941. It was rebuilt (by architect Gilbert Scott) preserving the essential features of Barry's work and was completed in 1950.

1 June

1938: Superman makes his very first appearance in Action Comics, *issue No. 1*

A few not-so-super facts about Superman, and some uplifting ones

- Superman was created by Jerry Siegel and Joe Shuster. They sold the rights for $130 between them. That's $65 each.

- When Superman became a multi-billion-dollar character known across the globe they didn't get a single cent from royalties for films, TV series, anything.

- In 1975 they began a public relations campaign against Warner Communications, the film studio behind the upcoming *Superman: The Movie*, starring Christopher Reeve. Joe Shuster even wrote a letter putting a curse on the movie!

- With the success of the film, Warner Communications agreed to give Siegel and Shuster $35,000 a year each for life. It was also agreed that, in future, they would be credited as his creators.

- Joe Shuster died in 1992.

- Jerry Siegel died in 1996.

- In 1999, Siegel's heirs won a court case and now have half-ownership of the Superman character.

- George Reeves (with an 's'), who'd played Superman in the 1950s, apparently committed suicide in 1959.*

- Christopher Reeve (without an 's'), who was in four *Superman* films between 1978 and 1987, broke his neck in a riding accident in May 1995. He died in October 2004.

- Tragically, Reeve's wife, Dana, died of cancer in 2006. Before they died, they established a paralysis foundation, helping paraplegics and quadriplegics throughout the world.

* The subject of the 2006 film *Hollywoodland*.

2 June

1692: the first woman* is found 'guilty' and convicted at the Salem Witch Trials in Massachusetts, USA

Ten basic requirements for being a witch (should they exist)

1. Pointy black hat
2. Flying broomstick
3. Warty toad
4. Warty nose and/or hairy mole (of the skin variety)
5. Cauldron
6. Eye of newt
7. Wing of bat
8. Cackling laugh
9. Tatty leather-bound book of spells (some ineffectual)
10. Crystal ball (but only sometimes)

*Bridget Bishop.

3 June

1937: Edward Duke of Windsor, formerly King Edward VIII, marries Mrs Wallis Simpson, the woman he gave up the British throne for

A (fairly large) handful of facts about Nick Park's 'Wallace and Gromit' films

- The four films so far are: *A Grand Day Out* (1989), *The Wrong Trousers* (1993), *A Close Shave* (1995) and *The Curse of the Were-rabbit* (2005).

- It took Park seven years to complete *A Grand Day Out*.

- Nick Park claims that Wallace is based on his dad, and Gromit – the dog! – on himself.

- Wallace's favourite cheese is Wensleydale, and a North Yorkshire creamery has paid £40,000 for the rights to use Wallace and Gromit to promote their cheese!

- My favourite, favourite, *favourite* Wallace and Gromit villain is the penguin lodger, Feathers McGraw, in *The Wrong Trousers*, who wears a rubber glove on his head to disguise himself as a hen!

- Each of the first three films is only around 25 minutes long but, using stop-frame animation, used up around 35,000 frames of film EACH.

- A potential disaster was averted when, in 1996, Nick Park left the Wallace and Gromit models in the back of a New York taxi. The taxi driver returned them safe and sound.

- Less happily, in 2005, a warehouse fire destroyed numerous Wallace and Gromit models and sets but – in public at least – Nick Park has been more philosophical than upset.

4 June

1783: the Montgolfier brothers give the first public demonstration of their invention, the hot-air balloon

Nine things I like (✓) and dislike (✗) about balloons

1. They can burst with a very loud bang. **✗**

2. You can rub them on your hair to make it stand up on end. **✓**

3. Doing No. 2 can make your hair feel a bit funny. **✗**

4. If you rub them on a sweater, they should stick to the ceiling. **✓**

5. If you put the clear sticky tape in the right place, you can stick a knitting needle through a balloon without it bursting. **✓**

6. The ones with air inside don't float upward and bob about as in children's illustrations. **✗**

7. Pre-filled helium-filled balloons do float upward – because helium is lighter than air – and are usually silver and silly-shaped, rather than having that traditional balloony look.* **✗**

8. If you draw features on them and give them cardboard feet, they can be your special friend.** **✓**

9. Balloons don't last forever.*** **✗**

* Unless they're SpongeBob-SquarePants-shaped balloons, because my brother likes those.
** Like my one-time balloon friend Brunjak.
*** Sob. Gone but not forgotten (see No. 8).

5 June

1988: Kay Cottee becomes the first woman
to sail non-stop, solo, around the world

A number of reasons for believing the world is flat*

1. We would fall off it if it was round.
2. I've never kept walking in a straight line
   and ended up back where I started from,
   which must eventually happen if it's round.
3. How could it be anything but flat?
4. Er . . .

* Not smoothly flat. I can see that it's wrinkled with hills
and mountains and ravines and stuff. I mean flat as in
NOT ROUND!

6 June

*1844: the YMCA (Young Men's Christian Association)
is founded by George Williams*

Some of the people who peopled Village People*

The original Village People
GI/Soldier: Alex Briley
Construction worker: David Hodo
Native American: Felipe Rose
Leatherman/Biker: Glen Hughes**
Cowboy: Randy Jones
Cop/Police Officer: Victor Willis

The current line-up (on the day of writing this)***
GI/Soldier: Alex Briley (original member)
Construction worker: David Hodo (original member)
Native American: Felipe Rose (original member)
Leatherman/Biker: Eric Anzalone (since 1995)
Cowboy: Jeff Olson (since 1980)
Cop/Police Officer: Ray Simpson (since 1979)

* Whose hits included: 'YMCA', 'Macho Man', 'In the Navy' and 'Go West'.
** Glen Hughes died on 4 March 2001.
*** With a few changes of line-up in between.

7 June

1946: BBC restarts regular TV transmissions, which were halted at the outset of the Second World War*

Ten famous movie mice

1. Mickey Mouse, who first appeared in *Steamboat Willie.*
2. Timothy Q. Mouse, who gives Dumbo the 'magic feather' in *Dumbo.*
3. Roquefort, the real hero of *The Aristocats* and my hero too.
4. Basil in *Basil the Great Mouse Detective.*
5. Fievel in *An American Tail.*
6. Stuart Little in – er – the *Stuart Little* films.
7. & 8. Bernard and Bianca in *The Rescuers* and *The Rescuers Down Under.*
9. Jerry of *Tom & Jerry.*
10. That put-upon mouse in *Mouse Hunt.*

* Transmission ended in September 1939 with a Mickey Mouse cartoon . . . and began again in 1946 with the same one.

8 June

Excuses for not eating your vegetables**

- Scientists have proved that eating anything green can cause you yourself to turn green and to fly into terrible rages, increasing in size, and splitting your trousers.***

- Vegetables have been found to be more intelligent than human beings and are taking names and addresses of people who eat them, so that the victorious vegetable forces can take you away, come the uprising.

- Some vegetables contain a substance which will keep you awake all night. Every night.

- A *very* recent survey showed that children who eat their vegetables do worse at school.

- Children who don't eat their vegetables are 52% more likely to help around the house than those who do.

- Bill Gates never ate his vegetables, and he's one of the richest men in the world *and* kind with it.

- You don't like them.****

---

* Not the King Edward after whom King Edward potatoes are named.

** Not that I'm claiming a single one of these is a legitimate excuse, let alone true. (If they were, this wouldn't be an absolutely useless list.)

*** If you're wearing any.

**** If, like me, you DO like most veg, you'll probably have skipped this list anyway.

9 June

1781: engineer George Stephenson is born

A trainful of facts about the Rainhill Trials

- A competition was announced to see whose design of steam locomotive would be built to pull the trains on the first public railway, the Liverpool-to-Manchester line. Five engines were entered, and were to be put to the test at the Rainhill Trials in October 1829.

- In the end, only four locomotives actually started the competition.

- The first to drop out was the *Perseverance* (which was rather unfortunate, when you consider the name). It didn't have enough power.

- The next to drop out was the *Sans Pareil*, which means 'without equal'. That was true: two of the trains were obviously better than *it* was! The *Sans Pareil* not only required ENORMOUS amounts of fuel to keep it going, but broke down during its eighth run.

- The two remaining steam engines were the *Novelty* and Stephenson's *Rocket*.

- The *Novelty* was very popular with the crowds, but it kept on stopping!

- The *Rocket* was the clear winner, steaming along the track at an average speed of 14 mph (23 km/h).

- Less than a year later, on 15 September 1830, the Liverpool-to-Manchester line was officially opened, using Stephenson's trains.*

---

* This great occasion was marred by the death of local MP William Huskisson, who was hit by a train (becoming the first public railway fatality).

10 June

2000: the official opening of London's Millennium Bridge (aka 'the wobbly bridge'), which swayed so much that it had to be closed the selfsame day for checks

Some facts about a famous building that moved

- The Great Exhibition was to be held in Hyde Park in 1851, celebrating ideas and inventions from all around the world. It was the brainchild of Queen Victoria's German husband, Prince Albert.

- Albert was unpopular at the time, a foreigner seen as being 'a paper Royal Highness' (by marriage). The British Parliament refused him funds for the project.

- Albert held a competition to design the building that would house the exhibition. Of the 234 entries, Joseph Paxton's design for the Crystal Palace won.

- Paxton had designed greenhouses for the Duke of Devonshire!

- The Crystal Palace was larger than the average greenhouse or conservatory.

- Building materials included:
  - ◆ around 300,000 panes of glass
  - ◆ 24 miles of guttering
  - ◆ 4,572 tonnes of iron

- It was 564 metres long and covered an area of about 4 km².

- The biggest fear was that, if there was a hailstorm, hailstones might shatter the glass. In reality, the biggest problem turned out to be BIRDS roosting in the trees inside the building and, more to the point, the bird poo they generated.

- The Duke of Wellington offered the solution: not shooting them (with all that glass about) but sparrowhawks!

- The exhibition officially opened on 1 May 1851. Its motto was *'The Earth is the Lord's and all that therein is'*.
- The Chinaman He Sing, who captained a junk – a Chinese sailing ship – moored in the Thames, somehow got mixed up with the important dignitaries at the ceremony, and was treated as a VIP for the day. He even appears in the officially commissioned oil-painting.
- He Sing was more used to charging people a shilling to look around his vessel!
- The 14,000 or so exhibits were divided into four sections: Raw Materials, Mechanical Inventions, Manufacturers and Works of Art.
- One of the stranger exhibits was a telescopic coffin, adjustable to fit a body of any size.
- The Great Exhibition closed on 15 October 1851, after over SIX MILLION paying visitors had passed through the doors of Paxton's Crystal Palace.
- In 1854, the Crystal Palace was moved to a new site near Sydenham, south London, not by a gust of wind, but by its being dismantled and completely reassembled.*
- The area was renamed Crystal Palace in its honour.
- Sadly, the Palace was destroyed by fire in 1936.**

* It officially reopened on this day (10 June) in 1854.
** None of the main building survives, but strange stone dinosaurs can still be found lurking on the site of the old grounds in the park.

11 June

1847: English Arctic explorer Sir John Franklin dies

Twenty-two things I've learned about British explorers from watching old black and white films

1. All explorers speak with very posh accents, except for those called Jock or Taffy and, of course, all the soldiers and/or sailors who have to do all the hard work and heavy lifting.

2. All expeditions begin on a ship with a large wooden crate being lifted on board in a net by crane.

3. Someone usually has to drop out at the last minute – often due to a terrible accident involving a large wooden crate being lifted on board in a net by crane – and is replaced by someone who ends up playing a huge part in the success of the expedition.

4. Leaders of expeditions spend a lot of time writing in journals or letters home to their wives.

5. When a wife at home read these letters, she often hears her husband's actual voice inside her head.

6. Explorers are very fond of their dogs and horses and feel a bit sad when they have to eat them when the rations run out.

7. Rations always run out.

8. It is always either too cold or too hot. (The climate. Not the rations.)

9. Men in the common ranks sweat more than the leader of the expedition, unless the leader of the expedition catches a tropical disease.

10. Leaders of expeditions always catch tropical diseases.

11. When sick, the leader of an expedition always hallucinates about his wife or fiancée, or both. His recovery usually coincides with a break in the weather.

12. When people in the common ranks die on an expedition, it's not as sad as when someone upper-class dies.

13. There is always one snivelling coward who ignores the expedition leader's command and makes a break for it across the breaking ice/into the crocodile-infested swamp/through the patch of quicksand/into the shark-filled lake, and dies as a consequence.

14. The young man who's come along to sketch the flora and fauna is always a sensitive soul, but circumstances mean that he does at least one manly thing to save the day (and the native girls like him).

15. Native peoples are either friendly to begin with, then turn nasty, or are nasty to begin with and then turn friendly. They never seem to be consistently friendly or nasty throughout.

16. British explorers generally befriend a local boy who loves them like a father, but has a cheeky grin and gets up to mischief.

17. Befriended native boys are good at sneaking into enemy camp at night and freeing the captured explorers.

18. Vines hanging from trees in the jungle are always strong enough for a person to swing from.

19. Back in London, in a book-lined room with a prominent wooden globe, Lord Somebody in a tweed suit and a man in military uniform are drinking whisky and are convinced that 'the chaps' will never make it back alive.

20. They usually make it back alive . . .

21. . . . or die a hero's death.

22. At the moment they die, if they do die, one of their pets back in England has a funny turn.

23. If the leader of the expedition dies a hero's death, Johnny (who was with him at the end) is sent to tell his wife. Seeing Johnny's silhouette through the frosted glass of her front door, the wife thinks it's her husband returned. She runs and opens the door. When she opens it to see Johnny standing there, she realizes the worst and sobs in his arms.*

* It is a requirement of all fiancées or wives of expedition leaders to have at least one panel of frosted glass in their front door.

12 June

1897: the forerunner of today's Swiss Army knife is patented in Switzerland

The various gadgets I could play with on a top-of-the-range Swiss Army (pen)knife if only I was deemed responsible enough to have one*

- Ballpoint pen
- Blade (large)
- Blade (small)
- Bottle opener
- Can opener
- Chisel
- Corkscrew
- Electricians' blade
- Fish scaler
- Hook
- Hook disgorger
- Keyring
- Magnifying glass
- Metal file
- Metal saw
- Nail file and nail cleaner
- Pharmaceutical spatula
- Pliers & wire cutters/ crimpers
- Pruning blade
- Puncher & sewing eye
- Reamer
- Ruler
- Scissors
- Screwdriver (fine)
- Screwdriver (large)
- Screwdriver (mini)
- Screwdriver (Phillips/ starhead)
- Screwdriver (small)
- Spanner/wrench with:
  - ◆ 4mm & 5mm female hex drive
  - ◆ 4mm posidrive 0 & 1 bits
  - ◆ 4mm slotted bit
  - ◆ Phillips 2 bit
  - ◆ 4mm hex bit
  - ◆ Torx 8 bit
  - ◆ Torx 10 bit
  - ◆ Torx 15 bit
- Straight pin
- Toothpick
- Tweezers
- Wire bender
- Wire stripper
- Wood saw

All between shiny red sides.**

NB One of these gadgets must be for getting the stones out of horses' hoofs, but I'm not sure which!

* No wonder – they weigh 250 g and are 4.5 cm wide!

** One of the smaller ones even comes with a built-in watch!

13 June

323 BC: Alexander the Great dies

A bunch of Greats

- Alfred the Great (of cake-burning fame)
- The Great Wall of China (visible from space)
- Gonzo the Great (the remarkable Muppet)
- 'The Great Escape' (the 1963 film based on real events in the Second World War)
- The Great White Shark (the name says it all)
- The Great Zucchini (the Victorian escapologist)*
- The Great Lakes (in North America)
- Catherine the Great (Empress of Russia)
- The Great Outdoors (as opposed to indoors)
- The Great Train Robbery (a famous British robbery of the 1960s)
- The Great Depression (the economic downturn starting in 1929)
- The Great Ape (the big hairy ones)
- The Great War (aka the First World War)
- Peter the Great (the beard-hating Russian Tsar)
- The Great Pyramid of Giza (big and pointy)
- 'The Great Gatsby' (the novel by F. Scott Fitzgerald)
- The Great Unwashed (a dismissive term for most of us)

* From my splendid book 'Dreadful Acts'.

14 June

Famous fictional bald-folk*

- Blofeld, James Bond's evil nemesis
- Charlie Brown from PEANUTS© (Well, he looks pretty bald to me)
- Monty Burns from *The Simpsons*
- Darth Vader (under that mask) in *Star Wars*
- Dobby in the *Harry Potter* books
- Dr Evil and Mini-Me in the *Austin Powers* films
- Elmer Fudd from the Warner Brothers Looney Toons cartoons
- Gollum from *Lord of the Rings*
- Kojak, the New York cop in the TV series
- Lex Luthor from *Superman*
- Mr Maggs, a misunderstood man**
- Morpheus in *The Matrix*
- Jean-Luc Picard, Captain of the USS Enterprise in *Star Trek: TNG*
- Popeye in – er – *Popeye* cartoons
- Homer in *The Simpsons*
- Yoda in *Star Wars*

* Well, lack of hair can make your head look pretty round . . .
** Shameless promotion for my 'Unlikely Exploits' series.

15 June

1215: King John 'signs' the Magna Carta by imprinting his seal at the bottom

Seven circus acts you don't see so much of nowadays*

1. A chimpanzee tightrope walking, while wearing a tutu and carrying a brightly coloured umbrella.

2. Tigers jumping on to little stools and looking bored.

3. Small dogs jumping through hoops of fire.

4. A lion tamer cracking his whip and fending off lions with a white chair, before sticking his head into a lion's mouth.

5. Ponies galloping around in circles with people doing handstands on their backs.

6. An elephant raising its trunk and feet on command, before being ridden by a clown, a chimpanzee or a young woman in a sparkling outfit, or all three.

7. A seal clapping his flippers together and saying, '*Arf! Arf!*' before being encouraged to balance a large beach ball on his nose.

* Which, I've no doubt whatsoever, is a very good thing indeed.

16 June

A yell of famous battle cries

'Aera!' ('Wind!') A Greek army battle cry.

'Ahoy!' Originally a nasty Viking seafarers' yell.

'Allahu Akbar!' ('God is great the greatest!') Used by Muslim warriors.

'Arrrrrrrrrghhhhh!'

'Banzai!' ('Ten thousand years!') A Japanese battle cry.

'Chaaaaaaaaaaaarge!'

'Denique caelum!' ('Heaven at last!') A Crusaders' cry.

'Deus vult!' ('God wills it!') Another cry of the Crusaders.

'Dex Aie!' ('God aid us!') A cry used by Norman soldiers at the Battle of Hastings.

'Dieu et mon droit!' ('God and my right!') The cry of Edward III at the Battle of Crécy.)

'Eleleu!' Ancient Athenian cry copying the cry of the owl, the symbol of the goddess Athene.

'Faugh a Ballaugh!' ('Clear the way!') Irish cry.

'Geronimo!'

'Godamite!' ('Holy Cross!') The cry of the Saxons at the Battle of Hastings.

'Hakkaa paalle!' ('Cut them down!') A Finnish battle cry.

'Kadima!' ('Forward!') The cry of the Israeli army.

'Olicrosse!' ('Holy Cross!') Another Saxon cry.

'Remember the Alamo!' Cry of the Texan volunteers at the Battle of San Jacinto.

'Tora! Tora! Tora!' ('Tiger! Tiger! Tiger!') The cry of Japanese kamikaze pilots at Pearl Harbour.**

* Also known as Goyathlay, meaning 'One who yawns'.

** An English translation of the American 'Pearl Harbor'.

17 June

*1775: American forces are defeated by the British at the Battle
of Bunker Hill during the American War of Independence*

Eight good things about bunk beds (so long as you get to have the top one)

1. There are far fewer bunk beds than ordinary beds in the world, so sleeping in one is exciting.
2. Climbing up a ladder to bed makes bedtime far more interesting.
3. Getting the top bunk when someone else is stuck with the bottom one makes you feel superior.
4. You get a totally different perspective on your bedroom stretching out beneath you.
5. A top bunk is like your own private world.
6. You get to know a corner of wall and ceiling that no one else does.
7. You can play double-decker buses.
8. It's easier to throw cushions and pillows down on somebody than for them to throw them up at you.*

* Though neither the author nor publisher approves of such actions, of course.

18 June

The Eleanor Crosses

1. Edward I was married to Queen Eleanor of Castile.
2. They were very happy and had 16 children.
3. Eleanor died at Harby, near Lincoln, in November 1290.
4. King Edward ordered that her entrails (innards) be removed and buried in nearby Lincoln Cathedral, but her body embalmed.
5. Her embalmed body was then carried in a sombre procession from Lincoln all the way to Westminster Abbey in London.
6. At each place where the procession stopped for the night, Edward ordered a memorial cross to be erected in her honour.
7. The twelve stopping places where the Eleanor Crosses were built were:
   ◆ Lincoln
   ◆ Grantham
   ◆ Stamford
   ◆ Geddington
   ◆ Northampton
   ◆ Stony Stratford
   ◆ Woburn
   ◆ Dunstable
   ◆ St Albans
   ◆ Waltham (Cross)
   ◆ Westcheap
   ◆ Charing (Cross)
8. Today, the only remaining original crosses are those at Waltham Cross, Geddington and Northampton.
9. The Eleanor Cross outside London's Charing Cross station is a – rather ornate – reconstruction. The cross does,

* Near the village of Waterloo, south of Brussels. Not to be confused with Britain's largest railway station of the same name, covering an area of 10 hectares.

however, give its name to the station, the area being simply called 'Charing' before Queen Eleanor's body rested there.

10. Interestingly, during the 19th and early 20th centuries, a number of fake Eleanor Crosses sprang up around the country (to add local interest and romance) including those at Walkden (Lancashire) and Sledmere (Yorkshire).

19 June

Thirteen (unlucky) key points to remember when attempting to put together self-assembly furniture

1. The instructions have been translated from a foreign language by someone who doesn't actually know that language, but has used a pocket-sized dictionary plus a lot of guesswork and imagination.

2. The illustrations bear no relation to the written instructions, and have been so oversimplified that several pieces look exactly the same.

3. It is possible to put at least one piece in upside down and still be able to assemble the rest of the furniture correctly.

4. It is only when you have assembled the rest of the furniture correctly that you will discover that you have put at least one piece in upside down, with the chipboard side showing.

5. Although the box describes the furniture as 'quick assembly' or 'easy to assemble' and *implies* – if not categorically states – that one competent person can put it together in half an hour, the reality is that even an octopus with a degree in mechanical engineering will still need an extra pair of hands to complete it before midnight.

6. Not all the pieces are necessarily in the box.

7. Self-tapping screws don't really tap themselves and a 15 lb club-hammer may help the job go a little faster.

8. No one really uses the little sachet of white glue to fix the bottom of the drawers in place. They rely on the little tacks alone.

9. The bottom of the drawers require glue as well as the little tacks.

10. The white finish in the photo on the box may look fresh but, by the time you've assembled the bathroom cabinet, it looks old and in need of replacing.

11. Mirrors in self-assembly furniture never look quite as shiny, silvery or reflective as *proper* mirrors.

12. Although you think you could do a better job than the person who's doing the main assembly, when they shout, 'All right, then! *You* do better!' and stomp off, leaving you to it, you'll find you're just as bad.

13. Self-assembly furniture may appear to be cheaper than ready-assembled furniture but, when you add up the number of hours you spent working on it, plus the time and money spent on returning to the shop for the one missing part, one broken part and one unidentifiable part – which turns out to be a factory off-cut that shouldn't even have been in there – and then factor in the emotional strain on everyone in the family (including the pets which hid when the shouting started), it would probably have been cheaper to buy an antique piece of furniture made from jewel-encrusted gold.

20 June

1916: Johnny Morris, famous for introducing and giving the voices to real animals in the TV series Animal Magic, *is born*

A menagerie of characters to be found in Hugh Lofting's Doctor Dolittle books

- Polynesia the parrot
- Gub-Gub the pig
- Dab-Dab the duck
- Too-Too the owl
- Chee-Chee the monkey
- Jip the dog
- (Professor) Quetch the dog, curator of the Dog Museum
- Pippinella the canary
- The white mouse
- Cheapside the sparrow
- The Pushmi-Pullyu (rather like a cross between a goat and a llama, but with a head at both ends)
- PLUS, as they say, many, many more!

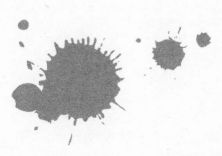

21 June

The original Wombles (as opposed to those in the TV series)

- The first Wombles book was published in 1968.
- The author, Elisabeth Beresford, was married to the presenter of one of television's first antiques programmes, *Going For A Song*.
- In Margaret Gordon's original illustrations, the Wombles look like small, very fat, teddy bears.
- Womble cook Madame Cholet wasn't really French. She chose her name from a town in France 'because she had once heard that was the country where cooking was wonderful'.*
- Tomsk drove a car/bus ('a small bus or a large car – depending on your point of view') called *The Silver Womble*, with the numberplate WOM 1.
- The London store Fortnum & Mason appears under the thinly disguised name of Fortune & Bason, containing boxes of chocolates the size of bicycle wheels.
- Great Uncle Bulgaria's middle name is Coburg.
- Apparently, a Womble was kidnapped from the common back in 1914 or 1915 (in the days before Great Uncle Bulgaria was in charge).
- The burrow is visited by American Womble, Cousin Yellowstone. He reveals that there are Womble communities in the Khyber Pass, Tibet, Australia and New Zealand. The suggestion is that Tibetan Wombles are, in fact, the yeti!

* The Wombles of Wimbledon Common chose their name from an old atlas in Great Uncle Bulgaria's room.

22 June

A rainbow of colourful E numbers*
to brighten up meal times

The following additives are intended to make up for natural colour lost in food processing.

E100 *Curcumin*: for giving margarine that yellow margariny look

E102 *Tartrazine*: for soft drinks

E110 *Sunset yellow*: for biscuits

E122 *Carmoisine*: for jams and preserves

E124 *Ponceau 4R*: for those dessert mixes

E127 *Erythrosine BS*: for making glacé cherries that extraordinary colour!

E128 *Red 2G*: for colouring sausages

E133 *Brilliant Blue FCF*: for canned vegetables

E142 *Green S*: for those green fruit pastilles

E154 *Brown FK*: for kippers

E155 *Brown HT*: for chocolate cakes

E163 *Anthocyanins*: for yogurts

E171 *Titanium dioxides*: for sweets

E175 *Gold*: for cake decorations!

* The 'E' stands for European, indicating that the additive meets EC safety standards.

23 June

Some data about the first computer

- The world's very first all-electric programmable computer was constructed in England in 1941.
- It was called *Colossus* and designed and built by Tommy Flowers at Bletchley Park in England.
- Mr Flowers was a telephone engineer before the Second World War. After the war, he returned to his old job.
- It wasn't until 1974 that the truth came out. Just one year before a US judge had declared that the first computer had been made in 1942 by an American called Atanasoff.
- During the war, Bletchley Park was home to the top-secret Project X, led by Alan Turing, and everyone involved signed the Official Secrets Act. Their silence wasn't broken for over 30 years.
- Flowers's computer could read information off paper at up to 60 mph.
- *Colossus* was built in the days before microchips, so valves had to be used. Valves generate heat, so the computer room became very popular in cold winters and unpopular in the summer.
- People would dry their laundry in the computer room.
- The purpose of *Colossus* was to crack enemy codes. It was successful and played an incredibly significant part in the Allies' victory in the Second World War.

24 June

Three subtle nationality name changes

Napoleon Bonaparte

The world's most famous Frenchman wasn't French. He was born in 1769 to Corsican parents on the island of Corsica, in the Mediterranean off Italy. His original surname was Buonaparte. He dropped the 'u' in 1796, in an effort to sound more French. He was also known as 'Paille-au-nez-Napollione', which means 'Straw-nose-Napoleon', and 'the Little Corporal' because of his diminutive stature.**

Marie Curie

Nobel Prize-winning scientist Marie Curie's name may sound French, but she was born Marja Sklodovska in 1867. Though married to Frenchman Pierre Curie, she was Polish and the radioactive element polonium was named after her mother country. Marie and her sisters' maiden surname was Sklodovska ending with an 'a', but their brother's was Sklodovski with an 'i'. This is the traditional Polish way of identifying a person's gender by surname alone.

Pope John Paul II

The previous pope*** (at the time of writing) was also Polish, born Karol Jozef Wojtyla. What I found more strange – though, if you think about it, it shouldn't be in the least bit surprising – is that at the Vatican, and in Italy, he was known as Giovanni Paulo II, and the English versions of his books also appeared under this name.

---

* Real name Giovanni Caboto, he was born in what is now Italy, and led an English-funded expedition, setting sail from Bristol.

** Small height.

*** A fuller title of someone holding such office is 'Bishop of Rome, Vicar of Christ, Successor of St Peter, Prince of Apostles, Supreme Pontiff of the Universal Church, Patriarch of the West, Primate of Italy, Sovereign of Vatican City and the only pope'. But 'pope' is easier to say.

25 June

*1997: underwater explorer and TV documentary
maker Jacques Cousteau dies*

Ten seriously wet thoughts

1. When we say 'underwater' what we actually mean is 'under
the *surface* of the water' or '*in* the water'.

2. The deepest point in all the world's seas and oceans is in
the Mariana Trench in the north Pacific Ocean. There, the
seabed is a whopping great 10,924 metres (35,840 feet)
below sea level.*

3. When a cartoon character's head fills with water, nine
times out of ten it is a *goldfish* we see swimming from eye
to eye.

5. The 20,000 leagues in the Jules Verne novel *20,000 Leagues
Under the Sea* don't refer to a depth of 20,000 leagues, but
the distance covered horizontally underwater (as with any
normal journey).

6. In cartoons, if an octopus isn't a one-man band, it always
seems to end up playing the drums (and usually has a non-
speaking part).

7. Some water is heavier than other water. The technical
name for the heavier water is heavy water.**

8. Jacques Cousteau invented the aqualung, an oxygen
supply actually carried by the diver him- or herself. Prior
to his invention, divers were attached to their vessel by a
line providing air.

---

* If Mount Everest was dropped into the Mariana Trench, after a big splash, it would not
only be completely covered by water, but there'd be over a mile of sea water between it
and the surface. We're talking DEEP here.

** Heavy water looks and tastes exactly like ordinary water. It is, however, more dense.
Ice made from heavy water sinks in normal water. It's not terribly good for you! Plants
watered with just heavy water will die. Heavy water (aka deuterium oxide) is a human-
made substance.

9. Scuba – as in scuba diving – is actually an acronym.*
   SCUBA stands for: Self-Contained Underwater Breathing
   Apparatus.

10. The current world record for holding one's breath
    underwater is just over NINE minutes.**

* An acronym is a word formed from the initial letters of other words.

** 9 minutes, 8 seconds,*** in fact, though this record may well have been broken
by the time you're reading this, which is why I'm not telling you the current record-
holder's name.

*** Without the aid of pre-inhaled oxygen. With pre-inhaled oxygen, the record in August
2007 was 15 minutes, 2 seconds.

26 June

A slice of famous pies

1. The one from which four-and-twenty** blackbirds emerged in the nursery rhyme.
2. The pies which Sweeney Todd the Demon Barber of Fleet Street made from his victims . . . but, have no fear, this was only a story!
3. Bellamy's veal pies, made famous by William Pitt the younger*** (prime minister) with his last words: 'I could eat one of Bellamy's veal pies.'
4. Those pies sold by the pieman Simple Simon met going to a fair.
5. Man – as in you and I – who, according to Scottish author and artist Alasdair Gray, in his book *Lanark*, 'is the pie that bakes and eats itself'.
6. Humble pie: a corruption of the word *umble*, being the innards – yuck – of a deer. The lord got to eat the venison, the huntsmen ate the umbles in a pie.
7. Frisbie pies, made by the Frisbie Pie Company of Connecticut, whose empty pie tins *may* have led to the invention of the Frisbee.
8. The pie in the sky which people refer to when they mean an idea that'll never be realized.
9. The printers' pie: a jumble of letters dropped on the floor back in the days when everything had to be composed using movable type (separate letters).
10. The horrendous pie served up at the end of Shakespeare's *Titus Andronicus*.****

* Pied simply means something of two or more different colours. He must have worn colourful clothing.

** Twenty-four to you and me.

*** Britain's youngest-ever prime minister at just 24 years old, he was the son of William Pitt the elder.

**** If you don't know what was in it, you don't want to. Honestly. Oh, all right. Villains Chiron and Demetrius are baked in the pie.

27 June

A flush of fairly well-known Louis, Lous, Lieus and Loos

- Cousin Louie/King Louie, the orang-utan king after the secret 'of man's red fire/flower' in Disney's version of *The Jungle Book* (voiced by Louis* Primo).
- Louis** Sachar, author of the splendid book *Holes*.
- Lou Carpenter currently co-owner of the General Store with Harold Bishop, in Australian TV soap *Neighbours*.
- Louisiana, named after Louis* XIV.
- Loo, slang for toilet/lavatory. Probably originates from the French words 'L'eau!', meaning 'Water!',*** which is what people are said to have shouted in warning before emptying their chamber pots out of the window into the street, in the days before flushing loos and underground sewers.****
- Lieu, short for Lieutenant Kojak (pronounced 'loo-tenant', rather than the English 'lef-tenant') in the TV series *Kojak* starring Telly Savalas.
- Louis* Vuitton, French fashion designer.
- Robert Louis** Stevenson, Scottish author and poet.
- Louis* Braille, inventor of the Braille alphabet for the blind.
- Louis* Armstrong, jazz musician, singer, film-star.
- Louis* de Bernières, author (probably best known for *Captain Corelli's Mandolin*)
- Louis* Pasteur, inventor of the pasteurization of milk, and developer (with Edward Jenner) of vaccination.

---

* Pronounced Loo-ee.
** Pronounced Lewis.
*** The full phrase was 'Gardez l'eau!' ('Watch out, water!')
**** Although the photographer Patrick Lichfield (aka Thomas Patrick John Anson, Fifth Earl of Lichfield) once claimed that the term 'loo' was inspired by a however-many-times-Great-Aunt Lou in his family (though perhaps he was being cheeky!).

28 June

Items most commonly found in Christmas crackers

1. Little slips of paper containing groan-inducing jokes, such as:

   Q: *Why is Father Christmas such a good gardener?*
   A: *Because he likes to hoe, hoe, hoe!*

   Q: *Why do Santa's little helpers get such good medical assistance?*
   A: *Because they're members of the National Elf Service.*

   Q: *Why does Comrade Rudolf make such a good weather forecaster, darling?*
   A: *Because Rudolf the Red knows rain, dear.*

2. Small novelties ranging from key chains and mini nail-clippers to plastic puzzles and whistles.

3. Balloons.

4. Paper crowns (just too small for most grown-ups to wear without them splitting – the paper crowns, not the grown-ups – down the seam).*

* It's usually too much Christmas lunch that makes grown-ups split down the seam.

29 June

Half a dozen different types of globe (not of the theatre variety), plus one extra

1. The *Boston Globe*: a US newspaper.
2. The *Globe and Mail*: a Canadian newspaper.
3. A globe: as in light bulb.
4. A globe: a spherical (ball-shaped) representation of the Earth, with a map on its surface.
5. Inflatable globe: like No. 4, but you have to blow it up.
6. The Globe Inn in Dumfries: popular drinking hole with poet Robbie Burns 200 years ago.
7. A snow globe: one of those water-filled 'glass'-domed ornaments – usually made of plastic nowadays – that you shake, to create the impression of it snowing on the inside.*

* If this was a things-to-make-and-do book, I could tell you how to make a snow globe out of a baby-food jar, filled with water and crushed egg shells, but it isn't. So I won't.

30 June

(Old) Money! Money! Money!*

- In the UK, in pre-decimalization days, the currency used to be pounds, shillings and pence.
- This was abbreviated to £.s.d. or L.S.D.**
- Coins & Notes:
  - farthing (phased out in 1960)
  - ha'penny (halfpenny)
  - penny (1d.)
  - shilling (1/-)
  - florin (2/-)
  - half crown (2/6d.)
  - crown (5/-)
  - ten shilling note (10/-)
  - 1-pound note (£1)
  - 5-pound note(£5)
  - 10-pound note (£10)
    (*plus* higher denomination notes)
- There were:
  - 2 farthings to a ha'penny (halfpenny)
  - 2 ha'pennies to a penny
  - 12 pennies to a shilling****
  - 20 shillings (240 pennies) to the pound
  - 1 pound, 1 shilling (21 shillings) to the guinea

---

* If you're too young to remember old money, and find it confusing, just be grateful you didn't have to learn to add and subtract it at school. I did.

** The 'D' comes from the Latin *denarius*, an old Roman coin. Originally worth enough for a Roman to buy 10 asses – which is how the coin got its name*** – the *denarius* (plural *denarii*) gradually became worth less over time.

*** Knowing Latin would help here.

**** If anyone tells you that they can remember the days when a shilling could buy them a fish supper for two, and still leave them with enough money to 'go to the pictures', they're either a) lying; or b) incredibly old.

- Decimalization day, when shillings disappeared and 100 new pennies made a pound, was known as 'D-Day' and occurred on 15 February 1971.
- In preparation, in 1968 new shillings and florins were issued as 5-pence pieces and 10-pence pieces (to get people used to the idea of change).
- In October 1969 the 50-pence piece replaced the 10-shilling note.
- Ten-shilling notes ceased to be legal tender on 22 November 1970.
- The ha'penny ceased to be legal tender on 1 August 1969.
- The half-crown was phased out on 1 January 1970.

1 July

Inventions made by Professor Calculus in the Tintin books*

Red Rackham's Treasure
- Soda-water maker
- Clothes-brushing machine
- Wall bed
- Shark-shaped electric-powered submarine

Destination Moon
- The Moon rocket itself

The Calculus Affair
- Ultrasound emitter

The Red Sea Sharks
- Motorized roller skates

The Castafiore Emerald
- 'Super Calcacolor' TV – colour TV with poor picture quality**
- A new breed of white rose, the 'Bianca'

Tintin and the Picaros
- Herbal tablets designed to put those with drinking problems – well, Captain Haddock, at least – off alcohol

---

* Written and illustrated by Hergé himself, thus excluding inventions which appear in the not-so-great *Tintin and the Lake of Sharks*, a book based on the animated film.

** Despite the appalling fuzzy picture quality, which leaves the viewers in tears and seeing everything else with wobbly lines, and despite the fact that colour television has already been invented, Calculus is inordinately proud of this big-screen invention.***

*** This is one of my favourite, favourite, FAVOURITE Tintin moments.

2 July

Composers whose names conjure up noise in themselves

Composer	Sound the name inspires
J. S. Bach (1685–1750)	'woof! woof!' of course
Samuel Barber (1910–81)	the snipping of scissors
Sir Harrison Birtwistle (1934–)	someone called Bert whistling
John Cage (1912–92)	the rattling of bars
Philip Glass (1937–)	'shatter! tinkle! crash!'
Christoph Gluck (1714–87)	water going down the plughole
Franz Joseph Haydn (1732–1809)	someone shouting: '. . . ninety-nine, one hundred! Coming, ready or not!'
Sir Peter Maxwell Davies (1934–)	breaking the seal to a jar of instant coffee
Jacques Offenbach (1819–80)	a dog yapping more often than Bach
Josef Suk (1874–1935)	someone enjoying a boiled sweet
Sir John Tavener (1944–)	a landlord shouting: 'Let me have your glasses now, ladies and gentlemen, please!'
Hugo Wolf (1860–1903)	howling at the Moon

3 July

1608: the French explorer Samuel de Champlain founds Quebec

A handful of words containing a 'Q' that isn't followed by a 'U', immediately or otherwise

QATAR - a state bordering Saudi Arabia on the Persian Gulf

QATARI - someone from Qatar

QIGONG - a Chinese system of physical exercise

QINTAR - one-hundredth of a lek (a monetary unit of Albania)

QOHELET(H) - the Book of Ecclesiastes in the Bible

QABALAH - an ancient Jewish tradition of mystical interpretation of the Bible (sometimes spelled Kabbalah)

QAWWALI - a type of Muslim devotional music

4 July

1968: Alec Rose, a 59-year-old British greengrocer, completes his 354-day single-handed circumnavigation of the globe

A dozen facts about Highgate Cemetery

1. There are over 168,000 people buried in more than 52,000 graves, vaults and mausoleums, with around 166,000 names engraved on to 51,000 headstones.

2. The cemetery – a graveyard which isn't attached to a particular church – covers an area of some 15 hectares but, with so much crammed into it, gives the impression of being much larger.

3. It was *the* place for people in fashionable Victorian society to be buried (but only after they were dead).

4. Modelled on ancient Egyptian ruins, the 'Egyptian Avenue' is a line of remarkable family vaults, the entrance to which includes a lotus-flower column and an obelisk.

5. The avenue leads to another spectacular area of family vaults: the Circle of Lebanon, a romantic and idealized vision of a mishmash of Egyptian, Gothic and Classical styles, surrounding a 300–400-year-old cedar tree.

6. Other notable sections of the cemetery – which includes a number of Grade 1 and Grade II listed buildings – are the Terrace Catacomb and the Columbarium ('place for urns').

7. Many notable Londoners are buried in the cemetery, including six Lord Mayors, 48 Fellows of the Royal Society, a number of Royal Academicians and the founders of many famous London businesses, including Foyles the bookshop.

8. There are carvings and statues of numerous different animals, one of the most famous of which must be Nero, a rather relaxed-looking lion. This monument is to the 19th-century showman George Wombell, owner of England's largest travelling menagerie of the day.

9. Nowadays, the cemetery is a haven to living, breathing animals, with some 50 species of bird and 18 of butterfly, as well as three rare breeds of spider, and numerous foxes.

10. The crowning glory of Highgate Cemetery is the mausoleum of Julius Beer, proprietor of the *Observer* newspaper. Built at a cost of £5,000 – which would buy you what £2m–£3m would today – it was constructed by Italian craftsmen and stands an impressive 1,000 ft (300 m) above sea level.

11. Karl Marx (co-author of *The Communist Manifesto* with Frederich Engels) is buried in the cemetery. A monument to his memory includes a HUGE bust of him, under which is written: *Workers of All Lands Unite. The philosophers have only interpreted the world in various ways; the point however is to change it.* Marx's grave can be found to that of the Elizabethan poet Edmund Spenser, creating the rather familiar pairing of Marx and Spenser.

12. Ernestine Rose (née Potowski) is buried alongside her husband, William Ella Rose. A truly great 19th-century American champion of women's rights and the abolition of the slave trade, Ernestine was a famous figure of her day, known as the Queen of the Platform for her rousing speeches (sometimes given in French and German to newly arrived immigrants).

5 July

Some explosive facts about Bikini atoll**

- Bikini atoll is one of the 29 atolls and five islands that make up the Marshall Islands, scattered over 357,000 square miles in the Pacific Ocean north of the equator.

- In 1945, with the Second World War ending in an Allied victory, US President Harry S. Truman ordered the testing of atom bombs on American warships. Because of its remote location – being far away from most regularly used sea and air routes – Bikini was chosen to be the nuclear testing ground.

- In February 1946, the military governor of the Marshall Islands visited Bikini and asked the islanders if they would be willing to leave temporarily, so that the US could test atom bombs for 'the good of mankind and to end all world wars'.

- Speaking on behalf of his people, King Juda, then leader of the 167 Bikinians, announced, 'We will go believing that everything is in the hands of God.'

- The Bikinians left their island home in March 1946.

- They were deposited on Rongerik atoll, some 125 miles to the east. It was six times smaller than Bikini, had inadequate food and water, and local tradition said that it was inhabited by evil spirits. The US left them with only enough supplies for two weeks. Within a couple of months the Bikinians were suffering from the effects of starvation and eating poisonous fish.

* The bikini isn't a particularly new design in swimwear. A Roman mosaic from the Piazza Armerina villa in Sicily shows two women exercising in two-piece garments remarkably like today's bikinis.

** An atoll is a ring-shaped reef, or chain of islands, formed of coral.

- There were two test explosions back on Bikini, with both atom bombs about the size of the nuclear bomb dropped on Nagasaki in Japan.

- Conditions worsened on Rongerik and the world's press became aware of the shabby treatment of the Bikini islanders. Plans were made to move them to Ujelang atoll and work even began on constructing houses there. This atoll was, however, eventually given to another set of relocated Marshall islanders!

- In March 1948 the malnourished and disillusioned Bikinians were transported to Kwajalein atoll, after two horrendous years on Rongerik, and were housed in tents right next to a US military runway!

- In November of that year, the Bikinians relocated to Kili island.

- On 1 March 1954 the US detonated its most powerful hydrogen bomb, causing a 15-megaton blast. The US government was aware that the nuclear fallout would blow in the direction of inhabited atolls (and the people on them) but decided to go ahead anyway, miscalculating just how dramatic the results would be.

- The local inhabitants of the Marshall Islands were not warned of the dangers of nuclear fallout, and there are many tragic stories of children playing in ash, everyone oblivious to the life-threatening radiation sickness this would cause.

- In 1967 the US explored the possibility of returning the Bikinian people to Bikini itself. In June 1968 President Lyndon B. Johnson promised them that they would now be able to return to their homeland and that it was the US's 'goal to assist the people of Bikini to build, on these once desolated islands, a new and model community'.

- By 1972 a number of Bikinians were living on the supposedly 'cleaned-up' island. In 1975, however, low levels of radiation were discovered in the urine of everyone living there.

- In October 1975 the Bikinians filed a lawsuit in a US federal court demanding that a complete scientific survey of Bikini and the northern Marshalls be conducted. In May 1977 it was concluded that the level of radiation in the well water on Bikini exceeded the US maximum allowed limits. This was only the first of many very serious discoveries.

- In May 1978 plans were announced to move the people from Bikini 'within 75 to 90 days', and so in September, once again, everyone was evacuated.
- In 1987 all the Bikinians' claims against the US government were dismissed, but the people of Bikini received two trust funds as compensation for giving up their islands.
- In April 2006 the islanders of Bikini atoll filed yet another lawsuit against the US government.
- Today the Bikinians remain scattered throughout the Marshall Islands, hoping one day to return to their atoll.

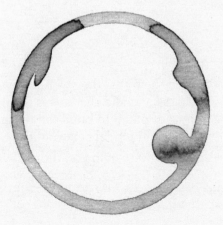

6 July

1535: Sir Thomas More is beheaded for high treason

One man and his beard

- Sir Thomas More was known as 'a man for all seasons'. He could be whatever his king (Henry VIII) wanted him to be . . . for a while.

- Henry made More lord chancellor after Cardinal Thomas Wolsey. Henry had hoped to execute Wolsey but – spoilsport – the cardinal died on the way to his trial.

- Thomas More didn't want the job of lord chancellor. Though a lawyer, not a churchman, he was a devout Roman Catholic and thought that Henry and his wife, Catherine of Aragon, should stay married for life. (Divorce wasn't allowed in the Catholic Church.)

- The king eventually persuaded More to take the job on the understanding that he wouldn't have to get involved in whole divorce/annulment* matter.

- Thomas More was more of a thinker than a doer, and one thing he certainly couldn't do was accept the idea of Henry having supremacy over the Church of England . . . so he refused to take the Oath of Supremacy and was thrown into the Tower of London.

- When the Constable of the Tower learned, in 1535, that Thomas More was to be executed, More was the one who cheered *him* up, rather than the other way around! 'Be of good cheer,' More said, assuring him that they'd meet up again in heaven and 'be merry and merry forever'.

- He sounded very brave and jolly. When he learned that Henry had changed his mind about torturing him before he was executed, More made a joke about the king being ever so merciful.

- Thomas More saved his best joke for his execution. He'd grown a long white beard while he'd been a prisoner all

---

* Annulment is official recognition that a marriage was never really a marriage in the first place, so doesn't count!

that time in the Tower. When he laid his head on the chopping block at Tyburn, he lifted his beard free of his neck, so that it trailed in front of him (rather than down the front of his neck). He declared that his beard had 'never committed treason' and, therefore, didn't deserve to get the chop along with him!*

* This merciful act towards his beard has earned Sir Thomas More great respect and a special place among beardies.**

** Members of the bearded community.

7 July

Famous folk ending in 'O'

Bozo*
Jumbo**
Dumbo**
The Great Soprendo***
Groucho****
Harpo****
Chico****
Zeppo****
Gummo****
Ringo Starr*****
Knocko******
Braggo******
Rhymo******
Coldfeeto******
Tightwaddo******
Sherlocko******
Wacko Jacko*******

* A clown.
** An elephant.
*** A not-so-great magician.
**** A Marx brother.
***** Drummer and ex-Beatle, born Richard Starkey.
****** A monkey character from the strip cartoons of Gus Mager (first published 1904).
******* More of a nickname actually.

8 July

Five famous train robberies

JESSE JAMES AND THE ROCK ISLAND LINE
21 July 1873

Outlaw Jesse James gained his reputation as a bank robber, but
he started robbing trains in July 1873, with a ruthless attack
on a passenger train west of Adair, Iowa, USA. His gang tied a
rope to a rail they'd prised loose, planning to pull it free just as
the train was about to go over it. The train's engineer (driver),
John Rafferty, however, spotted the rope and threw the engine
into reverse. Sadly he was too late and the train ran into the
gap caused by the now-missing rail. The locomotive and two
baggage cars were thrown from the track, landing on their side
and killing Rafferty and injuring the fireman. The gang stole
cash guarded by an express messenger and the passengers'
personal belongings. They had been hoping to steal $100,000-
worth of gold but, at the last minute, it had been decided to
send this on a later train.

THE WILCOX TRAIN ROBBERY
2 June 1899

In which six members of the Wild Bunch, including the
legendary Sundance Kid, held up a Union Pacific train
in Wyoming, USA, blowing up a bridge to prevent others
following by rail. Between $30,000- and $50,000-worth of
goods, including gold and the passengers' personal property,
were taken. It is believed that the robbery was masterminded
by Butch Cassidy,* though he didn't take part in the robbery
(having been pardoned by the then Wyoming governor
William A. Richards in January 1896 for earlier crimes). The
robbery was named after nearby Wilcox Station.

* Real name: Robert LeRoy Parker.

CANADA'S FIRST TRAIN ROBBERY
10 September 1904

Bill Miner, from Kentucky, USA, earned the nickname 'The Gentleman Bandit', serving several prison sentences for robbing stagecoaches. He moved to Canada and lived under the pseudonym George Edwards. On 10 September 1904 he and his gang of two accomplices robbed a Canadian Pacific Railway train in Canada's first train robbery.

BRITAIN'S FIRST GREAT TRAIN ROBBERY
15 May 1855

Unlike the robberies listed above, no one on board this particular train – except the criminals, of course – knew that a robbery had taken place. Three London firms had sent gold bars worth £12,000 from London Bridge, bound for Paris. They were packed in boxes in travelling safes, each with a double lock. The safes were guarded at all times. When the boxes were checked in France, it was found that they contained not gold but lead shot! Someone had switched the contents. But how? The British authorities blamed the French railway staff. The French blamed the British. The French were right. In prison for another crime – which he probably hadn't actually committed – one Edward Agar confessed to the robbery, and explained how it had been done.

With inside help from railway employee William Pierce, the mastermind behind the crime, Agar had managed to get wax impressions of the two keys that opened the safes. He travelled on the train a number of times to be absolutely sure that the keys would open the safes when the time came. The problem of the guard was easily overcome. He too was an inside man. Once the lead shot had been brought on board in small amounts, the rest was straightforward enough. What had seemed like an ingenious robbery was little more than people in trusted positions becoming untrustworthy.

If some of this seems vaguely familiar, you may have seen the film *The First Great Train Robbery** (aka *The Great Train Robbery*) written by Michael Crichton (of *Jurassic Park* fame). In this fictionalized version of events, the crime is far more ingenious.

* Starring Donald Sutherland.

THE GREAT TRAIN ROBBERY
8 August 1963

Late one Wednesday, a Travelling Post Office train – on which letters and parcels were sorted during the journey – was travelling from Glasgow to Euston, London. There was a High Value Package carriage in which registered mail was sorted, much of which contained money. The average amount of money on such a night would be £300,000. Because there had been a Bank Holiday in Scotland, however, the total that day was nearer £2.3 million (which has the buying power of between £30 million and £40 million today).

In the early hours of Thursday morning, the train driver, Jack Mills, stopped at a fake red light near Leighton Buzzard. The co-driver was thrown down the embankment when he got off the train to investigate. Jack Mills was knocked unconscious. The gang had planned to drive the engine and the two Post Office carriages further up the line to unload the money, leaving the other carriages behind. The gang member responsible for driving the engine found it was far more complicated than the ones he'd practised on and couldn't do it, so they had to revive the unconscious driver. While the two postal carriages were being robbed, the passengers in the carriages left behind had no idea anything was out of the ordinary.

Further down the line, the gang took two-and-a-half tons of money in 120 sacks from the train. Then one of them made a big mistake. He told the frightened postal workers to wait half an hour before calling the police, suggesting that the gang's hideout was no more than 30 minutes away!

The gang were eventually traced to Letherslade Farm in Oakley, Buckinghamshire, though they'd flown the coop by the time the police arrived. They'd been planning to lie low there for a number of weeks, but had been worried by a number of low-flying planes.* (It was actually a nearby resident who'd been suspicious of their comings and goings.)

The train robbers had paid someone to clear the farmhouse of all evidence, but this didn't happen. Police found

---

* These were, in fact, RAF pilots on training runs and had nothing to do with the massive manhunt.

fingerprints on a number of items, including a ketchup bottle and a Monopoly set. It later transpired that the robbers had played Monopoly using real money. One by one, the crooks were identified and arrested. The gang received a total of 307 years' imprisonment.

The judge said: 'Let us clear out of the way any romantic notions of daredevilry. This is nothing less than a sordid crime of violence inspired by vast greed . . . anybody who has seen the nerve-shattered engine driver can have no doubt of the terrifying effect on the law-abiding citizen of a concerted assault by masked and armed robbers in lonely darkness.'

9 July

An inferno of fires

The Great Fire of London, 1666
Probably the most famous fire of all time, it started on
2 September in a baker's shop in the aptly named Pudding
Lane. To begin with the authorities weren't overly worried
by the fire, thinking it to be a small affair. By the time it was
extinguished a few days later, more than 13,000 buildings
had been destroyed. Although there was no official death toll,
it's thought that the numbers of dead was surprisingly small.
There are vivid descriptions of events – including the burial of
valuables to escape the flames – in the diary entries of Samuel
Pepys. The London that rose from the ashes was to include
numerous churches by Sir Christopher Wren, including his
greatest triumph, the new St Paul's Cathedral.

The Great Chicago Fire, 1871
The US city of Chicago was a city of wood. Its houses were
wooden and so were most of the pavements. No one knows for
sure how the fire started, though local legend has it that, on
the evening of 8 October, a certain Mrs O'Leary's cow kicked
over a burning oil lamp during milking. Around 300 people
were killed and about 17,000 buildings destroyed. The great
centre of the city and much of its north side was gone.

The San Francisco Earthquake Fire, 1906
On 18 April 1906 the city of San Francisco suffered an
earthquake, but the aftershocks and the fires that followed
were much more devastating. There were four main reasons
for the fires: lamps and stoves being knocked over in the
quake; burst gas mains exploding or catching alight; accidental
fires caused by survivors' campfires; arson by owners of the
damaged or collapsed buildings. (The reason why so many
people burned their damaged homes was because they could
insure their homes against fire but not earthquakes!) Because

the water mains had burst, the firefighters' task was made all the more difficult. Entire blocks of buildings were dynamited to create firebreaks (gaps that the flames could not cross). Almost 300,000 buildings were destroyed as a result of the fire, and thousands of lives lost.

The Blitz, 1940–41

The word 'Blitz' comes from the German *Blitzkrieg*, meaning 'lightning war'. Thousands of planes, flown by Germany's Luftwaffe (air force), dropped thousands of bombs on London during this period of the Second World War. The Blitz began on 7 September 1940, when 348 German bombers, escorted by 617 fighters, dropped 600 tons of high explosives on the docks and East End: 448 Londoners were killed on that first night alone. On the night of 10/11 May 1941, the last and worst night of the Blitz, around 3,000 Londoners were killed. Incendiary bombs were used throughout the Blitz to create terrible firestorms, so much so that 29 December 1940 became known as the 'Second Great Fire of London'. It is estimated that over 30,000 civilians in London died in the Blitz, with another 50,000 injured. More than a million homes were damaged or destroyed.

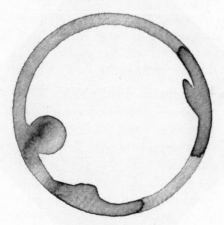

10 July

My ten shortest-lived ideas

1. To open a home for retired snowmen in Florida.
2. To run a stilt-walking mountaineering course for vertigo sufferers.
3. To create the perfect vegetarian hamburger from compost.
4. To invent a board game better than Monopoly.
5. To attract vultures to our garden bird table.
6. To develop a language understood by all animals.
7. To grow my own natural-fibre clothing.
8. To cultivate a mysterious limp.**
9. Oh, I give up . . .
10.

* She reigned for only nine days.
** I sometimes limp, but there's nothing mysterious about it.

11 July

1986: British newspapers are banned from publishing further extracts of Spycatcher, the already banned memoirs of former MI5 officer Peter Wright

What MI5* looks for when recruiting**

- team players
- loyalty
- personal integrity
- honesty
- objectivity
- a sense of proportion about your work
- knowledge of foreign languages (useful)
- women and people with disabilities***

* MI5 is short for Military Intelligence Section 5. In 1929 it was officially renamed the Defence Security Service. In 1931 it became the Security Service . . . but that doesn't stop everyone still calling it MI5 (the name it was first given in 1916).

** No mention of guns and international jet-setting. MI5 is a civilian organization and members of staff have no power to detain or arrest people. The MI5 website states: 'We do not kill people or arrange their assassination. We are subject to the rule of law in just the same way as other public bodies.'

*** MI5 is not exempt from equal opportunities legislation.

12 July

100 BC: Julius Caesar is born

What itching body parts* are supposed to foretell**

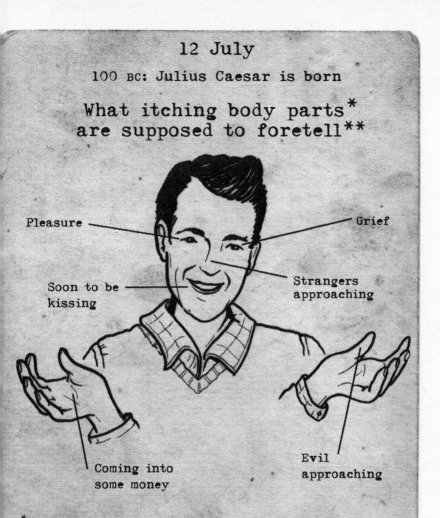

Pleasure

Grief

Soon to be kissing

Strangers approaching

Coming into some money

Evil approaching

---

* Caesar's most famous body part was probably his Roman nose, though Mark Antony did ask people to lend him their ears when coming to bury Caesar, not to praise him.

** Caesar's own death was foretold. He was warned to 'Beware the ides of March', the 'ides' simply meaning the 15th.

13 July

1985: Live Aid concerts take place in the Wembley Stadium, London, and the JFK Stadium, Philadelphia*

A few facts about the birth of the plaster (of the sticking kind)

- American Earle E. Dickinson, employee of Johnson & Johnson, is credited with having invented the plaster.

- His wife – Mrs Dickinson, of course – was, apparently, somewhat accident-prone and often needed patching up.

- Earle decided to be prepared! He stuck squares of gauze on to a roll of surgical adhesive tape and – *voilà!* – had pre-prepared dressings on hand.

- In 1920 he refined this technique and invented the plaster (called a 'sticking plaster' in the US).

- Rolls of sticking plaster first went on sale, through Johnson & Johnson, in 1921.

- 1924 saw the launch of pre-cut individual strips. They were a huge hit with the public.

* In the previous year, Live Aid organizers Bob Geldof and Midge Ure formed Band Aid** to perform a charity single to help the starving of Africa.

** Band Aid is the brand name of a make of plaster, but – in the US in particular – it is used generically to mean a plaster (in the same way people often say Coke – a registered trademark – when they mean any cola).

14 July

Ten very select groups of people
(not animals or things)

1. Actors who've played Doctor Who.
2. Captains of the *Starship Enterprise* who've captained the vessel throughout an entire series.
3. The friends in *Friends*.
4. People who've knocked out Mike Tyson.
5. Actors who've played a convincing Sherlock Holmes.
6. People who can't do Rubik's Cube but still enjoy trying.
7. Children who haven't let at least one of their Tamogotchi pets die.
8. Adults who don't get a tear in their eye watching the 'Daddy! My daddy!' scene in the film version of *The Railway Children*.
9. People who've been into space.
10. People who've travelled faster than the speed of sound.

15 July

A few taxing thoughts on the taxonomy of fish

1. Taxonomy is the branch of science concerned with classification.

2. Classification is the process of putting things – in this case fish – into various categories.

3. Fish are limbless cold-blooded vertebrate animals with gills and fins living wholly in water.

4. Limbless simply means that they don't have arms or legs.

5. Cold-blooded means that their blood isn't warm (like humans').

6. Vertebrate means that they have a backbone.

7. Gills are the respiratory organs that extract oxygen from water.

8. Fins are the flattened multipurpose appendages – good word that – on the bodies of fishes used for moving them through water, steering and balancing.

9. Water comes in two main types: fresh water (as in most streams, rivers and lakes) and salt water (as in the sea). Particular fish live in particular waters.

10. We still haven't got to the classification part.

11. That's because over the years there have been numerous (loads of) different systems for classifying fish. Even today, there are variations (and disagreements).

12. Most modern classifications divide fish into three distinctive types. They are:
    (i) **Class Agnatha:** jawless fish
    (ii) **Class Chondrichthyes:** fish with a cartilage** skeleton and a jaw
    (iii) **Class Osteichthyes:** fish with a bone skeleton

* Bream: 'a greeny-bronze-coloured deep-bodied freshwater fish'.
** Cartilage is a firm, whitish, flexible connective tissue.

13. Common examples of each class include:
  (i) **Class Agnatha:** lampreys
  (ii) **Class Chondrichthyes:** sharks, stingrays, skates
  (iii) **Class Osteichthyes:** eels, herrings, anchovies, piranhas, salmon, trout, cod and many, many more

14. Starfish aren't really fish, which is why, nowadays, we're encouraged to call them sea stars . . . but very few people do.*

* Perhaps we could start a trend: 'Sea stars! Sea stars! Sea stars!'**
** Stop! I'm seeing stars!

16 July

The seven chief labyrinths of antiquity (in other words: really old, really impressive structures which included maze-like passages)

1. The Cretan Labyrinth, home to the imprisoned Minotaur (half-man, half-bull). Here, sacrificial victims were left to be found by the beast . . . It was built by Daedalus, whose son Icarus flew too close to the Sun with home-made wings. Probably the most famous labyrinth of all time.

2. The Cretan Conduit. Not to be confused with the above, this had 1,000 tunnel turnings.

3. The Egyptian Labyrinth near Lake Moeris. Built around 1800 BC, it is said to have had over 3,000 apartments, half of which were underground.

4. The Lemnian Labyrinth was supported by Ionic columns so finely balanced that even a child could turn them.*

5. The Labyrinth of Clusium was built by Lars Porsena (the Etruscan king) in the 6th century BC as his own tomb.

6. The Samian Labyrinth, built around 540 BC.

7. The labyrinth at Woodstock (aka Labyrinthus) which was (according to Higden of Chester) built by King Henry II to protect his lover, the Fair Rosamond, from his wife, Queen Eleanor (who did manage to dispatch her in the end).

* If s/he wanted to, and I'd have been sorely tempted to try, given the opportunity.

17 July

Ten 'new' names probably chosen in the belief that they sounded fun or interesting

According to the UK deed-poll service (through which British citizens, among others, can legally change their names on all documentation), new names have included:

1. Donald Duck
2. Father Christmas
3. Hong Kong Phooey
4. Huggy Bear
5. Jellyfish McSaveloy
6. Jojo Magicspacemonkey
7. Nineteen Sixty-Eight
8. One-One-Eight Taxi
9. Ting A Ling
10. Toasted T Cake

* Apparently born Elinore Harris, and not Eleanora Fagan, as lots of people seem to think. So now you know, show-off.

18 July

A lucky thirteen Roman gods and their ancient Greek counterparts*

Roman	Greek	
Jupiter	Zeus	King of the Gods, God of Thunder & Lightning
Juno	Hera	Wife of Zeus, Goddess of Women & Childbirth
Neptune	Poseidon	God of the Sea[1]
Minerva	Athena	Goddess of Crafts & War
Mercury	Hermes	Jupiter's messenger, God of Trade & Thieves[2]
Diana	Artemis	Goddess of Hunting
Dis	Pluto	God of the Underworld[3]
Venus	Aphrodite	Goddess of Love & Beauty[4]
Mars	Ares	God of War
Vulcan	Hephaestus	God of Craftsmen & Forges[5]
Ceres	Demeter	Mother Goddess of Earth & Agriculture
Bacchus	Dionysus	God of Wine[6]
Apollo	Apollo	God of Music, Healing & Prophecy[7]

* The Romans 'borrowed' many of their gods from the Greeks, simply changing their names.

[1] Often depicted holding a trident.

[2] Wore those winged sandals.

[3] Had a three-headed dog.

[4] Often depicted hanging around in a big shell

[5] Space provided for you to make your own Mr Spock joke:

[6] Often depicted lounging about, nibbling a bunch of grapes.

[7] Not a typing error. Apollo was called Apollo in both cultures.

19 July

1545: the flagship of Henry VIII's battle fleet, the Mary Rose, *sinks off Southsea, near Portsmouth*

Five world-famous sinkings

1. The *Titanic*

Late on 14 April 1912, on her maiden voyage, the White Star liner hit an iceberg which ripped a 250 ft (75 m) hole in her hull. She sank early on 15 April. There weren't enough lifeboats for the number of passengers on board and 1,503 people died.

The wreck of the *Titanic* was discovered on 1 September 1985, 2.5 miles below the surface, 323 nautical miles off Newfoundland. It had broken in two, almost down the middle: the bow and the stern now lie some 2,000 ft (600 m) apart. Though the shape of the bow is in reasonable condition, the stern is extremely mangled.

Today it's possible for the public to visit the wreck on a tour aboard a mini submarine.

2. The *Lusitania*

The *Lusitania*, 'the greyhound of the seas' and the finest ship in the Cunard fleet, was sunk when sailing from New York to Liverpool. On 7 May 1915 she was hit by a torpedo fired by a U-boat (a German submarine) off the Old Head of Kinsale, Ireland. The ship sank in just 18 minutes, leaving 1,201 dead.

The site of the wreck was discovered in 1935, and one of the ship's huge quadruple screws – the propellers that moved the ship forward – was brought to the surface in 1982 and can be seen on the quayside at the Merseyside Maritime Museum in Liverpool's Albert Dock.

3. The *Bismarck*

The pride of the German navy, the *Bismarck* had many admirers, including Britain's wartime prime minister Winston Churchill, who described her as 'a masterpiece of naval construction'. On the warship's maiden voyage, however, she sank. It was May 1941 and, following a sea chase across the Atlantic – lasting over a week – a battle ensued in which the ship was holed by shell and torpedo fire. Around 2,085 people died, with just 115 survivors.

The site of the wreck was eventually located 15,000 ft (4,500 m) down, 380 miles south of Cork in Ireland. The site is officially a German war grave, so all visits to the wreck have to be cleared with the German authorities.

4. The *Belgrano*

On 2 May 1982, during the Falklands War, a British nuclear submarine fired two torpedoes into the Argentinian warship the *General Belgrano*, killing 323 men. Following a massive rescue operation, the remaining 770 crew members were saved. The torpedoing of the ship was a controversial act as she was said to be sailing away from the British 'exclusion zone' at the time.

In 2003 the Argentinian navy and the National Geographic Society launched a joint expedition to locate the wreck of the *Belgrano*, using similar equipment to that used to locate the *Titanic*. It failed. The wreck of the ship is still to be found.

5. The *Mary Rose*

Built between 1509 and 1511, the *Mary Rose* was the very latest in design; something between the cumbersome 'floating castles' of medieval times and the sleek galleons of the Elizabethan navy yet to come. Henry VIII described his flagship as 'the fairest flower of all the ships that ever sailed'. On 19 July 1545 the king was at Southsea to watch the *Mary Rose* set sail. The overladen ship capsized in the wind, taking in water through the lower gun ports (open portholes for cannons to fire through). Around 660 men are thought to have drowned, with less than 40 survivors.

Salvage work started in the very same year that the ship sank, because she wasn't that far below the surface. Weapons and equipment were brought up for reuse. Work on the wreck stopped by 1550, not least because much of the ship had been covered by silt. In the 1960s the wreck was investigated in great detail, culminating in 1982 with its raising. This was watched live by a television audience of an estimated 60 million people. Today the wreck is on display at Portsmouth's Historic Dockyard, behind glass screens, where it is constantly kept moist using a special preservative spray. (There are plans to start drying her out in 2008.)

20 July

Possessors of notable moustaches (real or otherwise)

Adolf Hitler: Real person. Real moustache.

Charlie Chaplin: Real person. (Usually) fake moustache.

Groucho Marx: Real person. (Usually) fake moustache.

Friedrich Nietzsche: Real person. Real moustache.

Duchamp's *Mona Lisa*: Depiction of real person. Fake moustache.

Lech Walesa: Real person. Real moustache.

Fu Manchu: Fictitious character with fictitious moustache.*

Pancho Villa: Real person. Real moustache.

Salvador Dali: Real person. Real moustache.

Mario: Fictitious character with fictitious moustache.**

NB Certain types of moustache traditionally go with certain types of character. For example, circus ringmasters and villains in melodramas are traditionally shown with thin moustaches with ends that they can curl. Old retired military types are often depicted with either handlebar or walrus moustaches.

---

* Fu Manchu is a creation of author Sax Rohmer. In the stories, the moustache is real.

** Mario is a Nintendo character. His moustache is real to him!***

*** Mario and his brother Luigi are sometimes referred to as the Mario Brothers, even though only one of them is called Mario and (according to Nintendo) they don't have a last name. This would be a bit like calling me and my brother the Philip Brothers, despite my brother's name being Martin.

21 July

Some sugary facts

- Sugar slows the setting of ready-mixed concrete and some glues.
- Some people claim that a teaspoon of sugar after a hot curry helps cool the spicy heat in their mouth.
- The bottles used in staged fights by stuntmen are often made of sugar, as is the 'glass' in those windows they get thrown through.
- Sugar is formed by plants, to store energy, using captured sunlight during the process of photosynthesis.
- A spoonful of sugar added to the water of freshly cut flowers will prolong their life.
- Chemical manufacturers often use sugar to grow penicillin.
- A teaspoon of sugar contains around 15 calories.
- Sugar hardens asphalt.
- The sweetness of sugar is believed to be the only taste humans are born craving.
- Sugar is converted to blood glucose, the fundamental fuel needed by the brain.
- Sugar has been used for centuries to help heal wounds. Sugar dries the wound, thus preventing the growth of bacteria.
- Sugar increases the life of jams and jellies by binding the water needed by mould and yeast for growth.

---

* Sir Henry Tate** not only donated his own collection of paintings but also paid for the gallery to be built. It was originally called the National Gallery of British Art but soon came to be known as the Tate Gallery. Today it is called Tate Britain.

** Tate's company Henry Tate & Sons merged with Abram Lyle and Sons to form Tate & Lyle in 1921.***

*** From the 1940s Tate & Lyle's 'mascot' was Mr Cube (finally replaced in 1999). It was Henry Tate who introduced the sugar cube to the UK.

- Sugar, as we know it, was first used by humans around 2,500 years ago, in as early as 510 BC.
- The Emperor Darius described sugar as the 'reed which gives honey without bees'.
- Sugar cane became known to western Europeans during the Crusades in the 11th century AD.
- Up until the 1500s sugar was so expensive it was used in tiny amounts as a medicine and a wine-sweetener, but not in food. It was presented as gifts to royalty.
- In Britain sugar was commonly sold in solid cones called 'sugar loaves' and required special pliers, called 'sugar nips', to break pieces off.
- In the 1500s a 100-tonne cargo of sugar would be worth around £1 million at today's prices.

1932: Florenz Ziegfeld,* US theatre manager, dies

The follies of Mad Jack Fuller

John Fuller (1757–1834) of Brightling, East Sussex, was better known as Honest John and even better known as Mad Jack Fuller. Local squire and Member of Parliament, he gained a reputation for eccentricity, even though he was involved in many good causes. These included the building of a (wooden) lighthouse at Beachy Head in 1828 and paying for Eastbourne's first lifeboat. He was also a founder member of the very well-respected Royal Institution. Mad Jack Fuller's most famous legacy, though, are his follies: structures built with no practical purpose, or no practical reason for looking the way they do. At the time of writing, they're all still standing and are:

The Sugar Loaf, aka Fuller's Point

So called because it resembles the conical shape in which sugar used to be supplied. Lying a few miles from Brightling, it's claimed that it was built (overnight) as a result of a wager. The story goes that, during a trip to London, Mad Jack Fuller bet a friend that he could see the spire of the church in the nearby village of Dallington from his home. On returning to Brightling, however, he discovered that there was a hill in the way! To win the bet, he quickly had the Sugar Loaf – in effect a spire without a church attached – built on a ridge of hills between his home and the village, so it appeared to be the spire poking over the top of the hill.

The Pyramid

It's not just ancient Egyptian pharaohs who are buried in pyramids. So is Mad Jack Fuller . . . in a Christian churchyard in East Sussex! It was, of course, all planned by the man himself during his lifetime. Tradition had it that his body was inside the tomb sitting at a table, wearing a top hat. Broken glass was strewn across the floor to stop the Devil walking in and getting him! (These stories were proven to be untrue when

---

* Ziegfeld was famous for his 'follies' in the 1900s: musical shows including female dancers in revealing clothing.

restoration work was carried out some years later.) Another part of the story is that the vicar only agreed to the pyramid being built in the churchyard if the new pub planned for opposite the church was relocated half a mile away!*

The Temple
Probably the most traditional of the follies, the temple is in a long tradition of follies simply built to add to the landscape to create an attractive view. It stands on private property in Brightling Park.

The Obelisk, aka the Brightling Needle
This 65 ft (20 m) folly stands at the edge of the village on Brightling Down. It's thought that Mad Jack Fuller had it built to commemorate the Battle of Waterloo in 1815 . . . but he didn't really need much of a reason, did he?

The Watchtower
A fantastic piece of medieval-looking nonsense, this 35 ft (11 m) round tower was apparently built so that Jack could keep an eye on the restoration of the genuinely 14th-century Bodiam Castle,** which he'd bought to save from demolition. It's a hollow shell standing in the middle of a field (and, the last time I was there, was surrounded by horses).

* For many years, and until quite recently, this pub was called the Jack Fuller.

** Bodiam Castle is now owned by the National Trust and is my favourite castle ruin in England, so I've a lot to be grateful to Mad Jack for.***

*** The locals have a lot to thank him for too. It's been pointed out that he might not have been quite so crazy after all. All his apparently hare-brained building schemes kept local labourers gainfully employed, putting food on their tables.****

**** As well as his follies, Fuller had a very impressive observatory built, containing some of the most up-to-date astronomical instruments of the day. Today it's a private home.

1888: US novelist Raymond Chandler is born

Quotes from Raymond Chandler as Raymond Chandler, and quotes from Raymond Chandler as his detective, Philip Marlowe

'Dinner tasted like a discarded mail bag and was served to me by a waiter who looked as if he would slug me for a quarter, cut my throat for six bits, and bury me at sea in a barrel of concrete for a dollar and a half, plus sales tax.'

'A dead man is the best fall guy in the world. He never talks back.'

'She had eyes like strange sins.'

'Ability is what you're capable of doing. Motivation determines what you do. Attitude determines how well you do it.'

'A good story cannot be devised; it has to be distilled.'

'A really good detective never gets married.'

'She looked as if it would take a couple of weeks to get her dressed.'

'If my books had been any worse, I should not have been invited to Hollywood, and if they had been any better, I should not have come.'

'At least half the mystery novels published violate the law that the solution, once revealed, must seem to be inevitable.'

'Chess is as elaborate a waste of human intelligence as you can find outside an advertising agency.'

'Everything a writer learns about the art or craft of fiction takes just a little away from his need or desire to write at all. In the end he knows all the tricks and has nothing to say.'

'From 30 feet away she looked like a lot of class. From 10 feet away she looked like something made up to be seen from 30 feet away.'

'I knew one thing: as soon as anyone said you didn't need a gun, you'd better take one along that worked.'

'I've found that there are only two kinds that are any good: slang that has established itself in the language, and slang that you make up yourself. Everything else is apt to be past before it gets into print.'

'She jerked away from me like a startled fawn might, if I had a startled fawn and it jerked away from me.'

'The streets were dark with something more than night.'

'He looked about as inconspicuous as a tarantula on a slice of angel food.'

'When in doubt, have a man come through the door with a gun in his hand.'

24 July

1901: US short-story writer O. Henry (William Sydney Porter) is released from prison after three years for embezzlement*

The magic of the Magi

- The Magi are also referred to as the Three Wise Men and the Three Kings. In Christian tradition they are known for bringing gifts to the baby Jesus and for alerting King Herod to Christ's birth.

- Magi is the plural of magus, meaning the member of a Persian priestly caste.

- The names most commonly given to them are: Caspar, Melchior and Balthasar (with variations in the spellings). Other alternatives include: Larvandad, Hormisdad and Gushnasaph.

- Not only does the Bible not actually name them, it doesn't say how many there were of them. Because it mentions three gifts – gold, frankincense and myrrh – it's possible that some people simply assumed that there must be three of them.

- Christian art depicts two, three, four and even *eight* magi.

- Oriental tradition says that there were twelve of them.

- Their gifts are said to be of symbolic value. Gold was to represent Christ's kingliness; frankincense was the purest incense, used in religious ceremony, and represented Christ's divinity; myrrh was used in medicine and was said to represent Christ's human side – his suffering and his care for others.

- It's often assumed that the Magi came from what was then Persia. All we know from the Gospel of St Matthew is that they 'came from the East'.

---

* In his most famous short story, 'The Gift of the Magi', Della has cut off and sold her hair ** in order to buy a watch chain for her husband, Jim, who has, meanwhile, sold the actual watch to buy Della a set of combs for her beautiful hair!

** You can still sell your hair, if it's long and undamaged. Blonde hair is worth more than brown or black.

- They are said to have followed the Star of Bethlehem to find Jesus's stable. Some believe that there really was such a star. Others suggest that it was a comet. Another suggestion is that there was a celestial conjunction between Jupiter and Saturn.

- Traveller and explorer Marco Polo claimed to have been shown the tombs of all three Magi in the 1270s. He wrote: '*In Persia is the city of Saba, from which the Three Magi set out and in this city they are buried, in three very large and beautiful monuments, side by side. And above them there is a square building, beautifully kept. The bodies are still entire, with hair and beard remaining.*'

- Cologne Cathedral claims to have their bones today (resting in the Shrine of the Three Kings).

25 July

A dozen things I vaguely recollect about Holland without ever having actually been there

1. It is very flat and looks a lot like the Norfolk Broads.
2. There are plenty of windmills (some inhabited by mice).
3. There are huge fields full of multicoloured tulips, with (flat) narrow lanes between them for people to cycle along.
4. Large numbers of Dutch people travel by bicycle.
5. The traditional footwear is wooden clogs, which can't make bike-riding very easy.
6. There are regular Edam-cheese markets, where the big round cheeses are laid out in cobbled market squares, so clog-wearing bike-riders have to swerve around them in order to avoid crashing.
7. The Dutch drink lots of weak tea and eat plenty of thin slices of Edam cheese.
8. In Amsterdam, all the houses are very tall and thin and next to a canal, so there must be a lot of canals too.
9. The main airports are Rotterdam and Schipol, Amsterdam.
10. Holland is one of the Benelux countries, the 'ne' of Benelux coming from the 'Ne' of Netherlands, another name for Holland. The 'Be' comes from Belgium and the 'lux' from Luxembourg. If they'd used the name Holland instead of Netherlands, they would be the Beholux countries.
11. Holland was occupied by the Germans in the Second World War.
12. Anne Frank and her family were hidden from the Nazis in secret rooms in a house in Amsterdam before being discovered and taken to Bergen-Belsen concentration camp, where she died in 1945. Her Amsterdam hiding place is now the Anne Frank Museum.

26 July

Five limericks written especially by me especially for you

A man by the name of C. Wren
Was given a shiny new pen
To design a great dome,
Like those ones there in Rome,
And the result's as well known as Big Ben.

A stylish young man I once knew,
Wore a shell in the place of each shoe.
They looked pretty neat
Down there on his feet.
Unlikely, I know, but it's true!

Brothers Wilbur and Orville Wright
Were excited by the idea of flight.
They achieved victory
In nineteen-oh-three
When the *Flyer* maintained a good height.

There was a young man from Khartoum
Whose nose became wedged in a loom.
Try as he might,
He was trapped day and night.
(Let's hope that they rescue him soon.)

Isambard Kingdom Brunel
Said, 'Cor, blimey! What a terrible smell!
All that smoke from the funnel
Is choking my tunnel
And making me feel unwell.'

* The first ocean-going propeller-driven ship.

27 July

1694: the Bank of England is created by Royal Charter

Things that sound as though they're people, but they're not

Britannia (she who rules the waves): the embodiment of Great Britain

Mother Nature: plain old nature

The Old Lady of Threadneedle Street: the Bank of England*

The Gentlemen in Black Velvet: moles**

* To be found in Threadneedle Street in the City of London.
** William III's horse stumbled over a mole hill in 1702, throwing the king to his death. As a result, the Jacobites (supporters of James II, who had been deposed by William III) traditionally toasted the health of 'the little gentleman in black velvet'.

28 July

1866: Beatrix Potter, children's author and illustrator, is born

Beatrix Potter's real live animal friends*

Benjamin Bouncer, aka **Bounce:** the first pet rabbit Beatrix ever owned. Bought secretly from a London shop, she smuggled him into the house in a paper bag. On the back of a photograph of him, she wrote: *This is the original 'Benjamin Bunny'.*

Peter Piper: a Belgian buck rabbit who used to enjoy lying in front of the fire, stretched out like a cat. Apparently he was clever at learning tricks. In a letter to a child, Beatrix wrote: *I saw him once trying to play the tambourine on a straw hat!*

Pig-Wig: a pedigree black Berkshire pig which, as a piglet, Beatrix bottle-fed day and night, and which slept in a basket beside her bed. He became a devoted pet, following her everywhere.

Spot: the Potters' spaniel, who loved riding in carriages. In adulthood Beatrix was to have many dogs of her own, preferring sheepdogs. She found dogs particularly difficult to draw, which is probably why they don't feature much in her books.

Mrs Tiggy-Winkle: a real hedgehog, not just a character in one of her stories, though her pet didn't do the other animals' laundry. Beatrix often took her pet hedgehog with her on journeys, claiming that travelling always made Mrs Tiggy-Winkle hungry.

Xarifa: a dormouse and one of Beatrix's favourite childhood pets. After the mouse died, she wrote in her diary: *I think she was in many respects the sweetest little animal I ever knew.* A dormouse named Xarifa appears in Potter's lesser-known (and only full-length) novel, *The Fairy Caravan.*

* In her childhood Beatrix's parents encouraged the care and study of animals. At one stage the schoolroom contained: one rabbit, one frog, one tortoise, one snake, two lizards and numerous newts.

29 July

Some of the many items the great consulting detective, Mr Sherlock Holmes, had to hand in his rooms at 221b Baker Street, London

- Persian slipper containing shag (tobacco)
- Pipe rack
- Pipes, including: clay, old brier and cherrywood
- Cigars in a box
- Bell-pull
- Unanswered correspondence nailed to the mantelpiece with a dagger
- Scientific equipment
- Dr Watson's scrapbook, containing clippings from newspapers, including the *Daily Telegraph*, the *Standard* and the *Daily News*
- Watson's copies of the *British Medical Journal*
- Crumpled newspapers in a pile by the sofa
- *Bradshaw's Railway Guide*
- Violin
- Gasogene (for creating fizzy water)
- Long row of yearbooks
- Dispatch cases filled with documents
- Massive manuscript volumes containing details of his cases

30 July

Football World Cup Finals

Year	Winner	Runner-Up	Host Nation
2006	Italy	France	Germany
2002	Brazil	Germany	Japan / Korea
1998	France	Brazil	France
1994	Brazil	Italy	USA
1990	West Germany	Argentina	Italy
1986	Argentina	West Germany	Mexico
1982	Italy	West Germany	Spain
1978	Argentina	Holland	Argentina
1974	West Germany	Holland	West Germany
1970	Brazil	Italy	Mexico
1966	England	West Germany	England
1962	Brazil	Czechoslovakia	Chile
1958	Brazil	Sweden	Sweden
1954	West Germany	Hungary	Switzerland
1950	Uruguay	Brazil	Brazil
1946	*Not held (Second World War)*		
1942	*Not held (Second World War)*		
1938	Italy	Hungary	France
1934	Italy	Czechoslovakia	Italy
1930	Uruguay	Argentina	Uruguay

31 July

1635: King Charles I allows the public to use the Royal Mail*

A bunch of right royal (French) Charlies

- **Charles II of France** was also known as Charles the Fat.** He was thrown off the throne in AD 877 and died, a pauper, in 888.

- **Charles III of France**, on the other hand, was nicknamed Charles the Simple, which sums up what people thought of him.

- **Charles VI of France** (aka the Mad) exhibited strange behaviour in a wide variety of ways. On one occasion he dressed as a 'wild man' at a dance, covering himself with feathers, and someone proceeded to set fire to his costume. On another occasion, he killed four of his *own* bodyguards.

- **Charles VII of France** didn't much like eating for two very specific reasons. Firstly, he had an extremely painful abscess in his mouth. Secondly, he was convinced that someone might try to poison him. As a result, he starved to death.

- **Charles VIII of France** was killed by hitting his head on the door frame of a chateau!

* Prior to this, it could only be used for the delivery of state documents.
** And, some claim, bald.

1 August

*1981: MTV broadcasts its first video: the aptly named
'Video Killed the Radio Star'* by Buggles***

Rhino facts

- The name 'rhinoceros' comes from Latin via ancient Greek:
  rhin = nose, and *keras* = horn.

- The plural of rhinoceros is rhinoceros or rhinoceroses.
  Take your pick.

- The rhino has been around for about 60 million years (or
  about for around 60 million years).

- A type of Mongolian rhino, now extinct, was the largest
  known land mammal: 18 ft (5.5 m) tall, 27 ft (8 m) long,
  weighing around 25 tons. It probably died out because of
  climate change.

- In 1298 Marco Polo understandably mistook the Sumatran
  rhinos for unicorns. He later wrote: *There are wild elephants
  in the country, and numerous unicorns, which are very nearly
  as big. They have hair like that of a buffalo, feet like those of
  an elephant, and a horn in the middle of the forehead, which is
  black and very thick.*

- A rhino's horn is made up of millions of heavily compacted
  hair-like fibres.

- Today, there are only five species of rhinos. All are close to
  extinction: the Sumatran, Javan, Indian and (in Africa) the
  Black and White Rhinoceros.

- During the 1970s, 50% of the world's rhino population
  disappeared.

- The White Rhino is faring better than the Black Rhino.

* On 27 February 2000 it also became the millionth video to be aired on MTV (after
  careful planning!).

** Produced by band member Trevor Horn.

- The White Rhino is neither white nor particularly pale. The word 'white' is a corruption of the Afrikaner word '*wijd*' meaning wide, referring to the animal's pronounced lips.

- According to the World Wildlife Fund (WWF):
  - Black Rhino numbers fell from 65,000 in 1970 to 2,550 in 1993, then went up a little to just over 3,600 in 2004.
  - In 2004 White Rhinos numbered around 11,000.
  - The Indian Rhino population was estimated to be about 2,090 in 2002.
  - In that same year the population estimate for Javan Rhinos was between just 50 and 70.

- The biggest cause of the rhino's endangerment isn't loss of habitat but poaching. Since at least the 5th century BC, there have been people who've thought the rhino's horn has particular medicinal properties or powers. Then there are those who prize it as a source of ivory for carving.

- Rhino horns fetch a very high price on the black market, although all trade in rhino horn is illegal.

- Although many rhinos are protected by armed guards in game reserves, such is their horns' value that some guards have been murdered by poachers to get at them.

- One solution is for officials to tranquillize rhinos and remove their horns, giving poachers no reason to kill them. The problem is that it's not known what effect the horn's removal has on the animals.

2 August

1100: William II, aka William Rufus, is killed
in the New Forest, Hampshire*

Events surrounding the death of William Rufus, according to Peter of Blois**

- There had come from Normandy, to visit King William, a very powerful baron, Walter Tirel by name.

- The king received him with the most lavish hospitality, and having honoured him with a seat at his table, was pleased, after the banquet was concluded, to give him an invitation to join him in the sport of hunting.

- After the king had pointed out to each person his position, and the deer, alarmed at the barking of the dogs and the cries of the huntsmen, were swiftly flying towards the summits of the hills, the said Walter incautiously aimed an arrow at a stag, which missed and pierced the king in the breast.***

- The king fell to the earth and instantly died; upon which, the body being laid by a few countrymen in a cart, was carried back to the palace . . .

- . . . on the morrow was buried, with but few manifestations of grief, and in an humble tomb; for all his servants were busily attending to their own interests, and few or none cared for the royal funeral.

- The said Walter, the author of his death, though unwittingly so,**** escaped from the midst of them, crossed the sea, and arrived safe home in Normandy.

* So called ('*rufus*' is Latin for 'red') either because of his ruddy complexion, fiery temper, or both.

** French diplomat, poet and chronicler, writing many years after the event.

*** According to some reports, the arrow was deflected off an oak tree, which was largely destroyed by souvenir hunters and no longer exists. The Rufus Stone now marks the spot.

**** There are those who believe that this was no accident.

3 August

1958: the USS Nautilus* reaches the North Pole**

Nautilus and Nemo

- The first submarine named *Nautilus* was built in 1800 by Robert Fulton, who went on to invent the first commercially viable steamboat.

- The name is probably derived from the 'chambered nautilus', a large mollusc (though *nautilos* – with an 'o' – is Greek for 'sailor').

- Probably the most famous *Nautilus* was the fictional submarine in the Jules Verne*** novel *Twenty Thousand Leagues Under the Sea*.

- The captain of Verne's *Nautilus* is Captain Nemo (meaning No Man).

- In a later book, *The Mysterious Island*, readers discover that Nemo is an Indian who took to life under the waves following the suppression by the British of the Indian Mutiny of 1857, in which his family was killed.

- In an earlier draft of the story, Verne had Nemo as Polish rather than Indian and his family killed by the Russians in the January uprising of 1863. (Verne's publisher requested the change because the British were far more unpopular than the Russians in France at the time.)

- One thing which remained unchanged – perhaps missed by the editor – was that Nemo still has a portrait of Tadeusz Kościuszko, a Polish national hero, aboard the *Nautilus*.

- It's more than likely that Nemo, the clownfish hero of Disney/Pixar's *Finding Nemo*, was named after the captain.

* The world's first nuclear submarine.
** Passing under the Arctic ice cap.
*** A Frenchman. (It's relevant later.)

4 August

1914: following Germany's invasion of Belgium, Britain declares war on Germany

Animals at war

- It's believed that around 16 million animals assisted the armed forces during the First World War.
- Horses were needed by cavalry divisions and, by 1916, there were over a million of them in service.
- The canine hero Rin Tin Tin was a real-life dog found on the Western Front as a puppy.
- In the First World War lanterns could not be used in the trenches at night because the bright light might attract enemy snipers or shells. Important messages were, therefore, often read by the bluey-green light of glow-worms.
- More than 100,000 pigeons served in the First World War.
- More than 200,000 pigeons served in the Second World War.
- In the First World War doves and rats were often sent into tunnels behind enemy lines to check for poisonous gas.
- Rats have been trained to sniff out landmines. They have a nose for them, and are too light to trigger off an explosion. Rightly or wrongly, trained rats are still used in this field today.
- During the Second World War elephants were used in Burma (now Myanmar) to build roads and transport humans.
- Cats were used on board ship in both wars, and in the trenches of the First World War to help get rid of rats.
- Dogs were trained for a wide variety of purposes:
  - ◆ as guard dogs
  - ◆ as watchdogs
  - ◆ for search and rescue

- for message delivery
- for mine detection
- for wire laying (for field telephones)
- for company morale-boosting

● Bears were often regimental mascots. The most famous military bears must be Winnie-the-bear* from the First World War and Wojtek from the Second World War.

● Wojtek (pronounced Voytek) was the mascot of 22nd Company, Polish Army Service Corps (Artillery). Rescued as a cub, he grew up to help carry supplies and ammunition, stood guard and was an extraordinary morale-booster. After the war, he retired to Edinburgh Zoo.

● During the Second World War the US considered using Mexican free-tailed bats as living incendiary bombs. Once freed over Japanese towns and cities, it was hoped that the bats would roost in attics. Timers would then set off the tiny firebombs, killing the bats and burning down the houses. This was never put into operation.

● The Dickin Medal,** which was created in 1943 by Maria Dickin, is awarded to animals for acts of bravery. So far only 60 animals have received the Dickin Medal:
- 32 pigeons
- 24 dogs
- 3 horses
- 1 cat

---

* Which is probably where Winnie the Pooh got his name from.

** On which is written: 'For Gallantry' and 'We also Serve'.

5 August

*1981: President Ronald Reagan fires 11,359
US striking air-traffic controllers*

Twenty tell-tale signs that you and your family are flying with a *very* low-cost, no-frills airline

1. The pilot is reading a well-thumbed copy of *Flying For Dummies*.

2. The 'automatic pilot' setting is a brick tied to the accelerator.

3. The person serving you your drink is the same person who checked you in.

4. The drink they're serving you is water, shared between all the passengers, in one chipped enamel mug.

5. The safety demonstration for 'in the event of landing in water' involves a beach ball to cling to and a clothes-peg for the nose.

6. The 'clearly marked exits' are holes in the sides of the plane.

7. The departure lounge and the aeroplane hanger are in the same building.

8. That building is an old cow shed.

9. The old cow still lives there.

10. The runway looks suspiciously like a farmyard.

11. The animals certainly seem to think so.

12. Your seatbelt is a piece of knotted rope.

13. It's the same piece of knotted rope you all had to climb up to board the plane.

14. The cabin crew look very young and are wearing a strangely familiar uniform.

15. It's your [old] school uniform.

273

16. In-flight entertainment is a performance by the crew using sick-bag glove puppets.
17. In-flight shopping is a raffle for the one parachute.
18. The airport you land in is a three-hour train journey from the city that it's named after.
19. The three-hour train journey starts at a railway station that's a six-hour coach ride from the airport.
20. The boarding passes are written in wax crayon.

6 August

1889: the Savoy Hotel opens in London

Items commonly removed from hotel rooms*

- towels
- dressing-gowns
- coat hangers
- mugs and cups
- TV remote controls
- clothes brushes
- clock radios
- table lamps
- mirrors
- irons
- ironing boards
- pictures
- minibar fridges

* Excluding all the little complimentary things: bottles of shampoo, bubble bath, conditioner and moisturizer, as well as soaps, cotton-wool balls, earbuds, shower caps, shoe shiners, sewing kits and slippers, plus tea bags, coffee granules, sugar, long-life milk and the contents of the minibar.**

** And the stuff you came in with, of course.

7 August

1782: George Washington creates the Badge of Military Merit for American soldiers wounded or killed as a result of enemy action*

Messages commonly found on Love Hearts**

All Yours	Funny Face	Kiss Me	Say Yes
Angel Face	Good Pals	Like Me	Slick Chick
Bad Boy	Great Fun	Like You	Smile
Be Mine	Great Lips	Love Bug	Sweet
Be My Love	Grow Up	Love You	Sweet Kiss
Blue Eyes	Guess Who	Lucky Day	Take It Easy
Bye Bye	Happy Birthday	Lush Lips	Tease Me
Canny Lad	Heart Throb	Luv U 24/7	Tickle Monster
Catch Me	Hello	Marry Me	Too Much
Cheeky Girl	Hi Baby	Meet Me	True Lips
Cool Dude	Hold Me	Miss Me	Trust Me
Cool Kid	Hot Lips	My Angel	Wicked Lover
Cuddle Me	Hug Me	My Boy	Wild Thing
Cute Kid	Hunk	My Girl	Will You
Cutie Pie	I Like You	My Hero	Wow
Dear One	I Surrender	My Pal	You And I
Doh!	I Want U	My Pet Love	You Cutie Pie
Dream Girl	I Won't Tell	My Wee Girl	You're Fab
Email Me	In Love	Nice Girl	You're Gorgeous
Ever Yours	It's Love	Oh Boy	You're Mine
Find Me	Just Me	Only You	
First Love	Just Say No	Page Me	
For Keeps	Kiss	Real Love	

* Later known as the Purple Heart.

** A registered trademark of the UK company Swizzels Matlow, Love Hearts sweets were first made in 1933. (Not to be confused with the US company Necco's Sweetheart Conversation Hearts, which date back to 1902).

8 August

Cans, canning and can-openers

- The tin can was patented by Peter Durand in 1810.

- In 1813 John Hall and Bryan Dorkin opened the world's first commercial canning factory in England.

- In 1846 Henry Evans invented a machine that speeded up the can-making process. In the past, the rate was six per hour. Evans increased this to sixty.

- Tin cans originally had to be hammered open. This was because they were so thick. As cans became thinner, proper can-openers were invented. The first was patented in 1858 by Ezra Warner of Connecticut, USA.

- Warner's can-opener was used by troops in the field during the American Civil War.*

- In 1866 J. Osterhoudt of New York, USA, patented a special kind of tin can which came with a key, the type still used for cans of sardines.

- The original version of the classic can-opener, familiar to this day – with that wheel that rolls and cuts around the rim of a can – was invented by William Lyman. Lyman patented his can-opener in 1870.

- It wasn't until 1925 that anyone could improve on Lyman's design, when the Star Can Company of San Francisco added a serrated edge to the wheel.

- Today, there are electric versions of this classic design, the first going on sale in 1931.

- In 1935 the world's first beer-in-a-can went on sale: Krueger Cream Ale from the Krueger Brewing Company of Richmond, Virginia, USA.

- The ring pull (enabling you to drink straight from the can without needing a can-opener) was invented by

* His *design* of can-opener, I mean. There was more than one actual can-opener to go around . . .

Ermal Cleon Fraze from Dayton, Ohio, USA, in 1959 and patented in 1963. Pulling a ring tore a tab off the top of the aluminium can.

- In 1975 a ring pull in which the tab remained attached to the can was invented. These are know as either 'stay tabs' or 'ecology tabs'. Not only could the old detachable ring-pull tabs cause cuts to customers, but they created a great deal of litter.* The stay tab solved this problem.

- The UK now manufactures around 8.5 billion cans a year, from either steel or aluminium, with continental Europe producing a further 24.5 billion.

- Steel drinks cans are coated on either side with a thin layer of tin, to stop the can corroding and to act as a lubricant during the actual can-making process.

* I liked linking the torn-off ring pulls together to make tasteful necklaces. Not that I should necessarily mention that in print.

9 August

Popular varieties of potato grown in the UK and what they're best for*

Variety: **Best uses:**

Variety:	Best uses:
Belle de Fontenay	boiling & salads
Cara	boiling, wedges, baking & chipping
Carlingford	boiling & wedges
Charlotte	boiling & salads
Colmo	boiling
Desiree	boiling, wedges, baking, chipping, roasting & mashing
Duke of York	boiling
Dundrod	boiling
Estima	boiling, wedges & baking
Fianna	baking, chipping, roasting & mashing
Golden Wonder	boiling & roasting
Kerr's Pink	roasting & mashing
King Edward	baking, chipping, roasting & mashing
Linzer Delikatess	boiling & salads
Marfona	boiling, wedges & baking
Maris Bard	boiling
Maris Peer	boiling, wedges & chipping
Maris Piper	boiling, wedges, baking, chipping & roasting
Minerva	boiling
Nadine	boiling, wedges & roasting
Nicola	salads

* According to the British Potato Council.

Pentland Javelin	boiling
Pink Fir Apple	boiling & salads
Premiere	boiling & chipping
Rocket	boiling
Romano	boiling, baking, roasting & mashing
Sante	boiling, wedges, chipping & roasting
Saxon	boiling, baking & chipping
Wilja	boiling, chipping, roasting & mashing

10 August

Reclassification of planets*

- As a result of the discovery of numerous objects in space beyond Pluto, the International Astronomical Union (IAU) decided that there was a need to redefine exactly what a planet is.

- The controversy over how to define Pluto itself started when it was discovered to be much smaller than was originally thought when discovered in 1930.

- Even early data suggesting that Pluto was large enough to affect the orbits of Neptune and Uranus turned out to be nothing more than observational errors.

- Options under consideration included calling any round object orbiting the Sun, and larger than an agreed size, a planet. If this minimum size was set small enough to include Pluto, it would also have to included UB313, a celestial body identified in 2005 from a photo taken in 2003, and unofficially known as Xena, now Eris.

- Another option was to call any orbiting object sufficiently large for gravity to pull it into a round shape a planet. This would have included Pluto, Xena and Ceres (an object long considered an asteroid that orbits between Mars and Jupiter).

- In August 2006 a decision on reclassification was made at the IAU's 26th General Assembly in Prague.

- At a later date, these decisions were reported to the world's press by:
  - ◆ Dr Luboš Perek, Emeritus Professor at the Czech Academy of Sciences

---

* There should be no real legal implications arising from the reclassification of planets. In the two most important space-related agreements – the Outer Space Treaty of 1967 and the Moon Agreement – the term celestial body is used instead of planet anyway.**

** And the IAU has agreed that both planets and dwarf planets classify as celestial bodies, so that's all right then.

- ◆ Dr Gerhard H. Schwehm, Head of Solar System Science & Operations Division, European Space Agency
- ◆ Mr Leslie I. Tennen, Former Commissioner, Arizona Space Commission
- ● The General Assembly ruled on three categories:
  1. **Planets**, which, in this solar system, are: Mercury, Venus, Earth, Mars, Jupiter, Saturn, Uranus and Neptune.
  2. **Dwarf Planets**, including celestial bodies such as Pluto. These must (among other things) be in orbit, have a round shape generated by their own rotation and cannot be satellites of another planet. (Such celestial bodies beyond the orbit of Neptune will now be referred to as *Trans-Neptunian Objects*.)
  3. **Small Solar System Bodies** which might be large asteroids or moons.
- ● This reclassification hasn't met with universal approval. Some experts believe that the original nine planets should remain planets. (But, as others argue, what is a dwarf *planet*, if not a planet?)

11 August

Letters from the past

- Before the building of Hadrian's Wall (c. AD 122–130) there were a number of military posts on the northern frontier between England and Scotland. One of these was the Roman fort of Vindolanda in what's now Northumberland.

- In 1973 a number of writing tablets were discovered there, since when hundreds more fragments of letters have been excavated.

- These were found among the rubbish buried in and around the Roman commanding officer's quarters. Waterlogged conditions helped to preserve these finds.

- The majority of the tablets are official military documents. Some, however, are private letters sent to or written by the serving soldiers.

- They are written on wafer-thin slices of wood, rather than wood and wax, which was believed to have been the most commonly used writing material then, along with papyrus.

- The Vindolanda letters are the earliest surviving examples of handwritten messages in Britain and are now at the British Museum in London.*

- They include:
  - one from slave Serverus to fellow slave Candidus, regarding the festival of Saturnalia (the day on which slaves and their masters traditionally swapped duties)
  - an account of sums received, including cash sums for specific goods
  - a letter to Cerialis, a unit commander, wishing him good luck at a meeting with the governor of the province of Britain

* Which is a gobsmackingly brilliant place, and you can get in free.**
** Not *for* free, because free means 'for nothing' so saying 'for free' is like saying 'for for nothing' . . . which is a bit odd and a waste of a 'for'. . . but you *can* get into the museum for nothing.

- a Roman birthday invitation, in which a Claudia writes to her friend Sulpicia, which begins (in Latin): 'On 11 September,* sister, for the day of the celebration of my birthday, I give you a warm invitation to make sure that you come to us . . .'**

- In a survey of British Museum curators, carried out for *Our Top 10 British Treasures* broadcast on BBC 2 on New Year's Day 2003, the Vindolanda letters came out top: they were voted the museum's greatest treasures.

- You can find out more on the British Museum website: www.thebritishmuseum.ac.uk

* Oooooh! That's my birthday too.
** Claudia didn't write all the letter herself. She simply added a quick message at the bottom.

12 August

1851: production begins of the first sewing machines for the home*

Well-known blind singers

Arizona Dranes (gospel)

Ray Charles (soul)

Stevie Wonder (soul)

Art Tatum (jazz)

Blind Lemon Jefferson** (blues)

Blind Willie McTell (blues)

Blind Willie Johnson (blues)

Sonny Terry (blues)

Blind Boy Fuller (blues)

*Invented by Isaac Singer.

** The first well-known male blues singer.***

*** All the early bluesmen were African American and a significant number were blind.****

**** So much so that when white (and fully sighted) jazz musician Eddie Lang wanted to create a black persona, he called himself Blind Willie Dunn!

13 August

Famous walls past and present

The Great Wall of China

Can't be seen from the Moon. Can't be seen from outer space. *Can* be seen from space. Designed in an effort to keep marauding raiders and nomads out of China's heartland. Not a total success, as the Mongol hordes swept over and around the Great Wall, seizing China.

Phil Spector's Wall of Sound

A background accompaniment in 1960s rock 'n' roll so full of orchestration that not an ounce of silence could slip through it. Invented by US producer Phil Spector, it even permeated into the Beatles' *Let It Be* album.

The Wailing Wall (aka the Western Wall, the Kotel, HaKotel HaMa'aravi and Al-Buraq)

On Temple Mount in Jerusalem, the Wailing Wall is believed to be the remains of one of the colonnades enclosing the Second Temple, built by Cyrus the Great around 516 BC (and destroyed by the Romans in AD 70). A place of pilgrimage for many Jews, who travel there to pray.

Pink Floyd's *The Wall*

The album from which comes the well-known schoolkids' anthem of the 1980s, 'Another Brick in the Wall' Part 2, with an animated video using the drawings of Gerald Scarfe. Later the name of a film, starring Bob Geldof, based around the album. Best known for the lines 'We don't need no education/ We don't need no thought control', suggesting why they did, in fact, need educating; the correct grammar being: 'We don't need any education,' or, better still, 'We do not require educating.'

The Berlin Wall

The East German government built the wall (which stood from 1961 to 1989), claiming that it would protect its subjects from the corrupting Western influence. The West argued that the wall was designed to keep people *in*. In 1989 the wall came down, and, just over a year later, East Germany ceased to exist.

Great Zimbabwe
Constructed over 700 years ago, in the country now known as Zimbabwe, the walled ruins of Great Zimbabwe cover a site of about 1,800 acres or 740 hectares. (The word 'zimbabwe' means 'house of rock' in Shona, the language of one of the tribes of the country.) It's not known exactly why Great Zimbabwe was built or why the civilization behind it declined by the 1600s. They left neither written records, nor passed down their history by word of mouth.

Wall's Pork Sausages
In 1786 Richard Wall opened his pork butcher's business in St James's Market, London, quickly earning a reputation for his superb quality cuts of meat and great sausages. In 1812 he received his first Royal Appointment as 'Pork Butcher to the Prince of Wales'. The business then went on to receive Royal Appointment from five reigning monarchs. A popular joke based on an old saying goes: 'Walls may have ears, but not in their sausages.'

Hadrian's Wall
Hadrian's Wall was built by Roman legionaries between c. AD 122 and 130 by order of the Emperor Hadrian, when Rome occupied England. It was 73 miles long, running east to west from what is now Wallsend-on-Tyne to Bowness-on-Solway. (The Romans would have considered it 80 miles long because their miles were shorter than ours.) The wall started out 5 metres high and 3 metres wide but, as work went on, it was only 1.8 metres thick in places (perhaps to speed up the building work). Along some stretches, turf was initially used and then replaced with stone later. The idea was to keep out the untameable Picts and Scots. Every (Roman) mile along the wall there was a fortified gateway, allowing Roman soldiers to pass through it.

The Wall of Jericho
Jericho has been inhabited since around 9000 BC. That's around 11,000 years ago. When, according to the Old Testament, Joshua's trumpeters blew down its wall, the town had already been rebuilt many times.

14 August

1867: novelist and playwright John Galsworthy is born

Fabulous pigs and piggies

- Miss Piggy from TV's *The Muppet Show*
- Wilbur the pig in E. B. White's *Charlotte's Web*
- Link Hogthrob, captain of the *Swine Trek*, in the Muppets' 'Pigs in Space'
- Babe from Dick King-Smith's *The Sheep Pig*
- Piggy Snead* from John Irving's short story *Trying to Save Piggy Snead*
- The pig with the ring in the end of his nose in *The Owl and the Pussycat* by Edward Lear
- Napoleon, Snowball and Old Major (among others) in George Orwell's *Animal Farm*
- Porky Pig the stuttering pig from Looney Tunes who says, 'That's all Folks!'
- Piggy* from William Golding's *Lord of the Flies*
- Olivia the pig heroine of Ian Falconer's books
- Hamm the piggy bank from the *Toy Story* films
- Squealer the pig, one of Ty's nine original Beanie Babies
- Rasher the pig from 'Dennis the Menace'
- Piglet from *Winnie the Pooh*. No list of pigs would be complete without him
- Gub-Gub from Hugh Lofting's Dr Dolittle books
- Gouger, Snouter, Rooter and Tusker, who pull the Hogfather's sleigh in Terry Pratchett's Discworld novels
- Pigling Bland from Beatrix Potter's *The Tale of Pigling Bland*

* This Piggy was a person, not a pig.

15 August

1967: pirate radio stations are made illegal in Britain

Basic requirements for being a pirate captain*

Eyepatch

Wooden leg or hook hand

Curly black wig (or curly black hair)

Moustache

Cruel streak

Frock coat with gold brocade

Pretence of being a gentleman

Parrot on shoulder (optional)

Treasure chest

Fiery temper

Idiot / cheery crew

Young nemesis

(Swash)Buckle shoes

Cutlass and / or rapier

Love of gold doubloons

Ability to put crosses on treasure maps

A pirate ship to be in charge of

* There are no footnotes on this page. Oops!

16 August

1960: Joseph Kittinger parachutes from a hot-air balloon 102,800 feet (31,330 metres) above the ground, setting three world records: for the fastest speed by a human without an aircraft, the highest-altitude jump and the furthest free fall

Fantastic falls

Falling Paint

In September 2005 116 gallons of white paint fell into the River Aker in Oslo, capital of Norway. It left the river looking as though it was flowing with milk. The accident happened when a lifting belt broke on a lorry delivering a pallet of paint to a paintshop. A spokeswoman for Oslo's Department of Water and Sanitation said that she had no idea if the paint would be harmful to humans but it was hardly the time of year for people to be wading in the river anyway!

Snow Fall

Lieutenant I. M. Chisov fell around 22,000 feet (6,700 metres) without a parachute in January 1942 after his Russian Ilyushin IL-4 bomber was attacked by German fighter planes. He landed in a snow-covered ravine and ended up at the bottom. Though severely injured, he survived the experience.

Falling Penguins?

In November 2000 UK scientists headed to the South Atlantic to discover whether there was any truth in the claim that penguins fall over backwards when they look up to watch aircraft flying overhead. They tested the theory with the help of British naval helicopters and 17 flights over more than a thousand penguions in the course of five weeks. The project was based on board HMS *Endurance* and led by Dr Richard Stone of the British Antarctic Survey. He believed the story to be a myth and he was proved right. The birds didn't like the noise of the aircraft and those without eggs to look after wandered off, but not one penguin fell over. Some people suggested that the myth grew up because the idea of penguins toppling like skittles or dominoes was such an immediately visual one.

Caught at the Railway Station

In January 1943 Alan Magee was a US gunner aboard a B-17 bomber which went into a spin. He was thrown from the plane above France, falling 22,000 feet (6,700 metres) into a skylight on the roof of St Nazaire railway station. He completely recovered from all his injuries!

The High Diving Horse

In 1929, the world-famous 'High Diving Horse' made its debut on Steel Pier in Atlantic City, USA. Other novelty animal acts included Sharkey the Hurdling Seal, Rosie the Elephant and Rex the Wonder Dog, who rode the waves on an 'aqua-plane'. (There was also a dolphin show and various boxing kangaroos.) The world-famous High Diving Horse (and its rider) leaped – and fell – from a 40-foot (12-metre) tower at the end of the pier.

A Miraculous Escape

Nicholas Alkemade was tail gunner aboard a Lancaster bomber attacked by German fighter planes during the Second World War. When the crew bailed out, Alkemade realized that his parachute pack was in the cabin . . . so he jumped without one. Falling 18,000 feet (5,500 metres), his fall was broken first by trees, then underbrush, then snowdrifts. His worst injury was a twisted knee!

17 August

1896: Bridget Driscoll becomes one of the first people, if not the first person, to be killed in a car accident*

A run-down on the tragic facts of being run down

- Bridget Driscoll was a 44-year-old woman.
- She was knocked down in the grounds of the Crystal Palace, London, on the way to a folk-dancing display with her teenage daughter Mary.
- The car that hit her was being used to give demonstration rides.
- It was built by the Anglo-French Motor Car Company.
- The driver was a Mr Arthur James Edsall.
- An eyewitness said that the car had been travelling at 'a reckless pace . . . like a fire engine'.
- Mr Edsall claimed he'd been going at 4 mph.
- His passenger, Alice Standing, asserted that they'd been going much faster.
- An 'expert' who studied the car announced that it couldn't have been travelling at more than 4.5 mph.
- At the inquest, held in Croydon, the jury passed a verdict of 'accidental death', so Mr Edsall was not prosecuted.
- The coroner, Percy Morrison, summed up by saying that he hoped such a thing would never happen again.
- Since 1896, around 30 million people have been killed on the world's roads. Every year, a further 1.2 million are killed.

---

* Some believe that the dubious honour of being the first car-accident fatality should go to Mrs Mary Ward in Ireland. In 1869, she was travelling in a steam-powered car, home-made by her cousins, the Parsons brothers, when she fell out of the vehicle and under the wheels at a bend in the road. She broke her neck.

18 August

1868: French astronomer Pierre Jules César Janssen discovers helium*

Stuff about party balloons

- Party balloons come in two main types: those made of latex (rubber) and those made of mylar (foil).
- Latex is not only biodegradable, it also breathes (but not down telephones as a prank).
- It's best to store latex balloons away from heat and light to preserve their quality (so a furnace wouldn't be a good idea).
- Air-filled latex balloons can stay perky for days, if not weeks.
- Helium-filled latex balloons lose their bounce after a day or so, rising less and less before eventually trailing along the ground like an exhausted puppy.
- A helium-filled foil balloon, however, can stay up in the air for a couple of weeks.
- It's best not to leave a bunch of helium-filled latex balloons in a hot car before a party. They'll go saggy on you.
- A knot is still the most effective way of sealing a balloon but, if you have hundreds of balloons to inflate in a matter of hours, you can see why lots of people settle for clips or seals.**
- With helium-filled foil balloons, it's not easy to detect a leak at the time of inflation. It becomes obvious later.
- Though people*** talk about filling balloons with helium (a lighter-than-air gas), the gas put in balloons is actually around 97% helium and 3% other gases.****
- The party trick of inhaling helium from balloons, to make your voice squeaky, really CAN BE HARMFUL and it's not just boring old grown-ups trying to spoil your fun.

---

* Though he doesn't know what it is.
** Not of the 'arf-arf' fish-eating, ball-balancing variety. That would be plain silly.
*** Including me. I don't deny it. You can't make me.
**** No, I'm not going to tell you what they are.

1977: Groucho Marx dies

Some words of wisdom spoken by the late, great Groucho Marx*

'A child of five would understand this. Send someone to fetch a child of five.'

'Don't look now, but there's one too many in this room and I think it's you.'

'Don't point that beard at me, it might go off.'

'Either this man is dead or my watch has stopped.'

'From the moment I picked your book up until I laid it down I was convulsed with laughter. Some day I intend reading it.'

'Go, and never darken my towels again.'

'He may look like an idiot and talk like an idiot but don't let that fool you. He really is an idiot.'

'I cannot say that I do not disagree with you.'

'I didn't like the play, but then I saw it under adverse conditions – the curtain was up.'

'I have nothing but confidence in you, and very little of that.'

'I love everything about you. Your lips, your eyes, your voice. The only thing I can't stand is you.'

---

* US comedian Groucho Marx (born Julius Marx) teamed up with his brothers Chico,[1] Harpo,[2] Gummo[3] and Zeppo[4] to perform vaudeville and musical comedy as the Marx Brothers. Gummo left before they made their first film in 1929. Zeppo left after four films, leaving the famous trio of Groucho, Chico and Harpo. On screen Groucho wore glasses, had a painted-on black moustache and often held a cigar.

[1] Real name Leonard, the character of Chico always spoke with an Italian-American accent and played the piano.

[2] Real name Adolph, Harpo wore a curly wig and hat, played the harp beautifully and never spoke, communicating by wild gesticulation, whistling and honking a horn.

[3] Real name Milton.

[4] Real name Herbert.

'I must say that I find television very educational. The minute somebody turns it on, I go to the library and read a book.'

'I never forget a face, but in your case I'll be glad to make an exception.'

'I was going to thrash them within an inch of their lives, but I didn't have a tape measure.'

'I'd dance with you until the cows came home. On second thoughts, I'd rather dance with the cows until you came home.'

'I'm not a vegetarian, but I eat animals who are.'

'I've had a perfectly wonderful evening. But this wasn't it.'

'Money will not make you happy, and happy will not make you money.'

'Now there sits a man with an open mind. You can feel the draught from here.'

'Only one man in a thousand is a leader of men; the other 999 follow women.'

'Outside of a dog, a book is man's best friend; inside of a dog, it's too dark to read.'

'Please accept my resignation. I don't want to belong to any club that will accept me as a member.'

'Room service? Send up a larger room.'

'She got her good looks from her father. He's a plastic surgeon.'

'There is one way to find out if a man is honest. Ask him. If he says yes, you know he is crooked.'

'Those are my principles. If you don't like them I have others.'

'Time flies like an arrow; fruit flies like a banana.'

'You'd better beat it. You can leave in a taxi. If you can't get a taxi, you can leave in a huff. If that's too soon, you can leave in a minute and a huff.'

'Who are you going to believe, me or your lying eyes?'

20 August

*1970: footballer Bobby Moore is cleared of
stealing emerald bracelet in Colombia**

More Moores

Alan Moore (1953–): comic-book writer whose credits
include *Miracleman*, *V for Vendetta* and *Watchmen*. Has an
EXTREMELY IMPRESSIVE BEARD.

Bob L. Moore (1932–): US bass guitarist and session musician
with over 17,000 recording sessions to his credit. Has
worked with the likes of Elvis Presley, Frank Sinatra,
Bob Dylan, Quincy Jones, Andy Williams, Roy Orbison,
Connie Frances and even Julie Andrews.

Dudley Moore (1935–2002): British comedian, actor and
pianist. Originally best known for being a part of a
double act with Peter Cook, he carved out a new career in
Hollywood, starring in films such as *10* with Bo Derek and
Arthur with Liza Minnelli.

Gordon Moore (1929–): co-founder of Intel, who admitted,
'If you asked me in 1980, I would have missed the PC. I
didn't see much future for it.' Awarded Presidential Medal
of Freedom, the US's highest civilian award.**

Grace Moore (1898–1947): US opera singer and film actress,
known as the 'Tennessee Nightingale', killed in a plane
crash which, among others, also killed Prince Gustaf Adolf
of Sweden, father (at the time of writing) of the present
Swedish king.

Henry Moore (1898–1986): British sculptor best known for
his large-scale abstract cast bronze and carved marble
sculptures.

Julianne Moore (1960–): Fabulous US film actress, born Julie
Anne Smith. Moore was her dad's middle name.

---

* It is believed Moore was set up, either to blackmail him and get publicity for the
jewellery shop or even to damage England's morale ahead of the World Cup.

** My late grandfather was awarded one of those (with oak leaf), and he's not even
American!

Mandy Moore (1984–): US actress and singer.

Mary Tyler Moore (1936–): US actress and comedienne and star of the TV series *The Mary Tyler Moore Show*.

Michael Moore (1954–): campaigning documentary film-maker and author.

21 August

A trio of audacious art thefts*

Painting: Leonardo da Vinci's *Mona Lisa*
Stolen: 1911

One of the most famous art thefts in history was also one of the most straightforward to execute. Vincenzo Perugia, a former Louvre worker, simply walked into the museum, took the painting off the wall, removed it from its frame and walked out with it under his arm! Legend has it that when the police searched his apartment in Florence, he had it hidden on his table under a tablecloth, and they even signed documents on top of it. He kept the painting in a trunk for two years, apparently as a patriotic act: to bring it back to Italy. (What he can't have realized was that Leonardo da Vinci had originally given the painting to the King of France in the first place!) Perugia was eventually caught trying to sell the *Mona Lisa* to a Florentine art dealer. It was exhibited across Italy before being returned to the Louvre in 1913. Perugia was only jailed for just over a year.

Painting: *The Duchess of Devonshire***
Stolen: 1878

Adam Worth, a German-born 'gentleman criminal' (possibly the basis for Sherlock Holmes's fictional nemesis Moriarty) stole this famous painting by Thomas Gainsborough from the London art dealers Agnew & Agnew. He wasn't after money and he didn't want to keep the painting. He planned to hold it for ransom, using it as a negotiating tool for the release of a fellow thief from jail. The only problem was that it turned out his friend had already been released . . . so there was a change of plan. Worth decided to ask for money instead. It wasn't until

---

* The world's most often stolen painting (so far) is probably Rembrandt's *Jacob de Gheyn III* which has been taken four times (so far).

** A painting of Georgiana Spencer. Diana, Princess of Wales (Lady Diana Spencer) was descended from Georgiana's brother, the Second Earl Spencer.

1901 that a deal was struck, via the Pinkerton Detective Agency, and the painting returned.*

Paintings: one Rembrandt and two Renoirs
Stolen: 2000

Three armed thieves ran into the National Museum of Fine Arts in Stockholm, Sweden, snatching the three paintings and escaping in a boat they had moored in front of the museum. They delayed the police by setting fire to cars in the street. In 2001, the police recovered one of the missing Renoirs and eight men were found guilty of the robbery. In March 2005 the second Renoir was recovered, this time in Los Angeles.** In September of the same year, following a tip-off from the FBI, the Swedish, Danish and US police mounted an elaborate sting operation at the Scandic Hotel in Copenhagen, Denmark. A US police officer worked undercover, posing as an interested buyer, and four men were subsequently arrested. The Rembrandt was recovered.

Artwork: Statue of Horatio Nelson
Date: 1975

The 17-ft- (5-m-) high statue of Nelson, by E. H. Bailey, disappeared overnight from the top of the column in Trafalgar Square, London, by a method unknown to the authorities even to this day. It was found by Simon Watts, a bank clerk, five days' later, lying, face down, in a row of bushes in St James's Park, having suffered only minor damage to its base. There was no evidence of a crane having been used, no reports of any low-flying aircraft on the night in question, and security guards at the nearby National Gallery, overlooking the square, reported having neither seen nor heard anything out of the ordinary. Whether intended as a prank or something more serious, it was planned and executed with extraordinary precision. No one has ever claimed responsibility for the act because it never

---

* Even in death Adam Worth hides behind a pseudonym. The name on his tombstone in Highgate Cemetery, London, apparently reads: Henry J. Raymond.

** Interestingly, the authorities had discovered the whereabouts of the Rembrandt (in the US) prior to this. They didn't remove it or announce the discovery, because they wanted to trap those trying to sell it.

happened. This list is entitled a *trio* of audacious art thefts, and this – the fourth entry – is a complete fabrication.*

NB I haven't included one of Stéphane Breitwieser's art thefts, because there were too many to choose from. Building up his own private collection of stolen art, he finally admitted to stealing 239 artworks from across Europe. In 2005 he was imprisoned (for just over two years). Tragically, for some reason his mother chopped up over 60 of the paintings, including the work of such masters as Brueghel. And this is all true.

---

* As a tribute to Orson Welles. In his film *F for Fake* he informs the viewer, 'For the next hour everything in this film is strictly based on the available facts.' Confident that the average viewer won't be timing the film, however, when the hour runs out, Welles adds a fictitious forgery of his own; something he only reveals at the very end of the film. So this entry in my list is art imitating life imitating art imitating life.

A drop in the ocean (or a splash in the loch) of some reported sightings of Nessie, the Loch Ness Monster

St Columba, AD 565

According to legend (written down over a century later), St Columba was travelling in Scotland when he reached Loch Ness and needed to cross it. On the banks of the lake he saw some local men burying one of their own who'd been killed by a monster when swimming in the water. They'd managed to pull the man's body clear before the creature had a chance to eat it. Seeing a boat moored on the other side, Columba ordered one of his followers to swim across to get it! This the follower did, only for the monster to resurface. The onlookers were horrified, except for Columba. Putting his trust in God, he raised his hand, made a sign of the cross and bellowed: 'Thou shalt go no further, nor touch the man; go back with all speed.' The monster fled and the man was saved. Or so that particular version of the story goes.

Mr and Mrs Spicer, 22 July 1933

George Spicer and his wife claimed to have seen 'a most extraordinary form of animal' cross the road some distance in front of their car. Apparently, it lurched towards the loch, leaving a trail of broken undergrowth behind it. Although they claimed that they couldn't see its limbs, because of a dip in the road, they described the animal as having a large body – about 25 feet (7 metres) long – and a long, narrow neck, 'slightly thicker than an elephant's trunk' and as long as the width of the road (which was around 12 feet or 4 metres wide). The neck, they added, had a number of 'undulations' in it.

Arthur Grant, 5 January 1934

Arthur Grant claimed that he almost ran into the creature with his motorbike on the approach to Abriachan, on the

* Or so the story goes ...

north-eastern shore of the loch. It was bright moonlight, which, he explained, was how he was able to see the creature's long neck and small head. He jumped off the motorbike and followed the direction it had taken, only to see ripples where it must have entered Loch Ness. There are claims, however, that he later admitted that he'd made the whole thing up as a joke for a friend.

Margaret Munro, 5 June 1934

Working at that time as a maid, Margaret Munro claimed to have watched the monster for around 20 minutes. It was about 6.30 in the morning, she said, when she spotted it on the shore about 200 metres away. She described it as having 'skin like an elephant's', a long neck, a small head and two short forelegs, which might have been flippers. After 20 minutes, it slipped into the water and out of sight.

G. E. Taylor, 1938

Mr G. E. Taylor, a South African tourist, took a 3-minute colour film of something in the loch with his 16mm camera. A still from the film has appeared in a book, but the film isn't in general circulation.

C. B. Farrel, May 1943

While on duty, C. B. Farrel of the Royal Observer Corps claims that he saw the Loch Ness Monster about 800 feet (250 metres) away from him. He said it had a 20–30 foot (6–9 metre) body, and its neck stretched about 5 feet (2 metres) out of the water. He also claimed that it had a fin, and very large eyes.

Rival III, December 1954

The fishing boat *Rival III* picked up sonar readings in the loch of something keeping pace with it 480 feet (145 metres) beneath it, for half a mile. Believers in the monster were quick to claim that it must have been Nessie.

Tim Dinsdale, 1960

Aeronautical engineer Tim Dinsdale filmed a 'hump' going across the surface of Loch Ness, a powerful wake trailing behind it. Some claim that it was just a boat, others that it was an animate object and others that it was Nessie for sure.

The multiple sightings of 17 June 1993

Edna MacInnes and David Mackay reported watching Nessie for around ten minutes. They were on land and the monster about a mile offshore, they claimed. They said that the monster had swum on the surface before sinking out of sight. Apparently, it had a long neck which it held high above the surface. They then claimed to see it again forty minutes later, at which point Mackay tried to take a photo of it, but only managed to get a picture of what he claimed was its wake. The next alleged sighting was later that evening, by James MacIntosh of Inverness and his son – er – James MacIntosh. The final alleged sighting that night was reported by Lorraine Davidson. Apparently she didn't see the monster but a large wake, even though there were no boats for miles.

Robert Kenneth Wilson, '19 April 1934'

Possibly the most famous of all 'Nessie photos' was that thought to have been taken by Harley Street gynaecologist, Colonel Robert Kenneth Wilson. (It is often referred to as the Surgeon's Photograph.) He let the picture speak for itself, saying only that he'd 'photographed something in the water'. Some argued that it was nothing more than an otter or even a piece of wood. Others thought that it was convincing proof of the monster's existence. It was later revealed to be a hoax by Christian Spurling, the stepson of the big-game hunter Marmaduke 'Duke' Wetherell.

Embarrassed at being taken in by an earlier (schoolboy) hoax – which led to him being ridiculed by the *Daily Mail* – Wetherell had decided to create a bigger and better hoax to get his own back on the paper. According to the by then 90-year-old Spurling, he had created the 'monster' himself, which they attached to a toy submarine and photographed. They then passed the undeveloped photo to Robert Wilson. Wilson, in turn, sold it to the *Daily Mail*. The intention had probably been to expose the fake soon after, thus giving the newspaper a taste of its own medicine. As it was, the picture raised an enormous amount of interest . . . so the hoaxers thought it best to say nothing! Spurling only made the confession just before dying, some 60 years after the event.

Scientific Searches

From 1967 to 1968 Professor D. G. Tucker, chairman of the Department of Electronic and Electrical Engineering at the University of Birmingham, was among the experts and amateurs making up the Loch Ness Phenomena Investigation Bureau's investigations at the loch. His prototype specialist sonar equipment picked up large moving objects reaching speeds of up to 10 knots. He didn't think they were fish, and – whatever they were – there was more than one of them. Andrew Carroll of the New York Aquarium's sonar study of October 1969 picked up what might have been an animal of about 20 feet (6 metres) in length. Other investigations included those by American Robert Rines in 1972, 1975 and 2001. He took a number of underwater photographs purporting to show parts of a monster or monsters. The most famous of these is of the rhomboid, or diamond-shaped flipper (which some argue is nothing more than an extreme close-up of a fish fin).*

NB Those convinced that Nessie is genuine, even if not all the sightings and photographs are, have suggested that it is a plesiosaur, a long-necked aquatic reptile thought to have become extinct millions of years ago, but with a small colony of them somehow surviving in the loch. Others have suggested that it is some kind of hitherto-unknown long-necked seal.**

---

* In 1975 well-known British naturalist Sir Peter Scott announced that the scientific name of the Loch Ness Monster should be *Nessiteras rhombopteryx* (which is ancient Greek for 'the Ness monster with diamond-shaped fin') on the basis of one of Robert Rines's grainy photos. It was later noted that *Nessiteras rhombopteryx* is also an anagram of 'monster hoax by Sir Peter S'!

** Non-believers suggest logs, branches, eels, boat wakes and even a swimming elephant from a passing circus taking a dip.

23 August

1968: Ringo Starr temporarily walks out on the Beatles during the recording of the White Album *

Films starring Peter Sellers as Inspector Clouseau

1. *The Pink Panther* (1963) **
In which the character of Inspector Clouseau is unleashed on the world. The bumbling policeman was supposed to be secondary to that of Sir Charles Lytton, played by David Niven, but he stole the show.

2. *A Shot in the Dark* (1964)
Based on a stage play, this film was, in fact, made before *The Pink Panther* but released after it. (The role of Clouseau was originally offered to Peter Ustinov.)

3. *The Return of the Pink Panther* (1975)
In which Christopher Plummer assumed the Niven role of Sir Charles Lytton.

4. *The Pink Panther Strikes Again* (1976)

5. *Revenge of the Pink Panther* (1978)

6. *Trail of the Pink Panther* (1982)
This film only just scrapes into the 'starring Peter Sellers' category of Pink Panther films. Clouseau's role in the film is created using previously unused clips of Peter Sellers as the character – which had ended up on the cutting-room floor in earlier films – and body doubles. His widow, Lynne Frederick, sued the makers of the film for insulting his memory. She won over a million dollars.

---

* And spent time on Peter Sellers's yacht.

** The Pink Panther in the films was a fabulous diamond. The title sequences introduced the cartoon Pink Panther, who went on to have his own TV series.

24 August

Ten pieces of invented useless information I made up which once won me a prize in a *Spectator* competition**

1. The Tibetans have no word for 'shoe'.
2. Clear honey is banned on the Isle of Skye.
3. Charles Darwin's beard was fake. (It covered an iguana bite.)
4. Maxim, inventor of the machine gun, also invented crêpe bandages.
5. Julius Caesar was born with three nipples.
6. Eyebrow hairs are the first recorded form of currency.
7. The 'qwertyuiop' keyboard came about as the result of a typing error.
8. The word 'ear lobe' appears in the Bible 420 times.
9. The first dog in space was posthumously awarded the freedom of the City of London.
10. The real Maria von Trapp was only 4 ft 2 in tall.

---

* It's often stated that the White House got its name when the burn marks were covered with white paint. It was, however, called the White House long before 1814, and was first painted white back in 1798 . . . so this is a lie!

** This isn't a lie. It was Competition No. 2374.

25 August

The World Wide Webby

1. There are over 37,000 species of spider.

2. According to Ovid, the ancient Roman poet, a young woman named Arachne faced the goddess Athene in a weaving contest, having boasted that she was a better weaver. When it became clear that she was losing, Arachne tried to hang herself . . . and Athene turned her into the first spider: a creature which weaves, and hangs by a thread.

3. The word 'arachnid' comes from Arachne's name, but doesn't mean spider. It is a term for *all* eight-legged animals without wings or antennae: spiders, scorpions, mites and ticks.

4. Spiders produce more than one kind of silk. There are seven different types, though there's no one single spider that can produce all of them. The silk ranges from the extra sticky variety for wrapping up the prey in their larder to extra-strong threads. Different types are produced by different silk glands and nozzles, which are called spinnerets.

5. As well as web-building and prey-catching, spiders also use their silk to make parachutes as a means of transport.

6. Bolas spiders eat moths, and fish for their prey by dangling a sticky strand of silk. This silk is impregnated with a substance similar to the pheromone that moths use to attract mates. (Some South Pacific native peoples use fishing nets made from spiders' webs spun between bamboo shoots.)

7. A variety of spider called orb weavers make silk the strength of tensile steel. If it was possible to collect enough of this silk, it's argued that it would be an excellent material for making bullet-proof vests!

26 August

A clump of yew trees

- Yew trees are a common sight in many English churchyards.

- They are poisonous and not favoured by sheep.

- Yew trees can live for many thousands of years. Their branches touch the ground and often re-root.

- John Wesley made a number of famous sermons beneath yew trees.

- Clippings from *Taxus baccata*, the English Yew, are collected and used to produce Taxol for cancer medicines.

- Yew wood was the favoured material for archers to make their bows. (Many yeomen held archery practice after church on Sundays.)

- Traditionally, the heartwood* of the yew is faced on the inside of the bow with the sapwood** on the outside. This is to take advantage of the natural properties of the wood. The heartwood can withstand compression, while the sapwood is elastic, allowing the bow to stretch.

- In many parts of Britain, providing an archer for the defence of a local lord was a good way for a farmer to work his way up to the 'middle classes'. In return for supplying a yew man, he would become a yeoman.

- A yeoman would be granted the freehold of his farm, and the authority to pass it on to his sons. He'd suddenly become a man of property, which, by definition, granted him yet further rights.

- Sometimes, yeoman farmers signified their position by planting a yew tree outside their home, which was also useful as a source of wood for the bows and arrows.

* Wood which has died and become resistant to decay.
** Freshly cut wood (with sap in it).

27 August

Some warming thoughts about solar power

- Over the space of a year, on average, the Sun deposits around 342 watts of energy into every square metre of the Earth.

- In reality, most of the Sun's heat is deposited into the tropics.

- The amount of solar heating of the North and South Poles varies a great deal throughout the year. In their summers, the polar latitudes get almost as much solar energy as the tropics, but during their winters they get no solar heat whatsoever.

- There are three main ways in which we can harness the energy of the Sun:

  1. by designing houses as heat absorbers: facing in the right direction for maximum rays, and incorporating large glass windows.

  2. by heating water with the Sun's rays: installing thin water pipes (so they can warm through more quickly), painting them black (to absorb the heat), and putting them in an insulator like a greenhouse (to maximize the heat).

  3. by converting sunlight directly into electricity using photovoltaic cells. These have been used in calculators – including mine – for years. Now there are photovoltaic-cell (PV) roof tiles.

- Photovoltaic roof tiles have many benefits:
  1. they're easy to install.
  2. they replace existing materials (such as ordinary roof tiles).

---

* Red, white and green solar-powered lights illuminate the bridge at night.

3. they can be used as easily in built-up areas as in the country because they don't need any extra land to house them.

● As with most renewable-energy systems, the set-up costs are quite expensive. In the long term, though, the savings on electricity bills should make up for this. (Houses with solar roof tiles often generate more electricity than is needed, which can be sold back to the local electricity company.)

28 August

1963: Martin Luther King Jr makes his 'I Have a Dream' speech at the Lincoln Memorial in Washington, DC, USA*

Ten of the most common dreams, in no particular order (I wouldn't dream of compiling a top ten)

1. Being chased.
2. Being naked in a public place.
3. No privacy when going to the loo.
4. Missing a train/bus/aeroplane/(other).
5. Losing property.
6. Losing someone in your care.
7. Being able to fly.
8. Being totally unprepared for a test/exam/interview.
9. Water.
10. Falling.

Martin Luther King Jr's speech began:

'I am happy to join with you today in what will go down in history as the greatest demonstration for freedom in the history of our nation.'

. . . and ended:

'And when this happens, when we allow freedom ring, when we let it ring from every village and every hamlet, from every state and every city, we will be able to speed up that day when *all* of God's children, black men and white men, Jews and Gentiles, Protestants and Catholics, will be able to join hands and sing in the words of the old Negro spiritual:

Free at last! Free at last!

Thank God Almighty, we are free at last!'

* Martin Luther King Jr was assassinated on 4 April 1968.

29 August

The Beatles and royalty (but not royalties)

- January 2007 saw the Royal Mail issuing six stamps showing the Beatles' following album covers:
  - *Sgt Pepper's Lonely Hearts Club Band*
  - *Abbey Road*
  - *With the Beatles*
  - *Help!*
  - *Revolver*
  - *Let It Be*

  – which means that Paul McCartney** and Ringo Starr will be in the unusual position of being able to send letters to people with pictures of themselves on the stamps, an honour usually reserved for HM the Queen alone.

- The song 'Her Majesty' runs at just 23 seconds on the album *Abbey Road* and is the Beatles' shortest official release. On the first printing of the album cover, 'Her Majesty' was not listed. It was, however, shown on the record label.

- Prince Philip, the Duke of Edinburgh, is quoted as having said in 1965 that the Beatles were 'on the wane'. (Which isn't quite as embarrassingly wrong as the Decca recording executive who, in 1962, said of the group: 'We don't like their sound, and guitar music is on the way out.')

- In 1963 the Beatles headlined at the Royal Variety Performance, where John Lennon*** famously said '. . . those of you in the cheaper seats clap your hands,' then – with a side glance to the Royal Box – added, '. . . the rest of you just rattle your jewellery.'

---

* Though they did play on the roof of the Apple offices in London in 1969.

** McCartney has used numerous pseudonyms over the years, including: Paul Ramone, Bernard Webb, A. Smith, Apollo C. Vermouth and Percy 'Thrills' Thrillington.

*** John Lennon also used a number of pseudonyms over the years, including Dr Winston O'Boogie, Mel Torment (not to be confused with the real Mel Tormé) and the Reverend Fred Gherkin (with his wife, Yoko Ono, calling herself Ada Gherkin).

30 August

1901: Hubert Cecil Booth receives a
British patent for the vacuum cleaner

All the words in the
English language containing
two 'u's side by side*

1. Continuum
2. Vacuum**

* Unless you count duumvir, duumvirate, menstruum,
residuum and triduum, which, of course, you should do.
This list is absolutely useless!
** You think the writing's a little on the large side? Well,
I had to fill the space somehow.

31 August

1997: Diana, Princess of Wales, dies in a car crash

A dozen or so famous* car fatalities

1935 **Queen Astrid of Belgium**

1940 **Nathanael West**, US writer

1955 **James Dean**, US film star

1960 **Eddie Cochran**, US musician

1967 **Jayne Mansfield**, US film star

1968 **Jim Clark**, British F1 racing driver

1977 **Marc Bolan**, British rock star (T-Rex)

1982 **Gilles Villeneuve**, Canadian F1 racing driver

1982 **Princess Grace of Monaco**, princess and former film-star

1994 **Ayrton Senna**, Brazilian F1 racing driver

1997 **Diana, Princess of Wales**, British ex-wife of heir apparent

2002 **Ben Hollioake**, cricketer

2002 **Lisa 'Left Eye' Lopes**, singer (TLC)

* Well, people I've heard of anyway.**
** Come to think of it, if I haven't heard of them, I can't include them, can I?

1 September

Three great wagers

1. The most expensive meal in history?

In 41 BC Mark Antony, one of the most powerful men in ancient Rome, summoned Cleopatra,* Queen of Egypt, to Tarsus (in what is now Turkey). There were probably a number of reasons for this, ranging from answering the charges that she'd been as thick as thieves with Cassius, who – along with Brutus and others – had conspired to assassinate Julius Caesar***, to trying to get her armies to support his own. And, oh yes, because he probably fancied her rotten and wanted to spend some quality time with her.

On arrival, Cleopatra proceeded to throw a wildly extravagant banquet for the visiting Roman official, which went on for days. Mark Antony and Cleopatra seemed to hit it off, and she made a friendly wager that she could host the most expensive dinner party ever. The bet was for a great deal of money, but the banquet would cost even more! Mark Antony accepted.

The following day, a further fantastic meal was held. The Roman had to admit that it had been incredible, but certainly wasn't the most expensive there'd ever been.

On hearing this, Cleopatra simply removed one of her exquisitely rare, large pearl earrings and dropped it in a goblet of wine vinegar with a plop. The pearl dissolved in the liquid, which the queen then proceeded to drink. That single pearl has been valued at 10,000,000 *sesterces*, 100,000 gold *aurei*, and – perhaps more usefully – 'the value of 15 countries'. Mark Antony conceded defeat and paid up in full.

For those who say, 'But a pearl wouldn't dissolve in vinegar!' there are versions of the story saying that she crushed the pearl into a fine powder before tipping it into a drink. The original version, outlined above, comes from Pliny the Elder's *Natural*

---

* Actually Cleopatra VII, but the previous VI** were far less famous than her.

** VI = 6.

*** And, of course, succeeded.

History. It is worth pointing out, however, that pearls are primarily calcium carbonate – like stalagmites and stalactites* – so will dissolve in vinegar . . . but a whole great big pearl would have taken a day or two if it hadn't been pulverized beforehand.

2. A big fat bet

The Seventh Earl of Barrymore (1769–93) died at the age of 24 when he accidentally shot himself in the eye, but he managed to fit much into his short but extraordinary life. Barrymore was incredibly fit. Once he bet a large sum that he would win a race against a Captain Parkhurst. What made it more interesting, however, was that he'd be on foot and the captain on horseback! It was the best of four races and, despite Captain Parkhurst's apparent four-legged advantage, the whole thing was declared a draw after two wins apiece.

With the Earl's love of a good wager well known, a very large butcher named Mr Bullock approached him with a proposition. He bet Barrymore that he could not beat him in a 100-metre dash if Barrymore would agree to two basic criteria: firstly, the butcher would be given a 35-metre head start and, secondly, the butcher would choose the course. The Earl agreed in an instant. Mr Bullock was not only very, VERY round but he also had an 'unhealthy complexion'. What chance did he have – 35-metre head start or no 35-metre head start – against a man who could keep up with a horse? Then Mr Bullock showed what a clever chap he really was.

The course the butcher chose was Black Lion Lane in Brighton, which had the distinction, of being one of the narrowest roads in Britain. In some places it's only one metre wide. Of course, Mr Bullock's 35-metre head start put him in front so, when the starting pistol fired and the Earl of Barrymore caught up with him in next to no time, there was no way he could get past the butcher. Barrymore had to admit defeat. Mr Bullock had proved that a fit mind can win races too!

3. There's winning and there's winning

Fonthill Abbey, near the city of Bath, was an amazing gothic-fantasy of a house which, sadly, no longer stands today. It

---

* Stalactites are the ones which hang down from cave roofs, stalagmites are the ones that stretch up. The way to remember which is which is that stalac*tites* have to hold on *tight*.

had an octagonal tower nicknamed Beckford's Folly* and the building looked more gothic than anything actually built in medieval times! It also housed the stunning art treasures of its owner, William Beckford (1760-1844), a very rich and very eccentric man who liked to keep himself very much to himself.

In Chapter Seven of the painter W. P. Frith's *My Autobiography and Reminiscences* (1887), he describes an encounter his (un-named) distant cousin had with Beckford at Fonthill Abbey as a result of a wager. Though surrounded by a seven mile wall, twelve feet (four metres) high, the cousin had bet that he could not only get to walk in the gardens but would set foot in the house itself.

Frith's cousin managed to gain entry to the grounds when the wife of the porter at the lodge house forgot to close the gates after a tradesman had been. He then walked around the gardens, admiring their beauty. It was then that he came across a man with a potato in one hand, who asked what he was doing. Frith's cousin explained that he'd 'found' the gates open and couldn't resist looking around.

The man, whom Frith's cousin took to be the gardener, then offered to show him around the house itself. 'Are you sure Mr Beckford won't mind?' he asked. 'I've heard he is so very peculiar.' The man assured him that Mr Beckford would be fine about it.

So Frith's cousin won the wager . . . but things didn't end there. The potato-wielding man later revealed himself to actually *be* William Beckford and invited him to stay to dinner. And what a fantastic dinner it was too, after which the cousin dozed by the fire. He was awoken by a footman, who said: 'Mr Beckford's compliments. I am to say that since you found your way into Fonthill Abbey without assistance, you may find your way out as best you can – and he hopes you will take care to avoid the bloodhounds that are let loose in the gardens every night.'

Once outside, Frith's cousin climbed into the branches of the first tall tree he could find and spent the entire night scared witless at what the dogs might do to him! He may have won his wager, but Mr Beckford had won a moral victory.

* It certainly was a folly. It fell down!

2 September

1752: Britain's last day using the Julian Calendar (the following day not being 3 September 1752, but 14 September, using the new Gregorian Calendar)

Days of the week and stuff

Sunday
Unlikely derivation: a corruption of sand day (a day for lying around on the beach).
Actual derivation: sun day.

Monday
Unlikely derivation: corruption of 'mundane day' (it being a boring start to the week).
Actual derivation: moon day.

Tuesday
Unlikely derivation: two's-day (it being the second day of the week . . . if you don't count Sunday).
Actual derivation: Tyr's day (Tyr being the one-armed Norse god of war).*

Wednesday
Unlikely derivation: corruption of Widnes-day, a day when people celebrated the existence of the town of Widnes.
Actual derivation: Woden's day, Woden being another name for Odin, the one-eyed chief of all the Norse gods.**

Thursday
Unlikely derivation: corruption of fur's day (a day for wrapping up in animal skins).
Actual derivation: Thor's day (after the two-armed two-eyed Norse god of war and thunder).

---

* He lost his other arm in the jaws of Fenris, having placed it between the giant wolf's teeth to show the beast that he should trust the gods . . . knowing full well that they were about to betray him.

** Who went around with a raven on each shoulder: Hugin and Munin.***

*** Those were the names of his ravens – who were his advisers – not his shoulders.

Friday

Unlikely derivation: frying day (for frying Friday's fish, of course).
Actual derivation: Frigga's day (Old Norse goddess wife of Odin).*

Saturday

Unlikely derivation: corruption of sat-around-day (for a lazy start to the weekend).
Actual derivation: Saturn's day (A Roman god at last!).

PS Derivation of the months' names:

January: Janus, Roman god of gateways, doorways, beginnings and endings.
February: Februa, a Roman feast of purification.
March: Mars, the Roman god of war.
April: *Aprilis*, Latin for 'the month of opening'.
May: Maia, the Roman goddess of springtime, growth and increase.
June: Juno, the Roman goddess of women and childbirth, wife of Jupiter.
July: Julius Caesar, after whom the Julian Calender itself was named.
August: Augustus, the first Roman emperor.
September: *septem*, Latin for seven (September originally being the seventh month in the Roman calendar of Romulus).
October: *octo*, Latin for eight (October originally being the eighth month in the calendar of Romulus).
November: *novem*, Latin for nine (November originally being the ninth month in the calendar of Romulus).
December: *decem*, Latin for ten (December originally being the tenth month in the calendar of Romulus).

---

* Frigga was by far the most powerful of all the Norse gods and goddesses.

3 September

Animal break-outs (which get less pleasant as you read on)

Goldie flies free (March 1965)

Goldie the male golden eagle enjoyed just 12 days of freedom but became a media sensation. He managed to escape from Regent's Park (aka London) Zoo when the keepers were cleaning out his cage. He spent the majority of his (free) time, out of reach in the trees of Regent's Park, though he was spotted in Euston, Tottenham Court Road and Camden Town. It was food which finally led to his recapture. He'd tried killing and eating one of the US Ambassador's ducks (successfully) and two pet terriers (unsuccessfully),** but the dead rabbit offered to him by the zoo's head keeper was too much to resist and he was caught.***

The bear and the bike in Berlin (August 2004)

Chunky 294-lb (130-kg) Juan the Andean spectacled bear broke out of his enclosure at Berlin Zoo by first paddling across a moat using a log for a raft, then climbing a wall. He headed straight for the playground, and toyed with a bicycle before he was cornered by staff with brooms and shot with a tranquillizer gun. Men, women and children fled, though quite a few dads were seen taking photos rather than keeping an eye on their kids. The zoo's deputy director was quoted as saying that bears such as Juan eat vegetables and meat, 'but children tend not to be on the menu'. Juan was carried back to his enclosure, where the logs were removed to stop him making any future escape bids.

Little Joe's first bid for freedom (August 2003)

Though known as 'Little Joe', this gorilla was 11 years old and weighed around 300 lb (135 kg) when he escaped from the 'gorilla habitat' at the Tropical Forest exhibition of the US's

* So, for Britons, that's when war officially broke out.
** Their owner beat him off.
*** Goldie had four more days of freedom when he escaped again that December!

Boston Zoo. On that occasion he didn't get out of the exhibition, let alone the zoo. How he'd managed to get across a 12-ft-high, 12-ft-deep moat (4 metres!) puzzled zoo officials, who promptly added electric wires around his enclosure to discourage further escape attempts.

Midnight feasts at the Battersea Dogs' Home (October 2004)

Staff at the Battersea Dogs' Home arrived at work on a number of occasions to find dogs running loose and dog food scattered everywhere. Not having CCTV cameras, they enlisted the help of a TV company and were amazed at what they discovered. Red, a three-year-old lurcher, was breaking out of his own kennel by opening the bolt with his nose and teeth, and then freeing other dogs (up to a maximum of nine). He only ever seemed to release dogs he was known to be friendly with, and that always included Lucky, the dog he was originally found with. A sturdy new lock on his kennel put a stop to these nocturnal antics!

Little Joe's second bid for freedom (September 2003)

In the month following his first escape attempt, the gorilla not only got past the electric wires, across the moat and over the wall, he also managed to escape from the zoo, just before midnight. Two hours later he was spotted at a bus stop (though not necessarily waiting for a bus). Police had to hold back crowds of onlookers while Little Joe was sedated and recaptured. Little Joe had scratched and bitten a few terrified people along the way.

Jabari's short-lived taste of freedom (March 2004)

Things ended tragically when 13-year-old Jabari, a 340-lb (155-kg) gorilla, escaped from the wilds of Africa exhibition at Dallas Zoo in the USA, attacking visitors and, at one stage, grabbing a toddler in his teeth. About 300 people were evacuated from the animal compound, while others hid in places such as the restaurant. How he had scaled a wall that was not only 15 feet (4.5 metres) high but also concave – bending back on itself – baffled zoo staff and gorilla experts alike. No people died but, sadly, Jabari was shot dead.

A terrible chimp attack (March 2005)

Two male chimpanzees named Buddy and Ollie had somehow learned how to unlock their cage in the Animal Haven Ranch, California. They attacked 62-year-old St James Davis, causing him horrible injuries (including biting his nose off and ripping out an eye).* The ranch-owner's son-in-law shot both chimps dead. After six months in hospital, Mr Davis was discharged.

Bruno and the mass break-out (April 2006)

In 1995 the 100-acre Tacugama Chimpanzee Sanctuary was founded in Sierra Leone for Bruno the chimpanzee. Eleven years later, the chimp led a mass break-out of over 30 chimps, ending in the death of a driver taking around three US sightseers. Bruno smashed the windscreen of the car, pulled out the driver and attacked him. Four chimps returned of their own free will. The rest were rounded up by the police and army over the next few days. The majority of chimps at the sanctuary – between 40 and 50 – hadn't joined in the escape in the first place.

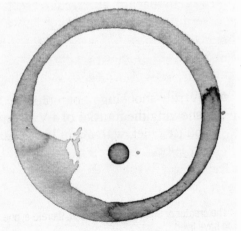

* I did warn you it wasn't pleasant.

4 September

1888: inventor George Eastman registers the Kodak trademark and is granted a patent for his roll-film camera

A gallery of famous photos

- A picture of Alice Liddell – the real Alice who inspired *Alice in Wonderland* – taken by Charles Dodgson who, as Lewis Carroll, wrote the *Alice* books.

- A photo of Frances Griffiths with the dancing 'Cottingley Fairies' taken by her cousin Elsie Wright (in 1917) was declared genuine by Sir Arthur Conan Doyle,* and as being 'untampered with' by the experts at Kodak. (It was a hoax. The 'fairies' were cut out from magazines and kept in place with hatpins.)

- A photo of British prime minister Neville Chamberlain waving a piece of paper and proclaiming, 'Peace in our time!' Less than twelve months later, Britain was at war with Germany.

- The picture of Vietnamese children fleeing in terror after a napalm attack taken by Nick Ut in 1972, during the Vietnam War.

- The publicity photo of Marilyn Monroe posing over the updraught from a New York subway for the film *The Seven Year Itch*.

- A truly shocking photograph by Eddie Adams showing the murder of a Vietcong man by the Saigon police chief, with a gun to his head, taken in Vietnam in 1968.

* The creator of Sherlock Holmes and, therefore, one of the greatest people ever to have lived.

323

- The most reproduced photo of the 20th century is the centrepiece of the US Marine Corps War Memorial in the Arlington National Cemetery. Taken by photographer Joe Rosenthal during the battle for the small Pacific Island of Iwo Jima in 1945, it shows five Marines and a Navy corpsman raising the US flag at the top of Mount Suribachi.*

- Murray Becker's photographs showing the *Hindenburg*, a Zeppelin airship, bursting into flames as it comes in to land in 1937.

- The extremely powerful image of a single male protester taunting the line of tanks in Beijing's Changan Boulevard after Chinese forces crush pro-democracy demonstrations in Tiananmen Square in 1988.

* It was actually recreated the following day for the camera.

5 September

1174: Canterbury Cathedral catches fire

A selection of fantastic cathedral-related stuff you'll find in the Canterbury* Cathedral gift shop, if you have a good rummage about**

- Becket Shrine Rye Tile
- Bookmarks:
  - ◆ Black Prince
  - ◆ Pulpit Canopy
  - ◆ Tudor Rose
- Candlesticks in the design of the famous western crypt columns
- Canterbury Cathedral chess set
- Canterbury Cathedral ornament
- Canterbury Cross roof boss***
- Lady in a Snood roof boss
- Pilgrim tokens:
  - ◆ Becket exile
  - ◆ Becket shrine
  - ◆ Murder of Becket
- Plumtre Missal range
- Shrine of St Thomas Becket mouse mat
- St Thomas of Canterbury roof boss
- Stained-glass magnet (large 42-piece magnet depicting the first of the Bible windows found in the south-west transept of Canterbury Cathedral)

* I used to live there in the 1970s.

** But please don't tell them I sent you.

*** An ornamental carving – often round – at the point in a ribbed ceiling where the ribs cross.

- Stained-glass replicas:
  - ◆ Adam delving
  - ◆ Angel Uriel
  - ◆ Becket and King Henry II
  - ◆ Canterbury pilgrims
  - ◆ Flight into Egypt
  - ◆ Floral quatrefoil
  - ◆ Madonna and Child
  - ◆ St Thomas Becket
  - ◆ the Three Kings
- St Thomas Becket and Henry II fridge magnet (fridge not supplied)

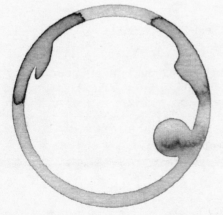

6 September

1852: the UK's very first free public
lending library opens in Manchester

Most borrowed children's authors from libraries 2005-6 according to PLR (Public Lending Rights)

1. Jacqueline Wilson
2. Janet* and Allan Ahlberg**
3. Mick Inkpen
4. Roald Dahl*
5. Lucy Cousins
6. Lucy Daniels
7. Eric Hill
8. Enid Blyton*
9. Francesca Simon
10. Nick Butterworth

* Deceased.
**OK, so this is TWO people . . .

7 September

1838: Grace Darling, the lighthouse keeper's daughter, helps to rescue nine with a rowing boat in raging seas, becoming a national heroine

Other famous Darlings – people, places and things – of fact and fiction

- **Captain Kevin Darling**, a character played by Tim McInnerny in the BBC TV series *Blackadder Goes Forth* by Richard Curtis and Ben Elton. (The surname was suggested by Stephen Fry.)

- **Darling Harbour, Sydney, Australia,** named after Lieutenant-General Ralph Darling, Governor of New South Wales from 1825 to 1831. Formerly part of the commercial port, it's now a mainly pedestrianized area, with – among other things – museums, a casino, cinema, market and hotels. (Exciting stuff!)

- **The Darling family** in J. M. Barrie's play and book *Peter Pan*,* the most famous of whom was probably Wendy.

- **Alistair Darling**, the MP who was voted the Most Boring Politician in Britain in 2002 in a poll held by CyberBritain.com . . . and who is currently the Chancellor of the Exchequer!

- *The Darling Buds of May*, a book by H. E. Bates, later a TV series which launched the career of the current Mrs Michael Douglas, Catherine Zeta Jones.

- **Darling**, a town near Cape Town in South Africa.

- *Darling*, the 1965 John Schlesinger film starring Julie Christie as Diana Scott, a model everyone just called Darling.

* And the splendid sequel *Peter Pan in Scarlet* by Geraldine McCaughrean.

8 September

1966: the very first episode of Star Trek *is broadcast. Called 'The Man Trap', it concerns an alien who appears in different forms to different people*

A distortion of impostors

George Psalmanazar, the man from Formosa

In around 1700 George Psalmanazar (1679–1763) began gaining attention in northern Europe with the claim that he was the first Formosan to visit the continent. Formosa, he explained, was a faraway island where he and his fellow islanders worshipped the Sun and the Moon. He went on to publish a very popular book entitled *An Historical and Geographical Description of Formosa*, 'revealing' many extraordinary things about his homeland. According to this, the Formosans had cannibalistic priests (who ate the bodies of the 18,000 or so young men whose hearts were annually sacrificed to the gods), though the Formosans' main source of food, he said, was serpents. Psalmanazar – who looked surprisingly European – went on lecture tours and even 'translated' various works into Formosan. In 1706, after hoodwinking the likes of the prestigious Royal Society in London, Psalmanazar grew tired of his remarkably successful prank and publicly admitted that he'd made it all up!

Mary Baker, the Princess Caraboo

In 1817 an exotically dressed and apparently confused young woman was found wandering around a village near Bristol. She seemed to be speaking an unintelligible language. People tried to find someone – *anyone* – who could understand her until, eventually, a Portuguese sailor apparently translated her story. She was, he announced, Princess Caraboo from the island of Javasu in the Indian Ocean. She'd been captured by pirates, but had managed to jump overboard in the Bristol Channel and swim ashore to safety. For the next ten weeks she became the toast of the town, and her actions were reported in the local press. She fenced, swam naked, used a bow and arrow and prayed to her god, 'Allah Tallah'. The truth was far more mundane: she was eventually exposed as being Mary Baker, born Willcox, (1791–1864) from Devon. She was a maid and a cobbler's daughter. As for the language, she'd made it up!

Mr Cole and HMS *Dreadnought*

On 10 February 1910, the Emperor of Abyssinia, accompanied by three Abyssinian dignitaries and Herbert Cholmondely of the Foreign Office, along with an interpreter, were taken on a tour of HMS *Dreadnought*. When shown things of particular interest, they would cry 'bunga bunga' to show their appreciation. This diplomatic nicety had been arranged by the Royal Navy following a telegram from Foreign Office Under-Secretary Sir Charles Hardinge . . . though things were not quite as they seemed. The telegram had, in truth, been sent by prankster William Horace de Vere Cole (1881–1936), who also played the role of Herbert Cholmondely. The apparently dark-skinned turban-wearing Abyssinians and their interpreter were fellow practical-jokers (including one Virginia Stephen, stick-on beard and all, who later became the world-famous novelist Virginia Woolf). Cole had dreamed up the whole scheme for fun rather than financial gain. He revealed his trick to the *Daily Mirror*, which published a picture of them in their disguises. The Royal Navy were embarrassed and furious in equal measure.

Wilhelm Voigt, the crafty so-called captain

With nothing more than a Prussian army officer's uniform, made from items bought from second-hand shops, Wilhelm Voigt (1849–1922) perpetrated the most ingenious of crimes. He went to an army barracks in Köpenick, Germany and stopped a number of soldiers outside, ordering them to follow him. He then had them arrest both the mayor and town secretary for financial irregularities! Having 'confiscated' 4,000 marks and issued a receipt, he commandeered two carriages, ordering some of the soldiers to take the prisoners to Berlin for questioning. He had the remaining men 'guard' the offices they'd just raided. Voigt, in the meantime, caught a train and changed back into his civilian clothes. He was caught, tried and convicted – of forgery, impersonating an officer and wrongful imprisonment – but his antics captured the public imagination, which is how Kaiser Wilhelm II came to grant him a pardon. Voigt was a free man.

Victor Lustig and the Eiffel Tower

Victor Lustig (1890–1947) is probably best remembered for pretending to be a government official and selling the Eiffel Tower for scrap. His skill was spotting an opportunity. There were articles in the press about the cost of upkeep of the tower, and the Parisian authorities' problems in meeting it. Rather than simply 'selling' it to the first scrap-metal dealer he could find, Lustig contacted six with an invitation to tender for the business! Once he'd awarded the contract to one of them and received the money, he caught a train to Vienna with a suitcase full of francs, before he could be found out! When it finally dawned on the scrap-metal dealer that he'd been the victim of an audacious con, he was too embarrassed to go to the police.

Fred Demara and Dr Cyr

Throughout the 1940s American Fred Demara (1921–82) held a number of important positions in a variety of religious orders, from a psychologist and university lecturer to a prison warden . . . all obtained on non-existent qualifications. In 1951, he moved to Canada and became 'Brother John', a novitiate monk in Grand Falls. During this time he became friends with a Dr Joseph Cyr and, in March of that year, assumed the man's identity. Calling himself Cyr, Fred Demara was commissioned into the Royal Canadian Navy as a surgeon-lieutenant. Somehow, Demara managed to get away with pretending to be a doctor – even removing the ship's captain's tooth – until that October, when instructions reached the ship that he was an impostor. The real Dr Cyr's mother had read a report in a newspaper about her son performing emergency surgery on the deck of a ship, when she knew that he was a civilian doctor with a practice on dry land! Amazingly, the bogus doctor was not only given an honourable discharge from the navy but also several hundred dollars in back pay. Fred Demara left Canada, eventually becoming a genuine clergyman, under his own name!

Frank William Abagnale Jr, *Catch Me If You Can*

Frank Abagnale (1948–) was played by Leonardo di Caprio in the film *Catch Me If You Can*, based loosely on his life of crime. Over five years in the 1960s he took on eight fictitious identities, not counting all the names he used for cashing over $2.5 m of bad cheques. He masqueraded as a PanAm pilot called Frank Williams for about two years. (He didn't want to actually fly planes but to get free rides around the world on scheduled flights.) For almost a year he impersonated a paediatrician in a Georgia hospital. Having forged a Harvard University law diploma, he genuinely passed the bar exam of Louisiana and managed to land a job at the office of the State Attorney General of Louisiana! He was finally caught and now runs his own anti-financial-fraud consultancy.

David Hampton, *Six Degrees of Separation*

David Hampton (1964–2003) pretended to be Hollywood film-star Sidney Poitier's son, calling himself David Poitier. An African-American, Hampton suddenly found himself accepted in celebrity circles. He got everything from free meals in restaurants to staying in people's homes, and 'borrowing' money. His victims included Melanie Griffith and Calvin Klein. After his story came to light following his arrest in 1983, his life became the inspiration for a play and film called *Six Degrees of Separation.**

Christophe Rocancourt, the master impostor

Christophe Rocancourt (1967–) made his first illegal millions by masquerading as a French member of the Rockefeller family. From very poor beginnings – he was placed in an orphanage, aged five – he forged the deeds to a property he didn't own and then managed to sell it for a very large sum. Rocancourt then

* The theory of 'six degrees of separation' is that no two people in the whole world are more than six people apart from being related.**

** A game based around this theory is 'Six Degrees of Kevin Bacon': trying to connect a person to film-star Kevin Bacon – he was probably chosen because he's been in so many films and his name has the same number of syllables as the word 'separation' – within as few people as possible.

Let's take me as an example. Short of working with Mr Bacon – unlikely at present – which would give me a Bacon Number of 1, or actually becoming him – he is, of course, the only person on the planet with a Bacon Number of 0 – the lowest Bacon Number I can hope to achieve is 2. As I'm not an actor, it's no good simply saying 'I met someone who met Kevin.' My links have to be someone with whom I was involved in an artistic endeavour who was in turn involved in an artistic endeavour and so on, to Bacon himself. So far, however, I've only been able to come up with a 'Bacon Number' of 3:

1. I wrote a book with Paul McCartney.
2. Paul McCartney was in *The Magic Years,* vol. 1 (1987) with Phil Collins.
3. Phil Collins was in the film *Balto* (1995) with Kevin Bacon . . . which isn't a bad start, I suppose.

used some of the money to get to the US, where he assumed numerous identities. He pretended to be a close relative of everyone from Sophia Loren to Dino de Laurentis. At one stage he was living with film-star Mickey Rourke. Once in Canada, he wrote a book about his cons, naming his victims and ridiculing them for being taken in . . . only to be extradited to the US, and imprisoned. He estimates his cons netted him at least $40 million but he could be lying. He is a conman, remember!

9 September

1956: Elvis Presley makes his first appearance on US TV's influential 'The Ed Sullivan Show'

Kings who aren't really

- King Kong (a fictitious giant ape)
- Nat King Cole (a fabulous singer and piano player)
- The King of the Beasts (lions)
- The Three Kings (wise men)
- Elvis Presley (a legend)
- Burger King (a burger outlet company)
- King Cotton (er – cotton)
- The King of Terrors (Death with a capital 'D')
- The Factory King (Richard Oastler, dedicated to improving the working conditions of factory workers, especially children)
- King of the King (Cardinal Richelieu)
- The King of Misrule (elected to oversee much silliness)
- The King of Bath (Richard 'Beau' Nash of the city of Bath)
- The Bean King (in charge of the revelry on Twelfth Night)
- King Charles Spaniel (a breed of dog)

10 September

*1977: murderer Hamida Djandoubi becomes the last person to be executed in France using the guillotine**

The children of Charles Dickens**

1. Charles Culliford Dickens, aka Charley (1837–96)
2. Mary Dickens, aka Mamie (1838–96)
3. Kate Macready Dickens, aka Katie (1839–1929)
4. Walter Savage Landor Dickens (1841–63)
5. Francis Jeffrey Dickens, aka Frank (1844–86)
6. Alfred D'Orsay Tennyson Dickens (1845–1912)
7. Sydney Smith Haldimand Dickens (1847–72)
8. Henry Fielding Dickens, aka Harry (1849–1933)
9. Dora Annie Dickens (1850–1)
10. Edward Bulwer Lytton Dickens, aka Plorn (1852–1902)

NB Their mother was Catherine Dickens (née Hogarth) whom Dickens married in 1836. They separated in 1858, which was a lot less common in those days.***

---

* Dr Joseph Ignace Guillotin didn't invent the guillotine, though it is named after him. He was the Deputy of Paris, who, in 1789, proposed that all condemned criminals should be beheaded by this method as it was the least cruel. This was agreed and became the official method of capital punishment in 1792. Many aristocrats were guillotined during the 'Reign of Terror' in the French Revolution

** Author of, among many others, the French Revolution novel *A Tale of Two Cities* beginning: 'It was the best of times. It was the worst of times . . .'

*** All of the children apart from Charley lived with Dickens after the separation.

11 September*

1961: Philip Ardagh, the author of this book, is born. (Oooh! That's me!)

A handful of people with whom I'm happy to share my birthday

1. 3 BC, **Jesus Christ****
2. 1862, **O. Henry**, US author (best known for his short stories)
3. 1885, **D. H. Lawrence**, English novelist***
4. 1917, **Herbert Lom**, brilliant film actor who, more often than not, played baddies or troubled souls****
5. 1969, **Gaby Morgan**, the editor of this book

* This was also the date on which, in 1895, the FA cup was stolen from the window of a Birmingham shop. In 1963 – some 68 years later – an 83-year-old man confessed to the crime. He claimed to have melted it down to make fake coins!

** According to the late Ernest L. Martin (1932–2002), who claimed that he had based this on the fact that 11 September in the year 3 BC was when the Moon moved in a rare pattern with Venus, generating the appearance of the bright celestial object referred to in Christian scriptures as the Star of Bethlehem. (No Christian scholar thinks Christ was actually born on 25 December.)

*** Auspicious literary company to be sharing such a special day with.

**** And played Chief Inspector Dreyfus, driven mad by Inspector Clouseau in the *Pink Panther* films.

12 September

1940: four boys looking for their dog discover the prehistoric cave paintings at Lascaux, France

Excuses involving dogs

1. The dog broke it. Honestly. I saw him do it.
2. The dog ate it. (Homework/Last slice of cake/TV remote.)
3. I'm late? The dog got off his lead and I've been trying to catch him all this time.
4. I have to go now. I've got to take the dog for a walk.
5. I know I'm under eighteen but my dog slipped off its lead and I'm sure I saw him run in here.
6. Of course I didn't bite/lick/push you! That was my dog.
7. I would have phoned but the dog ran off with my mobile.
8. Why would I be going through your bin? A stray dog knocked it over.
9. Of course I'm not spying on you. I ran up this tree to escape from a vicious dog!
10. That puddle on the floor has nothing to do with me!

13 September

1788: New York becomes the capital of the USA. For a bit.

The Empire State Building

- The Empire State Building gets its name from the nickname of the state of New York State itself.

- From 1931 to 1972 (when the World Trade Center's North Tower was completed), it was the tallest building in New York and the world.

- Since the destruction of the World Trade Center by terrorist attacks on 9/11 (11 September 2001), it has become the biggest building in New York once again. (The tallest building in the US is currently the Sears Tower in Chicago. The tallest in the world depends on your definition.)*

- At the same time as the construction of the Empire State Building, the Chrysler Building and 40 Wall Street were also being built. Both were the world's tallest building for short periods until the Empire State finally reached higher than them.

- The Empire State Building is 102 storeys high (the ground floor counting as the first).

- It's approximately 1,250 feet (381 metres) to the top of the 102nd floor, and 1,453 feet (and a bit) (443 metres) to the top of the antennae.

- Work began on preparing the site on 22 January 1930.

- Construction began on the building on 17 March 1930. It took just 410 days to complete. At one stage it was being built at the rate of one storey a day!

- Between 3,400 and 3,500 people worked on the building, mostly European immigrants, along with hundreds of Mohawk iron workers (famous for supposedly having a head for heights).

* Does the building have to be primarily for human habitation? If so, should the majority of its height be divided into floors for occupation? Should you include spires? Certainly not flag poles, but what about antennae?

- Five workers died during construction.
- It has:
  - 1,860 steps from street level to the 102nd floor
  - 73 lifts
  - 6,500 windows
  - a total floor area of 2.2 million square feet (200,000 square metres).
- It was officially opened by President Herbert Hoover on 1 May 1931, from Washington, DC, where he pressed a button which illuminated it in New York City!
- The building was originally intended as a landing platform for dirigibles (airships). This proved impractical and dangerous.
- In July 1945 a B-25 bomber crashed into the north side of the building – between the 79th and 80th floors – in thick fog. Fourteen people were killed but, amazingly, lift operator Betty Lou Oliver survived a plunge of 75 storeys inside a lift.
- In 1979 a woman jumped from the 86th floor, only to be blown back into the 85th floor. She had nothing physically worse than a broken hip.
- In the original *King Kong* film, the giant ape falls in love with a woman played by Fay Wray and later climbs the Empire State Building (only to be attacked by biplanes). When Fay Wray died in 2004 the lights in the building were switched off for a full 15 minutes in her honour.
- During Elizabeth II's Golden Jubilee in 2002, the building was illuminated in purple and gold in her honour and as a 'thank you' to the British people following the attacks on the twin towers of the World Trade Center on 9/11.

14 September

A few facts about the world's first manned balloon flight (and not just hot air)

- Frenchmen Joseph-Michel Montgolfier and Jacques-Étienne Montgolfier were two of 16 children.

- Their father Pierre owned a successful paper business in the small town of Vidalon, near Annonay, in southern France.

- While working for their father, Joseph and Étienne (as they were better known) had an active interest in science and undertook various experiments.

- In 1782 they discovered that if heated air was collected inside a large lightweight paper (or, later, fabric) bag, it caused the bag to rise up.

- They thought they'd discovered a new lighter-than-air gas formed in the heat which – surprise, surprise – they swiftly called 'Montgolfier Gas'. The truth was, however, that it was nothing more than hot air . . . which rises (because it becomes more buoyant when heated).

- They first demonstrated their discovery in public on 4 June 1783 at the marketplace in Annonay. They burned straw and wool under the large opening at the bottom of their bag.* This first balloon** rose somewhere between 1,000 and 2,000 metres into the air and stayed up there for about ten minutes, before coming back to Earth over a mile and a half away.

- They repeated the experiment in Paris and then travelled to Versailles.

---

* The bag is what we now call the envelope of a balloon. The basket beneath is the gondola.

** Although the Montgolfier brothers spelled their name without an 'e' at the end, their balloons were referred to as Montgolfière balloons.

- Here, on 19 September 1783, they not only employed a bigger balloon but also some passengers. The world's first balloon passengers were: a sheep, a rooster and a duck. The flight lasted about eight minutes and the balloon landed safely about 2 miles away. The spectacle was witnessed by Louis XVI, Marie Antoinette and the French court.

- Surprisingly, the first people to go up in a balloon were not the Montgolfier brothers themselves. This honour belongs to Jean-François Pilâtre de Rozier and François Laurent (better known as the Marquis d'Arlandes). Pilâtre de Rozier was a science teacher, and the Marquis d'Arlandes an infantry officer.

- The first manned free flight – in other words, the balloon wasn't tethered to the ground with a very long rope – took place on 21 November 1783. Jean-François Pilâtre de Rozier and the Marquis d'Arlandes flew for 5½ miles over Paris for about 25 minutes, making them the world's first human air travellers.

- Two of the most vital pieces of equipment on board were a bucket of water and a sponge . . . in case the balloon caught fire!

- In 1983 there were many events to commemorate the 200th anniversary of this historic flight. Martini, the drinks company, even ran a press ad in the UK saluting the achievement, pointing out that the Montgolfière balloon could have landed 'anytime, any place, anywhere' . . . which was the drink's advertising slogan at the time!*

- Joseph and Étienne Montgolfier were honoured by the French Académie des Sciences. They had invented air travel.

* I should know, I wrote that tribute ad myself!

15 September

A quick puff and pant around Britain's contribution to the modern Olympic movement

- In ancient Greece, the Olympic Games started in 776 BC and were held at Olympia over five days every four years. All wars between the Greek city-states were put on hold until the games were finished!*

- Events in the original Olympics included: running, wrestling, boxing, horse racing, chariot racing and the pentathlon (running, jumping, discus and javelin throwing).

- The last official Olympics were probably held in AD 393, the games being banned by the Christian Emperor Theodosius in AD 394. (There is now some archeological evidence, however, to suggest that the smaller versions of the games might have continued unofficially for a while.)

- In England, 'Mr Robert Dover[']s Olympick Games upon the Cotswold Hills' were under way by 1612 on Dover's Hill in Chipping Campden, Gloucestershire. Robert Dover was a local lawyer.

- The Cotswold Olympics were held on the Thursday and Friday of Whitsun (usually in May or June).

- Robert Dover personally presided over the games on his horse. He was dressed in finery that used to belong to the king himself. Spectators from all walks of life came to watch. The gentry were provided with tents and commoners were given rugs to sit on. There was plenty to drink!

- Competitors were called to the hill by the sounding of a hunting horn and the events themselves were started by the firing of a cannon.

---

* This was an all-male games. Married women weren't even allowed to spectate.

- Prizes included everything from silver cups to yellow favours.*
- The Cotswold Olympics included, among the more conventional sports: sword-play, cudgel-play,** sledgehammer-throwing and chess.
- The Civil War (between the Parliamentarians and Royalists) brought the games to an end in 1652. Ironically, the playing fields were the scene of battles between the forces. (Some sources say that Robert Dover died, aged 70, in that year. Others say that he died in 1641, aged 66!)
- After the restoration of the king (Charles II) in 1660, the games were reintroduced on a smaller scale. By the 1740s they were certainly popular once more but, over time, this popularity faded.
- The Cotswold games were firmly re-established in 1963, on the same site, and are a part of Chipping Campden's Scuttlebrook Wake (festival), attracting thousands of visitors.
- Whether or not Dr William Penny Brookes of Much Wenlock in Shropshire knew about the Cotswold Olympics, he held the first 'Brookes's Olympian Games' in his home town in 1850.
- Over time, the number of events increased, to include: football, cricket, running, long jump, quoits and even pig racing and a blindfold wheelbarrow race!
- Brookes was keen that the games were for 'every grade of man'; in other words, from every class and background.***
- Prizes included cash, medals and a laurel-wreath crown.****

***

* In the same way that, before a medieval joust, a lady would give a knight a favour showing her colours.
** A cudgel being a very large and unpleasant club!
*** And he did mean 'man' not 'human'. As with the ancient games, women were excluded.
**** As in the ancient Greek games.

- In 1865 Brookes founded the National (British) Olympic Association, holding the first games at the famous Crystal Palace in London. He was disappointed that it didn't attract the leading sportsmen because he couldn't get sponsorship.

- He did, however, attract the interest of a certain Frenchman named Baron Coubertin. The two men began corresponding in 1889 and, in 1890, the baron visited Much Wenlock to witness the games.

- As a result, Coubertin took up the cause which had long been Brookes's dream: to set up a modern, international Olympic Games. The baron had a few things that the Englishman didn't: power, wealth and influence. He turned the dream into a reality. Baron Coubertin founded the International Olympic Committee (IOC) in 1894.

- The first modern Olympics took place in Athens in 1896.

- Dr William Penny Brookes died a matter of months before this historic event, aged 86.

- Although Baron Coubertin is hailed as the father of the modern Olympic movement, Brookes's contribution is undeniable and fully recognized today.

- The baron incorporated the Englishman's idea of holding the Olympics at different venues, rather than at one permanent site. He also liked Brookes's idea of a grand opening procession and ceremony.

- In 1994, the then head of the IOC, Juan Antonio Samaranch, paid a special visit to Much Wenlock, where he laid a wreath on Brookes's grave. He acknowledged his enormous contribution to the modern Olympic movement by saying, 'I came to pay homage and tribute to Dr Brookes, who really was the founder of the modern Olympic Games.'

16 September

1620: the Mayflower * *sets sail from Plymouth bound for the New World****

Fish-shop favourites

- Around half the fish eaten in the UK is bought from fish 'n' chip shops.

- Cod is still the firm favourite fish in British fish 'n' chip shops, with haddock coming in second.

- Of the pies, steak-and-kidney still comes ahead of chicken-and-mushroom.

- Curry sauce is far more popular in northern fish 'n' chip shops than those down south. The same can also be said of mushy peas.

- Whether the saveloy is more popular than the sausage-in-batter or vice versa is hotly debated, with regional variations.

- Nearly everyone asks for their takeaway chips to be salted, and by far the majority have vinegar (or a cheaper vinegar substitute called 'non-brewed condiment', a solution of acetic acid, water and caramel, for colouring) too.

- The Maris Piper seems to be a favourite potato for making chips, though some sing the praises of Lincolnshire Whites.

- If anyone knows the average length of time a pickled egg or pickled onion sits in those big jars on top of the counter, they're not telling me.

- There are around 8,500 fish 'n' chip shops in the UK.

* Its passengers were the 'Pilgrim Fathers' but, as they included women and children, this is rather a misleading name to modern ears.**

** Whatever a modern ear may be.

*** They arrived at Cape Cod nine weeks later.

- A fish 'n' chip supper is no longer the cheap and cheerful meal it used to be – with fish prices rising by 11% and potatoes by 12.3% in 2006,* along with rises in gas and electricity prices. In 2007 the price of potatoes shot up too!

- More and more people seem to want to eat fish nowadays. Oily fish contains Omega 3, which is good for you, and – rightly or wrongly – people were put off eating chicken and turkey by the bird-flu outbreaks, so turned to fish.

- Many fish 'n' chip shops have silly names, often based around the pun 'fryer/friar'.

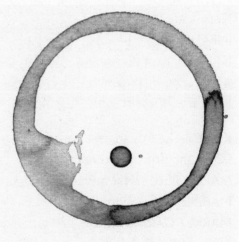

* According to the Office for National Statistics.

17 September

Some deadly serious operations involving British Forces on the Western Front in 1944 . . . by code name

ASTONIA: the Anglo-Canadian assault on Le Havre

BLUECOAT: the Anglo-Canadian advance to the River Vire

BRAVADO: mine-laying around the Kiel Canal

CLIPPER: the Anglo-American assault on Geilenkirchen

COMET: an early version of operation **MARKET GARDEN**

DIVER: the defence of London against V-1 rocket attack

EPSOM: the British assault west of Caen, Normandy

GAMBIT: the use of X-craft mini-subs as navigation beacons off Sword and Juno beaches

GOODWOOD: the largest British break-out attempt from Normandy**

INFATUATE: the final phase of the Battle of the Scheldt

JERICHO: the precision air raid on Amiens prison in an effort to free French Resistance prisoners

JUPITER: the British attack to occupy and hold Hill 112, near Caen

KITTEN: the British and Canadian advance to the River Seine

LOST: the British raid on Brittany

MAPLE: allied naval mine-laying operations

MARINE: mine-laying in the Rhine

MARKET GARDEN: the Allied airborne attempt to cross the lower Rhine at Arnhem

OVERLORD: the Allied landings on the Normandy beaches

* The basis for the film *A Bridge Too Far*.
** In fact, the largest tank battle the British army has ever fought.

PIRATE: Anglo-Canadian training exercise for D-Day, held at Studland Bay, England

PLUTO: the construction of undersea oil pipelines between England and France (Pipe Line Under the Ocean)

POMEGRANATE: the preparation for operation **GOODWOOD**

POSTAGE ABLE: landing-beach surveys using X-Craft mini-subs and divers

TIGER: Disastrous Allied training exercise for D-Day, held near Slapton, England

TONGA: British airdrop in Normandy, east of the Orne River

TOTALISE: Allied attempt to trap German armour in Normandy

TRACTABLE: the continuation of **TOTALISE**

TROUSERS: the Anglo-Canadian training exercise for D-Day, held near Slapton, England

18 September

A smattering of the more unusual entries to be found in Dr Johnson's famous dictionary

Dull: not exhilaterating;* not delightful; as, *to make dictionaries is dull work.*

Far-fetch: a deep stratagem. A ludicrous word.

Jobbernowl: loggerhead; blockhead.

Kickshaw: a dish so changed by the cookery that it can scarcely be known.

Lexicographer: a writer of dictionaries; a harmless drudge that busies himself in tracing the original, and detailing the signification of words.

Oats: a grain, which in England is generally given to horses, but in Scotland supports the people.

Pastern: the knee of a horse.**

Politician: 1. one versed in the arts of government; one skilled in politicks. 2. a man of artifice; one of deep contrivance.

---

* I suspect he might have meant 'not exhilarating'.

** This is an incorrect definition. When Johnson was later asked how he made the error he apparently said, 'Ignorance, Madam, pure ignorance.'***

*** This information, along with so much of what we know about Johnson, comes from his friend Boswell's biography *The Life of Johnson* (often referred to as *Boswell's Life of Johnson*).****

**** When Sherlock Holmes says 'I'm lost without my Boswell' he's referring to Dr John Watson, who committed so much of his life to paper.*****

***** If either had existed. Of course, they were both the creation of Sir Arthur Conan Doyle.******

****** Who used to be buried in the garden of the house where my maternal grandmother later lived out her final days.

19 September

The key differences between Dodie Smith's *The Hundred and One Dalmatians* and the Disney animated version

- For starters, they have subtly different titles. The 1956 children's novel is entitled *The Hundred and One Dalmatians* while the 1961 film is called *One Hundred and One Dalmatians.**

- In the book, Pongo marries Missis Pongo. When she has 15 puppies, they're worried how she'll cope until their 'pets' – which is what the dogs call their owners – find an abandoned Dalmatian to help with their upbringing, whom they call Perdita (meaning 'lost'). In the film, Pongo marries a dog named Perdita, and there is no stray.

- In the book, the dogs' 'pets' are called the Dearlys. In the film, they're Roger and Anita.

- In the book, Mr Dearly is a financial wizard who wiped out the government's National Debt. In the film, he's an impoverished songwriter.

- In the book, they have two nannies: Nanny Cook (who cooks) and Nanny Butler (who butles). In the film, there's just one.

- In the book, we discover that the odious Cruella de Vil is married to a furrier (a man who deals in animal furs). She also has a white Persian cat whom you might assume would be against the Dalmatians (dogs being a cat's natural enemy) but not at all. Cruella has drowned her kittens in the past, and the cat is biding her time until she can get her revenge.

* The 1996 live-action remake was entitled *101 Dalmatians.*

- In the book, the parent dogs' journey from London to Suffolk is told in much more detail, meeting more animals along the way.

- In the book, the Dalmatians are helped by a human too: Tommy Topkins* – the 'pet' of Colonel, the Old English Sheep Dog – who gives his toy hay cart to the Dalmatian puppy Cadpig to ride home in on their return journey.

- In the book, Cadpig is the runt of the litter. In the film it's Lucky.

- In the book, the 101st Dalmatian is the abandoned dog Perdita's lost love, Prince. They are reunited.

- The film** really is a Disney classic and surprisingly faithful to the book. The book, however, is even better still.***

* I wish it had been me. Imagine being a part of the greatest escape in canine history.

** It was the first animated film to use a new photocopying technique . . . which was very useful, what with all of those Dalmatian spots to draw!

*** There's a newish edition illustrated by David Roberts, who's illustrated nine of my books (so far).

20 September

1863: Jacob Grimm (one of the Brothers Grimm of Grimms' Fairy Tales fame) dies

A sneer of nasty fairy tales*

- The version of the *Three Little Pigs* in which the wolf comes down the chimney of the house made of bricks and is boiled alive in a large cooking pot.

- *Jack and the Beanstalk*, in which Jack not only trespasses and steals from an ogre living up in the clouds but also kills him – or, at the very least, causes him serious injury – by hacking down the beanstalk while the giant is chasing him down.

- *Hansel and Gretel*, which involves a cannibalistic old witch.

- The version of *Cinderella* in which the two ugly sisters have their eyes pecked out by pigeons – yes, pigeons – for being so cruel to poor little Cinders.

- The version of *Snow White* in which the huntsman who spares her life kills a passing young bear, cutting out its lungs and liver, and in which the queen is forced to put on red-hot iron slippers and dance until she drops down dead.

- The version of *Little Red Riding Hood* in which the wolf is disembowelled to free whoever it was he swallowed whole.

- *Three Billy Goats Gruff*, in which three goats terrorize a troll who lives under a bridge and then physically assault him.

* And these are just the well-known ones. The names of many lesser-known fairy tales give away just how nasty they are. These include: *The Girl Without Hands* and *Godfather Death*.

21 September

A coterie of pretenders to the English throne

In this instance, the term 'pretender' refers to someone claiming the title of being the rightful King or Queen of England (and probably Ireland, Scotland and Wales too) usually while someone else already has that role and is on the throne. The word 'pretender' rather suggests that they're making the whole thing up – pretending to be something that they're not – but, in some instances, some pretenders had very legitimate claims indeed. History, remember, is written by the victors.

Lady Jane Grey

When Henry VIII died, his son Edward became king. Edward had two sisters: Mary Tudor and Elizabeth (later Elizabeth I). Edward VI was persuaded that when he died, rather than let his elder sister succeed him, he should make his cousin, Jane, queen. He agreed, but Parliament didn't. When Edward died, Lady Jane Grey did become queen in 1553 . . . but only for nine days. Mary Tudor then claimed her rightful place on the throne. Jane was executed, poor thing: a pawn in a political game.

James Francis Edward Stuart

When Charles II died, his Catholic brother James VII of Scotland was crowned King James II of England. In 1688, five lords and two commoners invited William of Orange to become king and restore Protestant rule. He landed with an army of 15,000 and James II fled. After James's death, his son James Francis Edward Stuart claimed the throne, and was supported by the Jacobites, who thought William and his successors had no right to be monarchs. James Stuart became known as 'the Old Pretender'.

Charles Edward Stuart

Charles was the son of James Francis Edward Stuart and grandson of the former King James II. Known as the Young Pretender, his claim to the throne was, therefore, a pretty legitimate one though not, of course, in the eyes of his enemies (or not publicly, at least). Also known as Bonnie Prince Charlie, he arrived in Scotland in 1745, where a number of Highland clans came to fight in his name. He took the city of Edinburgh, defeated the British force at Prestonpans and advanced as far south as Derby before having to retreat. In April 1746 his forces were utterly routed at Culloden Moor. Despite being hunted by the English for over five months, he was never betrayed by the Highlanders who hid him. He eventually escaped to France. Charlie was both born and died in Rome.

Henry Benedict Stuart

When Charles – who thought of himself as Charles III – died in 1788, his brother Henry Benedict Stuart assumed the Jacobite claim, calling himself Henry IX of England. Since his death in 1807, the Jacobite 'monarchs' have never publicly used their titles or pushed their claims.

Franz Bonaventura Adalbert Maria Herzog von Bayern

Born 14 July 1933, His Royal Highness* The Duke of Bavaria is head of the former ruling family of the Kingdom of Bavaria. He is a great-grandson of the last King of Bavaria, Ludwig III, who was deposed** in 1918. Franz's family were opposed to the Nazis and in October 1944 (when he was just 11) he and his family were sent to a number of concentration camps. He was liberated in April 1945. What gets him on this list, however, is the fact that he's considered by 21st-century Jacobites to be the current rightful ruler of Great Britain.

Franz is another descendant of England's Catholic King James II who was deposed in 1688 and replaced by the Protestant William of Orange. In Jacobite circles, therefore, Franz is known as King Francis II of England. Unmarried and without children, the title will pass to his brother Prince Max on his death. On Max's death, the position of heir of the House of Stuart – and, therefore, some would argue, the rightful ruler of Great Britain – will go to his daughter Sophie.

* An honorary title.
** He was overthrown and the monarchy ceased to exist.

NB Being a Jacobite – a supporter not of the monarch on the throne but a pretender overseas – was a dangerous business. Many people hid their true beliefs. The deposed James II (and his descendants, in turn) was referred to as 'the king over the water'. Traditionally, the first toast – as in raising of glasses after dinner – was to the king, at that time King George. A Jacobite might, however, simply say, 'The King!' and raise his glass over a water decanter on the table . . . in other words, he was making a toast to the king *over the water*: a secret code as to where his true loyalty lay.

22 September

British prime ministers from Walpole to Brown, according to the Prime Minister's own website

1. 1721–42, Sir Robert Walpole
2. 1742–3, Spencer Compton, Earl of Wilmington
3. 1743–54, Henry Pelham
4. 1754–6, 1757–62, Thomas Pelham-Holles, Duke of Newcastle
5. 1756–7, William Cavendish, Duke of Devonshire
6. 1762–3, John Stuart, Earl of Bute
7. 1763–5, George Grenville
8. 1765–6, 1782, Charles Wentworth, Marquess of Rockingham
9. 1766–8, Earl of Chatham, aka William Pitt 'the Elder'**
10. 1768–70, Augustus Henry Fitzroy, Duke of Grafton
11. 1770–82, Lord North
12. 1782–3, William Petty, Earl of Shelburne
13. 1783, 1807–9, William Bentinck, Duke of Portland
14. 1783–1801, 1804–6, William Pitt 'the Younger'***
15. 1801–4, Henry Addington
16. 1806–7, William Wyndam Grenville, Lord Grenville
17. 1809–12, Spencer Perceval
18. 1812–27, Robert Banks Jenkinson, Earl of Liverpool
19. 1827, George Canning
20. 1827–8, Frederick Robinson, Viscount Goderich
21. 1828–30, Arthur Wellesley, Duke of Wellington
22. 1830–34, Earl Grey
23. 1834, 1835–41, William Lamb, Viscount Melbourne

* Though he was actually called 'first minister'. The official term 'prime minister' didn't come in until 1905.

** When the world was younger.

*** When the world was older.

24. 1834–5, 1841–6, Sir Robert Peel*
25. 1846–51, 1865–6, Earl Russell
26. 1852, 1858–9, 1866–8, Earl of Derby
27. 1852–5, Earl of Aberdeen
28. 1855–8, 1859–65, Viscount Palmerston
29. 1868, 1874–80, Benjamin Disraeli
30. 1868–74, 1880–85, 1886, 1892–4, William Ewart Gladstone
31. 1885–6, 1886–92, 1895–1902, Robert Gascoyne-Cecil, Marquess of Salisbury
32. 1894–5, Earl of Rosebery
33. 1902–5, Arthur James Balfour
34. 1905–8, Henry Campbell-Bannerman
35. 1908–16, Herbert Henry Asquith
36. 1916–22, David Lloyd George
37. 1922–3, Andrew Bonar Law
38. 1923, 1924–9, 1935–7, Stanley Baldwin
39. 1924, 1929–35, James Ramsay MacDonald
40. 1937–40, Arthur Neville Chamberlain
41. 1940–45, 1951–5, Sir Winston Leonard Spencer Churchill
42. 1945–51, Clement Attlee
43. 1955–7, Anthony Eden
44. 1957–63, Harold Macmillan
45. 1963–4, Sir Alec Douglas-Home
46. 1964–70, 1974–6, Harold Wilson
47. 1970–74, Edward Heath
48. 1976–9, James Callaghan
49. 1979–90, Margaret Thatcher
50. 1990–97, John Major
51. 1997–2007, Tony Blair
52. 2007–, Gordon Brown

* After whom the police got the nicknames peelers and bobbies.

23 September

1846: Johann Galle discovers Neptune*

Things we often call something else

- A fork's prongs are actually called *tines*.

- A bar of soap used to be a great big block that one cut smaller pieces off. The thing we (should) wash our hands with is really a *cake* of soap.

- Alsatian dogs should technically be called *German Shepherd* dogs.

- MI5 stopped being called MI5 in 1929 but that doesn't stop everyone calling it MI5, even MI5 themselves on their own MI5 website.

- The MOT of MOT simply stands for Ministry of Transport. 'An MOT' is really an MOT *test* or *certificate*.

- ID isn't short for 'Identity' but stands for *Identity Document* so, technically, it's nonsense to ask for 'proof of ID' or for 'ID papers'.

- The correct term for a coin's head and tails is *obverse* and *reverse*.

- It's wrong to call a *koala* a koala bear because they aren't bears.

- Technically, there are no burglaries during daylight hours but, before you express amazement at this apparent drop in crime, I hasten to add that there are break-ins. Burglaries happen after dark.

* The Roman sea god Neptune (and his Greek counterpart Poseidon) carried a trident: a three-pronged spear.

24 September

1940: King George VI institutes the George Cross, the civilian equivalent of the Victoria Cross*

Some very heroic people indeed

The most recent award

At the time of compiling this list, the most recent recipient of the George Cross is Corporal Mark Wright of the 3rd Battalion, the Parachute Regiment. He was awarded his George Cross posthumously having died on 6 September 2006 from injuries he sustained when entering a minefield in Afghanistan to try to save injured soldiers. Despite further mine detonations, and being badly injured by a mine he himself stepped on, he managed to keep up the morale of other wounded men. He died in the helicopter taking him to a field dressing station.

The most recent civilian award

This award was also awarded posthumously. The recipient was Sergeant Stewart Guthrie of the New Zealand police. He was killed during efforts to apprehend a crazed gunman in the 'Aramoana Massacre' on 13 November 1990.

The largest collective award

In April 1942 King George VI conferred the George Cross on the Mediterranean island of Malta. The king's letter to its governor, Lieutenant General Sir William Dobbie, included the announcement:

> 'To honour her brave people I award the George Cross to the Island Fortress of Malta to bear witness to a heroism and devotion that will long be famous in history.'

This was in recognition of the their courage under sustained enemy attacks during the Second World War. As a result, the George Cross was added to the Maltese flag.

* And for military personnel 'for gallant conduct which is not in the face of the enemy'.

The youngest (individual) recipient

Early in the morning of 19 October 1952 a fire started downstairs in the home of the Bamford family in Newthorpe. Mr Bamford and his eldest son John (then aged 15 years, seven months) managed to get Mrs Bamford and three other children out, but that left two boys (aged two and six) still trapped inside. By now the stairs were ablaze and in danger of collapse but John fought his way through the flames and found his frightened brothers huddled together. John managed to throw both of them out of the window to their father below. Badly burned and about to lose consciousness, he then managed to follow them through the window. John Bamford was in hospital for the next four months and underwent numerous skin-graft operations.

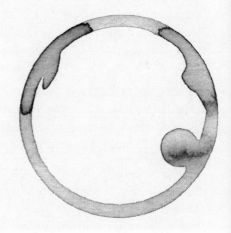

25 September

Headlines with something to shout about (which sometimes put their foot in it)

TITANIC SUNK – NO LIVES LOST
A tragically inaccurate headline from the *Daily Mirror* in 1912.

DEWEY BEATS TRUMAN
screamed the *Chicago Daily Tribune* headline in the 1948 US presidential election . . . In fact, Harry S. Truman won!

IF KINNOCK WINS TODAY WILL THE LAST PERSON TO LEAVE BRITAIN PLEASE TURN OUT THE LIGHTS
The *Sun's* subtle hint that voting for Labour in 1992 might cause a mass exodus from Britain.

GOTCHA!
This was the tasteless headline the *Sun* newspaper ran when the Argentinean ship the *Belgrano* was sunk during the Falklands War in 1984.

KILL AN ARGIE AND WIN A MINI METRO
The headline for a fictitious competition on a spoof *Sun* cover produced by satirical magazine *Private Eye*. (Today, some people who remember the headline, or being told about it, remember it as a genuine *Sun* headline.)

POPE ELOPES!
Another made-up headline, this time by famous American wit Dorothy Parker, who came up with a sensational headline in just two words . . . however unlikely it might be.

IT'S A BOY! EXCLUSIVE – MACCA BABY A MONTH EARLY!
It wasn't. Still, the *Mirror* had a 50% chance of getting the sex of Sir Paul McCartney's latest child, Beatrice, right.

FREDDIE STARR ATE MY HAMSTER

A genuine headline in – you guessed it – the *Sun* again, but
that doesn't mean that the story was true. It was apparently
'placed' by media guru (?) Max Clifford.

SO WHERE ARE THEY, MR BLAIR?

asks the *Independent on Sunday*'s 2003 headline of Saddam
Hussain's non-existent weapons of mass destruction.

SUPER CALEY GO BALLISTIC, CELTIC ARE ATROCIOUS

A pun on Mary Poppins's special word 'supercalifragilistic-
expialidocious', this headline for a Scottish football story
appeared in the *Sun* in 2000.

26 September

*1580: Francis Drake sails into Plymouth in the
Golden Hind, having sailed around the world*

Some of the round-ish things in my office today*

- Wall clock
- CDs and DVDs
- Coffee cup rim
- Telephone buttons on the fax machine
- Little bits of paper from the hole-punch
- Goliath fob watch (aka a turnip, aka a very LARGE fob watch)
- Dial on my repro retro Bush radio
- 'I'm a rare breed' sticker from the Rare Breeds Farm
- The 'O's on the cover of my 2007 desk diary
- The base of my *Deutscher Jugendliteraturpreis* statuette
- Wire-mesh** pen-holder
- A colourful thingy covered in glitter and twirly pipecleaners made by my son at nursery
- Little black magnet on the back of my Moominpapa fridge magnet***
- Lid off the Pritt stick
- Tip of the jack plugs for my laptop computers
- Magnifying-glass lens
- Lenses in my glasses
- Adjustable pencil-width dial on my desk-mounted pencil-sharpener

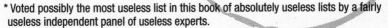

* Voted possibly the most useless list in this book of absolutely useless lists by a fairly useless independent panel of useless experts.

** The holder, not the pens.

*** Not currently being used on a fridge. (I hope that's legal?)

- Lid to a jar of pennies
- Pennies themselves
- Roll of Sellotape
- Caran d'Ache logo on my Caran d'Ache pens
- Big metal-rimmed holes* in the spines of my fatter ring binders
- Face of my wristwatch
- Glass eyes of my hand-made Malcolm the stuffed stoat soft toy**
- Ribs of my paper lampshade***

* I've no idea of their function.
** Though please don't tell him I called him that.
*** Cheapskate.

27 September

*1389: Cosimo de' Medici, the great statesman
and financier from Florence, is born*

A quick spin on
*The Magic Roundabout**

- Regular characters (original French name in *italics*):
  - ◆ Zebedee (*Zebulan*), the springy chap with the big moustache, who used to say 'Time for bed!'
  - ◆ Florence (*Margotte*), the big-booted girl
  - ◆ Dougal (*Pollux*), the sugar-lump-loving shaggy dog and real star of the show)**
  - ◆ Brian (*Ambroise*), the boater-wearing snail
  - ◆ Dylan (*Flappy*), the laid-back guitar-wielding rabbit
  - ◆ Ermintrude (*Azalée*), the flower-chewing cow
  - ◆ Mr Rusty (*Père Pivoine*), the owner of the roundabout
  - ◆ Mr MacHenry (the gardener)
  - ◆ The train (a train)
  - ◆ Plus other children

- The original UK BBC TV series was by Eric Thompson*** or, more to the point, he took the original Serge Danot episodes and wrote an English soundtrack, using the stories and dialogue which he thought best fitted the visuals (and rarely had much to do with Danot's scripts). They were deliberately much more witty and (sometimes) anarchic than the French originals.****

- A song by 1960s Liverpudlian group the Scaffold – made up of Mike McGear (Paul McCartney's brother Michael McCartney), Roger McGough (the poet) and John Gorman –

---

* Created by Frenchman Serge Danot in 1965, *Le Manège Enchanté* ran for over 400 episodes.

** Briton Ivor Wood, famous for the stop-frame puppets in many UK TV programmes including *Postman Pat*, worked for Danot at the time and came up with the idea for a dog character (with legs 'hidden' so he could really run on wheels!)

*** Father of Oscar-winning actress Emma Thompson.

**** And was by far the most popular programme on British TV, with over eight million viewers at its peak.

included the lines: 'Now we hurry home to see / Brian the snail and Zebedee.'

- In 1992 Channel 4 bought hitherto untranslated episodes for which Nigel Planer* did the English scripts and narration.

- 1972 saw the release of *Dougal and the Blue Cat*, a disturbing full-length feature film in which a blue cat takes the regular characters prisoner. Surreal and chilling, it's WEIRD, to say the least!

- In 2005 the brand-new *The Magic Roundabout*** film was released, which needlessly came up with new-look characters, employed celebrity voices and surgically removed much of the charm of the original.

* Neil from BBC TV's *The Young Ones*.
** Called *Doogal* in the US, as is Dougal!

28 September

No loitering: short stays at the top

- Pope Benedict V's papal reign was one day shorter than John Paul I's, at just 33 days in AD 964.

- The Pope with the shortest reign – not counting Pope Stephen, because the Vatican itself no longer does – was Urban VII in 1590. He reigned for 13 calendar days and died before consecration.

- Lady Jane Grey was Queen of England for just nine days in 1553, though many historians don't count her as a 'proper' monarch.

- At the time of writing, the person who was the world's oldest person for the shortest time was Emma Tillman. She died on 28 January 2007 aged 114, having been the world's oldest for just four days. Her parents had been former slaves and she had been a nurse to film-star Katharine Hepburn.

- A number of Miss Worlds have either resigned or been stripped of their title. The one with the shortest reign to date was the 1980 winner Gabriela Brum of Germany. Her reign lasted less than a day. She was forced to resign after it was discovered that she'd appeared nude in photos in a magazine.

- Edward V ruled England for just two months in April 1483 before being deposed by his uncle, who then became Richard III. It's thought that he and his younger brother were murdered in the Tower of London.

- King Louis X of France – also known as Louis the Quarreller, Louis the Headstrong and Louis the Stubborn – reigned for just two years, dying after a game of *jeu de paume,* a kind of tennis without rackets.*

* You used your hands.

29 September

1829: London's Metropolitan Police Force
is founded*

Different types of nose (some incorporating mouths)

Category A:
Beak
Bill

Category B:
Trunk
Proboscis

Category C:
Roman
Aquiline
Snub
Button

Category D:
Broken
Bloody
Blocked up

Misc:
Pierced
Electronic

* Slang terms for the police include the 'Old Bill'

30 September

At least twenty films filmed, in part at least, at Pinewood Studios

1. *Alexander*
2. *Batman* series
3. *Carry On* series
4. *Charlie and the Chocolate Factory**
5. *Chitty Chitty Bang Bang*
6. *The Da Vinci Code*
7. *Doctor in the House* and the other *Doctor* films
8. *Dr No* and most of the other Bond films
9. *Eragon*
10. *The Fifth Element*
11. *Interview with a Vampire*
12. *Lara Croft: Tomb Raider*
13. *Miss Potter*
14. *Mission Impossible*
15. *The Mummy*
16. *Nanny McPhee*
17. *Planet of the Apes**
18. *Superman* series
19. *Thunderbirds*
20. *Trouble in Store***

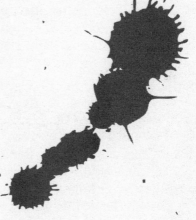

* The Tim Burton one.
** With Norman Wisdom.

1 October

1868: St Pancras Station opens in London

A few facts about a saint whom most people seem to think of as a railway station

Name: St Pancras
aka: St Pancritas or St Pancratius
Saint's Day: 12 May
Born: AD c. 290
Place of Birth: Phrygia (Turkey)
Died: AD c. 304
Place of Death: Rome
Cause of Death: Beheaded

Patron Saint of: oaths, treaties, headaches, cramps, children, against false witness and perjury

In Life

As a 14-year-old orphan, Pancras was brought to Rome by his uncle, (St) Dionysius, and converted to Christianity. Here, he publicly proclaimed his new-found faith, which was punishable by death. He became a martyr when he was executed along with St Nereus, St Achilleus and St Domitilla.

In Death

St Pancras was buried on the Via Aurelia, Rome: the place of his execution. Centuries later, Pope Symmachus (Pope from 498 to 514) built a church over his tomb. His relics were interred in St Pancras Church, Rome, but were destroyed in 1798. St Pancras's head – he was beheaded, remember – is still in the basilica* of St John Lateran, also in Rome.

Pope Vitalian (Pope from 657 to 672) sent some of his relics to England to help spread Christianity. The very first Christian church in England was a former pagan temple in Canterbury, re-dedicated to St Pancras by St Augustine. Many English churches (and the railway station) are named after him.

* The title given by popes to special churches remarkable for their age or historical associations.

2 October

1870: Rome becomes capital city of the newly founded Italy

Ten untrue sayings

1. 'All roads lead to Rome.' No they don't.

2. 'Sticks and stones may break my bones but words can never hurt me.' Oh yes they can.

3. 'A watched pot never boils.' It does if it's heated long enough.

4. 'A stitch in time saves nine.' You what?

5. 'No man is an island.' Well, they could be a very small one.

6. 'All work and no play makes Jack a dull boy.' It depends upon the job.

7. 'Never apologize. Never explain.' I'm sorry?

8. 'Let sleeping dogs lie.' What if they're blocking a fire exit?

9. 'Time is a great healer.' It also gives you an opportunity to bleed to death.

10. 'A bird in the hand is worth two in the bush.' It depends on whether you're a taxidermist or an RSPB officer.*

* Shouldn't these asides really be footnotes?**
** Probably, Philip, but you really should stop talking to yourself.'

3 October

A recipe of rationing during the Second World War

- *The weekly ration (amounts varying over time):*
  4 oz (113 g) bacon or ham
  2 oz (57 g) butter
  1–2 oz (28–50 g) cheese
  1 egg per week or 1 packet (makes 12 'eggs') of egg
    powder per month
  2 oz (57 g) fat or lard
  2 oz (57 g) jam (1 lb every two months)
  2 oz (57 g) margarine
  1s 6d (approximately 1 lb 3 oz or 540 g) of meat**
  3 pints (1.7 litres) of milk per week or one packet of milk
    powder per month
  2 lb (907 g) onions
  3–8 oz (85–225 g) sugar
  3 oz (85 g) sweets
  2 oz (57 g) tea
  + 16 'points' per month for tinned and dried food

- Everyone was issued with a ration book containing
  coupons. When paying for food, people had to hand over
  the relevant ration coupons at the same time. No coupon,
  no ration of that particular food.***

- Pregnant women were given special green ration books
  to get extra food rations. Breastfeeding mothers received
  extra milk.

- Bread was never rationed. The 'National Loaf' was
  introduced, made to a set recipe across the nation.

---

* It wasn't until 4 July 1954 that all rationing ended (sweet rationing ended 5 February 1953).

** Sausages weren't rationed but were very rare.

*** Unless you bought food illegally and at inflated prices on the black market.

- The government set the price of food.
- Potatoes, coffee, vegetables and fruit weren't rationed either, though choice and availability was limited. Many people grew their own veg and kept hens for eggs.
- Meals eaten out in restaurants, cafes and canteens weren't 'on the rations' (you didn't need to use any of your ration coupons). This meant that those with more money could eat far better. To try to lessen this gap between the rich and poor, a cap of five shillings on a meal at a restaurant was set in 1942.
- Because food was scarce, people were discouraged from 'wasting' it on feeding the birds. Sparrows were nicknamed 'Hitler's feathered friends'!
- It wasn't just food that was rationed: petrol and clothing were too.

4 October

1931: the first Dick Tracy *comic strip is published*

A mobile phone by any other name . . .

- Dick Tracy's two-way radio wristwatch
- 'Kirk-to-Enterprise' *Star Trek* communicator
- *The Man from U.N.C.L.E.* (United Network Command for Law and Enforcement) pen radio transmitter
- *Get Smart's* Maxwell Smart's in-shoe-heel two-way radio
- Inspector Gadget's hand phone . . . Not hand held, it actually came out of his hand: an aerial from one finger, ear-piece and mouth-piece from others
- James Bond's clothes-brush communicator with radio and Morse code transmitter;* CIA two-way car cigarette lighter;* his quartz watch teletype;** his two-way radio Seiko wristwatch with digital message readouts***

---

* *Live and Let Die.*
** *The Spy Who Loved Me.*
*** *For Your Eyes Only.*

5 October

The end of the airship era

- The *R101* was designed and built at Cardington, Bedfordshire, by the Royal Airship Works.

- When designing the airship, all measurements were made in millimetres, centimetres and metres, even though at the time Britain still officially used the imperial measurements of feet and inches (right up to metrication in 1971).

- The shape of an airship was usually determined by moulding flexible wooden laths. In the case of the *R101*, it was calculated using a mathematical curve devised by Dr Harold Roxbee Cox, who was instrumental in the ship's design.

- At 237 metres (777 feet), the *R101* was for a time the largest flying object ever built.

- When returning from the Hendon airshow in June 1930, the airship went into a 150-metre nosedive before regaining control. There were a number of other glitches on the flight.

- There remained a number of technical problems that the team needed to iron out but Lord Thompson, the Secretary of State for Air, insisted that it be ready for a flight to India on 4 October 1930. (It was no secret that he had political ambitions in the subcontinent.) Regarding whether or not the *R101* was ready to fly, however, he did write: 'You mustn't allow my natural impatience or anxiety to start to influence you in any way. You must use your considered judgement.'

- A test flight of 17 hours over two days took place prior to the actual voyage and the airship was deemed flightworthy by the captain and those responsible.

- Dr Roxbee Cox wanted to go on the *R101*'s first all-important flight to India, but lost his place to the VIPs who wished to travel. This turned out to be extremely fortunate for him.

- 4 October came, and a crowd of over 3,000 came to

witness its departure. There were 42 crew, six officials and six passengers on board.

- Things went wrong early on. Because the airship was overloaded, some of the ballast had to be dropped overboard, strong winds made steering difficult and – if that wasn't enough – the aft (rear) engines broke down.

- At around 2 o'clock the following morning, the *R101* passed over the French city of Beauvais, north-west of Paris. She went into a dive and hit the ground.

- The official inquiry noted that the *R101* had reduced to a ground speed that would have been ideal for a perfect landing: 13.8 mph. The airship bounced a little, slid forward around 20 metres and then stopped.

- It was after it had come to a halt that it burst into flames.

- Of the 54 people on board, 48 people died in the tragedy. All six survivors were crew members.

- There was an enormous outpouring of national grief. The victims were accorded full state honours, their bodies brought back aboard HMS *Tempest* to Dover, where special trains brought them to Victoria Station.

- The bodies were taken to Westminster Hall at the Palace of Westminster, where they were laid in state. Thousands of members of the public filed past the coffins. The bodies were then taken by a special train to be buried in a communal grave in a small churchyard in Cardington village.

- There was also a memorial service at St Paul's Cathedral on 11 October.

- The plan to build fleets of airships as part of the 'Airship Scheme' was cancelled.

- An official inquiry later determined that the terrible disaster had not been caused by a design fault but by a hydrogen leak.

- Dr Roxbee Cox, later Sir Harold, and later Lord Kings Norton, went on to have a number of key roles in aviation, and worked closely with Frank Whittle, inventor of the jet engine.

6 October

1889: the Moulin Rouge opens in Paris

A skyful of windmill-related stuff

'A Windmill In Old Amsterdam'

Not an actual windmill but a song about one or, more to the point, about the mice who live in it. It starts out as one mouse but soon becomes a (happy) infestation. By Ted Dicks and Myles Rudge, the song begins 'A mouse lived in a windmill in old Amsterdam' and contains the memorable lines: 'I saw a mouse! Where? There on the stair . . .'

The windmills of Holland / the Netherlands / call it what you will

There are estimated to be around 1,150 working windmills in Holland, with more currently under restoration. There are over 4,000 either vanished, ruined or no longer in use. Some were used for grinding grain, others for pumping out water for drainage.

The Windmill Theatre

A London theatre famous for showing nude tableaux (in which the naked people weren't actually allowed to move) and for the slogan 'We Never Closed',* referring to the fact that it stayed open throughout the Blitz, when London was being repeatedly bombed by the German Luftwaffe in the Second World War. This period of the theatre's history was the subject of the 2005 film *Mrs Henderson Presents,* starring Dame Judi Dench and Bob Hoskins.

The windmills of old Amsterdam

There used to be 89 or 90 windmills in the Dutch capital of Amsterdam. There are still eight working windmills dotted around the city.

'Tilting at windmills'

A phrase meaning attacking enemies that don't even exist. Tilting in this case refers to the thrust of a lance when

* Sometimes adapted to 'We're Never Clothed'.

jousting. The phrase is derived from Cervantes's 1605 novel*
Don Quixote.** In the novel, Quixote plans to attack a group
of windmills, believing them to be giants. In 1644 it was
commented in print that 'the Quixotes of this Age fight with
the Wind-mills of their owne Heads' but, apparently, the oldest
printed record of the actual phrase 'to tilt at windmills' doesn't
appear until 1937 and Agatha Christie's *Death on the Nile*.***

'The Windmills of Your Mind'

An extraordinarily haunting song by Alan and Marilyn
Bergman and Michel Legrand used as the theme for the original
1968 film *The Thomas Crown Affair*. Begins with: 'Like a circle
in a spiral, like a wheel within a wheel / Never ending or
beginning on an ever spinning reel . . .'

---

* Originally published as *The Ingenious Knight of La Mancha*.

** For years pronounced *don quick-so* in the UK, but nowadays, the more correct *don kee-ow-tee*, since he's Spanish.

*** Surely not!?

7 October

1931: Desmond Tutu, Nobel Prize winner, archbishop
and anti-apartheid campaigner, is born*

Clothes named after people rather than people who share names with clothes

Cardigan
This can either be described as a button-fronted sweater or a knitted jacket, being one and the same. Especially designed to keep British soldiers warm in the freezing Russian winters, the cardigan is named after the Seventh Earl of Cardigan** who led the Charge of the Light Brigade.***

Garibaldi jacket and Garibaldi shirt
Bright-red woollen garments with military detailing in black braiding or embroidery, popular in the 1860s. Though named after the Italian revolutionary Giuseppe Garibaldi,**** they were worn by women.

Ike jacket
(sometimes referred to as the Eisenhower jacket)
A waist-length, Second World War military jacket more correctly called the Jacket, Field, Wool, M-1944.***** It gained its name from the fact that it was commissioned by Dwight Eisenhower (then a general).

Mao jacket
A lapel-less jacket with a raised collar, similar to that worn by Chairman Mao (Mao Tse Tung/Mao Zedong) and people in China during the Cultural Revolution. Very plain and often grey.

* Also the name of a female ballet dancer's costume.
** James Brudenell.
*** In the Crimean War.
**** Who also had the 'squashed-flies' biscuit named after him.
***** Based on the British Army's battledress jacket.

Nehru jacket

Similar in many ways to a Mao jacket but with a longer length. Collarless and lapel-less, it was made popular by Jawaharlal Nehru, the first prime minister of independent India.

Wellington boots

The traditional wellington boot was a smooth boot designed to go under the trouser leg rather than over it (unlike earlier boots with fold-down tops, more popular when trousers were shorter). These original wellies weren't rubber and were based on the Hessian boot worn in Germany. They got the name from the First Duke of Wellington, Arthur Wellesley, who was a big fan of them.

NB

Chinos – the trousers – aren't named after a person but from the Spanish meaning 'toasted' because they're often toast-coloured!

Sweaters are sometimes called jumpers because they resemble a 'jump', meaning a short jacket.

T-shirts are called T-shirts because, you guessed it, they look like the letter T when laid flat (which is why you should always spell T-shirt with a capital T).

8 October

Mini-Me

- Mini-Me is the character who appears in the *Austin Powers* films played by actor-cum-stuntman Verne Troyer who, among many other roles, also appeared in *Harry Potter and the Philosopher's Stone*.

- A miniature clone of Dr Evil, Mini-Me is described as being 'one-eighth' the size of the doctor.*

- Mini-Me copies Dr Evil's mannerisms but rarely speaks, apart from an 'Eeeeeeeeee' or two. On one occasion when he sings, his voice is very deep and manly.

- Mini-Me has a kitten called Mini-Mr Bigglesworth, to complement Dr Evil's own cat.

- Mini-Me's arch-rival is Dr Evil's son, Scott Evil. Scott Evil has referred to him as that 'Chihuahua thing'.

- Dr Evil has also referred to Mini-Me being 'like a dog or something' and has even kept him on a lead!

- Mini-Me has a particular penchant for Belgian chocolate.

- There are a number of strong contenders for the inspiration behind the character:

1. Both the bald Dr Evil and Mini-Me look remarkably like the film version of James Bond's arch-enemy Blofeld (with cat to stroke and all), who had a clone in *Diamonds Are Forever*.

2. Another major contender is Dr Moreau's sidekick in the 1996 film version of *The Island of Dr Moreau*,** in which he not only dresses identically to the doctor but also duets with him on the piano!

3. At the top of the list, though, comes Scaramanga's henchman, diminutive Nick Nack in the James Bond adventure *The Man with the Golden Gun*.

* Though he actually looks much larger. (Troyer is 2 ft 7 in tall.)
** In which Dr Moreau is played by Marlon Brando.

9 October

1701: Yale University is founded in the USA

Twenty problems I've had with my keys over the years

1. Losing them.
2. Having them stolen.
3. Thinking I've lost them (then finding them later).
4. Thinking I've had them stolen (then finding them later).
5. Forgetting where I've put them (but managing to find them).
6. Putting the wrong key in the lock.
7. Putting the right key in the wrong lock.
8. Putting the wrong key in the wrong lock.
9. Putting the right key in the right lock, but with great difficulty in the dark.
10. Putting the right key in the right lock, but with great difficulty because a dog is tearing at my trouser leg/I've been 'celebrating'/I have a headache/I am distracted.
11. Their eventually rubbing a hole in my trouser pocket.
12. Their being painful to roll over on to while in a pocket.
13. The 'whistle-and-I'll-bleep' keyring they're attached to arousing the suspicion of the US secret service during a tour of the White House in 1991.
14. Their setting off various metal detectors during moments of absent-mindedness.
15. Hurting my teeth when clenching a key between them.
16. Bending back my thumbnail very painfully when trying to put a new Yale key on a keyring that doesn't have one of those easy-open links.
17. Dropping a big bunch of keys in the audience during a theatrical performance, causing much tutting and a reaction on stage.

18. Hiding my keys in my left slipper when in hospital, then jamming my toes up against them when I'd forgotten all about it.

19. Using my front-door key as a prop during a photo-shoot, then worrying that someone may trace round it, have a duplicate cut and use it to get into my house and take things.

20. Using them as a subject for a list in this book, and trying to come up with twenty problems!

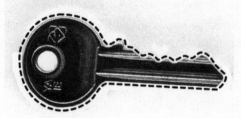

10 October

1966: Simon and Garfunkel release the album
Parsley, Sage, Rosemary and Thyme

A pinch of herbs and what they're supposed to be good for, but don't take my word for it. Seek advice before going anywhere near any of them

Angelica root: good for digestion and respiration.

Bayberry: a blood purifier and detoxifier, and good for stopping colds developing.

Catnip: not just popular with cats, this is good for calming nerves and helping to relieve nausea and diarrhoea.

Dandelion: bitter-tasting and, apparently, liver-nourishing. The roots are good for the glands.

Elderberry flowers: for ridding the body of toxins, increasing circulation and even purifying the blood.

Fennel: good for detoxification and the removal of waste materials from the body.*

Garlic: quite apart from protecting you against vampires,** it's also an antibiotic and fungicide, and provides nourishment for the urinary, circulatory and immune systems.

Hops: the stuff in beer is a relaxant, a tonic and helps against pain and insomnia.***

Irish moss: good for glands, lungs and kidneys.

Juniper berries: help eliminate excess water and toxins.

Kelp: a type of seaweed, contains almost 30 different minerals helping to balance the metabolism and is good for the brain.

Licorice: yup, of All-Sorts fame, is good for combating stress and for the heart, spleen and respiration.

* Erch!
** If they existed.
*** Hic!

Marshmallow: soothing properties and nutritionally supports the respiratory and gastrointestinal systems.

Noni: popular among the Polynesians, it seems to have a huge variety of uses.

Oatstraw: good for the bones.

Parsley: good for the blood.

Quercetin: defence against harmful micro-organisms.

Rhubarb: good for the colon.*

Sage: helps combat excessive mucus.

Thyme: a powerful tonic and antiseptic.

Valerian root: helps with sleeping and calming the nerves.

Watermelon seeds: help to eliminate excess water.

Yellow Dock root: high in iron, it purifies the blood and is good for the liver.

* THE LEAVES ARE HIGHLY POISONOUS.

11 October

1910: Theodore Roosevelt becomes the first man to have held the office of American president and to have flown in an aeroplane*

People who are 'firsts' yet may never be identified as such, let alone recognized and lauded for such firstiness**

1. The first British prime minister to have eaten an orange.
2. The first British actor to have trodden in spilt yogurt.
3. The first Italian traffic warden to have heard Abba's *Knowing Me, Knowing You.*
4. The first US postal worker to have smelt pancakes burning (whilst on his or her mail route).
5. The first Japanese diplomat to have used superglue.
6. The first Welsh schoolchild to have had a pet cat and dog *and* goldfish, all at the same time.
7. The first Liverpudlian to be given incorrect change in a newsagent's when buying a newspaper and a few other things, including a packet of biscuits.
8. The first woman to appear on British television with a very slight tummy upset, nothing to do with feeling nervous.
9. The first French doctor to have switched from a fringe to a centre-parting on the advice of friends.
10. The first European police officer (above the rank of inspector or equivalent) to have a desk-mounted pencil-sharpener.
11. The first member of the British royal household to eat genetically modified sweetcorn.
12. The first Russian diplomat to have dialled a wrong number.

---

* Or 'airplane' as he'd have called it, being American . . . which is fair enough, what with the Wright brothers, who built the first successful one, being Americans themselves.

** If there was such a word.***

*** Which there isn't.

13. The first member of the Royal Academy to have been involved in a minor road accident involving an animal.

14. The first rocket scientists to have said, 'It's not rocket science!' then, remembering that it is, to have laughed about it.

15. The first heart-transplant surgeon to have been disappointed by the breakfast at the conference hotel.

16. The first Scottish schoolteacher to have repaired their own puncture on their bicycle in the rain.

17. The first member of a British expedition to have lost a game of Scrabble to their daughter at home.

18. The first serving member of the Salvation Army to have found an amusing article in a newspaper or magazine and shown it to their friend.

NB If not an absolute certainty in every single case, it is statistically extremely likely that each and every one of these people exists (or existed), if only we knew who they were, to give credit where credit's due . . .

12 October

1609: the first published version of Three Blind Mice *appears in Thomas Ravenscroft's* Deuteromelia

The first lines of five non-existent nursery rhymes which sound like they might be rather interesting if they did exist (in my opinion, anyway) and one complete one (which we can all see for ourselves is truly splendid)

1. THE TINY MAN WITH NEEDLE TEETH
The tiny man with needle teeth,
Lived beneath a big brown leaf . . .

2. ABLE JOHN
Two bears, one frog and Able John
Built a boat to sail upon.
They made the hull from bark and string
Then found a lake to sail it in . . .

3. HEY, DIDDLE DUMPLING!
Hey, diddle dumpling, dance and shout!
What's this nursery rhyme about?

4. UP UPON THE WINDOW SILL
Up upon the window sill,
I can see a distant hill
Up upon the distant hill,
I can see yet further still . . .

5. PITTER PATTER PATTERSON
Pitter Patter Patterson
Make batter for my better son
Not for Pat my bitter son
For that would be quite wrong . . .

6. FOOTNOTES ACROSS LONDON

(Believed to date from the first decade of the 21st century)

Up the Gherkin,[1]
Dodge the sheets,[2]
Around the Eye,[3]
And down the Streets.
Across the bridge
With drunken gait,[4]
To ultra-modern Mr Tate.[5]
Meanwhile, poor Charlie,[6]
All alone,[7]
Captured by the living stone.[8]
Raise the Standard![9]
Share the News![10]
London has gone down the Tubes![11]

Philip Ardagh

[1] Probably not a line in praise of the vegetable, but a reference to a tower block with that nickname.

[2] Possibly sheets of glass rather than of the bed variety. There were (allegedly) some teething problems concerning the Gherkin's glazing.

[3] Likely to be the Millennium Wheel, aka the London Eye.

[4] Believed to refer to the wobbling of the Millennium Bridge.

[5] Tate Modern, the art gallery, named after Mr Tate of 'and Lyle' fame.

[6] The statue of King Charles in Trafalgar Square.

[7] Following the redevelopment of the square, the statue became stranded on its own as a traffic island.

[8] Not so much a reference to sculpture but a more dreadful pun of uncertain meaning.

[9] More fully known as the *Evening Standard*, this is a London newspaper.

[10] The *Evening News* was incorporated into the *Standard*.

[11] Not an inference of London's demise, but reference to Londoners' heavy use of public transport, particularly in defiance of terrorist attack.

13 October

1905: actor Sir Henry Irving dies *

Just about everything that keeps people awake at night

- Worry
- Bad dreams
- Pain
- Nightmares
- Fear
- Heat
- Cold
- Uncomfortable beds (too lumpy/too hard/too soft)
- Bright lights
- Annoying pillows
- Noise (in the room, next door and/or miles away)
- Thinking too much
- Coughing and sneezing
- Hypnotism
- Ghosts
- Uninvited guests
- Strong smells
- A sinking feeling***
- Allergies
- Animals (including pets walking across your head)
- Storms
- Insomnia
- Severe obstructive sleep apnoea****

* Famous for playing, among others, Macbeth.*

** Who 'murdered sleep'.

*** Particularly common for those sleeping on punctured waterbeds or punctured inflatable mattresses.

**** Unlike sufferers of insomnia, who know that they're not sleeping, sufferers of severe obstructive sleep apnoea assume that they're sleeping, unaware that they stop breathing many hundreds of times in the night, each time waking up struggling for breath . . . so can go for years without a proper night's sleep without realizing it (getting tireder and tireder all the time).

14 October

1982: in an extraordinary ceremony, 11,674 people – that's 5,837 couples – get married at the same time in Seoul, Korea

Terms married people use for their married partner (excluding their actual names, embarrassing nicknames, terms of endearment, and things they call them when they're angry or trying to attract their attention from a distance)

My husband

My significant other

My spouse

Father**

My old man

She Who Must Be Obeyed***

My cell mate****

Me/The missus

My old Dutch******

My wife

My other half

Mother*

My ball and chain

My partner

My soul mate

Her indoors*****

Me hubby

* Referring to the mother of his children (rather than his own mother).

** Referring to the father of her children (rather than her own father).

*** A reference to the title character in Sir Henry Rider Haggard's novel *She*, She Who Must Be Obeyed was popularized as a term for a wife by the character Rumpole in the books and TV series *Rumpole of the Bailey* by Sir John Mortimer.

**** A variation on soul mate, it refers to the other partner sharing the same 'stretch' (sentence of marriage).

***** Popularized by the character of Arthur Daley, played by George Cole, in the TV series *Minder*.

****** The song 'My Old Dutch', which begins with the line 'We've been together now for 40 years', deals with the – thankfully now long gone – practice of separating husbands and wives when putting them in 'homes' in their old age, because there were separate homes for men and women.

15 October

1581: what is considered by many to be the world's first true ballet (Le Ballet Comique de la Reine*) is performed in Paris*

What we all know (or think we know) about ballet

1. Ballet often takes place in opera houses although it is ballet not opera.
2. Ballet is like opera but, whereas in opera fat people stand around singing, in ballet thin people leap around dancing.
3. No one speaks in ballet. The only sound is the music, the noise of people's feet landing on the stage and (sometimes) noisy scenery.
4. Female ballet dancers are called ballerinas and wear costumes called tutus with dresses that stick out like Queen Elizabeth I's ruff.
5. Male ballet dancers aren't called ballerinas. They don't wear tutus but they don't wear bottom-halves either, except for tights. So you can't see their dangly bits, they wear something like a cricket box inside their tights, called a codpiece.
6. Male ballet dancers have to be fit and strong so that they can grab hold of, hold up and spin around ballerinas while making it look really easy.
7. Ballerinas have to be fit and strong so that they can take their entire body weight on their pointes, which means the tips of their toes.
8. Most ballets involve a princess, princes, swans, a castle and a woodcutter, not necessarily in that order. Come Christmas, you can add a nutcracker and a sugarplum fairy to the mix.
9. Famous traditional ballets often contain classical music which people like to listen to without feeling the need to see the dance moves that go with it.

10. Many modern ballets contain scores which people would rather not hear again even if they like the dance moves that go with them.

11. It's fun to take ballet dance classes as a girl.

12. If you're a boy and you want to learn ballet, you still might get teased a bit but not quite so much since *Billy Elliot* was such a big hit and – hey – what do those jerks know anyway?

16 October

1958: 'Blue Peter' is broadcast for the very first time

Some 'Blue Peter' presenters I prepared earlier . . .

1. Christopher Trace
2. Leila Williams
3. Anita West*
4. Valerie Singleton
5. John Noakes
6. Peter Purves
7. Lesley Judd
8. Simon Groom
9. Christopher Wenner
10. Tina Heath
11. Sarah Greene
12. Peter Duncan**
13. Janet Ellis
14. Michael Sundin
15. Mark Curry
16. Caron Keating
17. Yvette Fielding
18. John Leslie
19. Diane-Louise Jordan
20. Anthea Turner
21. Tim Vincent
22. Stuart Miles
23. Katy Hill
24. Romana D'Annunzio
25. Richard Bacon
26. Konnie Huq
27. Simon Thomas
28. Matt Baker
29. Liz Barker
30. Zoe Salmon
31. Gethin Jones
32. Andy Akinwolere

* A presenter for just 4 months in 1962, she was left off the official BBC list of 'Blue Peter' presenters for many years.
** Left, then came back again.

17 October

Anagrams of the names of the rich and famous**

Albert Einstein: Ten elite brains

Alec Guinness: Genuine class!

Arnold Schwarzenegger: He's grown large 'n' crazed

Britney Spears: Best PR in years

Chairman Mao: 'I am on a march!'

Clint Eastwood: Old West action

Elvis Aaron Presley: 'Seen alive? Sorry, pal!'

Emperor Octavian: Captain over Rome

Jennifer Aniston: Fine in torn jeans

Justin Timberlake: 'I'm a jerk, but listen!'

Madonna Louise Ciccone: One cool dance musician

Margaret Thatcher: That great charmer

Marilyn Monroe: I marry loon men

Paul McCartney: Pay Mr Clean-Cut

Princess Diana: End is a car spin *and* Ascend in Paris

Sean Connery: On any screen

Sharon Stone: No near shots

Steve Martin: I'm star event

William Shakespeare: I am a weakish speller
and I'll make a wise phrase

William Shatner: Will is Earthman

* 'Worthy hair? Ta!'
** None of which I claim as my own.

18 October

1867: Russia sells Alaska to the USA*

Purchases too big to take home on the bus

1. Alaska
2. A bus . . .

THIS IS A RIDICULOUS WASTE OF TIME!

* The sale of Alaska to the United States, for a staggering $7.2 million, seemed like an excellent deal for Russia at the time: Alaska being little more than an icy waste. The deal (and Alaska) became known as Seward's Folly (after the US Secretary of State who went ahead with it). When gold and later black gold - oil - were discovered, however, it turned out to be the Americans who got a great deal.**

** If only I could turn around this list in the same way. Success from failure and all that.***

*** Hang on! Maybe I could suggest that the expanse of white space on this page represents the great white expanse of Alaska itself and, as Alaska hides its black gold beneath, so the white of this page hides the beauty of my own black gold: the printed words beneath . . . my own priceless prose!****

**** Or maybe not.

NB There were, of course, people already living in Alaska when the US bought it. In the 1970s they were compensated with $963 million and 44 million acres. The US government could easily afford it, with all that income from gold and oil. It's funny how things turn out, huh?

19 October

Eighty-one male variations on the name John (from the Hebrew word for 'God is gracious')

1. Anno
2. Ean
3. Eian
4. Eion
5. Eoin
6. Euan
7. Evan
8. Ewan
9. Gian
10. Giannes
11. Gianni
12. Giannis
13. Giannos
14. Giovanni
15. Hannes
16. Hanno
17. Hans
18. Hanschen
19. Hansel
20. Hansl
21. Iain
22. Ian
23. Ioannes
24. Ioannis
25. Ivan
26. Ivann
27. Iwan
28. Jack
29. Jackie
30. Jacky
31. Jan
32. Jansci
33. Janek
34. Janko
35. Janne
36. Janos
37. Jean
38. Jeanno
39. Jeannot
40. Jehan
41. Jenkin
42. Jenkins
43. Jens
44. Jian
45. Jianni
46. Joannes
47. Joao
48. Jock
49. Jocko
50. Johan
51. Johanan
52. Johann
53. Johannes
54. John-Carlo
55. John-Michael
56. Johnn
57. Johon
58. Johnie
59. Johnnie
60. Johnny
61. Jon
62. Jona
63. Jonnie
64. Jovan
65. Jovanney
66. Jovanni
67. Juan
68. Juanito
69. Juwan
70. Sean
71. Seann
72. Shane
73. Shaughn
74. Shaun
75. Shawn
76. Vanek
77. Vanko
78. Vanya
79. Yanni
80. Yanno
81. Zane

20 October

1955: JRR Tolkein's The Lord of the Rings: The
Return of the King *is published*

A handful of rings

Claddagh rings

Usually gold, though sometimes silver, moulded in the form
of two hands holding a crowned heart. The crown represents
loyalty, the hands friendship and the heart – you guessed it
– love. If the tip of the heart faces the hand, the wearer is 'taken'
(having a sweetheart). If the tip of the heart faces towards the
fingertips, then they are free. The ring gets its name from the
Irish town of Claddagh, which, I believe, no longer exists. Such
rings are worn by both men and women.

Engagement rings

Often containing diamonds – sometimes just one (big one)
called a solitaire – engagement rings are traditionally worn by
women who are betrothed (have promised to marry). It's worn
on the ring finger of the left hand.*

Eternity rings

Rather than a cluster of jewels, those in an eternity ring are set
in the band itself, side-by-side all the way around the ring, so
you can't see where they begin and where they end: they go on
in an eternity,** like the giver of the ring's love for its receiver
(usually a woman).***

Gimbal rings

From the Latin *geminus*, meaning 'twin',**** the gimbal ring is
made of two wavy halves than can be worn by two separate

* The ring finger of the left hand is traditionally 'reserved' for the engagement and
wedding ring only. Ancient Egyptians believed that a 'vein of blood' ran exclusively from
this particular finger all the way to the heart, making it special. People in Britain didn't
start wearing wedding rings on this finger until the 1700s, Protestants before Catholics.

** For ever and ever.

*** In Victorian times there was a craze for the first letter of each gem in eternity-style
rings spelling out a word, for example *diamond, emerald, amethyst, ruby, emerald,
sapphire, topaz* spelled out 'dearest' and *ruby, opal, sapphire, emerald* the name 'Rose'.

**** As in Gemini, the Heavenly Twins.

people, usually lovers – to show that they go together to make one – or as one ring, locked together like a puzzle.

Gimmal rings (*see* Gimbal rings)

Half-eternity rings

If eternity means forever, then half-eternity means half-of-forever, which is impossible! What it refers to in this instance is that, instead of the gemstones going all the way around the band as in an eternity ring, in a half-eternity ring, they only go around the top. Traditionally a woman's ring.

Jimmal rings (*see* Gimbal rings*)

True-love-knot rings

Usually made of gold or silver, and often made to look like tiny pieces of string or rope, the knot represents true love. Traditionally a ring worn by both men and women but, nowadays, more women than men.

Wedding rings

Traditionally a plain gold band denoting marriage, worn by both men and women on the ring finger of the left hand.

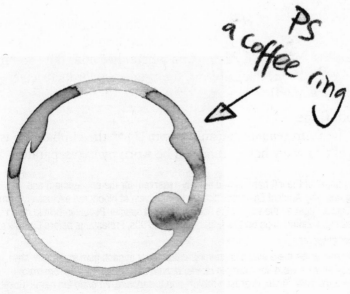

PS a coffee ring

* Again!

21 October

Nelson, Trafalgar and his column

- A pivotal naval battle in the Napoleonic Wars, the Battle of Trafalgar gets its name from Cape Trafalgar, east of Cadiz, in Spain.

- The battle was between the British fleet, led by Admiral Lord Nelson, and a combined Franco-Spanish (French and Spanish) fleet.

- At this final stage of his career, Horatio Nelson had one good eye (having lost the sight in the other* at the Battle of Calvi) and one arm, having lost the other* at the Battle of Santa Cruz de Tenerife in 1797.

- As the fleet prepared to engage – to attack each other – Nelson ran up a 31-flag signal to the rest of his fleet, spelling out the famous phrase: 'England expects that every man will do his duty'.**

- The *Victory* succeeded in crippling the French flagship, *Bucentaure*, which gave the British a great morale boost and psychological advantage. She then moved on to the French ship the *Redoutable*, and the two vessels became entangled.

- Snipers in the rigging, crow's nest and fighting tops of the *Redoutable* repeatedly fired down on to the naval officers and sailors on deck of the *Victory*. The victims included Nelson himself. A single bullet entered his shoulder,

---

* His right (eye and arm). It was to this blind eye that Horatio Nelson famously put his telescope at the Battle of Copenhagen, so that he could ignore orders to cease action by claiming he couldn't see the signal to do so! (He probably never wore an eyepatch, whatever you may think.)

** Nelson had originally intended that his signal read: 'Nelson confides that every man will do his duty', with 'confides' meaning that he was confident that they would do their duty. The signal officer asked to substitute the word 'expects' for 'confides' because it required fewer flags, so would be quicker to signal! As for substituting 'Nelson' for 'England', that was another officer's idea, and Nelson readily agreed. The flag signal was run up the HMS *Victory*'s mizzenmast*** and became a part of history.

*** The mast immediately aft (behind) the ship's mainmast, towards the stern of a ship.

pierced his lung, and then became lodged at the base of his spine.

- Despite his terrible injuries, Nelson remained conscious for around four hours, which was long enough for him to learn that he had been victorious: the British fleet had won.

- Nelson's last words were neither 'Kiss me, Hardy,' nor 'Kismet, Hardy' (whichever they were*) but either 'Thank God I have done my duty' (if William Beatty, the *Victory's* surgeon is to be believed) or 'Drink, drink. Fan, fan. Rub, rub' (if his chaplain and steward are to be believed). He was mortally wounded, remember!

- The bullet that killed Nelson was removed from his body after death and is now there for all to see at Windsor Castle.

- Nelson's Column and Trafalgar Square were laid out and built between 1829 and 1841 in honour of Nelson's final victory. The column is a Grade 1 listed structure. The statue of Nelson at the top the column is made from Craigleith sandstone. The Craigleith quarry in Scotland closed over 60 years ago. The most recent repairs on the statue were made using Craigleith sandstone salvaged from Donaldson's School for the Deaf in Edinburgh, when it too was undergoing repairs.

- The most serious damage to the statue has been to Nelson's left arm. It was struck by lightning in the 1880s.

- The four giant bronze lions at the bases were sculpted by Edward Landseer and are (incorrectly) shown sitting like big dogs, rather than the big cats that they are. Landseer is probably most famous for having painted the *Stag at Bay*.

- The height of Nelson's Column was originally thought to be 185 feet (56 metres) from street level to the top of Horatio's hat. In 2006, it was found to measure only 169 feet (51 metres).

* See 13 January.

22 October

Some superstitions in the air

- A number of US, European and Asian airlines don't have a seat row numbered 13 in their aircraft, because many consider it an unlucky number. (The row numbers go straight from 12 to 14.)

- Many airlines don't have a flight number 13 and, at a few airports, there isn't even a gate number 13.

- The Japanese airline Nippon leaves out seat rows numbered 4 and 9 too. Why? Because the Japanese word for 'four' sounds very similar to the Japanese word for 'death' and their word for 'nine' sounds remarkably similar to their word for 'torture'!

- As well as not having a row 13, Lufthansa, the German airline, doesn't have a row 17. In Italy, the number 17 is considered unlucky because the Roman numerals for 17 – XVII – can be rearranged to spell the Italian word VIXI which means 'I lived' . . . suggesting that you no longer do and are now dead!***

- In the West the numbers 7 and 11 have traditionally been considered lucky, so much so that there have been internal flights to America's gambling capital Las Vegas deliberately numbered 777 and 711 to encourage the superstitious punter to use them!

- Tragically, flights 77 and 11 were not lucky for the passengers and crew aboard the ill-fated hijacked American Airlines planes on 11 September 2001 (aka 9/11).

---

* 3,000 feet (915 metres) from a balloon – not a plane** – and on purpose, not in an emergency. The feat was performed by a Monsieur Andre-Jacques Garnerin, above Paris.

** Because they hadn't been invented yet.

*** What's weird is that Italy's national airline, Alitalia, isn't bothered and *does* have seat rows numbered 17 in their planes!

- In certain dialects of Chinese, the word for 'eight' sounds a hair's breadth away from the word meaning 'to acquire wealth', which is why Continental Airline's flight from China's capital to Newark in the US is numbered 88 (and was launched at a special $888 price)!

- In 2007, at some expense, Brussels Airlines had to change its logo – including all the livery on its aircraft – from 13 (unlucky) balls to 14, by adding an extra one! This came as a result of floods of emails and calls from worried potential flyers.

- Not that a superstitious Chinese traveller would then choose to fly with Brussels Airlines. The Mandarin Chinese word for the number 14* sounds similar to the Mandarin phrase meaning 'to want to die'! You just can't win, can you?

- Most pilots refuse to fly their aircraft under ladders. Not because they're superstitious, but because their aircraft wouldn't fit and, anyway, it would be a very stupid thing to go and do.

* Or, more accurately, one-four.

23 October

Ten titles for ten very short lists

1. Suns in our Solar System
2. UK's Current Reigning Monarchs
3. Dogs That Breathe Underwater
4. Boy Band Members Who Play Their Own Instruments on Their Songs
5. Internationally Successful Danish Pop Groups
6. Vegetables Popular with All the Family
7. Sure-Fire Ways of Keeping Toddlers Occupied for Car Journeys Over Five Hours Long (Which Don't Involve Sleeping)
8. Teachers Who <u>Really</u> Appreciate a Good Practical Joke
9. Britons Who've Never Heard of Harry Potter
10. People Who Seriously Believe that Posh is the Talented One Out of Posh and Becks

---

* Quitting due to ill health just seven months later, making his one of the shortest terms in office.

24 October

2003: the final Concorde's final flight

Twelve things about Concorde which are not true but which, if you read, you may forget are made-up and start thinking of (and telling others) as being facts

1. The earliest design for a Concorde-style aeroplane was a sketch by Leonardo da Vinci. Because he used mirror writing, if built, it could only have flown from right to left rather than left to right.

2. The word 'concorde' comes from the French, *con* meaning 'fool' and *corde* meaning 'string', thus literally meaning 'fool's string' or 'elastic thread', suggesting the speed with which the aircraft would *TWANG!* past.

3. A joint British and French venture, it was agreed for the prototype that the two countries would each build half of Concorde. When it came to put the two together, it was found that they'd both built front halves and there was no tail end.

4. As the world's first supersonic – faster than the speed of sound – passenger plane, people often had to complain about the terrible noise Concorde made before they'd even heard it.

5. Concorde's nose cone had three positions: straight during flight, down when landing, and turned up when looking down on inferior (US) aircraft.

6. The Russians claimed to have come up with a remarkably similar-looking aeroplane quite by coincidence, which was nicknamed Concordski.*

7. Concorde flights between London and New York were so expensive to begin with that it would have been cheaper to box up New York and bring it to London by boat.

* Hang on! This one's true!!!!

405

8. For Comic Relief, darts-player Jocky Wilson flew one of the last Concordes into a mile-high giant foam dartboard built especially by the BBC props department. The stunt raised over £30 for the charity (and cost £7.3 million to stage).

9. The Duke of Edinburgh once piloted Concorde for a full six minutes before realizing that it wasn't a flight simulator.

10. The person to pilot the very last Concorde for the very last time was Captain Andrew 'Hairy Hands' McConnaught (who gained his nickname from having very hairy hands). He so missed the aeroplane that he officially changed his name to 'Captain Concorde' and had plastic surgery to make his nose resemble the aircraft's nose cone. He was Britain's highest-earning children's party entertainer until 2005, when he was overtaken by Sprat the Talking Seal.

11. Concorde was voted Most Recognizable Silhouette of the Year for four out of five years in a row. (The year it didn't win, the Most Recognizable Silhouette was Homer Simpson.)

12. Fewer people have flown Concorde as full-paying First Class passengers than have walked on the Moon.

25 October

*1854: the Light Brigade charges, as in
'The Charge of the Light Brigade'*

Some enlightening thoughts about light and where that leads us

- In a vacuum,* light travels at around 299,792,458 metres per second.
- That's about 186,000 miles per second or a staggering 669,600,000 miles per hour.
- Light travels in a straight line.**
- Speed can bend light.
- If light itself can't bend, then something else must be bending: the space and time that the light is travelling through (speed being the measurement of the time it takes an object to travel through a certain space or distance).
- For an astronaut in a spaceship accelerating at a constant 9.8 metres per second per second (m/s^2), it would feel the same as being on Earth: the pull of the acceleration on his body matching the pull of gravity when on Earth.
- If acceleration bends space and time, and gravity behaves like acceleration, then gravity must also bend space and time.***
- In other words, the Sun, the planets, the moons and the stars all have different masses and gravity of different strengths, so they are all bending time and space around them to different degrees . . . which means that, in space, time can go more quickly or more slowly relative to time on Earth.

* A place without gas or air, such as space.
** If it didn't there wouldn't be shadowy corners, the light would simply bend around them to fill them with light.
*** The quickest way between two points is a straight line. If time is bent, it must be taking longer or going slower.

- This means that, in theory, an astronaut who travels far enough could return to Earth to find that he's aged much more quickly than the people he left behind . . .
- And if you've understood the information in this list, you're well on your way to understanding Einstein's Theory of Relativity.*

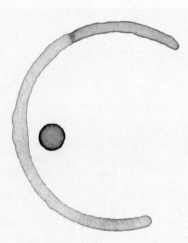

---

* Smartypants.

26 October

1881: the infamous 'Gunfight at the OK Corral' takes place in Tombstone, Arizona, USA

No need for tombstones: people back from the dead (or buried by mistake!)

- **Oran:** one of St Colomba's monks, he was buried alive in error. On being rescued, he babbled on about having seen both Heaven and Hell. The story goes that he was promptly reburied alive. Deliberately this time! (6th-century Scotland)

- **Thomas [of] Kempis:** famous for having written *The Imitation of Christ*. There are some claims that scratch-marks from his fingernails were found on the *inside* of his coffin lid, suggesting that he'd been buried alive in error. (13th-century Germany)

- **Matthew Wall:** fell from his coffin as it was being carried at his funeral, which woke him up. (16th-century England)

- **Anne Greene:** hanged for a crime, her body was about to be dissected when she woke up . . . and lived for many more years. (17th-century England)

- **Marjorie Elphinstone:** found to be alive when grave robbers tried to steal her jewellery. (17th-century Scotland)

- **Marjorie Halcrow Erskin:** deliberately buried in a shallow grave by the local sexton so that he could steal her jewellery later. She awoke when he tried to cut off a finger to steal her rings! (17th-century Scotland)*

- **William Duell:** hanged for murder in 1740, at England's famous gibbet in Tyburn, he survived the experience, so was sent back to prison!

---

* What is it with the 17th-century Scots and trying to steal jewellery off the undead called Marjorie, huh?

- **Nicephorus Glycas:** the Greek Orthodox Bishop of Lesbos, he lay in state in an open coffin for two days in 1896 while mourners filed past paying their last respects. Suddenly he sat up, wondering what on Earth was going on!
- **Sipho William Mdletshe:** declared dead after a traffic accident in South Africa in 1993, the 24-year-old spent two days shut in a metal container in the local morgue before his cries for help were heard.

27 October

Twenty-one things the Brits are famous for (justified or otherwise)

1. A stiff upper lip
2. Queuing
3. Being polite
4. Football hooliganism (at home)
5. Football hooliganism (abroad)
6. The Dunkirk spirit
7. Jolly Cockneys
8. A love of roast beef
9. Playing by the rules
10. Cricket
11. A love of warm beer
12. Being class conscious
13. Winning lots of wars
14. Ruling the waves
15. Enduring hosepipe bans
16. Sayings such as 'What ho!', 'Jolly hockey sticks!' and 'Cor, lumme!'
17. Once governing much of the world
18. Giving foreign Johnnies a sporting chance
19. Wearing knotted hankies on the head
20. Losing the home-grown film industry
21. Not liking the term 'Brits'

28 October

1886: a gift to the American people from the French,
the Statue of Liberty* is officially dedicated

The Statue of Liberty's vital statistics

Height from her heel to the top of her head: 33.86 m (111 ft 1 in)

Height from the ground to tip of her torch: 92.99 m (305 ft 1 in)

Waist: 10.67 m (35 ft)

Length of her right arm: 12.80 m (42 ft)

Length of hand: 5.00 m (16 ft 5 in)

Length of index finger: 2.44 m (8 ft)

Width of head from ear to ear:** 3.05 m (10 ft)

Width of an eye: 0.76 m (2 ft 6 in)

Length of her nose: 1.37 m (4 ft 6 in)

Width of her mouth: 0.91 m (3 ft)

Her tablet:

Length: 7.19 m (23 ft 7 in)

Width: 4.14 m (13 ft 7 in)

Thickness: 0.61 m (2 ft)

* Which was, believe it or not, used as a lighthouse for a number of years.

** Where to where?

29 October

1618: Sir Walter Raleigh is executed

Three things for which Sir Walter Raleigh is most famous . . . but never did

1. Laying his cloak over a puddle so that Elizabeth, the Virgin Queen, could walk across it without muddying her shoes.*
2. Introducing the potato to England in 1586.***
3. Introducing England to tobacco when he brought back a shipload of it from Virginia in 1586.****

NB Sir Walter didn't invent the Raleigh Chopper bicycle either.

* This event-that-never-happened was probably an invention of the 17-century historian Thomas Fuller, who is well known for heavily embellishing the truth. Sir Walter Scott did much to give the cloak-'n'-puddle thing a whole new lease of life in his fabulous 1821 novel *Kenilworth*.**

** An abridged copy of which I got as a school prize (for short-story writing) in 1971.

*** The evidence seems to point to this honour actually going to a certain Thomas Harriot, a mathematician. Queen Elizabeth herself probably never tasted a potato. A bunch of her nobles tried the stem and leaves (which are poisonous) and threw away the potato part!!! Potatoes were already being grown in Continental Europe by 1585.

**** Sir Walter Raleigh never set foot on the North American mainland, though he was in charge of others establishing offshore island settlements. He named the colony Virginia after his Virgin Queen, but that's not the Virginia we know today. The islands are part of what we now call North Carolina. It was the Frenchman Jean Nicot – who has the dubious honour of having nicotine named after him – who introduced tobacco to France in 1560. It was from France, apparently, not the Americas directly, that tobacco was introduced to England.

30 October

1938: a radio-play version of The War of the Worlds, *performed as live news broadcasts, causes nationwide panic in the USA*

BBC Radio April Fool's Day hoaxes designed to fool some and amuse other listeners but not cause fear of a Martian invasion

- In 1973 the BBC broadcast a radio interview with a bumbling doctor who said that a Dr Emily Lang of the London School of Pathological and Environmental Medicine had discovered that certain people could catch Dutch Elm Disease from infected trees. Those most susceptible were believed to be redheads and those with a blood count similar to the soil conditions in which diseased trees grow. They could find their hair turning yellow – like leaves in autumn, of course! – and falling out. They were advised to steer clear of woods and forests. This elderly and rather eccentric academic was played by none other than ex-Goon Spike Milligan.

- In 1975 it was the turn of world-famous naturalist David Attenborough to play the fool, on Radio 3. He announced the discovery of a hitherto-unknown species of tree mice on the Sheba Islands in the Pacific. What made them so special was that they sang at night. Known as Musendrophilus, the mice were said to have webbed feet, used by the local population as reeds for their musical instruments!

- In 1980 the Beeb caused a rumpus when they announced that the clock tower in Big Ben was to lose its hands and be adapted to a digital readout. The BBC Japanese Service went so far as to offer the old hands on sale to the first lucky listeners to phone in!

- In 1987 star-gazer Patrick Moore could be heard on Radio 2 announcing that, at 9:47 that morning, a unique astronomical event would occur. Pluto's passing behind

Jupiter would have a direct effect on Earth's gravity, meaning that people would be able to jump higher and feel lighter – like an astronaut – for a brief window of time. It seems that some listeners genuinely imagined they were experiencing such feelings, while others – either joining in the hoax, or wanting to be a part of something big – made wild claims (aka lies) about giant leaps or floating to the ceiling.

● In 1999 it was announced on Radio 4's prestigious *Today* programme that the existing National Anthem of 'God Save the Queen' was being dropped in favour of a new European anthem, sung in German. This was then performed on air by pupils of a German school in London. Even Prince Charles's office at St James's Palace telephoned the BBC to ask for a copy of the new anthem . . . though they later insisted that this was to play along with the joke.*

* A likely story!

31 October

1864: Nevada becomes the 36th state of the USA

Twenty things to do when lost in the middle of the desert

1. Wear plenty of sunscreen.
2. Wear a sun hat/knotted hankie/something on your head.
3. Remember not to stare directly into the sun through a pair of magnifying glasses.*
4. Be polite to your camel because:
   (i) it might spit at you
   (ii) it might trample you
   (iii) it might get you out of there
   (iv) you might have to live off it in the knife-and-fork sense
5. Be on the lookout for waterholes.
6. Do your best not to be tricked into thinking that a mirage is a waterhole.
7. Do your best not to think that a waterhole is a mirage.**
8. Watch out for sidewinders.
9. Look up 'sidewinders' in your pocket dictionary and discover that they're snakes.
10. Make sandcastles. (It'd be a missed opportunity not to try.)
11. Dress up a cactus in a spare Hawaiian shirt for company. (It's lonely out there.)
12. Bury yourself in the sand at night for warmth (but see No. 8).
13. Bury yourself in a copy of *Philip Ardagh's Book of Absolutely Useless Lists for absolutely every day of the year* for entertainment.
14. Tear out the pages for loo paper.

* Probably best not to do this anywhere, ever EVER, come to think of it.
** Or you might fall in.

15. Try to attract the attention of passing aircraft with a mirror.*

16. Try not to attract the attention of passing biker gangs riding futuristic vehicles stripped to their bare essentials.**

17. Ration what little food and water you might have.

18. Remember not to eat that delicious golden sand, however appetizing it might look.

19. Ask your driver where you are. (This could be the taxi driver or the camel driver.)

20. Switch on your Global Positioning System.

---

* Don't throw it at the plane, but try to catch the sun's rays in it. The glinting of the reflected light will let the pilot – or whoever – know that there's someone down there.

** The bikes, not the bikers.

1 November

1922: the BBC introduces the licence fee

Thirteen things we should (but don't) need a licence for

1. Having children
2. Wearing LOUD ties or non-matching accessories
3. Eating microwaved fruit pies
4. Kicking a ball against the wall of a house (when someone's try to sleep/read/eat/watch TV inside)
5. Sporting a Mohican haircut
6. Playing in that playground with the nasty stain – I'm sure it's blood – by the swings
7. Eating mangoes in the bath
8. Wearing non-matching socks
9. Watching a documentary about how lampshades are made when there's a good film on another channel
10. Mixing fruit punch in the bath
11. Keeping smelly trainers in an airless locker
12. Eating a pickled onion in a built-up area
13. Singing loudly and embarrassingly in public while listening to music through earphones

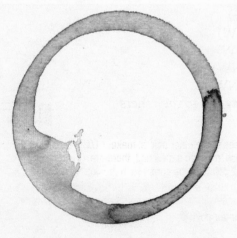

2 November

The 32* – that's right:
32 – points of the compass

- **The four cardinal points**
1. North (N)
2. South (S)
3. East (E)
4. West (W)
. . . at 90 degrees to each other.

- **The four half cardinal points****
Between the cardinal points, these are:
1. North-East (NE)
2. South-East (SE)
3. South-West (SW)
4. North-West (NW)
. . . at 45 degrees to the four cardinal directions (1/8th of a circle).

- **The eight false points:*****
The directions dividing the cardinal and half cardinal points:
1. North-North-East (NNE)
2. East-North-East (ENE)
3. East-South-East (ESE)
4. South-South-East (SSE)
5. South-South-West (SSW)
6. West-South-West (WSW)
7. West-North-West (WNW)
8. North-North-West (NNW)
These points are at 22.5 degrees to the others
(1/16 th of the circle).

* The quarter points (at 2.8125 degrees to the other points, making 1/128th of a circle) are very rarely shown on the compass 'rose' on a map and, therefore, do not count among the 32 points. Reciting the 32 points of the compass in the correct order is known as 'boxing the compass'.

** aka quadrantal points.

*** aka intermediate points or three-letter points.

● The 16 by points

1. North by East (N by E)
2. North-East by North (NE by N)
3. North-East by East (NE by E)
4. East by North (E by N)
5. East by South (E by S)
6. South-East by East (S-E by E)
7. South-East by South (S-E by S)
8. South by East (S by E)
9. South by West (S by W)
10. South-West by South (SW by S)
11. South-West by West (SW by W)
12. West by South (W by S)
13. West by North (W by N)
14. North-West by West (NW by W)
15. North-West by North (NW by N)
16. North by West (N by W)

● Put these 32 points together and you get

Point	Direction	Azimuth*	Point	Direction	Azimuth
0	North	0° 0'	16	South	180° 0'
1	N by E	11° 15'	17	S by W	191° 15'
2	NNE	22° 30'	18	SSW	202° 30'
3	NE by N	33° 45'	19	SW by S	213° 45'
4	NE	45° 0'	20	SW	225° 0'
5	NE by E	56° 15'	21	SW by W	236° 15'
6	ENE	67° 30'	22	WSW	247° 30'
7	E by N	78° 45'	23	W by S	258° 45'
8	East	90° 0'	24	West	270° 0'
9	E by S	101° 15'	25	W by N	281° 15'
10	ESE	112° 30'	26	WNW	292° 30'
11	SE by E	123° 45'	27	NW by W	303° 45'
12	SE	135° 0'	28	NW	315° 0'
13	SE by S	146° 15'	29	NW by N	326° 15'
14	SSE	157° 30'	30	NNW	337° 30'
15	S by E	168° 45'	31**	N by W	348° 45'

* The horizontal angle or direction of a compass bearing.

** Thirty-two in total, because North starts as 0.

420

3 November

Middle names, existing and non-existent

- In America, NMN stands for 'No Middle Name'.
- George Washington didn't have a middle name.
- Paul McCartney's middle name is Paul. (No, he's not Paul Paul McCartney. His first name is James.)
- The J in Homer J. Simpson doesn't stand for anything.
- Captain Kirk's middle name is Tiberius but, in the *Star Trek* episode 'Where No Man Has Gone Before', his middle initial is incorrectly shown on his tombstone as R.**
- If he has one, the middle name of Squidward J. Tentacles – neighbour of SpongeBob SquarePants – is currently not known.***
- It's hard to say what F. Scott Fitzgerald's middle name was, because he had *four* names in total, so there wasn't one in the middle. If he'd just been F. Scott Fitzgerald – the 'F' being for Francis – then the honour would clearly have gone to the name Scott. As it was, his *full name* was Francis Scott Key Fitzgerald, Francis Scott Key, after the man who wrote the words to the USA's national anthem****and a distant relation.

---

* Born Hiram Ulysses Grant, the S didn't stand for anything. The name came about as an error made by a congressman on a nomination for Grant's acceptance into the United States Military Academy, and it stuck.

** Apparently *Star Trek* creator Gene Roddenberry was originally planning to call him James Rice Kirk.

*** Despite his name, Mr Squidward is not a squid but an octopus, even though he doesn't appear to have the requisite eight legs.

**** 'The Star-Spangled Banner'.

4 November

1922: the steps to Tutankhamun's tomb are uncovered

Types of dance plus one wild animal (which you have to spot as the odd one out)

Ballet
Ballroom
Belly dancing
Break-dancing
Capoeira
Cha-cha
Exotic dancing
Flamenco*
Foxtrot
Hip hop
Jazz
Kabuki**
Lambada
Line dancing***
Merengue****
Military two-step
Moshing
Ocelot
Quickstep
Salsa
Samba
Square dancing
Swing
Tango*****
Techno
Waltz

*Not to be confused with flamingos.

**Based on Japanese Kabuki theatre moves (all extremely slow).

***Not to be confused with ambling around a room with your thumbs hooked into the belt loops of your jeans.

****Not to be confused with a meringue, of course.

*****You guessed it: not to be confused with an orange fizzy drink.

NB The odd one out, spelled backwards, is toleco.

5 November

The Gunpowder Plotters

The key players:
- Robert Catesby
- Guy Fawkes
- Thomas Wintour
- Thomas Percy
- Thomas Bates
- Christopher Wright
- Robert Wintour
- John Grant
- John Wright
- Robert Keyes
- Ambrose Rookwood
- Sir Everard Digby
- Francis Tresham
- John Wintour
- Humphrey Littleton
- Stephen Littleton
- Thomas Habington

An A to Z of others arrested and questioned:
- **Abraham** (aka **Abram**), **Robert**: retainer of Sir Everard Digby
- **Acton, Robert**
- **Andrew, William**
- **Askew, Robert**: servant to Robert Catesby
- **Ater** (aka **Archer**), **Christopher**: servant to Ambrose Rookwood
- **Bartlett, George**: servant to Robert Catesby
- **Bates, John**: son of Thomas Bates
- **Batty, Matthew**: servant to Lord Monteagle
- **Bickerstaff, Edward**: servant to John Grant
- **Bonne, Stephen**: servant to Sir Everard Digby
- **Browne, William**: servant to Robert Wintour
- **Conyers, Robert**: servant to Ambrose Rookwood
- **Cooke, William**
- **Darler, Thomas**: servant to Robert Monson

- **Daye** (aka **Dey**), **Richard**: servant to Sir Everard Digby
- **Digby, Sir Robert**
- **Eadale, William**: servant to Sir Everard Digby
- **Edgin, Thomas**: servant to John Wintour
- **Facklins, John**
- **Flower, John**: servant to Ambrose Rookwood
- **Fowes, John**: servant to Robert Wintour
- **Fuller, Ambrose**
- **Garvey, James**: servant to Sir Everard Digby
- **Grant, Francis**
- **Grant, Thomas**
- **Higgins, Robert**: servant to John Grant
- **Howson, William**
- **Huddleston, Henry** (later Sir Henry)
- **Johnson, William**: servant of Robert Keyes
- **Kirke, Stephen**: servant to Ambrose Rookwood
- **Kyddall, William**: servant to Robert Tyrwhitt of Kettleby
- **Leeson, Bennett**
- **Maunder, Thomas**: servant to Robert Wintour
- **Miles, Reginald**: servant to Sir William Engleston
- **Morgan, Henry**: friend of John Grant
- **Ockley, Edward**: retainer of Robert Wintour
- **Ockley, Thomas**: retainer of Robert Wintour
- **Osborne, Robert**
- **Parker, Richard**: servant to Robert Catesby
- **Pelborough, Michael**: servant to Ambrose Rookwood (and blacksmith)
- **Petty, William**: servant to Robert Catesby
- **Prior, Francis**
- **Richardson, Thomas**
- **Rookwood, Robert**
- **Rookwood, Thomas**
- **Sergeant, Henry**: servant to Henry Huddleston
- **Singleston, Father John**
- **Snow, Will**
- **Strange, Father Thomas**
- **Thornberry, William**: servant to Henry Huddleston
- **Townsend, Robert**
- **Westberry, Richard**
- **Wranford, Richard**
- **Yorke, Richard**

6 November

1896: Queen Victoria officially opens the rebuilt Blackfriars Bridge

Friars of various hues

Christian friars come in various orders. The most important ones are the four great orders, and then there are the lesser orders. The four great orders are:

- The Dominicans, formerly known as the Black Friars; so called because they wore a black mantle (or cappa) over their white habit. They were founded by St Dominic in 1215. They are sometimes referred to as the Friars Preachers.

- The Franciscans, or Grey Friars, were founded by St Francis of Assisi. They are also referred to as the Friars Minor.*

- The Carmelites, or White Friars; so called because of the white cloak covering their brown habits. They are divided into two sections: the Calced and the Discalced Carmelites.

- The Augustinians, also known as the Austin Friars, were founded by the Bishop of Hippo. They also go by the name of the Hermits of St Augustine.

Unlike monks, friars didn't cut themselves off from the community, but saw their involvement within it as of key importance. All four of the above orders were 'Mendicant friars'. Such friars originally made a vow of poverty, renouncing all proprietorship. Unlike monks, this applied not only to individuals but also to the entire order, which had to rely on the support and charity of others. No prizes for guessing, therefore, how they got the nickname 'begging friars'.

* A branch of Franciscan friars called the Capuchin has been made famous by coffee drinkers the world over. The cappuccino – with its white frothy top over the light brown coffee beneath – matches the colours of the Capuchin Friars' habit!

7 November

1974: Lord Lucan disappears

Types of magic (of the trick variety)

Close-up magic, as the name suggests, is performed close-up, often with the magician mingling among the audience (even strolling around a party). Close-up magic usually involves cards, coins, boxes of matches and other small (apparently) everyday objects. Since it sometimes requires a tabletop – whether on stage, in a pub or at home – close-up magic is also called table magic. Audiences for close-up magic can't be huge, because not many people can get that close to a magician at one time, particularly if s/he wants you to witness things from a certain angle! ('Don't stand there! You can see up my sleeve!').

Stage-magic is the biggie. This is the kind of magic with the elaborate props and big effects. Though not always performed on stage – for TV appearances of world-famous magicians, stage-magic venues have included the Great Wall of China – the home of such magic is usually the large auditorium. These wow-factor effects can be well appreciated from a distance. One of the most famous exponents of stage magic is magician David Copperfield.*

Cabaret magic is closer to stage magic than close-up, but is usually performed at medium-sized venues much closer to the audience than a stage magician.

Children's magic is, as its name suggests, magic for children. Usually young children. Usually *very* young children. The majority of tricks are stock tricks (bought from magic shops) combined with plenty of audience participation and slapstick humour.**

Street magic is not so much a new form of magic but a mixture of stage and close-up magic brought to the masses. Attracting an audience – sometimes pouncing on the unsuspecting (hence its other name, guerrilla magic) – it can be anything from a

---

* Born David Seth Kotkin.
** Oh no it isn't! Oh yes it is!

simple 'find the lady' card trick or the traditional 'cup and balls' performed on top of a suitcase, to a whole raft of mind-boggling effects (from 'your chosen playing card inside a beer bottle', to 'your sweetheart's name written in ash on someone's arm'). Such magic has been made famous (and cool) by David Blaine.

Bizarre magic, existing magic styles wrapped up in a pseudo-Gothic/mystical/horror approach. Be afraid . . . Be very afraid.

Mentalism, best known in the UK through the work of Derren Brown, is magic designed to give the impression that the magician is not a trickster but really does have special mind powers. Again, the actual tricks are traditional enough, it's just the ingenious way in which they're presented. (This is also popular with David Blaine.)

Shock magic* is intended to – no surprises here – shock, so often involves fake blood, loud noises and apparently unpleasant pastimes, such as appearing to eat razor blades **WHICH YOU SHOULD NEVER ATTEMPT.**

NB My favourite trick of the sawing-a-person-in-half variety is firing-the-girl-from-a-cannon-into-a-locked-box-hung-from-the-ceiling . . . and I know how it's done!

* BOO!**
** Sorry. I didn't really mean to frighten you.

8 November

Ten of the world's most famous paintings

- *The Mona Lisa** by Leonardo da Vinci (1503–6)
- *The Laughing Cavalier*** by Frans Hals (1624)
- *Seaport with the Embarkation of the Queen of Sheba* by Claude Lorrain*** (1648)
- *The Hay Wain***** by John Constable (1821)
- *Rain, Steam and Speed* by J. W. M. Turner***** (before 1844)
- *The Starry Night* by Vincent van Gogh (1889)
- *The Scream******* by Edvard Munch (1893)
- *Four Dancers* by Degas (c.1899)
- *The Tragedy* by Pablo Picasso (1903)
- *Water Lilies******** by Claude Monet (1903)
- *Campbell's Soup Cans********* by Andy Warhol********* (c.1962)

* Also known as *La Gioconda*.
** He's not really laughing. He just has a cheery moustache!
*** aka Claude Gellée from Lorraine.
**** Or *Haywain* or *Hay-Wain* (among others).
***** Nicknamed 'the painter of light'.
****** There's more than one version.
******* aka *The Clouds*.
******** Which is exactly what it says on the tin.
********* Born Andrew Warhola.

9 November

1947: a pre-recorded programme is broadcast on BBC television for the first time*

Repeats: programmes that seem to be on TV all the time

Only Fools and Horses

Judge Judy

Little Britain

Two Pints of Lager and a Packet of Crisps

Star Trek

Star Trek: The Next Generation

Star Trek: Deep Space Nine

Star Trek: Voyager

Star Trek: Enterprise

Inspector Morse

* Until now, everything had been shown live. At least one earlier recording of a British TV programme had been made – including both sound and vision – but this was not intended for later broadcast.

10 November

1728: Irish playwright Oliver Goldsmith is born

Goldsmith and Ardagh

- The name Ardagh (*Árd Archadh* in Gaelic) means 'the high field'.

- There are a number of places in Ireland called Ardagh, including those in Limerick, County Mayo and County Longford.

- The town of Ardagh in County Longford used to be an important centre for pre-Christian worship, with commanding views of the surrounding countryside.

- The Fetherston family settled in Ardagh, building the existing Ardagh House in the 1700s.

- In 1744 Ardagh House was visited by Oliver Goldsmith, who mistook it for a grand inn.

- He also mistook the Fetherston daughters for servant girls and – to put it politely – tried to 'court' them!

- Rather than put the whole embarrassing incident behind him, Goldsmith made it the basis for his most popular and successful play, *She Stoops to Conquer*.

- Today Ardagh House is a convent school. Its current proportions look a little strange because it used to be three storeys high but is now only two. The top storey was destroyed by fire in 1949.

- Ireland's most famous treasure, the Ardagh Chalice,* is one of the world's finest examples of 8th-century Celtic metalwork and is made from silver, bronze and gold. It gets its name not from the Ardagh in County Longford but in County Limerick, where it was discovered.

- Ardagh is also the name of one of Britain's greatest living children's authors.**

* Currently in the National Museum of Ireland.
** Though I may need to have this fact verified.

11 November

1920: the bodies of two First World War unknown soldiers are prepared to be laid to rest, one in Westminster Abbey, London and the other* in the Pantheon, Paris

Famous quotes from Clint Eastwood** and the characters he played

'If you want a guarantee, buy a toaster.'

'Abuse of power isn't limited to bad guys in other nations. It happens in our own country if we're not vigilant.'***

'Go ahead, make my day.'

'I have strong feelings about gun control. If there's a gun around, I want to be controlling it.'

'I know what you're thinking. Did he fire six shots or only five? Well, to tell you the truth, in all this excitement, I've kinda lost track myself. But being as this is a .44 Magnum, the most powerful handgun in the world, and would blow your head clean off, you've got to ask yourself one question: Do I feel lucky? Well, do ya punk?'

'I tried being reasonable, I didn't like it.'

'See, my mule don't like people laughing. He gets the crazy idea you're laughing at him. Now if you apologize, like I know you're going to, I might convince him that you really didn't mean it . . .'

'There's only one way to have a happy marriage and as soon as I learn what it is I'll get married again.'

'They say marriages are made in Heaven. But so is thunder and lightning.'

'This film cost $31 million. With that kind of money I could have invaded some country.'

* Before being buried under the Arc de Triomphe.
** Famous for playing the Man with No Name.
*** After Thomas Edison, of inventing fame.

12 November

*1911: Chad Varah, the founder of the Samaritans
telephone helpline, is born*

Some fictitious New Testament characters
(the ones no one claims were real)*

- The Good Samaritan
- The Prodigal Son
- The Sower (and his seed, come to that)
- The Labourers in the Vineyard (each given the same pay, no matter how long they worked)
- The Good Shepherd (hunting his lost sheep)
- The Rich Fool
- The Unjust Steward
- The Beggar Lazarus (not to be confused with the Lazarus risen from the dead)
- The Unjust Judge and the Importunate Widow
- The Two Debtors
- The Pharisee and the Tax Collector
- The Unmerciful Servant
- All ten of the Ten Virgins

* All of the above are characters in Jesus's parables – 'Earthly stories with heavenly meanings' – supposedly made up by Christ to illustrate simply various aspects of his teachings.

13 November

1002: King Ethelred the Unready orders the killing of all Danes in England

Anglo-Saxon kings of England from 802 to the Battle of Hastings

1. Egbert (reigned AD 802-839)
2. Ethelwulf (AD 839-856)
3. Ethelbald (AD 856-860)
4. Ethelbert (AD 860-866)
5. Ethelred (AD 866-871)
6. Alfred, the Great (AD 871-899)
7. Edward I, the Elder (AD 899-924)
8. Athelstan (AD 924-939)
9. Edmund I (AD 939-946)
10. Eadred (AD 946-955)
11. Eadwig aka Edwy (AD 955-959)
12. Edgar (AD 959-975)
13. Edward II, the Martyr (AD 975-979)
14. Ethelred II, the Unready (AD 979-1016)
15. Edmund II, Ironside (AD 1016)

    DANISH RULE (AD 1016-1042)[*]

16. Edward III, the Confessor (AD 1042-1066)
17. Harold II, Godwinson (AD 1066)[**]

[*] All of the Anglo-Saxon kings listed were from the Royal House of Wessex. There was a period between 1016 and 1042 when England was ruled by the Danes:
- Canute (1016-1035)
- Harold Harefoot (1035-1040)
- Hardicanute (1040-1042)

[**] He was killed by William the Conqueror's forces at the Battle of Hastings (though not with an arrow in his eye).

*1940: much of the city of Coventry is destroyed
by German bombing and hundreds die*

Being shunned and keeping quiet

1. BOYCOTTING

The term 'boycott' – as in, for example, refusing to buy South
African goods when the country was run by a minority white
apartheid regime – is a eponym; it's named after a particular
person. In this case, it was an English captain called Charles
Cunningham Boycott, land agent to the Earl of Erne in County
Mayo, Ireland. The earl himself was an absentee landlord living
in England. After the failure of the Irish harvest in 1880, Captain
Boycott refused the pleas of tenants to reduce rents during these
tough times, even though failed crops meant little, if any, income.
He threatened to evict the earl's tenants from their homes if they
couldn't pay every penny in full. Rather than letting him get away
with such cruel treatment, the locals rebelled against him, but
not with violence. Instead, everyone shunned him. His servants
deserted him. No one would sell him anything: not even food
and drink, and people turned their backs on him. This approach
proved so successful that Boycott not only quit his job but also the
country. He went back home to England!

2. KEEPING MUM*

Keeping mum means keeping quiet. In this instance, the word
'mum' probably comes from the sound you make if trying to
talk with your mouth closed: a cross between a mumble and a
'mmmmm!'; or something 'imitative of a sound made with lips
closed' as a dictionary might put it. (Traditionally mummers were
actors who performed mime: actions without words.) During
the Second World War there were two famous British posters
employing the phrases KEEP MUM. SHE'S NOT SO DUMB and
BE LIKE DAD. KEEP MUM. The idea behind these was the same
as that of LOOSE LIPS SINK SHIPS – beware of what you're

* The word 'Mum' or 'Mummy' (as in female parent) is a much more recent word than
'mum' as in silent. People didn't start calling their mums 'Mum' until the 18th century.
Before that it would have been Mam or Mammy.

saying, you never know who might be listening – but it also reveals a very different attitude towards women back then!

3. SENDING TO COVENTRY

'Sending someone to Coventry' means deliberately ignoring them; shunning them; not speaking to them; treating them as if they don't exist. Like so many phrases in the English language, there seems to be a healthy dispute as to the origin of the phrase, with a few contenders. These are based on the fact that:

- During the English Civil War, many Royalists (Cavaliers) were imprisoned in Coventry by the victorious Parliamentarians (Roundheads) . . . so being 'sent to Coventry' was no fun.
- Coventry was a garrison town, packed with soldiers who were unpopular with the locals. Any women seen talking to a soldier lost their good reputation . . . so much so that no one spoke to them or the soldiers. Being stationed in Coventry meant being shunned by just about anyone and everyone.
- Coventry is possibly a corruption of 'covin-tree'; a tree used as a gibbet – a hangman's tree – in medieval times. (You certainly would be silenced if hanging from a noose, dead, but the last of these possible explanations does seem rather unlikely, doesn't it?)

4. BEING AS SILENT AS THE ORANGE*

There is no such phrase as 'being as silent as the Orange', but there should be, the Orange in question being a person and not a fruit. William I, Prince of Orange (1533–84), earned the nickname William the Silent, though William the Gobsmacked might have been equally appropriate. In conversation with King Henry II of France, when hunting in 1559, the French king revealed his plans to massacre vast numbers of Protestants in Holland and France (assuming that William would support him). Orange was surprised, shocked and horrified, and wisely chose to say nothing . . . though he was completely opposed to the idea.

---

* If you use start using the phrase 'as silent as the Orange' – engineering conversations in the right direction just so that you can – then, in next to no time, this could become a genuine saying, leaving lexicographers scratching their word-filled heads. Go on. Give it a go!

15 November

Three different punchlines to the same joke*

The Joke

A petty crook ends up in jail and is kept awake his first night by fellow prisoners shouting out numbers to each other, then guffawing loudly. When the crook asks his cellmate what's going on, he's told that one of the most popular books in the prison library is a joke book. Rather than telling the jokes, the prisoners simply call out the page numbers of their favourite ones. The crook decides to give it a go and calls out, '73!'

Punchline A:

Nobody laughs. There's not even a titter.

'What did I do wrong?' asks the crook.

His cellmate shakes his head. 'They've all heard that one before,' he explains.

Punchline B:

There's silence.

'Why didn't anyone laugh?' asks the crook.

His cellmate shrugs. 'Some people are just no good at telling jokes,' he replies.

Punchline C:

There's much laughter but, long after the others have stopped, one guy in the cell next door is still laughing.

'What's with him?' asks the crook.

His cellmate grins. 'He's not heard that one before.'

* A version of which my father told me when I sat on his knee.**
** Or some other low-down joint.***
*** Which is also a very old joke.

436

1959: the stage version of The Sound of Music *premieres in New York*

Nuns on TV

1. For some reason, nuns in cartoons are often mistaken for penguins and vice versa.
2. Sometimes, cartoon nuns get knocked down like skittles, or is that penguins?
3. We never see the nuns' legs or feet.
4. Nuns always appear to glide as though they're on castors.
5. At some stage, at least one nun will produce a guitar and start singing.
6. The Mother Superior always seems stern but turns out to have a heart of gold (as all real nuns should have).
7. At least two of the so-called nuns will turn out to be male prisoners on the run (probably for a crime they didn't commit).
8. All TV nuns seem to live in convents, never nunneries.
9. All the convents are in a state of disrepair and need renovating.
10. Help usually comes in the form of a seemingly bumbling young priest and a bunch of street urchins.
11. A young humourless nun – who probably slaps the back of the children's hands with a ruler – will, at some stage, be chased by a goose, ostrich or some other long-necked bird.
12. The plain-looking nun with glasses will turn out to be stunningly beautiful with gorgeous hair when she has to remove her wimple, having swum across the swollen river to save the little Chinese boy at the mission.
13. At least one nun in a foreign mission will be able to fix the broken-down ex-army truck using a huge spanner.
14. Nuns can hide small children, priceless works of art and important religious relics under their habits without batting an eyelid.
15. Their prayers are answered, even if only in the last five minutes.

17 November

1973: US President Richard Nixon famously publicly announces, 'I'm not a crook.'

Ten unusual subjects of some websites specializing in these topics alone

1. Men who look like Kenny Rogers
2. Humorous vegetables
3. Dumb crooks
4. Toy presidents
5. Disturbing auctions
6. Turtle watching
7. Tall people
8. Fish paintings
9. Animal law
10. Timber poles

18 November

1901: George Gallup, opinion-poll guru, is born

Good old basic radio sound effects

- Punching a person: punching a cabbage
- Stabbing a person: stabbing the same cabbage*
- Galloping horses: banging coconut halves together or on a board
- Twanging arrow: twanging a ruler on the edge of a table
- Thunder: shaking a metal sheet
- Rain: frying bacon (!)
- Mixing a drink with ice in a cocktail shaker: rattling old flashbulbs in a can of water
- Bat hitting a ball: snapping a match in two (very close to the microphone)
- Animal noises: people making animal noises!
- Crackling fire: crinkling cellophane
- The click of a Geiger counter: twisting the dial on a combination padlock
- Getting out of a saddle: flexing a leather wallet near the microphone
- Chirping crickets: running a fingernail along the teeth of a comb
- Skating on ice: rubbing two knife blades together
- Writing with a scratchy-nibbed pen: scratching paper with unbent paper clip
- Opening a safe: twisting the dial on a combination padlock
- A wet dog shaking itself: strips of bicycle inner tubing flailed about
- Boiling water: blowing through a straw into water
- Popping champagne cork: popping a balloon
- Breaking bones: snapping a stick of celery
- Breaking glass: dropping little squares of sheet metal

And my personal favourite:

- A fire suddenly igniting: speedily opening a gent's umbrella**

* Or sometimes a melon.

** You'll be amazed how convincing it sounds.

1850: Alfred, Lord Tennyson becomes Poet Laureate

Some of the worst lines from the worst poems of William McGonagall,* thought by many to be the worst published poet in the English language**

Therefore, ye sons of great Britain, come join with me,
And welcome in our noble Queen's Jubilee;
Because she has been a faithful Queen, ye must confess,
There hasn't been her equal since the days of Queen Bess.
    – from 'An Ode to The Queen On Her Jubilee Year'

Then hurrah! for the mighty monster whale,
Which has got seventeen feet four inches from tip to tip
    of a tail!
Which can be seen for a sixpence or a shilling,
That is to say, if the people all are willing.
    – from 'The Famous Tay Whale'

Beautiful Moon, with thy silvery light,
Thou cheerest the fox in the night,
And lettest him see to steal the grey goose away
Out of the farm-yard from a stack of hay.
    – from 'The Moon'

Oh, mighty city of New York, you are wonderful to behold –
Your buildings are magnificent – the truth be it told –
They were the only thing that seemed to arrest my eye,
Because many of them are thirteen storeys high;
And as for Central Park, it is lovely to be seen –
Especially in the summer season when its shrubberies are green
    – from 'Jottings of New York'

---

* Following Tennyson's death in 1892, McGonagall went to Balmoral to ask Queen Victoria if he could be the new Poet Laureate. He was informed that she was out.

** McGonagall was ridiculed in his own lifetime, often pelted with vegetables.

Pity the sorrows of the poor blind,
For they can but little comfort find;
As they walk along the street,
They know not where to put their feet.
They are deprived of that earthly joy
Of seeing either man, woman, or boy;
Sad and lonely through the world they go,
Not knowing a friend from a foe.
— from 'The Sorrows of the Blind'

Your 'Tam O'Shanter' is very fine,
Both funny, racy, and divine,
From John O'Groats to Dumfries
All critics consider it to be a masterpiece,
And, also, you have said the same,
Therefore they are not to blame.
— from 'Robert Burns'

The firemen tried to play upon the building where the fire
    originated,
But, alas! their efforts were unfortunately frustrated,
Because they were working the hose pipes in a building
    occupied by Messrs Smith & Brown,
But the roof was fired, and among them it came crashing down.
— from 'The Miraculous Escape of Robert Allan, the
Fireman'

Beautiful Railway Bridge of the Silv'ry Tay!
Alas! I am very sorry to say
That ninety lives have been taken away
On the last Sabbath day of 1879,
Which will be remember'd for a very long time.
— from 'The Tay Bridge Disaster'*

* Possibly McGonagall's most famous (dreadful) poem.

20 November

1947: Princess Elizabeth (now the Queen) marries Philip Mountbatten (now Prince Philip)*

Famous grandmothers and grandfathers, real and imaginary**

- Grandma in 'Little Red Riding Hood', famously impersonated by the wolf.

- Grandpa from 'The Simpsons'.

- Margaret Thatcher who, as prime minister, once proudly announced, 'We are a grandmother,' even though there was only one of her.

- Grandpa Joe, Grandma Josephine, Grandpa George and Grandma Georgina from 'Charlie and the Chocolate Factory'.

- Grandma Moses (born Anna Mary Robertson), a famous American folk artist who lived to be 101 and didn't start painting until she was in her seventies.

- Grandpa (who slept hanging upside down in a cupboard) in 'The Munsters'.

* Both share a great-great-grandmother: Queen Victoria.

** Many well-known people were raised by a grandparent or grandparents. These include: former James Bond Pierce Brosnan; supermodel Naomi Campbell; rock legend Eric Clapton; movie actors Morgan Freeman, Al Pacino and Samuel L. Jackson; singer/actor Curtis '50 Cent' Jackson; author Sir Walter Scott; and country 'n' western stars Willy Nelson and Tammy Wynette.

21 November

1877: Thomas Edison announces his invention of the world's first sound-recording machine: the phonograph

The early days of sound recording

- The very first word ever recorded was 'Mary'. It was spoken by Thomas Edison himself when he recited 'Mary had a little lamb'.*

- The first recordings were on to wax cylinders. These were later replaced by foil cylinders, later records** and – later still – magnetic tape, before everything went digital.

- A recording of Florence Nightingale's voice still exists today.

- Queen Victoria had her voice recorded, on the condition that the recording be destroyed once she hard heard it played back. This was done.

- Other famous Britons to have their voices recorded in those early days included:
  - prime minister William Gladstone
  - Poet Laureate Alfred, Lord Tennyson****
  - poet Robert Browning

- The first full-length 'talking picture' (film with sound) was *The Jazz Singer***** starring Al Jolson.

* He re-recorded this in 1927.
** Spinning 78 revolutions per minute ('78s'), followed later by 33 ⅓s*** and 45s.
*** Former Beatle George Harrison released an album entitled *33⅓* – the speed at which the record revolved, and also his age at the time.
**** Who recited his most famous poem, 'The Charge of the Light Brigade'.
***** Released in 1927.

22 November

Hair-related nicknames

- Goldilocks: she of the golden locks of hair, who trespassed into the three bears' home
- Bluebeard: the murderous fairy-tale nobleman
- Red/Rusty/Carrot-top/Ginger: just about anyone with red hair!
- Blue/Bluey: a common Australian nickname . . . for people with red hair. Hmm.
- Mr Twit*/Fuzzy-Face: a bearded person
- The Silver Fox: silver-haired Australian professional poker player Mel Judah
- Blondie: a blond(e)-haired person (usually female)
- Dreads: a person with dreadlocks
- Curly: a common nickname for someone with curly hair . . . or used ironically for someone with particularly straight hair or, perhaps, no hair to speak of
- Goldie: aka Clifford Joseph Price. Many people think he got the nickname from his gold teeth. In fact, he used to have gold dreadlocks
- Shaggy: the shaggy-haired dropout in cult cartoon *Scooby-Doo*

* From Roald Dahl's *The Twits*.

23 November

1852: Britain's first post boxes are installed*

Things that change colour

- Leaves
- Cephalopods (cuttlefish etc.)
- Chameleons
- Specialist candles
- Babies' eyes (from blue)
- Kapuas mud snakes (Enhydris gyii)
- Some politicians
- Litmus paper
- Embarrassed people
- Light-sensitive glasses
- Zebra fish
- Traffic lights
- Fading photographs

* They were green rather than red and erected in Jersey, in the Channel Islands.

445

24 November

1974: comic writer, actor and director Stephen Merchant is born*

Tall-ish people who don't actually break any records of note

2-metre-tall people
Chris Evans (the DJ and TV-personality one)
Dave Prowse[1]
Hulk Hogan
James Arness[2]
James Cromwell[3]
Joey Ramone[4]
Kevin James[5]
Krist Novoselic[6]
Long John Baldry
Montell Jordan
Peter the Great[7]
Philip Ardagh[8]
Stephen Merchant
William Wallace[9]

- Average height of female members of the Tall Persons Club of Great Britain and Ireland: 6 ft 1 in (1.85 m)
- Average height of male members of the Tall Persons Club of Great Britain and Ireland: 6 ft 5 in (1.96 m)

---

* Probably best known for co-writing and co-directing *The Office* and *Extras* with Ricky Gervais.

[1] Darth Vader of *Star Wars*, when he has his helmet on.

[2] In TV's *Gunsmoke*.

[3] Playing George Sibley in *Six Feet Under* and, at the time of writing, the tallest person to have been nominated for an Oscar – which isn't really a proper world record now, is it?

[4] Of – you guessed it – The Ramones.

[5] Currently Britain's tallest soccer player (again, no big deal).

[6] Bass player for band Nirvana.

[7] Tsar of Russia (and beard-hater).

[8] Beard-lover.

[9] General all-round historical Scottish hero.

Well-known tall female tennis players
Venus Williams, 6 ft 1½ in (187 cm)
Maria Sharapova, 6 ft 2 in (188 cm)
Lindsay Davenport, 6ft 2½ in (189 cm)

Well-known 6-ft (183-cm) women
Elle MacPherson
Brooke Shields
Geena Davis
Uma Thurman
Macy Gray
Beth Orton
Saffron Burrows

25 November

1952: Agatha Christie's The Mousetrap *opens in London. At the time of writing, it's running still and is the world's longest-running play*

The patter of tiny feet

- The word 'mouse' comes from an ancient Sanskrit word meaning 'thief'.
- Mice bred for pets come in around 70 different colours and combinations.
- A mouse's tail is as long as its body. It's scaly to help the mouse grip when climbing.
- A mouse can climb vertical surfaces, so long as they're rough enough to grip, and it can walk along thin ropes and wires.
- A mouse's whiskers are used to sense the texture of surfaces – rough or smooth – changes in temperature, and breezes.
- A mouse has poor eyesight but sees best in dim light.
- A mouse's incisors (front teeth) never stop growing. If they didn't grind down with all that gnawing, they could grow up to 13 cm a year!
- A mouse can squeak at very high frequencies, often outside the range of human hearing.
- A mouse has an average life expectancy of two years.*
- A female mouse produces 6 to 10 litters of 5 to 10 pups a year, which means up to 100 mouse pups from one mum in 12 months.
- A mouse pup begins breeding at just two months old!
- Mice also can transmit diseases. These include: salmonellosis (bacterial food poisoning), hantavirus, pulmonary syndrome, leptospirosis, lymphocytic choriomeningitis, rat-bite fever, rickettsial pox and tularaemia.

* Born in 1928, however, Mickey Mouse will – at the time of writing – soon be eighty!

- Mice also carry mites, a bite from which can give a human lyme disease and dermatitis.
- In folklore, eating mice was suggested as a cure for: tummy aches (ancient Egypt), smallpox, whooping cough, measles and – if their ashes were eaten with honey – earache (ancient Greece). Eating fried mice was also supposed to cure bed-wetting.*

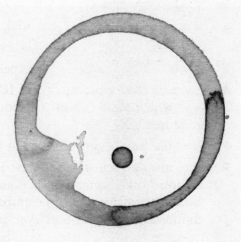

* Which can't have been much fun for the mice or the bed-wetters.

26 November

1983: gold worth around £26 million is stolen from Heathrow Airport, London, in the 'Brinks Mat' robbery

A matter of security

Background

- Jack has a secret message that he wants to send to Jill.
- Jill wants to be able to send her own secret message as a reply.
- They have one box (which can be locked with padlocks).
- Each has a padlock with only one key.

Question

- How can Jack send a secure message in the box to Jill?
- How can Jill read the message and send a secure reply to Jack that he, in turn, can read?

Note: neither ever sends the other their key or a copy of it.

Pause for thought

- Hmm.
- Ready? GO FOR IT!

ANSWER
HOLD UP TO MIRROR

- Jack puts his secret message in the box, locking the box using a padlock for which he has a key. He then sends Jill the box.

- Jill adds her padlock to the box – looping it through the same hasp, or an additional hasp – then sends it back.

- Jack then unlocks and removes his padlock and sends the box back to Jill.

- Jill now unlocks her padlock with her key, reads the message and replaces it with her reply. She then locks the box with her padlock and sends it to Jack.

- Jack adds his padlock and sends the box back to Jill.

- Jill then removes her padlock with her key and sends the box back to Jack.

- Now all Jack has to do is unlock his own padlock with his key and read the reply. Mission accomplished!

NB Apparently, there's a mathematical equivalent of the chest-and-padlocks concept called the discrete logarithm problem. If you want to send a secret number to someone by email you can apply a 'padlock' to the number that only you can remove. You apply this padlock by taking the secret number and calculating the *discrete exponentiation function* using your secret key number as the exponent . . . so now you know!

27 November

1701: Anders Celsius is born. He goes on to create the Celsius scale for temperature*

Upside down and topsy-turvy

- Traditionally, Britons think of Australians walking upside down on the other side of the world.

- Also, traditionally the opposite side of the world to the USA is said to be China (hence the term 'the China Syndrome' for the result of a serious nuclear accident. This was based on the alarmist thought that material from a molten nuclear-reactor core would burn a hole right through the centre of the Earth and come out the other side in China). It has been pointed out by some spoilsports, however, that a line drawn from the USA through the centre of the Earth actually ends up in the Indian Ocean!

- The bat isn't the only animal to spend plenty of time hanging upside down. Others include the sloth, the slow loris and plenty of apes, but not – according to the Opossum Society of the US** – the opossum. That's an urban myth.***

- There's an animal called an upside-down jellyfish (with tentacles pointing upwards), and there's an upside-down catfish too.

- Gecko lizards can walk upside down across ceilings.

- The two types of performer most commonly upside down in the Big Top are acrobats (doing handstands, walking on their hands or forming human pyramids) and trapeze artists.

---

* Celsius fixed water as freezing at 100 degrees and boiling at 0 degrees. Later this was swapped around.

** And they should know.

*** Not that I know many urban opossums.****

**** Not that I know *any* opposums, come to that.

452

- The story goes that in 1961 MOMA, the Museum of Modern Art in New York, displayed the painting *Le Bateau* (*The Boat*) by Henri Matisse the wrong way up for 47 days, with the reflection of the boat at the top and the actual boat at the bottom. Some claim this is just an urban myth. Others are adamant that it's T-R-U-E.

- The Wonderworks building in Orlando, Florida, has deliberately been built to look as though it's been ripped out of the ground and turned upside down, going so far as to have a thick layer of 'earth' on the top, with upside-down palm trees growing downwards towards the street below.

- With a pineapple upside-down cake, you place the pineapple at the bottom of the baking tin and, just before serving, turn the whole thing upside down so that the pineapple ends up on the top. Hence the name.*

- Inversion therapy is a method of hanging upside down to improve your mood.

- Aerobatic (stunt) pilots often go into a roll and then fly their planes upside down. They need a fuel-injected engine or specially adapted fuel tanks, otherwise gravity would pull the fuel away from, rather than towards, the engine, causing the aircraft to stall.

- The painter Wasilli Kandinsky once walked through a gallery, stopping to admire an unfamiliar painting for some time, greatly appreciating its 'extraordinary beauty glowing with an inner radiance' . . . before realizing that it was one of his own works hanging the wrong way up! This is said to have inspired him to try abstract – non-representational – art.

* A tarte tatin uses the same approach but with apples and sounds less interesting (if just as tasty).

28 November

Funny trousers/breeches/hose
in the arts

- In the 16th-century play *Gammer Gurton's Needle* (*Grandma Gurton's Needle*), the missing needle – her only one – is eventually found in someone's breeches. This comedy was probably originally staged in 1553, long before William Shakespeare had his first play produced.

- British farce is a very particular kind of British comedy, involving lots of people hiding from lots of other people – with doors slamming and people very nearly being found out – and often contains the side-splittingly funny moment of *someone's trousers falling down*.

- The traditional cartoon substitute for missing trousers is a barrel with braces.

- In the Wallace and Gromit short film *The Wrong Trousers*, the sleeping Wallace is forced to take part in a jewel theft while wearing a pair of ex-NASA 'techno trousers', adapted for remote-controlled use and manipulated by Feathers McGraw, a penguin disguised as a chicken. This was based on a true story.***

- For an actor to 'give up funny trousers' means that they've turned their back (legs and bottom) on Shakespeare plays and costume dramas. What they wear in their own time is their own business.

- The TV series *Monkey Trousers*, starring Steve Coogan, Vic Reeves and Bob Mortimer is very strange indeed, and includes the character of an evil toyshop owner.

* In 1809 *Knickerbocker's History of New York* was published, supposedly written by one Diedrich Knickerbocker, who was actually a creation of Irving's. Baggy trousers – like those worn by Dutch settlers in New York** – came to be known as knickerbockers after him.

** Originally named New Amsterdam.

*** OK, no it wasn't.

- Many people think that golfers wear funny trousers of the loud-checks-wouldn't-be-seen-dead-wearing-them-anywhere-else variety. If you think they're funny, you should see those tasselled golfing shoes!*

- Snufkin in the brilliant Moomin books wears the same pair of old, well-worn trousers throughout. In *Comet in Moominland*** he almost buys a new pair but ultimately declines to do so. His returning this pair of new trousers leads to the kindly elderly lady shopkeeper deducting their value from some additional purchases – exercise book, lemonade, star and looking-glass (with rubies) – even though they're hers in the first place.

* I know golf isn't really an art so much as a sport, but I really really wanted to mention golfing trousers.

** One of my favourite books of all time, ever.

29 November

People with appropriate (or inappropriate) names for their professions or activities

- Possibly one of the most inappropriately named people has to be Cardinal Sin. Cardinal Jaime Sin was Archbishop of Manila, in the Philippines, from 1974 to 2003!

- According to the Associated Press, another inappropriately named person is Mr Keifer Bonvillain. He allegedly tried to extort $1.5 million from Oprah Winfrey . . . but got arrested for his troubles. If he does turn out to be a villain, he certainly isn't a *bon** one.

- According to contributions to the *New Scientist*, appropriately (and inappropriately) named people include:
  - ◆ Ashley Burns, a fireman
  - ◆ Brian Mole, head of security at University of Sheffield
  - ◆ Mr Brake, an executive at a company making brake components
  - ◆ Bill Webb, a web-designer at the *Tacoma News Tribune*
  - ◆ Professor Michael Lean, Professor of Nutrition at the University of Glasgow
  - ◆ Alan Pee, a council sewage worker
  - ◆ David Butcher, the Executive Director of the Royal Society for the Prevention of Cruelty to Animals in New South Wales
  - ◆ David Nutter, producer of *The X-Files*

* *bon* = French for 'good'.

30 November

Countries that have abolished the death penalty for all crimes, and the years in which abolition occurred*

Andorra, 1990
Angola, 1992
Armenia, 2003
Australia, 1985
Austria, 1968
Azerbaijan, 1998
Belgium, 1996
Bhutan, 2004
Bosnia-Herzegovina, 2001
Bulgaria, 1998
Cambodia, 1989
Canada, 1998
Cape Verde, 1981
Colombia, 1910
Costa Rica, 1877
Cote d'Ivoire, 2000
Croatia, 1990
Cyprus, 2002
Czech Republic, 1990
Denmark, 1978
Djibouti 1995
Dominican Republic, 1966
Ecuador, 1906
Estonia, 1998
Finland, 1972
France, 1981
Georgia, 1997
Germany, 1987

Greece, 2004
Guinea-Bissau, 1993
Haiti, 1987
Honduras, 1956
Hungary, 1990
Iceland, 1928
Ireland, 1990
Italy, 1994
Liberia, 2005
Liechtenstein, 1987
Lithuania, 1998
Luxemburg, 1979
Macedonia, 1991
Malta, 2000
Mauritius, 1995
Mexico, 2005
Moldova, 1995
Monaco, 1962
Montenegro, 2002
Mozambique, 1990
Namibia, 1990
Nepal, 1997
Netherlands, 1982
New Zealand, 1989
Nicaragua, 1979

* According to Amnesty International. For more information, see: www.amnesty.org

457

Norway, 1979
Paraguay, 1992
Philippines, 2006
Poland, 1997
Portugal, 1976
Romania, 1989
Samoa, 2004
San Marino, 1865
Sao Tome and Principe, 1990
Senegal, 2004
Serbia, 2002
Seychelles, 1993
Slovak Republic, 1990

Slovenia, 1989
South Africa, 1997
Spain, 1995
Sweden, 1972
Switzerland, 1992
Timor-Leste, 1999
Turkey, 2004
Turkmenistan, 1999
Ukraine, 1999
United Kingdom, 1998*
Uruguay, 1907
Vatican City State, 1969
Venezuela, 1863

NB Countries that have NOT abolished the death penalty include the USA.

* In 1973 the death penalty in the UK was abolished for all 'ordinary crimes'. The last woman to be hanged in the UK was Ruth Ellis in 1955. The last people to be hanged in the UK died in 1964.

1 December

1761: Madame Tussaud,* of modelling-people-in-wax fame, is born

What the Swiss have given us apart from the cuckoo clock**

Cellophane: That see-through crinkly stuff was invented by Swiss Jacques E. Brandenberger in 1908.

Knorr: Cooking stuff.

Milk chocolate: The first successful solid milk chocolate (as opposed to drinking chocolate) was developed by Swiss Daniel Peter Masters in 1876. Famous for its fabulous chocolate, Switzerland's first chocolate factory opened under Francois-Louis Callier in 1819.

Rayon: In around 1855 the Swiss chemist Georges Audemars paved the way for the creation of the fabric.

Red Cross parcels: During the Second World War, the Swiss Red Cross supplied parcels for Allied Prisoners of War, among others. The contents included soap or toothpaste, treats such as chocolate, coffee and cigarettes, and FOOD.

The scanning tunnelling microscope (STM): Co-invented by the Swiss Heinrich Rohrer, it shows images of individual atoms on the surfaces of materials.

Skiing in the Alps: Strangely enough, the first skiing party in the Swiss Alps, which took place in 1893, included Sherlock Holmes's creator, Sir Arthur Conan Doyle, who had to order the skis from Norway.

* She was Swiss.

** In the film *The Third Man*, the character of Harry Lime, played by Orson Welles, famously says, 'In Italy for 30 years under the Borgias they had warfare, terror, murder, bloodshed – but they produced Michelangelo, Leonardo da Vinci and the Renaissance. In Switzerland they had brotherly love, 500 years of democracy and what did that produce – the cuckoo clock!'***

*** Actually, between you and me, the cuckoo clock is thought to be a German invention, not Swiss!

The discovery of high-temperature superconductivity in a new class of materials: This sounds more complicated than the others because it is. Alex Mueller, along with his colleague J. Georg Bednorz, working for IBM, Switzerland, was awarded the Nobel Prize in Physics in 1987 for this discovery.

Velcro: Yet another Swiss invention, this time the brainchild of George de Mestral, who was inspired by burrs in nature.

The list that replaces the list of Premiership football club chants which was going to go here until I found that most of them were unprintable,
aka
Those people whose images appear on the cover of the Beatles' *Sergeant Pepper's Lonely Hearts Club Band**

Albert Einstein *(Physicist)*
Albert Stubbins *(Soccer player)*
Aldous Huxley *(Writer)*
Aleister Crowley *(Dabbler in sex, drugs and magic)*
Aubrey Beardsley *(Illustrator)*
Bob Dylan *(Musician)*
Bobby Breen *(Singer)*
Carl Gustav Jung *(Psychologist)*
Cloth Figure of Shirley Temple *(by Jann Haworth)*
Cloth Grandmother Figure *(by Jann Haworth)*
Das Varga Girl *(by Artist Alberto Vargas)*
Diana Dors *(Actress)*
Dion (di Mucci) *(Singer)*
Dr David Livingstone *(Missionary and Explorer)*
Dylan Thomas *(Poet)*
Edgar Allan Poe *(Writer)*
Four-Armed Indian Doll
Fred Astaire *(Actor)*
Garden Gnome *(Almost a person)*

* Along with humanoid-shaped thingummies, and excluding Leo Gorcey (Actor), who was painted out – because he requested a fee – and Mohandas Gandhi (Indian leader), who was painted out by request of EMI, who feared it might cause offence.

George Bernard Shaw (*Writer*)
George Harrison
H.C. Westermann (*Sculptor*)
H. G. Wells (*Writer*)
Huntz Hall (*Actor*)
Issy Bonn (*Comic*)
Japanese Stone Figure
John Lennon
Johnny Weismuller (*Swimmer and Actor*)
Karl Marx (*Philosopher, Socialist*)
Karlheinz Stockhausen (*Composer*)
Larry Bell (*Artist*)
Legionnaire from the Order of the Buffalos
Lenny Bruce (*Comic*)
Lewis Carroll (*Writer*)
Mae West (*Actress*)
Marilyn Monroe (*Actress*)
Marlene Dietrich (*Actress*)
Marlon Brando (*Actor*)
Max Miller (*Comic*)
Oliver Hardy (*Comic*)
Oscar Wilde (*Writer*)
Paul McCartney
Petty Girl (*by Artist George Petty*)
Richard Lindner (*Writer*)
Richard Merkin (*Artist*)
Ringo Starr
Robert Peel (*Prime minister*)
Simon Rodia (*Creator of Watts Towers*)
Sonny Liston (*Boxer*)
Sri Lahiri Mahasaya (*Guru*)
Sri Mahavatara Babaji (*Guru*)
Sri Paramahansa Yoganandu (*Guru*)
Sri Yukestawar Giri (*Guru*)
Stan Laurel (*Comic*)
Stephen Crane (*Writer*)
Stone Figure of Girl
Stone Figure of Snow White
Stuart Sutcliffe (*Artist and Former Beatle*)

462

T. E. Lawrence (*Soldier, Lawrence of Arabia*)
Terry Southern (*Writer*)
Tom Mix (*Actor*)
Tommy Handley (*Comic*)
Tony Curtis (*Actor*)
Tyrone Power (*Actor*)
W. C. (William Claude) Fields (*Actor/Comic*)
Wallace Berman (*Actor*)
Wax hairdressers' dummy
Another wax hairdressers' dummy
Wax Model of George Harrison
Wax Model of John Lennon
Wax Model of Paul McCartney
Wax Model of Ringo Starr
William Burroughs (*Writer*)

3 December

1967: the world's first heart transplant is carried out by a team headed by white South African, Professor Christiaan Barnard

A 12-point plan to heal a broken heart, according to Dr Celia Gilberts* *plus* how to mend a puncture

1. Let yourself wallow in self-pity and 'grief' for a while, and don't be afraid to call on your friends and family for support. (They'll get fed up if this stage drags on and on and on.)

   A. *Release the brake callipers and remove the bicycle wheel, then remove the cap from the valve of the tyre, so that the valve will be free to pull through the hole in the rim.*

2. Don't look at the end of this, or any other relationship, as a sign of failure. Learn from what you think might have been 'mistakes' – we all learn from experience – and move on.

   B. *Use the tyre levers, provided in most puncture-repair kits, to remove just one side of the tyre from the rim. Now remove the inner tube.*

3. Tempting though it may be, revenge on your old partner – if they dumped you – isn't worth it. It leaves you stuck in the past rather than moving forward.

   C. *Carefully check the surface of the tyre for anything stuck in the rubber that might have caused the puncture, then – with great care – run your fingers around the inside of the tyre to check for any sharp objects. If you find one, remove it and then check again.*

---

* Though I'm not sure what kind of doctor she is. She may, for example, have a PhD in Geography, so I'd take everything she says with a pinch of salt.**

** She may not even be a real person. (I might have made her up.) I certainly don't believe everything I read.***

*** Or read everything I believe.

4. Take stock of what you want and need from a relationship. Have you been attracted to people who just aren't right for you?

   D. *Inflate the inner tube with a bicycle pump, placing the tube, section by section, in a bowl of water, applying slight pressure with the fingers. Bubbles will appear in the water when the puncture has been located.*

5. Just because you're single doesn't mean you shouldn't go out. If you don't like films and meals on your own, go with a friend.

   E. *Dry the inner tube and mark the location of the puncture with the chalk provided in your kit.*

6. Don't shut yourself away. There are millions of people in the world. Statistically, there should be someone out there right for you, but you need to be out there.

   F. *Be sure to check the rest of the inner tube, even when the puncture has created bubbles, to ensure that there isn't more than one puncture. When this has been done, thoroughly dry the tube in the area of the puncture/s.*

7. Treat yourself. Don't go mad on 'retail therapy' (buying loads of stuff to try to feel good), but there's no harm in splashing out on something special once in a while.

   G. *Use the sandpaper or the 'roughener' provided in the kit to slightly scuff the area around the puncture. This gives the glue a better surface to adhere to.*

8. Don't let yourself go. Take care of yourself. The better you look and the better you feel, the more attractive you'll be to the outside world.

   H. *Spread the glue thinly and EVENLY over and around the puncture and wait for the glue to dry enough for it to feel tacky to the touch. Now put a patch over the hole and apply pressure. (Some kits now come with peel-off sticky-backed patches.)*

9. Avoid the classic rebound. Don't jump into a relationship just because you need something to distract you, or because you think it might be your only chance of ever finding love again.

   I. *Slowly and gently pump up the tube. Place one edge of the tyre around the wheel rim and push the valve back into the rim hole. Starting from the valve, push the rest of the tube back into the tyre. Once the tube is back in position, return the edge of the (outer) tyre on to the rim. In the later stages, this will require the tyre lever. Be sure not to pinch the inner tube between tyre and wheel rim.*

10. Forgive yourself.

   J. *Slide the wheel back in place between the forks on the bike and tighten the nuts evenly, taking care to ensure that the wheel is aligned correctly in the frame. Re-connect the brakes. (I repeat: RE-CONNECT THE BRAKES.)*

11. Forgive your ex-partner. (You don't have to tell them you have. Forgiving them frees you.)

   K. *Pump up the tyre to its normal pressure, take it for a short test ride, to be sure that the tyre is repaired, the wheel correctly aligned and the brakes working.*

12. Move on.

   L. *Move off.*

466

4 December

1865: Edith Cavell is born

A variety of statues in the vicinity of Charing Cross, London, excluding Nelson and his column

Monument to Charles I

King Charles I's statue, currently standing on the edge of Trafalgar Square, had led a most interesting existence. Placed at Charing Cross during the king's lifetime, it was sold for scrap when he was executed and the Parliamentarians took power. The statue was bought by a certain John River, who, instead of scrapping it, buried it in his garden. He then proceeded to show the authorities some other pieces of scrap metal to 'prove' the job was done. After that, he sold a number of small bronze items, claiming that they were made from the melted-down statue. Cavaliers bought them out of respect for their dead king. Roundheads bought them as a reminder of their victory. On the restoration of the monarchy, with Charles II on the throne, the statue was promptly dug up and sold back to the authorities!

The statue had a genuine sword held in place by a separate buckler and strap (rather than being moulded on to the seated figure). On 13 April 1810 these fell from the statue and were picked up by a porter from the nearby Golden Cross Hotel. He, in turn, handed them to a Mr Eyre, a trunk maker, until he received instructions from St James's Palace about what should be done to them. This original – mid-17th century – sword apparently disappeared around the time of Queen Victoria's coronation, to be replaced with a (then) modern replica. As to what happened to the original, there were rumours but no one seems sure.

Today, the statue not only suffers the indignity of being dwarfed by the lions at the base of Nelson's Column – quite apart from Nelson's Column itself – but of having become a traffic island since the pedestrianization of the area in front of the National Gallery!

A Conversation with Oscar Wilde

Unveiled in November 1998, this statue by Maggi Hambling can be found in Adelaide Street, a wide paved area at the back of St Martin-in-the-Fields. A controversial statue, it depicts the head and shoulders of the Irish playwright carved in bronze, reclining or emerging from what appears to be a granite coffin, also intended as a seat for passers-by. Inscribed is a quote from Wilde's play *Lady Windermere's Fan*: 'We are all in the gutter, but some of us are looking at the stars'. Wilde was originally depicted holding a cigarette but this was sawn off as an act of vandalism and, on each occasion that it has been replaced, has been sawn off again.*

The Fourth Plinth

In Trafalgar Square there have been four plinths for many years, but only three statues. In 1999 the fourth plinth began its life as a temporary home for a variety of contemporary statues. These include:

- **Mark Wallinger's *Ecce Homo*** (erected July 1999): A standing image of a very human Christ.

- **Bill Woodrow's *Regardless of History*** (March 2000): The gigantic bronze showed the head of a man crushed under a giant book, both bound to the plinth by the roots of a dead tree.

- **Rachel Whiteread's *Monument*** (June 2001): Described by the artist as 'a pause . . . a quiet moment', this was a translucent mirror image of the plinth, somewhat reminiscent of a giant Fox's Glacier Mint.

- ***David Beckham*** (2002): This waxwork was erected without permission and removed very quickly indeed.**

- **Marc Quinn's*** *Alison Lapper Pregnant*** (2005): The 15-ft-high (4.5 m) white marble statue depicts artist Alison

---

* As I write (in 2007), the cigarette is missing and hasn't been replaced for some time.
** And is the only one of the statues in this list I haven't actually seen for myself.
*** Husband of Georgia Byng, author of the *Molly Moon* books.

Lapper naked and eight months pregnant. As a result of a congenital disorder called phocomelia, Ms Lapper was born with no arms and very short legs.*

Sir Henry Irving

Sir Henry Irving, the world-famous actor-manager, was the first British actor to be knighted and was buried in Westminster Abbey in 1905. The statue, erected in 1910, is located on the north side of the National Portrait Gallery, near an entrance to Leicester Square and in the heart of London's 'theatreland'. The statue was sculpted by Thomas Brock, who was also responsible for the ENORMOUS *Queen Victoria Memorial* in front of Buckingham Palace.

Edith Cavell

The statue to Edith Cavell, almost opposite the entrance to the National Portrait Gallery, was erected in 1920. It includes the words: *'COURAGE, DEVOTION, FORTITUDE AND SACRIFICE'*. Small wonder, when you consider that Cavell, a nurse, helped many British soldiers escape from German-occupied territories during the First World War. She was caught and executed by firing squad on 12 October 1915. Also inscribed on her statue are her final words: *'Patriotism is not enough. I must have no hatred or bitterness for anyone'*.

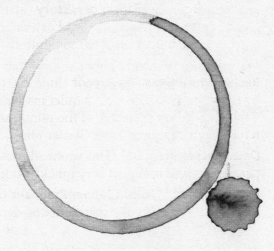

* At the time of writing, this statue is still on the fourth plinth, though that's bound to have changed by the time you're reading this. Life goes on.

5 December

A somewhat sceptical look at the Bermuda Triangle*

The Bermuda Triangle seems to get bigger when it suits writers who want to include disappearances within it. (It's usually said to be a triangular area in the Atlantic Ocean bounded, roughly, at its points by Miami, Bermuda and Puerto Rico.)

Folklore has it that there have been hundreds – perhaps thousands – of disappearances of ships and aircraft in the triangle over the centuries. Suggested reasons for this include:

The supernatural
- friendly alien intervention
- unfriendly alien abduction
- by-products of other extraterrestrial activity
- something to do with the Lost City of Atlantis
- people testing anti-gravity devices and accidentally interfering with ships and aircraft
- nasty people testing anti-gravity devices and *deliberately* interfering with ships and aircraft
- temporal shifts (i.e. time travel)
- vortices to and from other dimensions
- sea-monsters with very long tongues (that can catch aircraft like a frog catches flies)**

Forces of nature
- currents
- earthquakes
- hurricanes
- thunderstorms
- tsunamis
- magnetic fields
- releases of pockets of gas from the ocean bed

* The name was invented by Vincent H. Gaddis in an article for *Argosy* magazine in 1964, though he wasn't the first to claim the phenomenon.

** I'm sorry. I made this last one up. I should be taking this more seriously. Sorry. Again.

Human-induced

- pilot error
- general incompetence (including everything from running out of fuel to poor navigation)
- piracy
- unstable cargoes

Others, who don't believe in a supernatural solution, point out that no solution of any kind – strange or otherwise – is required in the first place, because there's no case to answer. They point out that the number of wrecks and disappearances in the so-called triangle is statistically insignificant for

- ◆ the size of the area
- ◆ the amount of shipping and aircraft traffic passing through it
- ◆ the time period involved

– especially when, on closer study, it's been noted that many of the incidents reported in popular literature on the subject include those which occurred way outside this shape-shifting triangle.

This theory was put to the test by the editor of *Fate* magazine in 1975. He checked the accident records kept by Lloyd's of London – responsible for insuring the world's shipping – and discovered that the Bermuda Triangle was no more dangerous than any other part of the ocean, something which the US Coast Guard had been saying all along.

Having said that, it's no mystery why this became a mystery, because it makes such a great story!

The 20th-century legend of the Bermuda Triangle grew from the disappearance of the five US bombers making up Flight 19 in 1945. It should, however, be pointed out that

- ◆ it was a training mission, which by its very nature means that most of those up there were not used to the conditions. They were students
- ◆ the trainees' aircraft weren't equipped with their own navigational instruments

- ◆ the lead pilot, Lt Charles Taylor, radioed in that his compass wasn't working
- ◆ it became clear from Taylor's radio transmissions that he had then miscalculated their position,* and it would only be a matter of time before they ran out of fuel
- ◆ there was a terrible storm, including 50-foot (15-metre) waves
- ◆ the bombers weighed 14,000 lb (6,350 kg) empty and would have sunk almost straight away if/when the planes ditched into the sea

The Navy Board of Investigation set up to determine the fate of Flight 19 was far from baffled. The board's original conclusion had been that it was a tragic accident caused by Taylor's confusion. Taylor's mother, however, apparently refused to accept this and managed to have the final report put the disappearance down to 'causes or reasons unknown'. Perhaps the phrase added fuel to the fire of an already seemingly interesting incident, when looked at superficially.**

Apparently, since then, accounts of many other disappearances have been distorted to make them seem more unexplainable:

- ◆ seas are described as 'dead calm' when, in truth, conditions were rough
- ◆ storms are conveniently overlooked
- ◆ wreckage later discovered is glossed over
- ◆ other embellishments are made***

* In those days, planes flying over large expanses of water had to depend on knowing their starting point, how long they had flown for, how fast they had flown and in what direction. A single mistake with just one of these figures could have catastrophic – even fatal – results. There were no landmarks over this stretch of ocean.

** And it wasn't helped by the fact that one of the rescue planes disappeared too, though a nearby ship witnessed an explosion. The plane, a Mariner, had a poor safety reputation and was nicknamed 'the flying bomb'. It's believed a fuel tank exploded.

*** In other words, whopping great lies are told. (Who was it who said, 'Never let the facts get in the way of a good story'?)

6 December

1958: animator Nick Park is born

Ten uses for Plasticine*

1. As modelling clay.**
2. As a less-effective Blu-Tak.
3. To remove fluff from something that needs de-fluffing.
5. To pick up nasty little slivers of broken glass.***
6. For blocking up small holes in plasterboard walls.
5. For making Morph, who used to appear on *Take Hart*.
6. To win Oscars.****
7. For making moulds for plaster casts.
8. For making an emergency false moustache (as part of a disguise intended only to be viewed from a distance).
9. To make imprints of coins and other stuff, just for the fun of it.
10. As one of those anti-stress squeezing toys.

PLEASE NOTE (OH, GO ON, *PLEEEEASE*): I don't recommend any of the above uses. Not even the modelling clay one. So don't blame me if you try any one – or all – of them and damage yourself, your house, or your furniture. Leave me out of it. OK?

* A putty-like modelling 'clay' made to a secret formula, invented by English art teacher William Harbutt in 1897, patented in 1899 and commercially produced from 1900. Non-toxic, soft and easy to mould, it doesn't dry on exposure to air (unlike, for example, Play-Doh).

** Other modelling clays are available.

*** After which you must throw the piece of Plasticine away.

**** As Nick Park did with Wallace and Gromit.

473

7 December

How fake pearls* are made

- There are natural pearls, formed naturally by oysters without human intervention, and there are cultured pearls, created by placing a tiny piece of grit inside an oyster, encouraging it to build a pearl around it. These are the only real pearls. All other types of pearl are imitations or fakes.**

- In AD 83, Chinaman Wang Chhung (aka Wang Chong) wrote something along the lines of: 'By following the proper timing, pearls can be created from chemicals, just as brilliant as genuine ones. This is the pinnacle of Taoist learning and a triumph of their skill.'

- In the 16th century the Venetians created iridescent glass. They blew this into pearl-sized bubbles which they filled with wax and – hey presto – you had faux pearls.

- Later, a rosary-maker in Paris, named Jacquin, observed that fish scales in water gave off an iridescent substance which floated on the surface.*** He took this and mixed it with a certain type of varnish to create *'essence d'orient'* ('essence of the orient') or pearlessence. Later, this was used to coat the inside of ordinary glass beads before adding wax to create a whole new type of imitation pearl. It takes around 2,000 fish to produce about a litre of pearlessence concentrate.

- Majorica pearls aren't real pearls, despite what the name might suggest. Made by a secret process created by German immigrant Eduardo Hugo Heusch in Spain in 1890, they're generally agreed to be the world's best faux

---

* Fake/faux pearls are supposed to be clearly identified as such . . . but probably aren't always, everywhere in the world, by everyone.

** Faux means fake but, unlike the word 'fake', it doesn't sound like you're trying to fool everyone. Sure, you want the pearls to look real, but you're not selling them as anything other than an imitation.

*** Quanine, an organic waste product.

pearls.* The process includes pearlessence and polishing between coating.

- Today, simulated pearls are made by coating pearl-sized plastic beads dipped into a pearl film which is made from the finely ground powder of genuine pearls and is, therefore, very expensive. The more coatings of the film, the more convincing the finished product and the more expensive the fake pearls. They can be very difficult for a layperson to tell apart from the real thing.

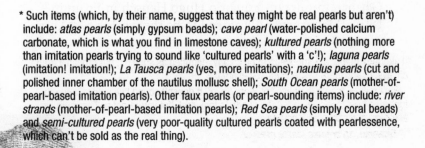

* Such items (which, by their name, suggest that they might be real pearls but aren't) include: *atlas pearls* (simply gypsum beads); *cave pearl* (water-polished calcium carbonate, which is what you find in limestone caves); *kultured pearls* (nothing more than imitation pearls trying to sound like 'cultured pearls' with a 'c'!); *laguna pearls* (imitation! imitation!); *La Tausca pearls* (yes, more imitations); *nautilus pearls* (cut and polished inner chamber of the nautilus mollusc shell); *South Ocean pearls* (mother-of-pearl-based imitation pearls). Other faux pearls (or pearl-sounding items) include: *river strands* (mother-of-pearl-based imitation pearls); *Red Sea pearls* (simply coral beads) and *semi-cultured pearls* (very poor-quality cultured pearls coated with pearlessence, which can't be sold as the real thing).

8 December

Miss Jekyll (with nothing to hide)

- Gertrude Jekyll, the fifth of seven children, lived from 1843 to 1932. Her father was a Grenadier Guardsman who retired young due to ill health.

- When she was 18, Gertrude enrolled in the South Kensington School of Art in London. As well as painting, she also studied botany, anatomy and optics.

- She created over 400 gardens, contributed over 1,000 articles to magazines and wrote 13 books (though she didn't start writing them until she was 55).

- Gertrude Jekyll ran a nursery-garden business and bred new plants right into her eighties.

- As well as a gardener, she was a painter, photographer, designer and a huge fan of the Arts and Craft movement.

- As Gertrude began to suffer from failing eyesight, she channelled her creative energies into garden design (though she did carry on painting for the rest of her life).

- Gertrude is probably best known for her work with the English architect Sir Edwin Lutyens. He designed or remodelled the houses while she created or redesigned the surrounding gardens.

- Her gardening philosophy was that there should be a sympathetic relationship between a house and its surroundings. Each plant should be chosen for its habitat, foliage and colour to achieve a 'practical, beautiful and appropriate effect'. She believed that a garden should also reveal unexpected views and 'pictorial surprises'.

- She created gardens in the UK, in Europe and in the USA.

- Gertrude's family connection with America included her great-great-grandfather, John Jekyll, who was Collector of Customs in Boston, Massachusetts, from 1707 to 1732.

(The famous 'Boston Tea Party'* didn't take place until the following year: 1733.)

● Gertrude's brother Walter was a friend of the author Robert Louis Stevenson who borrowed the surname for the title of his famous novel *The Strange Case of Dr Jekyll and Mr Hyde*.**

● Gertrude pronounced her name *Jee-kull*, whereas Dr Jekyll is generally pronounced *Jeck-ull*.***

● Her gravestone was inscribed by Edwin Lutyens with the words: ARTIST GARDENER CRAFTSWOMAN.

* The Boston Tea Party was no such thing. It is the name given to the action of those protesting against having to pay British taxes on tea. Dressed as Native Americans, a number boarded ships at anchor and tipped the cargo of loose tea into the water.

** He did ask permission first!

*** Robert Louis Stevenson is often called Robert *Loo-ee* Stevenson, but his name is correctly pronounced '*Lewis*'.

9 December

1960: the very, very, very first episode of TV series Coronation Street *is broadcast*

Words on *The Street*

- Commonly nicknamed *Corrie* or *The Street*, *Coronation Street* was originally only intended to be 13 episodes long, though some of those working at Granada – its makers – thought it might not even run that long. At the time of writing, it's still going!

- Only one of the original cast members remains: William Roache, who played Ken Barlow. He's the second-longest-serving actor in the history of TV soaps. Only Don Hastings, an actor in the American soap *As the World Turns* since *October* 1960 without a break, has played the same character longer.

- The opening titles have been reshot a number of times. When this was done in the 1970s, a cat wandered across a wall. This wasn't planned but, since then, a cat has always been deliberately included in any reshot title sequences.

- For ten years,* the Granada Studios Tour allowed members of the public to walk around the exterior set of Coronation Street. (It adjoined the Baker Street set for Granada's *Sherlock Holmes* series, starring Jeremy Brett in the title role.) The set was off-limits on Mondays, when exterior scenes were routinely shot.

- A few well-known people have appeared as themselves:
  - ◆ Wrestler Iain Campbell (in a bout with the character Stan Ogden)
  - ◆ The Duke of Bedford (encountered by the character Ena Sharples on a trip to his ancestral seat of Woburn Abbey)
  - ◆ HRH Prince Charles (on the show's 40th Anniversary episode in 2000)
  - ◆ Members of the rock band Status Quo

* 1989–99.

- Betty Driver, who later played Betty Turpin,* originally auditioned for the part of Hilda Ogden, a role which ended up being played by Jean Alexander.** Betty is godmother to one of William Roache's children.

- The actor Sir Laurence Olivier/Lord Olivier formed a fan club in honour of Hilda Ogden.

- Granada and ITV executives claim that *Coronation Street* is the world's longest-running soap opera. *The Guinness Book of Records* doesn't agree. The latter recognizes the US soap opera *Guiding Light* as the holder of that title, with over 50 years on television (plus an extra 15 on radio).

* Famous for her Lancashire hotpot.
** Jean Alexander was voted the 'Greatest Soap Opera Star of All Time' in a *TV Times* poll in September 2005.

10 December

*1851: Melvil Dewey, inventor of the Dewey
library classification system, is born**

Donald Duck and family

- Donald Duck's full name is Donald Fauntleroy Duck.

- In most films he appears under his own name and always
  seems to play the same character:** a duck with a very
  short temper trying not to get too annoyed. Despite this,
  he nearly always manages to get the audience on his side.
  Perhaps that's because he ultimately has a good heart.

- With the exception of a few hat-changes, Donald wears the
  same clothes in just about every appearance he makes: a
  sailor suit top half and sailor hat.

- Although he doesn't wear bottom halves, he still wraps a
  towel around his bottom half when stepping out of a bath
  or shower. This is to show a sense of propriety.

- Donald made his screen debut in the Silly Symphony
  (short) cartoon *The Wise Little Hen* on 9 June 1934. He
  looked a bit different back then, with a longer, thinner
  neck. (Perhaps it was the make-up.)

- Donald's first real starring – rather than scene-stealing –
  role was in *Don Donald* (1937), with love interest Donna
  Duck, whom – assuming she was the same duck –
  appeared in later films as Daisy Duck. The film is set in
  Mexico, and Donald spends much of the time wearing a
  sombrero.

- Donald appeared with a number of his animated friends
  in two South American-set films – *Saludos Amigos* (1942)***
  and *The Three Caballeros* (1945) – combining them with
  live action.

---

* Which, let me tell you, is exciting for a former highly unqualified library assistant such
as me.

** Unless, of course, they're documentaries.

*** Which means '*Hello Friends*'.

- During the Second World War, Donald appeared in the propaganda film *Der Fuehrer's Face* (1943), which included a song of the same name that was a HUGE hit.*
- Donald co-starred in the 3-D film *Working For Peanuts* (1953) with the cheeky little chipmunks Chip 'n' Dale.** Set in a zoo, there's plenty of 3-D action involving an elephant's trunk firing peanuts and the like!
- To celebrate Donald Duck's 50 years in show business – more loosely termed his '50th birthday',*** though he wasn't fresh out of the (duck) egg in *The Wise Little Hen*, CBS aired a US television special hosted by Dick Van Dyke on 13 November 1984.
- Donald has appeared in 128 films to date, and numerous TV shows, as well as being featured in comic strips and stories in newspapers, magazines and books.
- For much of his on-screen life, Donald Duck has lived with his identical-triplet nephews Huey, Dewey and Louie. Other regular family members include:
  - ◆ Scrooge McDuck, his uncle
  - ◆ Gladstone Gander, his cousin
  - ◆ Grandma Duck, his – er – grandma (aka Elvira Coot)
  - ◆ Della Thelma Duck,**** Donald's sister and mother of the triplets
- For some reason, Donald Duck's name is translated into different languages when he appears abroad. In Finland, I'd still be Philip Ardagh . . . but Donald Duck becomes Aku Ankka. (Perhaps he should complain to his agent.) Other versions of his name include:
  - ◆ Anders And (Danish)
  - ◆ Donal Bebek (Indonesian)

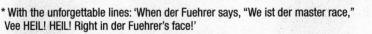

* With the unforgettable lines: 'When der Fuehrer says, "We ist der master race," Vee HEIL! HEIL! Right in der Fuehrer's face!'

** Chip 'n' Dale . . . Chippendale – like the furniture – geddit?

*** Donald's actual birthday is 13 March . . . or 16 September . . . or 9 June . . . That's the trouble with an actor called Donald Duck playing a character called Donald Duck. Fact and fiction blur!

**** Better known by everyone – including herself, for some strange reason – by the nickname Dumbella.

- ◆ Kalle Anka (Swedish)
- ◆ Lekker Hapje (Dutch)
- ◆ Ntonalt Ntak (Greek)
- ◆ Paja Patak (Serbo-Croat)
- ◆ Patoka Donald (Bulgarian)
- ◆ Tang Lao Ya (Chinese)

● Though now in his seventies, Donald Duck appears to have aged very little, if at all, and there's no suggestion that he's had plastic surgery. One of his favourite phrases – spoken in his oft-imitated voice, of course – is still: 'Oh, phooey!'

11 December

Toothy grins

Dentist (looking inside patient's mouth): Good Heavens!
You've got the biggest cavity I've ever seen . . . the biggest
cavity I've ever seen!
Patient: I'm scared enough without you saying it twice.
Dentist: I didn't! That was the echo.

Q: What does the dentist of the year get?
A: A little plaque.

Q: What does a dentist do on a roller-coaster ride?
A: He braces himself!

A husband and wife go to the dentist. The wife says, 'I need a
tooth pulled as soon as possible. We're in a hurry, so there's no
time for gas or anaesthetic. Just pull the tooth, so we can get out
of here, please.' The dentist looks surprised. 'You're a very brave
woman,' he says. 'Now, which tooth is it?' The wife turns to her
husband and says, 'Open wide and show him which one, dear.'

Q: How many dentists does it take to change a light bulb?
A: Three. One to administer the anaesthetic, one to extract the
light bulb and one to offer the socket some of that funny pink
mouthwash.

Father: Has your tooth stopped hurting since you went to the
dentist?
Son: I don't know, Dad. He kept it.

Q: What did the tooth say to the dentist going on his lunch?
A: Fill me in when you get back.

A man goes to a restaurant for a special occasion and realizes that he's forgotten his false teeth. Observing the situation, a young man at the next table leans across and pulls a pair of false teeth out of his pocket. 'Try these,' he says. The man tries them. 'Thanks, but they're too small,' he says. The young man produces another pair. 'What about these?' 'Too big,' says the man. 'No worries,' says the man at the next table. 'I do have one last pair.' The man slips them in and they're a perfect fit. At the end of the meal he turns to the young man who helped him out. 'Thank you so much,' he says. 'You must give me your business card. I could do with a good dentist.' 'I'm not a dentist,' says the young man. 'I'm the local undertaker.'

Dentist to patient in the chair: Would you be kind enough to give me a few of your loudest, most painful screams?
Patient: Why?
Dentist: There are so many people in the waiting room right now and I want to be home in time for *Home & Away*.

12 December

*1982: 30,000 anti-nuclear women protesters form a
ring around Greenham Common airbase, England*

Popular myths (or 'stuff which people think is true which often ain't')

The Twelve Days of Christmas

The song was neither a secret code song for Christians in non-
Christian countries where their faith was forbidden, nor for
persecuted Catholics living in England.* This myth surfaced in
the 1990s, with those claiming to have discovered it generally
unable to provide their original sources.

The US Presidential Seal

The US President's seal of office includes an eagle clutching
an olive branch – the symbol of peace – in its left talon (as
you face it) and what look like thunderbolts in its right. The
eagle faces left. Rumour has it that, in time of war, this seal
is changed for one with the eagle facing right, away from the
olive branch and towards the thunderbolts. This is not only
mentioned as fact in an episode of the fabulous *West Wing* TV
drama, but also in the novel *Deception Point*, by Dan Brown.**
In fact, this is not true. The eagle stays as it is. The confusion
may arise from the fact that, until President Truman had the
seal modified in 1945, the eagle did face the other way.

Mr Ed the Talking Horse

A popular 1960s US TV serial was *Mr Ed*, about a talking
horse. Back in the 1990s Snopes.com – an excellent website for
debunking urban myths – reported that the horse was, in fact,
played by a zebra! They were being naughty . . . and creating
an urban myth of their own. (Though there are clues in the

* The first is patently ridiculous, because it's obviously a song about Christmas: the
birth of Christ!

** Author of *The Da Vinci Code*.

485

entry to suggest that it shouldn't be taken too seriously.) Mr Ed was definitely played by an American Saddlebred horse.

Brass bands

Brass bands aren't called brass bands because all of the instruments are made out of brass. Brass instruments are technically those whose tones are produced by vibrating the lips through a resonator. Brass in this instance, therefore, refers to the type of sound they make.

'Ring a ring o' roses'

The nursery rhyme does not date back to the Black Death of the 14th century, with the ring representing the round red rash that was the first symptom of the plague. The earliest written record of the rhyme wasn't until Kate Greenaway's *Mother Goose or The Old Nursery Rhymes* of 1881. Had 'Ring a ring o' roses' been part of the oral* tradition some 400 to 500 years previously, you'd have expected it to have had a mention somewhere before. Apparently, the first written record of the plague interpretation was James Leasor's *The Plague and the Fire*, which wasn't published until 1961! But try telling that to some people. We all choose to believe what we choose to believe.

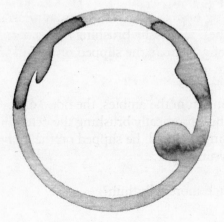

* Spoken/sung.

13 December

A rose by any other name . . .

The Windscale nuclear reactor was renamed Sellafield,
probably in the hope that people would forget that it was
Windscale. Here are a smattering of suggestions for some other
name changes, designed to make the world seem a friendlier
place:

- Oil spill: gloopy-doop
- Wasp: striper
- Broken glass: crystaleen
- Nettle: hair-plant
- Snake:** amble
- Spider: octogilly
- Traitor: nono
- Rash: sputtle
- Sting: zing
- Rusty: ruberish

Example 1
Running from the snakes, the traitor dashed between the
branches, frantically brushing the spiders from his hair.
Reaching the road, he slipped on the oil spill, landing on
broken glass . . .
would become:
Running from the ambles, the nono dashed between the
branches, frantically brushing the octogillies from his hair.
Reaching the road, he slipped on the gloopy-doop, landing
on crystaleen . . .

So much more jolly, huh?

---

* Which he later renames the *Golden Hind*.

** The word 'snake' has the disadvantage of beginning with the letters 'sn' in keeping
with a number of less-pleasant words in the language: sneeze, snot, snide, snappy,
snarl, snicker, snatch, snare, snitch, snivel, snob, snooty, etc., etc.

Example 2

Stung first by the wasps and then by the nettles, Trevor
watched in horror as a rash appeared on his skin. He stumbled
on to a rusty old can . . .

would become:

Zinged by the stripers and then by the hair-plants, Trevor
watched in horror as a sputtle appeared on his skin. He
stumbled on to a ruberish old can . . .

14 December

1911: Roald Amundsen becomes the first person to reach the
South Pole, beating the English expedition led by Robert Scott*

Ten Famous Roalds**

1. Roald Amundsen

2. Roald Dahl***

3.

4.

5.

6.

7.

8.

9.

10.

* In May 1926 Amundsen reached the North Pole aboard the airship the Norge, making
him the first person to have reached both poles. He disappeared in 1928 on a rescue
mission in a flying boat to find the missing aeronautical engineer (and fellow Arctic
explorer) Umberto Nobile. Nobile was later found safe and well. Amundsen's body was
never found.

** Uh-oh! I feel I might be on to a non-starter here!

*** Who was named after Amundsen in the first place. Both were Norwegian, though Dahl
was born in Wales. Roald Dahl Day is celebrated on 13 September (Dahl's birthday).
There's now a Roald Dahl Museum and Story Centre. You can find out more at:
www.roalddahlmuseum.org

15 December

1939: Gone with the Wind *premieres in Atlanta, Georgia, USA*

Film actors whose names sound similar to architectural features

Diana Dors

Clark Gable

Er . . .

OK, OK. Let's try something else:

Film actors whose names are somehow related to animals

Walter Pidgeon

Sandra Bullock

Kevin Bacon*

Brad Pitt**

Nicolas Cage***

Saffron Burrows****

Er . . .

This isn't really working, is it?

* It's what some pigs become.
** Wild animals are sometimes captured in pits.
*** And put in cages.
**** Think bunnies.

Ten things famous for not working

1. Aristocracy/the landed gentry.
2. Charles Babbage's mechanical computers, in his lifetime.
3. Chicken poo as a hair-restorer.*
4. Being able to cut glass with scissors underwater.
5. Anti-gravity boots.
6. Those X-ray glasses you could send off for in the back of kids' comics.
7. Me and boomerangs.**
8. Spinning gold from straw.
9. Finding an economical method of extracting gold from seawater.***
10. The Elixir of Eternal Youth/Eternal Life.

* Or so I'm told.
** I can't just blame the boomerangs, though I'd like to.
*** It is, I am assured by people with ENORMOUS brains, perfectly possible to extract gold from seawater. The problem is, however, that the cost of the process currently far outweighs the amount of gold that could be extracted each time.

16 December

A short list containing some famous diets and some larger-than-life people

- **The Atkins Diet:** a high-fat low-carbohydrate/no carbohydrate diet, designed to accelerate fat burning and loss of weight even when eating constantly. Yes to steaks. No to chips, pasta and fruit.

- **Fatty Arbuckle**

- **Zen macrobiotics:** a diet based on the ancient Chinese polarities of Yin and Yang, the most perfectly balanced food – between Yin (stimulating) and Yang (strengthening) – is brown rice, and, therefore, the staple of this culinary regime. Macrobiotics ('large-life') relies entirely on natural whole foods, locally produced.

- **Oliver Hardy** (of Laurel and Hardy)

- **The High Fibre Diet:** intended to lower cholesterol, provide protection against diverticulitis and heart disease, and help with weight control.

- **John Candy**

- **The Stillman (high protein) Diet:** unlimited amounts of lean meat, poultry and seafood, along with eggs and low-fat cheese, consumed in six small meals – rather than three big ones – a day. Bread, fruit and veg strictly prohibited, along with sugar and alcohol . . . and – oh yes – you must drink at least eight glasses of milk a day, and take vitamin pills.

- **Cyril Smith** (one-time Liberal MP)

- **The Scarsdale Diet:** a two-week crash diet or, for the longer term, two weeks on and two weeks off. A strictly regimented diet, limited to around 1,000 calories per day, comprised of 43% protein, 34.5% carbohydrates and 22.5% fats. By banning oils, butters and other fats, the body is encouraged to metabolize existing stores of fat. Specific menus are allocated to specific days.

- **Luciano Pavarotti**
- **The C Diet:** eating everything you see.
- **Alfred Hitchcock**
- **The F Plan Diet:** a very popular high-fibre, low-fat, calorie-controlled eating plan.
- **Henry VIII**
- **The Grapefruit Diet:** An 800-calories-a-day diet based around eating plenty of 'fat-burning' grapefruit in order to kick-start your metabolism, along with as much black coffee as you like, some boiled eggs and the occasional piece of dry toast.
- **Orson Welles**
- **The Blood Type Diet:** Not a diet of blood – thank heavens – but one which recommends that you follow a diet that's been specifically designed for your blood group!
- **Marlon Brando**

IMPORTANT NOTE 1: Never go on a diet without discussing it with me first. No, I'm sorry. That should read: Never go on a diet without discussing it with your doctor or health practitioner first.

IMPORTANT NOTE 2: The inclusion of well-known figures in the same list as these diets in no way implies that any one of them has ever been on any of these diets – or any other diet, for that matter – nor had or has any reason to be.*

IMPORTANT NOTE 3: You're standing on my foot.**

* I just heard a sigh of relief from the publisher's legal department.
** Another of my despicable lies.

17 December

1903: the Wright brothers' 'Flyer'
becomes the world's first heavier-
than-air machine to fly*

The names of the Wright brothers (and sisters) who weren't the famous Wright brothers (or sisters),** but were their brothers (or sisters) - because Wilbur and Orville weren't the only two

1. Reuchlin Wright (1861-1920) brother
2. Lorin Wright (1862-1939) brother
3. Otis Wright (1870-1870) brother (twin to Ida)
4. Ida Wright (1870-1870) sister (twin to Otis)
5. Katharine Wright (1874-1929) sister

None of the children had a middle name. Their father, Milton Wright, was a bishop. Wilbur was named after Wilbur Fisk, and Orville after Orville Dewey, both fellow clergymen their father had an admiration for . . . but Wilbur and Orville apparently called each other by the nicknames Ullam and Bubs!

Wilbur was Milton and Susan's third child (1867-1912), Orville their sixth (1871-1948).

* Flying 17 metres at Kitty Hawk, North Carolina, USA
** Not that there were actually any famous Wright sisters!

18 December

1737: Antonio Stradivari – better known as Stradivarius – dies

The world's most valuable violins, or not, as the case may be*

- A Stradivarius by the name of the Lady Tennant was purchased at a Christie's auction for $2,032,000 in 2005 and was referred to by some as being 'the world's most valuable musical instrument' when, in fact, it was simply the musical instrument for which the highest amount had ever been paid at auction. Made in 1699, the violin is now on 'indefinite loan' to the world-famous violin soloist Yang Liu.

- In May 2006, the title of 'musical instrument for which the highest amount had ever been paid at auction' then went to another Stradivarius violin: the Hammer. Again sold by Christie's, this instrument fetched $3,544,000.

- In the past, the Nippon Music Foundation of Japan purchased the Paganini Stradivari Quartet of instruments for an impressive $15,000,000; an average of $3,750,000 each. More recently, they acquired a number of Stradivarius instruments at prices ranging between $4,000,000 and $5,000,000.

- The world's oldest surviving violin was made by Andrea Amati in 1564 and can be seen at the Ashmolean Museum in Oxford. A violin from the same set – but made two years later, and now housed in the Civic Museum in Cremona – has been valued at $10,000,000 . . . so heaven knows how much the Ashmolean Museum one is worth! But it's a pretty safe bet that *this* is the world's most valuable violin.

* Antique instruments are valued on three main criteria: period, physical condition and their provenance (history). In the case of Stradivarius violins, those made after 1700 are generally the most valuable, reaching the highest prices for those made in about 1715. (This was because he became an even more skilled craftsman as time went on.) He is known to have created around 100 instruments – not all violins – of which around 65% are said to have survived.**

** In the mid-19th century violins were mass-produced because there was such a great demand for them. Many of them were labelled with famous makers' names, including that of Stradivarius. They weren't intended as forgeries, it was simply the fashion . . . Today, however, these 19th-century copies turn up now and again, fooling those who come across them into thinking they've unearthed an original and are about to earn a fortune!

19 December

1981: the Royal National Lifeboat Institute Penlee lifeboat, the Solomon Browne, *is lost with all its crew*

The crew members of the *Solomon Browne** – all volunteers – who gave their lives attempting to rescue those aboard the *Union Star***

- William Trevelyan Richards (56), Coxswain
- James Stephen Madron (35), Second Coxswain/Mechanic
- Barrie Torrie (33), a fisherman
- Charles Greenhaugh (46), the landlord of the Ship Inn in Mousehole
- Gary Wallis (23)
- John Blewett (43), Emergency Mechanic, a telephone engineer
- Kevin Smith (23)
- Nigel Brockman (43), Assistant Mechanic, a fisherman

Today, the old lifeboat house at Penlee Point stands empty, as a tribute and lasting memorial to its dead crew. All men were posthumously awarded RNLI medals for their bravery and sacrifice. A public appeal raised over £3 million for the victims' families, and increased awareness of the remarkable work carried out by RNLI volunteers around the British coast. To find out more about the RNLI, visit: www.rnli.org.uk

---

* A wooden 47-ft (14-m) Watson-class lifeboat crewed by men from the Cornish village of Mousehole launched at Penlee Point. All crew members – selected from the 12 who answered the 'shout' to assist – were experienced seamen. The *Solomon Browne*'s final radio message was: 'We've got four men off, hang on, we have got four at the moment. There's two left on board . . .'

** In appalling conditions with 50-ft-high (15-m) waves.

20 December

1901: US physicist Robert J. van de Graaff is born*

Some hair-raising facts

- Using the image of 'hairs standing on end' to mean scared probably first appeared in print in *Hamlet* in 1603, where Shakespeare wrote: *'I could a tale unfold, whose lightest word would harrow up thy soul, freeze thy young blood, make thy two eyes, like stars, start from their spheres, thy knotted and combined locks to part and each particular hair to stand on end, like quills upon the fretful porpentine.'* (A porpentine, I guess, being a porcupine.)

- The allusion to making your hair stand on end isn't a metaphor. It's real. Dogs' hackles rise when they're scared and we humans get goosebumps – or gooseflesh – causing our body hairs to rise when we're sc-sc-sc-scared.

- The word 'horripilation' appears in Thomas Blount's *Glossographia; or A Dictionary Interpreting All Such Hard Words of Whatsoever Language, now used in our refined English Tongue* of 1656, in which he defines it as: '. . . the standing up of the hair for fear . . . a sudden quaking, shuddering or shivering.'

- In 2004 Gillette introduced a new high-tech razor featuring a tiny battery-powered motor emitting vibrating pulses that cause the hairs on the skin to stand up so that they can be sliced off by the razor blade more easily.

- Rubbing a balloon on your hair (with a view to 'sticking' the balloon on the ceiling) creates static electricity and causes the hair to stand on end. You get the same effect if you rub the balloon on a sweater/jumper and then hold it to your hair.

- Your hair can also stand up in a thunderstorm. If that happens to you, good luck.**

* Inventor of the van de Graaff generator, which makes the hair on your head stand up like that porpentine Shakespeare mentioned. It's said to work even better if you wear rubber-soled shoes/wellies.

** Bang!

21 December

A few words about crosswords

- Before any Americans get too smug about coming up with such a great idea, I should add that, although the first crossword appeared in the fun supplement of *New York World*, it was devised by Arthur Wynne, a native of Liverpool working as a journalist in the US.

- This first crossword was, in fact, called a word-cross.

- Right up until 1924, *New York World* was the only newspaper publishing crosswords.

- It was in 1924 that a (then) small publishing company, named Simon & Schuster, brought out a collection of *New York World* crosswords in book form, followed by another and then another. They were bestsellers. Crosswords were suddenly all the rage, appearing in every kind of newspaper and magazine.

- In November of that year, the *New York Times* claimed that the crossword craze was causing 'temporary madness'!

- *Puzzles of 1925*, a Broadway musical revue starring Walter Pidgeon, included a sketch about crossword solvers.

- Puzzles soon caught on in Britain too, but *The Times* – whose cryptic crosswords are now considered some of the finest in the world – didn't publish its first puzzle until 1930.

- Having declared that the 'crossword epidemic' was over at the beginning of 1927, the *New York Times* didn't publish their first puzzle until 1942, and didn't start their weekly crosswords until 1950.

- One of the most bizarre incidents involving a crossword raised matters of international security during the Second World War. In May 1944 British MI5 officers doing a *Daily Telegraph* crossword, compiled by a 54-year-old headmaster named Leonard Dawes, were horrified to find the following answers to clues:

- Utah
- Omaha
- Mulberry
- Neptune
- Overlord

- The reason why the counter-espionage officers were so worried by what they read was because each of these words related to the top-secret D-Day landings:

  - Utah: one of the Normandy beaches on which Allied forces were due to land
  - Omaha: *as with Utah*
  - Mulberry: the floating harbour to be towed across the Channel
  - Neptune: the naval support unit
  - Overlord: the code name for the entire D-Day landings!

- Officers were sent to see Dawes to determine whether he was somehow trying to tip the Germans off. They concluded that it was nothing more than an absolutely extraordinary coincidence.

- There is an equally innocent possibility as to how these particular words came into Mr Dawes's head at the time. In 1939, his school had been evacuated from London to Surrey (to avoid the bombing). At that time, there were many members of the US Forces based in the area who could well have openly used the words – being *code words* no one else would have understood – and these may have been overheard by some of the pupils. The boys, in turn, may have suggested them to Leonard Dawes, who is known to have sometimes asked senior boys for ideas for words for inclusion in his puzzles. This is speculation, of course, but it could go some way to explaining one of the crossword world's most enduring mysteries!

22 December

Some uncomfortable facts in the Dreyfus Affair

- Alfred Dreyfus was a captain in the French army on the Army General's General Staff.

- He was also Jewish.

- Dreyfus's family was well established and prosperous, having made its money in Alsace when the province was still a part of France.

- When Alsace was absorbed into Germany, the Dreyfus family moved to Paris so as to remain French.

- In October 1894 Alfred Dreyfus was arrested out of the blue and then charged with passing military secrets to the Germans via the German Embassy in Paris.

- On this day in December 1894 he was convicted of treason by a military tribunal. The 'evidence' against him was a handwritten note listing offers of secret French military information. The list had been found in the office of the German military attaché Max von Schwartzkoppen. It had been fished out of his wastepaper basket by an Alsatian cleaning lady (working for French counter-intelligence).

- All that linked Dreyfus to the list was that he had access to much of the information being offered on it, and that the handwriting looked not dissimilar to his.

- Dreyfus was sentenced to life imprisonment in total isolation on Devil's Island, a notoriously dreadful prison island off the coast of French Guiana.

- Two years after Dreyfus's transportation, a new chief of army intelligence was appointed. Lieutenant Colonel Georges Picquart re-examined all the evidence and dug far deeper than the original tribunal. He concluded that the guilty officer was one Major Walsin Esterhazy, not Dreyfus.

- Despite being strongly anti-Semitic, Picquart believed in justice and in having the true culprit removed from the French army. He found himself thwarted at every turn and was then transferred to Tunisia.

- A military court did eventually try Major Esterhazy but, despite the strength of evidence, acquitted him.*

- There was much anti-Semitism in France at the time, and many prominent people were convinced that this had had a part to play in Dreyfus's arrest and conviction. They were sure that there had been a terrible miscarriage of justice.

- One of Dreyfus's strongest supporters was the world-famous French novelist Émile Zola, who wrote an open letter, *J'accuse!*, a detailed denunciation of the army's cover-up.

- As a result, Zola was found guilty of libelling the army and sentenced to prison, which he managed to avoid by fleeing to England.

- Dreyfus was retried in 1899 and found guilty again.

- In 1906 – 12 years after the first trial – the verdict was finally changed to *not* guilty.

- Amazingly, not only was Dreyfus restored to his original rank but he also chose to return to the army.

- Zola was given an amnesty and was also able to return to France.

* He too could, of course, have been innocent. It's just that Dreyfus was convicted on much lesser evidence.

23 December

1888: Vincent Van Gogh cuts off part of his ear with a razor

Characters in Robert Louis* Stevenson's *Treasure Island***

Ben Gunn: former pirate in Captain Flint's crew, marooned on Treasure Island for three years:

> 'From [tree] trunk to trunk the creature flitted like a deer, running manlike on two legs, but unlike any man that I had ever seen, stooping almost double as it ran.'

Billy Bones: the man with the map locating Captain Flint's treasure, he spends his days at the Admiral Benbow inn.

Blind Pew: the pirate in search of the map, who gives Billy Bones the black spot*** as a warning – or more of a threat – that he will die.

> He was plainly blind, for he tapped before him with a stick, and wore a great green shade over his eyes and nose; and he was hunched, as if with age or weakness, and wore a huge old tattered sea cloak with a hood, that made him appear positively deformed. I never saw in my life a more dreadful-looking figure.'

Captain Flint: the pirate who buried the treasure on Treasure Island before the story begins.

Cap'n Flint: the parrot often found on Long John Silver's shoulder, the bird's favourite cry being: 'Pieces of eight! Pieces of eight! Pieces of eight!' (A piece of eight being a Spanish dollar, equivalent to eight *reales*.****)

Captain Smollett: the first non-pirate in this list and (honest) captain of the *Hispaniola*. His crew, however, proves less reliable . . .

---

* Pronounced 'Lewis' not 'Loo-ee', remember.

** Favourite children's book of children's author and former Children's Laureate Michael Morpurgo.

*** The black spot is a piece of fiction, but so popular that many people think that pirates really did give them out as deadly warnings.

**** Hence the name.

Jim Hawkins: the main narrator of this tale, he becomes a cabin boy aboard the *Hispaniola* and is at the centre of much of the action.

Doctor Livesey: family physician to the Hawkins family, he's a good man and a good doctor, treating the wounds of friends and enemies alike.

Long John Silver:* once a member of Captain Flint's crew, he's now the cook aboard the *Hispaniola* before revealing his true pirate colours. Ruthless, cunning and treacherous, he has a genuine liking for Jim Hawkins:

> 'His left leg was cut off close by the hip, and under the left shoulder he carried a crutch, which he managed with wonderful dexterity, hopping about upon it like a bird. He was very tall and strong, with a face as big as a ham – plain and pale, but intelligent and smiling.'

Squire Trelawney: the (honest) man who finances the expedition to find Captain Flint's treasure. He buys the *Hispaniola* and picks the crew . . . unaware that many of its members are not what they seem!

Tom Redruth: the squire's gamekeeper, who accompanies him on this voyage of adventure. Poor man.**

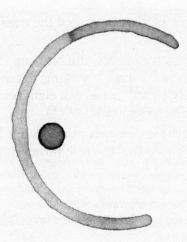

* With a missing leg, rather than ear.
** Ooops! A bit of a giveaway that he comes to a sticky end.

24 December

A whisper of silences

- that dreadful silence when a joke falls flat.
- the eerie silence after a terrible explosion or earthquake.
- John Cage's *4'33"* (4 minutes, 33 seconds), performed on any instrument in three (equally silent) movements.*
- the two minutes' silence in remembrance of the war dead on Armistice Day and Remembrance Sunday.
- 'Taking the Fifth', as in refusing to answer a question – remaining silent on a matter – on the grounds that an answer might be used against a person to convict them of a criminal offence.**
- the one minute's silence on 6 September 1997 to remember Diana, Princess of Wales.
- the right to remain silent without it suggesting one has something to hide.***
- the vow of silence taken by some religious orders.
- the silence in a Quaker meeting, to let the divine speak to the heart and mind.
- the strange calm before a storm.****
- the silence just before a gunfight in old black and white westerns, often accompanied by a tumbleweed or two rolling by in the wind.*****
- what comes to us all in the end.

---

* Originally written for piano, the world premiere of *4'33"* was given on 29 August 1952 at Woodstock, near New York, by David Tudor. He raised the piano lid at the start of each movement, played nothing, then lowered it at the end of each movement. After four minutes and thirty-three seconds, the piece was over without a note having been played.

** This is an American term, referring to the Fifth Amendment in the US Bill of Rights.

*** A hotly debated point of law.

**** And often afterwards too.

***** Many people assume tumbleweed to be a native North American plant, but it ain't. It's likely that it actually came to America by mistake, mixed up in flax seeds imported from the Ukraine.

25 December

Things I know about Father Christmas (aka Santa Claus) despite never having met him

- He is fat.
- He is jolly.
- He is kind.
- He is magical in a way that no one else is magical.
- He has a great big bushy white beard and moustache.
- He wears a red suit trimmed with white fur, often with shiny black boots.
- He chuckles 'Ho! Ho! Ho!'
- He is very, very old.
- He rides in a magic flying sleigh with sacks full of presents on Christmas Eve.
- He comes down the chimney, if there is one.
- He fills children's stockings with goodies.
- His sleigh is pulled by magic flying reindeer called: Dasher, Dancer, Prancer, Vixen, Comet, Cupid, Donner,* Blitzen and Rudolph (the one with the red nose).**
- He lives at the North Pole.

* aka Donder.
** Who was first brought to the attention of the world by one Robert L. May.

And if you were born on
Christmas Day . . .

- According to folklore, the Devil can't take your soul.
- When you're very young, you think all the fuss is because it's *your* birthday.
- Then you realize it's Jesus Christ's birthday.
- Then you realize that not even Christians think that Christ was actually born on 25 December. (It's just the date chosen to remember his birth.)
- Then you realize that many people who 'celebrate' Christmas simply enjoy the Christmas tree, decorations, cards, presents, food and the get-together part of the day, rather than necessarily the religious aspect.
- But what concerns you far more is the fact that you often end up with a combined birthday-cum-Christmas present instead of two separate ones!

1898: Pierre and Marie Curie* announce they've discovered radium

Some less-often repeated facts about Marie Curie

- Marie Curie won both a Nobel Prize for Physics (1903) and one for Chemistry (1911). What's less known is that she donated her gold Nobel Prize medals – along with her husband's – to the Allies' war effort in the First World War.

- She regularly carried test tubes containing radioactive isotopes in her pocket** and kept them in a desk drawer, unaware of the real dangers of radioactivity . . . though she did comment on their glow. Her notebooks are still highly radioactive today.

- Marie was a cycling nut. Her honeymoon with Pierre was a cycling tour of Brittany, and the record of expenses she kept in one of those aforementioned notebooks shows that she lavished a great deal on her bike.

- She and husband Pierre's laboratory was little more than a large shed with a glass roof. It was swelteringly hot in the summer and leaked in the winter.

- Marie had conducted her experiments with Pierre until his death in 1906. He stepped out in front of a horse-driven former milk-cart being used to transport surplus army uniforms.

- On her death in 1934, Marie was buried in a coffin on top of her late husband's in the cemetery at Sceaux (in Paris's outskirts).

- In 1995, Marie's and Pierre's remains were moved to the Panthéon in Paris. Interment in the Panthéon is seen as the highest honour from the French Nation for 'national heroes'. It's even more of an honour when you consider that Marie was born Polish.

* See 24 June.
** Florence Nightingale kept a little owl in hers.***
*** Not that it was a competition.

Those with noses of note

1. **Rudolph the Red-Nosed Reindeer:** the name says it all. As if being one of Father Christmas's magic sleigh-pulling reindeer isn't enough, he also has a glowing red nose!

2. **Rudolph I of Hapsburg:*** both King of Germany and Emperor of the Holy Roman Empire in the 13th century, he was said to have a nose so large that official portrait painters made a point of making it look smaller!

3. **Pinocchio:** some days, his nose looked proportionate to his head but, after a lie or two, took on epic proportions.

4. **Thomas Wedders:** has the distinction of having the longest known nose of any human in history (so far). It measured an extraordinary 7½ inches (19 cm). He was exhibited as nothing more than a circus freak in the 1700s.

5. **Mister Bignose:** a cartoon character drawn by Banx in the short-lived *Oink!* magazine, which lasted just 18 months in the 1980s.**

6. **Matthew Parker:** though his nose wasn't particularly large, his nosiness earns him a special place in this list, not least because he gave his name to the term 'a nosy parker' (meaning someone who sticks their nose into other people's business). Archbishop of Canterbury during Elizabeth I's reign, he gained the reputation for wanting to know *everything* about matters of the Church.

7. **Keyhole Kate:** a regular of the *Sparky* comic, cartoon character Keyhole Kate would poke her nose through keyholes, being such a – er – nosy parker! (She started life in the *Dandy* along with Hungry Horace, who also moved to *Sparky*.)

* aka Rudolf I of Hapsburg (spelled with an 'f' rather than a 'ph').
** And, sadly, I gave my copies away!

8. **Tycho Brahe**: the 16th-century Danish astronomer is more famous for the fake tip to his nose, replacing the real tip he lost in a swordfight. The replacement was made of gold.

9. **Cyrano de Bergerac:*** the dramatist and duellist is famously said to have fought over a thousand duels with those foolish enough to have insulted his humungous nose. What's even more surprising to some people is that Cyrano de Bergerac really was a real person, though made famous through Edmond Rostand's play.

10. **Jimmy Durante:** the piano-playing, song-and-dance comedic actor who starred in films, TV and on the stage had such a large nose – or snozzle – that he became better known as Snozzle Durante.

11. **Josef Myslivecek:** the 18th-century Czech composer cut off his nose as a quack cure to an unfortunate disease. He's probably equally – if not better – known today for his absence of nose than he is for his operas.

* Played by Gérard Depardieu.

28 December

1895: the world's first moving film, by the Lumière brothers, is shown in Paris

What some of those people do whose names appear under strange job titles – you know the ones – in the credits at the end of films

Best Boy: aka Best Boy Grip, Best Boy Electric, the Best Boy is usually the chief assistant of the *gaffer* or *key grip*. (Female chief assistants are usually called Best Boys rather than Best Girls.) They're in charge of the people and equipment, responsible for scheduling both in the required numbers for each day.

Dolly Grip: a *grip* who moves a dolly – a small truck, which rolls along dolly tracks, carrying the camera, along with some of the camera crew and, on occasion, even the director.

Grip: a highly skilled member of the crew responsible for setting up, adjusting and maintaining the equipment on the set. Their duties are related to mechanical rigging, lighting refinement and even camera movement. In the UK a grip only works with equipment on which the camera is mounted.

Foley Artist: aka Foley Operator, the person who creates foley sound effects, effects which are recreated in synchronization with the visual elements of the film. They're named after an early sound-effects man, Jack Foley.

Foley Editor: Edits the sounds created by a *foley artist*.

Foley Mixer: a sound mixer who works with the *foley artist* to mix and create sound effects.

Gaffer: aka Chief Lighting Technician, the head of the electrical department responsible for the design and execution of the lighting plan for a production. The name comes from the controlling of natural light in early films by use of tarpaulins held in place with long poles called gaffs.

Key Grip: the head of the grips, and often a construction co-ordinator. *Gaffers* and *grips* work closely.

Location Mixer: the sound mixer responsible for mixing sounds recorded on location, rather than in the studio.

Pyrotechnician: an expert on fire and explosions for special effects and stunts.

29 December

1809: William Gladstone, British prime minister, is born*

Twenty things I wouldn't want to have named after me

1. A musical loo seat.
2. An area of contaminated land upon which there are plans to build a children's hospital.
3. A particularly smelly cheese.
4. An equation that is compulsory for all children to learn to solve in Maths.
5. A constricting pair of pants.
6. One of those cans you open with a little key, that you always end up cutting yourself on.
7. A kind of mould often found festering in bathroom grouting.
8. Something electrical that emits a persistent low hum.
9. A deadly spider.
10. An exercise regime.
11. A TV recording device which always somehow manages to miss off the first ten minutes of what you really want to watch.
12. A breed of dog with a particularly shaggy underbelly that is difficult to clean and has a very 'doggy' smell when wet.
13. An extraordinarily complicated board game with pages and pages of instructions and rules.
14. A dentist's drill.
15. A leatherette/faux-leather pouffe.

* After whom the Gladstone bag was named.**

** Belisha beacons – those flashing orange balls at the top of stripy poles at some zebra crossings – are named after Isaac Leslie Hore-Belisha (First Baron Hore-Belisha) who was Minister for Transport*** in the 1930s.

*** In 1937 he became Secretary of State for War.****

**** He also rewrote the Highway Code.*****

***** Which is, today, one of the bestselling books in Britain.

16. A pen which leaks in the warmth of a pocket.

17. A style of open-toe sandal.

18. A kind of super glue which sticks your finger and thumb together while you're halfway through getting the cap off the !?$!!! thing.

19. Any stinging jellylike animal which lurks out of sight just below the surface of the sea near the shore of a holiday beach.

20. A brand of sticking plasters that really hurt when you pull them off.

30 December

1879: Gilbert and Sullivan's comic operetta The Pirates of Penzance *receives its world premiere*

Gilbert without Sullivan

W. S. Gilbert wrote the words. Arthur Sullivan composed the music. Sullivan was knighted in 1883. Gilbert had to wait until 1907.

● At a dinner party some time after Sir Arthur Sullivan's death:
GUEST: What is Sir Arthur doing these days?
GILBERT: He is doing nothing.
GUEST: Surely he is composing?
GILBERT: On the contrary, he is decomposing.

● A paraphrased conversation illustrating Gilbert's offstage wit:
MAN: Call me a cab!
GILBERT: You're a four-wheeler.
MAN: Why did you say that?
GILBERT: Well, I can hardly call you hansom.*

● And again:
GUEST: Mrs B—— was very pretty once.
GILBERT: Yes, but not twice.

● Gilbert didn't like Shakespeare's plays and liked *Hamlet* least of all. He once commented to the actor Herbert Beerbohm Tree of his performance in the tragic title role: 'I never saw anything so funny in my life, and yet it was not in the least vulgar.'

● Gilbert's near neighbours to his Stanmore home were the Blackwell family of Cross & Blackwell preserves and pickles fame. In those class-ridden days, the Blackwells had a reputation for trying to 'pass themselves off' as landed gentry rather than having made their money from manufacturing, heaven forbid! One day, Gilbert received a letter of complaint about his dogs having strayed on to the Blackwells' property. He wrote back: 'Dear Sir, I will

* A type of cab and a dreadful pun.

take care that in future my dogs do not trespass on your preserves. Kindly pardon the expression.'*

- As a young man, author P. G. Wodehouse met Gilbert and interrupted one of his stories by laughing so loud and so long that everyone else turned their attention elsewhere, leaving the end of the tale untold. As a result, Gilbert gave him one of his stares. Wodehouse later recalled: 'His eyes were like fire and his whiskers quivered. It was a horrible experience.'**

- On 29 May 1911 Gilbert was swimming with two young ladies in a lake in the grounds of his home when one of them – Miss Ruby Preece – got out of her depth and into trouble. Gilbert dived in to assist her but he didn't resurface. He died of a heart attack. Miss Preece, however, was fine.

- The inscription on the memorial to Gilbert, to be found along the Thames Embankment in London, reads: 'His Foe was Folly, and his Weapon Wit'.

* Which, as well as fruit preserved by cooking with sugar, can mean someone's domain . . . so is another dreadful pun.
** As told in *Bring on the Girls* by P. G. Wodehouse and Guy Bolton.

New Year's Eve, the last day of the year

Some last words about some famous lasts (but not some famous last words)

- **The last execution in the Tower of London** was a lot more recent than many people imagine. It took place on Thursday, 14 August 1941, when Josef Jakobs, a German spy, was shot by firing squad. He'd broken his ankle when parachuting into England so he couldn't stand. He was executed while sitting, tied to an old wooden chair.

- **The last known wild wolf in Britain** was – sadly – killed in Scotland in 1743.

- **The last Olympics where the gold medals really were made out of gold**, rather than gold-coloured metal, were the 1912 games held in Stockholm, Sweden.

- **The last person in Britain to be burned at the stake** was Phoebe Harrius. She wasn't convicted of being a witch – it was 1786 – but of 'coining false money', in other words making counterfeit cash, which was a crime of high treason in those days. She was burned at the stake in front of Newgate Prison, for all to see.

- **The last song that Elvis Presley ever performed at a public concert** was, somewhat surprisingly, Simon and Garfunkel's 'Bridge Over Troubled Water', in Indianapolis in June 1977.

- **The last married pope** was Pope Adrian II (867–872). He was married with a daughter before he was elected pope, and refused to give up his wife on election. Tragically, both wife and child were later assassinated.

- **The last Wimbledon at which wooden-framed tennis rackets were used** was in 1987 (the year that Pat Cash won the men's finals and Martina Navratilova the women's).

- **The last words spoken on the Moon** were those of Commander Eugene Cernan, of Apollo 17, on 11 December 1972: 'As we leave the Moon at Taurus-Littrow, we leave as we came, and, God willing, we shall return, with peace and hope for all mankind.'

- **The last slave-owning president of the USA** was Ulysses S. Grant. When he married Julia Dent in 1848, she already owned a slave, and received a second as a wedding gift. She later bought a third. Grant himself bought a slave, whom he later freed.

- **The last of Philip Ardagh's truly splendid *Further Adventures of Eddie Dickens*** was aptly named *Final Curtain*. The final picture shows Eddie tied to a railway track, but the text doesn't say *why*.

- **The last Olympics to feature tug-of-war** was the 1920 games held in Antwerp, Belgium. (The winners of the gold medals for tug-of-war were Great Britain.)

- **The last person to die from smallpox** was Janet Parker, an English medical photographer, on 11 September 1978. She was accidentally exposed to the virus, which was being stored in a laboratory downstairs from her dark room. In 1980 the World Health Organization (WHO) declared that the disease – once responsible for the death of *hundreds of millions* – had been eradicated.

- **The last of the American branch of the Bonapartes** was Jerome Napoleon Bonaparte who died in 1945 . . . as a result of tripping over his dog's lead in Central Park, New York.

- **The last entry in the last list in Philip Ardagh's *Book of Absolutely Useless Lists for absolutely every day of the year*** is this one . . . and there's not a footnote in sight. HAPPY NEW YEAR!

An Afterword

Aubergine.